Winning Business

Cashman Dudley
An imprint of Gulf Publishing Company
Houston, Texas

Winning Business

How to Use Financial Analysis and Benchmarks to Outscore Your Competition

Rich Gildersleeve

Winning Business

Copyright ©1999 by Gulf Publishing Company, Houston, Texas. All rights reserved. This book, or parts thereof, may not be reproduced in any form without express written permission of the publisher.

Cashman Dudley
An imprint of Gulf Publishing Company
P.O. Box 2608 ☐ Houston, Texas 77252-2608

10 9 8 7 6 5 4 3 2 1

Library of Congress Cataloging-in-Publication Data

Gildersleeve, Rich.
    Winning business : how to use financial analysis and benchmarks to outscore your competition / Rich Gildersleeve.
       p.   cm.
    Includes bibliographical references and index.
    ISBN 0-88415-898-5 (alk. paper)
    1. Ratio analysis. 2. Financial statements. 3. Benchmarking (Management)   I. Title.
HF5681.R25G55 1999
658.15'5—dc21   99-13911
                                                                                        CIP

Printed in the United States of America.

Printed on acid-free paper (∞).

The author and the publisher have used their best efforts in preparing this book. The information and material contained in this book are provided "as is," without warranty of any kind, express or implied, including, without limitation, any warranty concerning the accuracy, adequacy, or completeness of such information or material or the results to be obtained from using such information or material. Neither Gulf Publishing Company nor the author shall be responsible for any claims attributable to errors, omissions, or other inaccuracies in the information or material contained in this book, and in no event shall Gulf Publishing Company or the author be liable for direct, indirect, special, incidental, or consequential damages arising out of the use of such information or material.

Contents

Acknowledgments, xii

Introduction, xiii

Considerations, xv

Argo, Inc. Financial Statements, xvii

Chapter 1
Financial Statement Analysis Methods 1
    Using Vertical Analysis to Analyze Financial Statements 2
    Using Horizontal Analysis to Analyze Financial Statements 3
    Exploring Variance Analysis 4
    Studying Ratio Analysis 5

Chapter 2
Income Analysis 6
    Determining Gross Profit 7
    Examining the Gross Profit Ratio 9
    Calculating Income from Operations 11
    Examining the Operations Income Ratio 13
    Measuring Pretax Profit 15
    Evaluating the Pretax Profit Ratio 17
    Calculating Net Income 19
    Comparing Net Income to Sales 21
    Finding the Percentage of Net Sales and Net Income that are Domestic 23
    Finding the Percentage of Sales and Net Income that are Foreign.......... 24
    Determining the Cost of Capital 25
    Measuring Economic Value Added (EVA) 26
    Comparing Economic Value Added (EVA) to Net Income 27
    Examining the Size of Residual Income............................ 28
    Comparing Residual Income to Net Income 30
    Determining the Return on Equity (ROE)........................... 31

21	Finding the Return on Assets (ROA).	33
22	Determining the Return on Invested Capital (ROIC)	35
23	Comparing Cash Provided by Operations to Net Income	37
24	Comparing Short-Lived Income to Net Income	38
25	Determining the Significance of Short-Lived Sales to Net Sales	39
26	Comparing Cash Flow from Operations to Total Cash Flow	40
27	Comparing Cash Flow from Investing Activities to Total Cash Flow	42
28	Comparing Cash Flow from Financing Activities to Total Cash Flow	43

Chapter 3
Investment Analysis 44

29	Determining Revenues Earned Per Share of Stock.	45
30	Finding the Amount of Earnings Per Share of Common Stock	46
31	Examining Dividends Per Common Share	47
32	Calculating the Growth Rate of Revenues	49
33	Calculating the Growth Rate of Earnings	51
34	Finding the Common Stock Dividend Growth Rate	53
35	Determining the Price-to-Earnings (P/E) Ratio	54
36	Measuring the Price-to-Earnings-to-Growth-Rate Ratio (PEG)	55
37	Examining the Earnings Yield.	56
38	Determining the Market Price Return Ratio	57
39	Determining the Common Stock Dividend Return Ratio	58
40	Determining the Size of the Common Stock Dividend Payout	59
41	Determining the Size of the Dividend Payout in Relation to Operations Cash Flow	60
42	Determining the Preferred Dividend Return Ratio	62
43	Determining the Size of the Preferred Dividend Payout	63
44	Determining the Size of the Preferred Dividend Payout in Relation to Operations Cash Flow	64
45	Determining the Size of the Total Return on Common Stock	65
46	Computing the Cash Flow Per Share of Outstanding Common Stock	66
47	Computing the Operating Cash Flow Per Share of Outstanding Common Stock	68
48	Determining the Volatility, or Beta, of a Stock	70

Chapter 4
Product and Factory Costs 71

49	Calculating the Total Amount of Direct Costs Per Production Unit	72
50	Determining the Total Labor Cost Per Production Unit	73
51	Calculating the Total Cost Per Production Unit	74
52	Examining Variable Costs	75
53	Comparing Variable Costs with Total Costs	76
54	Examining Variable Costs Per Production Unit	77
55	Examining Fixed Costs	78
56	Comparing Fixed Costs to Total Costs	80
57	Finding the Fixed Cost Per Unit	82
58	Finding the Contribution Margin	83
59	Determining the Break-Even Point in Sales Volume	85
60	Determining the Break-Even Point in Sales Dollars	87
61	Finding the Sales Volume Necessary to Generate a Desired Operating Income	89
62	Finding the Sales Dollars Necessary to Generate a Desired Operating Income	91
63	Finding the Break-Even Plant Capacity	93

Chapter 5
Expense Analysis 95

64	Comparing the Cost of Goods Sold to Sales and Net Income	96
65	Calculating the Amount of Sales and Cost of Goods Sold Per Employee	98

66	Determining Sales, Net Income, and the Cost of Goods Sold Per Direct Labor Employee	99
67	Comparing the Cost of Direct Labor and Direct Labor Hours Worked to Sales, Net Income, and the Cost of Goods Sold	100
68	Comparing Direct Labor Costs, Direct Labor Employees, and Direct Labor Hours Worked to the Cost of All Labor	102
69	Finding the Labor Cost and Hours Worked Per Direct Employee	104
70	Determining the Percentage of All Employees Who Are Direct Laborers	106
71	Determining the Direct Labor Costs Per Production Unit and Other Direct Labor Efficiency Ratios	108
72	Comparing the Direct Overhead Cost to Sales, Net Income, and the Cost of Goods Sold	109
73	Comparing Raw Materials Costs to Sales, Net Income, and the Cost of Goods Sold	110
74	Comparing Other Direct Costs to Sales, Gross Profit, Net Income, and the Cost of Goods Sold	111
75	Comparing R&D Costs to Sales and Net Income	112
76	Comparing Selling, General, and Administrative Costs (SG&A) to Sales and Net Income	114
77	Comparing Individual Overhead Expenses to Total Overhead Expenses and Sales	115
78	Finding Plant Equipment Costs Per Hour	117
79	Comparing the Cost of Fixed Asset Maintenance to Sales	118
80	Comparing the Cost of Fixed Asset Maintenance to the Value of Fixed Assets	119
81	Relating Insurance Costs to Sales Revenue	120
82	Relating Insurance Expenses to the Value of Fixed Assets	121
83	Examining Book Depreciation	122
84	Examining Tax Return Depreciation	123
85	Relating Book Depreciation Expenses to Sales Revenue	124
86	Comparing Book Depreciation Expenses to the Value of Fixed Assets	125

Chapter 6
Assets ... 126

87	Determining the Size of Fixed Assets	127
88	Examining the Relationship Between Fixed Assets and Sales	128
89	Examining the Relationship Between Fixed Assets and Net Income	129
90	Examining the Relationship Between Fixed Assets and Operations Cash Flow	131
91	Comparing Fixed Assets to Total Assets	132
92	Assessing the Fixed-Asset-to-Equity Ratio	133
93	Determining the Relationship Between Fixed Assets and Long-Term Debt	134
94	Comparing Fixed Assets to Short-Term Debt	135
95	Examining Fixed Asset Turnover	136
96	Assessing the Age of Fixed Assets	137
97	Determining the Turnover Rate of Total Assets	138
98	Finding the Total Asset Coverage Ratio	139
99	Comparing Intangible Assets to Sales Revenue	140
100	Comparing Intangible Assets to Net Income	141
101	Comparing Intangible Assets to Total Assets	143
102	Comparing Intangible Assets to Owner's Equity	145
103	Comparing Changes in Intangible Assets to Changes in Net Income	146
104	Comparing Individual Intangible Assets to Sales	147
105	Comparing Individual Intangible Assets to Net Income	148
106	Comparing Individual Intangible Assets to Total Assets	149
107	Measuring the Rate of Fixed Asset Reinvestment	150
108	Determining the Productivity of Fixed Assets	151
109	Comparing Fixed Asset Replacement Cost and Book Value	152
110	Comparing High-Risk Assets to Sales Revenue	153
111	Relating High-Risk Assets to Total Assets	154

Chapter 7
Debt 155

- 112 Comparing Debt to Sales 156
- 113 Examining the Debt-to-Operating Income Ratio 157
- 114 Examining the Debt-to-Asset Ratio 158
- 115 Examining the Debt-to-Equity Ratio 159
- 116 Comparing Debt to the Market Value of Assets 160
- 117 Determining Debt Turnover 161
- 118 Comparing Debt and Total Invested Capital 162
- 119 Relating Short-Term Debt to Long-Term Debt 163
- 120 Determining the Cost of Debt Capital 164

Chapter 8
Equity 165

- 121 Comparing Equity to Sales Revenue 166
- 122 Comparing Equity to Total Assets 167
- 123 Comparing Equity to Total Debt 168
- 124 Determining the Turnover of Equity 169
- 125 Examining the Turnover of Invested Capital 170
- 126 Comparing Net Income to Invested Capital 171
- 127 Comparing Stock to Invested Capital 172
- 128 Comparing Retained Earnings to Invested Capital 173

Chapter 9
Liquidity 174

- 129 Finding the Current Ratio 175
- 130 Using the Acid Test 176
- 131 Determining the Cash Flow Ratio 177
- 132 Calculating Cash Turnover 178
- 133 Finding How Many Days of Cash Expenses are Available 179
- 134 Examining How Many Days of Sales in Cash are Available 180
- 135 Using Altman's Z-score to Determine the Probability of Bankruptcy 181
- 136 Comparing Sales to Current Assets 182
- 137 Comparing Liquid Assets to Current Liabilities 183
- 138 Relating Liquid Assets to Cash Expenses 184
- 139 Relating Current Debt to Sales 185
- 140 Comparing Current Debt to Total Debt 186
- 141 Examining Working Capital 187
- 142 Finding the Turnover of Working Capital 188
- 143 Comparing Working Capital to Sales 189
- 144 Comparing Working Capital to Net Income 190
- 145 Relating Working Capital to Current Debt 191
- 146 Relating Working Capital to Long-Term Debt 192
- 147 Relating Working Capital to Total Debt 193
- 148 Comparing Working Capital to Current Assets 194
- 149 Comparing Working Capital to Specific Current Assets Such as Cash and Inventory 195
- 150 Comparing Working Capital to Total Assets 196
- 151 Relating Liquid Assets to Total Current Assets 198
- 152 Relating Marketable Securities to Total Current Assets 199
- 153 Comparing Accounts Receivable to Total Current Assets 200
- 154 Comparing Inventory to Total Current Assets 201
- 155 Comparing Other Specific Current Asset Accounts to Total Current Assets ... 202
- 156 Comparing Specific Expenses Such as Interest and Taxes to Total Current Assets 203

Chapter 10
Solvency 204
- 157 Determining How Many Times Interest Expense is Earned 205
- 158 Comparing Operations Cash Flow Plus Interest to Interest 206
- 159 Finding How Many Times Debt Expenses are Covered 207
- 160 Comparing Operations Cash Flow Plus Debt Expenses to Debt Expenses 208
- 161 Finding How Many Times the Long-Term Debt is Covered 209
- 162 Comparing Operations Cash Flow to Long-Term Debt 210
- 163 Finding How Many Times Fixed Costs are Covered 211
- 164 Comparing Operations Cash Flow Plus Fixed Costs to Fixed Costs 212
- 165 Determining How Many Times Operating Expenses are Covered 214
- 166 Comparing Operations Cash Flow Plus Operating Expenses to Operating Expenses 215
- 167 Determining How Many Days of Operating Expense Payables are Outstanding 216
- 168 Finding How Many Times Asset Additions are Covered 217
- 169 Comparing Operations Cash Flow to Changes in Assets 218
- 170 Comparing Retained Earnings to Total Assets 219

Chapter 11
Leverage 220
- 171 Comparing Debt to the Market Value of Equity 221
- 172 Comparing Current Debt to the Market Value of Equity 222
- 173 Comparing Long-Term Debt to the Market Value of Equity 223
- 174 Determining the Funded-Capital-to-Fixed-Asset Ratio 224
- 175 Examining Financial Leverage 225
- 176 Examining Operating Leverage 227
- 177 Examining Total Leverage 229

Chapter 12
Accounts Receivable 231
- 178 Comparing Accounts Receivable to Sales 232
- 179 Determining the Turnover of Accounts Receivable 233
- 180 Determining How Many Days of Credit Sales are in Accounts Receivable . . . 234
- 181 Examining the Ages of Accounts Receivable (Aging Schedule) 235
- 182 Determining What Percentage of Current-Period Sales Will Be Collected in the Current Period 236
- 183 Determining What Percentage of Current-Period Sales Will Not Be Collected in the Current Period 237
- 184 Examining Bad Debt and Accounts Receivable 238
- 185 Relating Bad Debts to Sales 239
- 186 Determining if Credit Discounts Should be Accepted and Offered 240
- 187 Examining Accounts Receivable Factoring 242

Chapter 13
Accounts Payable 243
- 188 Comparing Accounts Payable to Sales 244
- 189 Finding the Turnover of Accounts Payable 245
- 190 Calculating the Number of Days of Purchases in Accounts Payable 246
- 191 Comparing Accounts Payable to Purchases 247
- 192 Finding How Many Days of Purchases Have Been Paid 248
- 193 Comparing Accounts Payable Cash Disbursements to Accounts Payable 249
- 194 Comparing Individual Accounts Payable Disbursements to Total Cash Disbursements 250

Chapter 14
Inventory 251
- 195 Relating Inventory and Sales Levels 252
- 196 Determining the Turnover of the Entire Inventory 253

197	Determining How Many Days of Inventory Are On Hand	254
198	Calculating the Turnover of Finished Product Inventory	255
199	Finding How Many Days of Finished Product Inventory Are Available	256
200	Determining the Turnover of Work in Process Inventory	257
201	Calculating How Many Days of Work in Process Are Available	258
202	Determining the Turnover of Raw Materials Inventory	259
203	Examining How Many Days of Raw Materials Inventory Are Available	260
204	Determining the Inventory Ordering Cost	261
205	Measuring the Inventory Carrying Cost	262
206	Determining the Optimum Inventory Order Quantity	263
207	Determining the Total Cost of Inventory Per Item	264
208	Determining the Timing of Inventory Reorders	265
209	Estimating the Size of Inventory Safety Stock	266
210	Examining Just-In-Time (JIT) Systems	267

Chapter 15
Product and Service Demand Types ... 268

211	Examining Elastic Demand for Goods or Services	269
212	Examining Inelastic Demand for Goods and Services	270
213	Understanding Unitary Elasticity for Goods or Services	271
214	Examining Cross-Elasticity for Goods or Services	272
215	Examining Price Elasticity of Supply	273

Chapter 16
Capital Investment ... 274

216	Determining the Payback Period	275
217	Determining the Payback Reciprocal	276
218	Finding the Discounted Payback Period	277
219	Finding the Accounting Rate of Return	278
220	Determining the Net Present Value (NPV)	279
221	Finding the Risk-Adjusted Discount Rate	281
222	Ascertaining the Benefit Cost Ratio	282
223	Finding the Internal Rate of Return (IRR)	283
224	Finding the Modified Internal Rate of Return (MIRR)	285
225	Determining the Certainty Equivalent	286
226	Determining the Future Value of $1	288
227	Finding the Future Value of an Annuity of $1	289
228	Calculating the Future Value of an Annuity Due of $1	290
229	Finding the Present Value of $1	291
230	Determining the Present Value of an Annuity of $1	292
231	Calculating the Present Value of an Annuity Due of $1	293
232	Examining Perpetuities	294

Chapter 17
Investment/Loan Interest Rate Information ... 295

233	Examining Simple Interest	296
234	Exploring Compounded Interest	297
235	Examining the Current Yield on Bonds	298
236	Examining the Yield to Maturity on Bonds	299
237	Examining the Effective Annual Yield on T-bills	300
238	Exploring the Rule of 72	301
239	Exploring Interest Rates and Their Significance: Federal Funds Rate	302
240	Exploring Interest Rates and Their Significance: Discount Rate	303
241	Exploring Interest Rates and Their Significance: Treasury Bills/Notes/Bonds	304

Chapter 18
External Indicators 305

- 242 Examining the Index of Leading Economic Indicators 306
- 243 Examining the Index of Coincident Economic Indicators 307
- 244 Examining the Index of Lagging Economic Indicators 308
- 245 Assessing the Gross Domestic Product (GDP) 309
- 246 Examining the Gross National Product (GNP) 310
- 247 Examining the Producer Price Index (PPI) 311
- 248 Assessing the Consumer Price Index (CPI) 312
- 249 Examining the Dow Jones Industrial Average (DJIA) 313
- 250 Exploring the Russel 2000 Average 314
- 251 Exploring the Wilshire 5000 Average 315

Chapter 19
Company Valuation 316

- 252 Determining the Book Value of a Company 317
- 253 Finding the Liquidation Value of a Company 318
- 254 Ascertaining the Market Value of a Company 319
- 255 Assessing the Price-to-Earnings Value of a Company 320
- 256 Valuing a Company on Discounted Future Cash Flow 321
- 257 Determining the Value of a Company with No-Earnings-Per-Share Dilution . . . 322

Appendix A 323

Appendix B 325

Appendix C 325

Abbreviations 326

References and Suggested Readings 326

Index 327

Acknowledgments

Many thanks to Dr. Kris Jamsa for his vision and encouragement in making this book a reality. Professor Gun Joh of California State University, San Diego also deserves accolades for his insightful suggestions. I am most appreciative and thankful for the support and love of my wonderful wife, Tammy, and our great kids, Sean and Tara.

Introduction

Winning Business and its interactive CD-ROM can help business managers, investors, small business owners, and students better understand, monitor, and improve company performance. Successful business people use indicators to monitor conditions such as return on assets, liquidity, profitability, and growth. This book helps you determine these critical performance indicators and supplies you with benchmarks to see how your company stacks up against the competition.

The book gives you 257 tips conveniently organized in categories so you can quickly focus in on areas of concern. The categories include income analysis, investment analysis, product and factory costs, expense analysis, capital investment, liquidity, solvency, accounts payable and receivable, product service demand types, investment and loan interest rate information, leverage, inventory, assets, debt, equity, and external indicators. Each tip presents a ratio to help you understand, monitor, and when applicable, improve company performance in the area of concern. You will also find an example with each tip to show you how to calculate the ratio. All examples are based on the financial statements of Argo, Inc., a fictitious concern, whose financial statements are detailed in Appendix A.

Many of the tips also provide industry benchmarks to enable you to compare your company's performance with many different-sized companies operating in a variety of industries. The companies included in the benchmark tables are shown below. The data comes from the financial statement information found in each respective company's annual report. In the sample tables below, Table 1 shows financial information reporting dates and Table 2 shows corresponding sales levels for that reporting period.

Table 1. Benchmark companies with financial information reporting dates.

Sector	Mid to large cap	Financial Reporting Date	Small to mid cap	Financial Reporting Date	Micro to small cap	Financial Reporting Date
Manufacturing	General Motors	12-31-97	Toro	10-31-97	Encad	12-31-97
Retail	Wal-Mart Stores	1-31-98	Bed Bath & Beyond	2-28-98	TCBY Enterprises	11-30-97
Food	McDonald's	12-31-97	Applebee's Int'l	12-28-97	Garden Fresh Restaurant	9-30-97
Technology	Microsoft	6-30-98	Cypress Semiconductor	12-29-97	Jmar Technologies	12-31-97
Finance	Morgan-Stanley Dean Witter	11-30-97	Franklin Resources	9-30-97	AmeriTrade Holding	9-27-97
Healthcare	Columbia/HCA Healthcare	12-31-97	Novacare	6-30-97	National Home Health Care	9-31-97
Service	Manpower	12-31-97	Air & Water Technologies	10-31-97	Market Facts	12-31-97
Media/Publishing	McGraw Hill	12-31-97	Scholastic	5-31-98	Thomas Nelson	3-31-98

Table 2. Sales levels of benchmark companies at the listed reporting period.

Sector	Mid to large cap	Sales (M$)	Small to mid cap	Sales (M$)	Micro to small cap	Sales (M$)
Manufacturing	General Motors	178,174	Toro	1,051	Encad	149
Retail	Wal-Mart Stores	117,958	Bed Bath & Beyond	1,067	TCBY Enterprises	91
Food	McDonald's	11,409	Applebee's Int'l	516	Garden Fresh Restaurant	90
Technology	Microsoft	14,484	Cypress Semiconductor	544	Jmar Technologies	21
Finance	Morgan-Stanley Dean Witter	27,132	Franklin Resources	2,163	AmeriTrade Holding	96
Healthcare	Columbia/HCA Healthcare	18,819	Novacare	1,066	National Home Health Care	35
Service	Manpower	7,259	Air & Water Technologies	456	Market Facts	100
Media/Publishing	McGraw Hill	3,534	Scholastic	1,058	Thomas Nelson	253

The interactive CD-ROM enables you to input standard company financial statement information, most of which can be found in annual reports, and then watch as the program automatically performs all of the ratio calculations for you. In an instant, you can have a vast array of critical performance characteristics mapped out for you. Using this information, you can determine when performance is high and when improvement is indicated. The CD-ROM also contains a full multimedia version of the book.

The following three examples demonstrate ways in which *Winning Business* can help managers and investors stay ahead of the competition. Suppose you are a business manager concerned with excessive and/or climbing inventory levels. You could flip to the *Winning Business* chapter on inventory that describes a number of useful ratios such as inventory turnover and inventory to sales. These ratios will help you understand and improve company performance in that area. After determining the size of these ratios, you can use the benchmark table to see how your company stacks up against others in a variety of industries. The tips offer potential causes, outcomes, and suggestions for the improvement of high and low inventory levels to help you take any desired corrective action.

Next, assume you are considering your next stock market investment. You could turn to the chapter on investment quality. There you could pick from several useful ratios such as earnings growth and dividend payout to analyze the investment potential of the company under consideration.

Finally, let's suppose you are a business manager considering expanding a business by starting a new product line. You would flip to the chapters on capital investment and income quality. There you would analyze the potential return on the investment by determining ratios such as the payback period, net present value, and the economic value added (EVA). These ratios should help you make more informed and objective decisions regarding the potential of the product line expansion.

Winning Business provides you with the tools to improve the health of your business and analyze the potential of your investments. Each of the 257 tips will help you understand, monitor, and improve company performance. With the interactive CD-ROM, you can easily perform sophisticated financial and business analysis with a minimum of effort. The tools provided in *Winning Business* can provide investors, managers, and students with a blueprint for success.

Considerations

Although ratio analysis can provide the business manager and investor with tremendously helpful information regarding company performance trends, you should weigh a number of factors when employing ratio analysis. Below are some of the issues to consider when using the information in this book:

1. Trends over time are often more insightful than one-time values. A high or low one-time value may be the result of an unusual event not likely to reoccur whereas a trend is often more indicative of an event that is likely to repeat in the future.
2. The ratios in this book are based upon the latest balance sheet values instead of an alternative method of averaging the last two or more balance sheet values.
3. When comparing ratios with other companies, you will generally realize more accurate and insightful results when comparing companies of similar size and in similar industries.
4. When the value of the ratio indicator that falls in the denominator approaches zero, the resulting ratio is very high and can give misleading information.
5. It is always important to consider risk when analyzing the potential of a business. Higher rewards are not necessarily better when there is a disproportionate degree of risk.
6. Financial ratios reflect the past and not necessarily the present or future.
7. Financial ratios are in large part dependent on the reliability of the information found in financial statements. If this information is misleading or inaccurate, the analysis results will likely also be incorrect.
8. Financial ratios are dependent upon the particular accounting principles used by the company. Although most companies adhere to generally accepted accounting principles, the manner in which these firms report financial performance can vary greatly. For example, some companies prefer to account for inventory on a last-in, first-out (LIFO) basis while others prefer a first-in, first-out (FIFO) accounting. In an inflationary period, a given inventory would likely have a larger value when the company uses FIFO instead of LIFO inventory methods even though the same type and volume of inventory are present. Both accounting methods are acceptable but can give seemingly very different inventory perspectives. It is thus important to check financial statement footnotes when comparing companies to account for differences in accounting methods.

9. The per-share ratios in this book are based upon the number of outstanding shares listed in company balance sheets.
10. The financial statements analysis methods discussed are targeted to U.S. corporations. Extra care should be taken when applying these methods for foreign companies, because varying accounting standards and definitions may give misleading results.

Argo, Inc. Financial Statements

The appendix details the financial statements of a fictitious company, Argo, Inc. This information is the basis of many of the example calculations explained in the book. The examples help illustrate where you can locate the information on a financial statement and how you can use this information to determine the ratio under consideration.

The Argo, Inc. financials include three of the most common instruments employed to communicate a company's financial state. These instruments are the income statement (also known as the **profit and loss statement,** the **statement of earnings,** and the **statement of operations**), the balance sheet (also called the **statement of financial condition**), and the cash flow statement.

The **income statement** conveys information regarding income streams and expenses over a period of time such as yearly, half-yearly, and quarterly. The top lines of an income statement describe the company's income streams. The statement lists expenses below the income-related information. The first expenses listed are most directly associated with the production of the company's products or services. You find other expenses as you proceed down the income statement until all expenses are accounted for, resulting in the company's financial net income, or bottom line, for the time period. The income statement is in some ways analogous to an organized personal checkbook statement that details an individual's salary, living expenses, taxes, and remaining balance after the owner has accounted for all forms of income and expenses.

The **balance sheet** relays information regarding a company's assets, liabilities, and owner's equity at any given time, typically the last day of a company's fiscal year. While the income statement covers a time period, the balance sheet conveys the financial status as a snapshot in time. This financial statement is aptly called the balance sheet because it "balances" assets, liabilities, and equity according to the accounting formula:

Assets = liabilities + owner's equity

Assets include all the items a company possesses that have value. They are typically listed according to liquidity. The most liquid assets, such as cash, are listed first, and longer term, less liquid assets such as buildings, machinery, and other long-term investments are listed further down the balance sheet.

Liabilities include all of the areas in which the company is indebted to others. Examples include bank loans, investor loans, trade credit, and taxes. Like the assets section, near-term liabilities such as notes payable to investors and accounts payable to trade creditors are listed before longer term obligations such as long-term loans.

The **owner's equity,** also called the **shareholders' equity,** includes primarily all the capital paid to the company by shareholders as well as the capital the company has earned that has been reinvested in the company. This latter portion is commonly called **retained earnings.**

Now that we've laid a small amount of groundwork, let's explore what the accounting formula, Assets = liabilities + owner's equity, conveys. A company that has a large amount of assets must have an equally large amount of liabilities and owner's equity for the equation to balance. If the company has an amount of liabilities equal to the amount of assets, there will be no owner's equity. In this situation, the company is highly leveraged since all assets are covered by liabilities such as loans from banks and trade creditors. Alternatively if the company has no liabilities, the owner's equity portion will be equal to the assets. In this situation, the company's assets are fully owned by the owners since there is no debt. The second company is in a generally sounder financial state since it is not leveraged. However, this information alone does not mean the second company is, or will be, more successful. It simply means that the company, for any variety of reasons, has elected or has not needed to acquire any debt. Many successful companies will acquire debt for assets such as machinery and extra inventory to help support the growth of the company.

Rearranging the accounting formula to solve for owner's equity gives

Owner's Equity = assets − liabilities

This equation shows that the larger the amount of assets relative to liabilities, the more equity the owners have in the company. When you look at the balance sheet in this manner, you can see that it is in many ways similar to an individual's net worth statement, in which the difference between all personal assets and liabilities equals the individual's net worth.

The **cash flow statement** describes where the company has generated and used cash over a period of time. Possible sources and uses of cash include manufacturing operations, service contracts, bank loans, and the sale and purchase of assets. An example may be the best way to describe the usefulness of the information contained within the cash flow statement. Consider two companies that each experienced an increase in cash of one million dollars. The first generated nine million from operations, invested six million in new factory equipment, and paid off two million in financed debt $(9 − 6 − 2 = 1)$. The second lost five million from operations, sold off another five million in factory equipment, and borrowed eleven million in cash $(−5 − 5 + 11 = 1)$. While both companies had a net increase in cash of one million, they clearly arrived at that point in vastly different manners. Everything else being the same, the first company is in a much sounder financial state than the second since operations are supplying a positive stream of cash, with a large portion of this cash reinvested in the company for future growth. The second company, on the other hand, is losing money in operations and selling assets that may be required for future sales.

In addition to the financial statements there are a number of qualitative aspects of the financial report that may provide further insight into company performance including management discussions, auditor's opinions, and the financial report footnotes. Management discussions help you gain an improved understanding of a company's financial performance because these discussions often disclose the stories behind financial numbers. For example, reduced sales levels may be caused by increasing competition, reduced demand, a fire that destroyed production facilities and subsequently hampered sales efforts, or any number of other reasons. An auditor's opinion typically accompanies the financial report and discloses how accurately the state of the business is portrayed. When a negative opinion is offered, the financial statement information disclosed can be misleading or totally in error. Extra care is warranted when using such information for business analysis. Footnotes also typically accompany the financial reports. These footnotes often provide the needed details to better understand the numbers disclosed in the financial reports.

CHAPTER ONE

Financial Statement Analysis Methods

This chapter describes commonly used methods of analyzing financial statements. You can use these analysis methods with many of the financial ratios discussed in this book to track income and expense performance over time and to compare one financial indicator to another to gain improved insight regarding company performance.

1 Using Vertical Analysis to Analyze Financial Statements

Vertical analysis is a method of analyzing financial statements in which you can compare individual line items to a baseline item such as net sales from the income statement, total assets from the asset section of the balance sheet, and total liabilities and owner's equity in the liabilities and owner's equity section of the balance sheet. The word *vertical* is used to describe this analysis method because the method generates a vertical column of ratios next to the individual items on the financial statements.

When to use indicator: You can use vertical analysis to compare trends in the relative performance of any financial statement line items over time. For example, from the income statement you may want to track the cost of goods sold and the net income as a percentage of sales. These two indicators let you know whether year-to-year costs are becoming unreasonable and whether net income trends are as desired. By tracking ratios over time, you can observe positive or negative trends so that you can begin any required corrective actions. You can also use vertical analysis to compare a company's performance relative to the performance of other companies operating in similar industries.

Example

Argo, Inc. Vertical Analysis Example		
Income Statement Fiscal year ending 31-Dec-97 (dollars in thousands)		
Net sales	85,420	100.0%
Cost of goods sold	54,212	63.5%
Gross profit	31,208	36.5%
R&D expenses	4,578	5.4%
Selling, G&A expenses	15,993	18.7%
Depreciation & amortization	1,204	1.4%
Operating income	9,433	11.0%
Nonoperating income	455	0.5%
Interest expense	784	0.9%
Pre-tax income	9,104	10.7%
Provision for income taxes	3,529	4.1%
Net income before extraordinary items	5,575	6.5%
Extraordinary items	−592	0.7%
Net income	4,983	5.8%

2 Using Horizontal Analysis to Analyze Financial Statements

Horizontal analysis is a method of analyzing financial statements in which a manager compares individual line items to their historical values. The word *horizontal* is used to describe this analysis method because the method generates horizontal rows of data.

When to use indicator: You can use this method to compare trends over time of any financial statement line items. For example, managers often want to track changes on the income statement in net sales and net income over time. If, in a particular reporting period, net sales increased 8% and net income rose 12% over the prior year, you can learn much information from this. First, compare the performance of the line items with forecasts to determine the level of company performance. Some companies would consider an 8% increase in net sales a dramatic failure while others would consider it a tremendous success; the relationship of performance to forecast is the key. Further, the relationship between distinct line items can give you a lot of insight into the health of the company. In this example, it is likely a very positive indication that net income rose at a much higher rate (12%) than did net sales (8%). When you use horizontal analysis over time, you can spot positive or negative trends.

Example

Argo, Inc. Horizontal Analysis Example

Income Statement
(dollars in thousands)

Fiscal year ending	31-Dec-97	31-Dec-96	Change in dollars	Change in Percent	Ratio of '97 to '96
Net sales	85,420	72,886	12,534	17.2%	1.172
Cost of goods sold	54,212	50,258	3,954	7.9%	1.079
Gross profit	31,208	22,628	8,580	37.9%	1.379
R&D expenses	4,578	4,877	-299	-6.1%	0.939
Selling, G&A expenses	15,993	11,265	4,728	42.0%	1.420
Depreciation & amortization	1,204	642	562	87.5%	1.875
Operating income	9,433	5,844	3,589	61.4%	1.614
Nonoperating income	455	687	−232	−33.8%	0.662
Interest expense	784	812	−28	−3.4%	0.966
Pre-tax income	9,104	5,719	3,385	59.2%	1.592
Provision for income taxes	3,529	1,856	1,673	90.1%	1.901
Net income before extraordinary income	5,575	3,863	1,712	44.3%	1.443
Extraordinary items	−592	−275	−317	−215.3%	2.153
Net income	4,983	3,588	1,395	38.9%	1.389

3 Exploring Variance Analysis

Equation

Variance = standard or budgeted amount − actual amount

Managers use **variance analysis** to track cost and revenue performance over time. This specific type of horizontal analysis compares items to the budget instead of comparing items to performance in previous years (see horizontal analysis, tip #2). Positive variances occur when actual costs are lower than budgeted costs or when actual revenue exceeds anticipated revenue. Positive variances thus yield better returns. Negative variances, and lower returns, occur when the opposite trends occur.

When to use indicator: Managers use variance analysis to compare performance to standards or budgets over time. This tool helps the manager keep on top of company expenditures and incomes by indicating how these items compare to forecasted standards. When the manager notices sizable variances, he can use the signal to determine if the causes of the variance are justified or not.

Example

Argo, Inc. Cost of Goods Sold Variance Analysis Example				
(dollars in thousands)				
Item	Actual	Budget	Variance ($)	Variance (%)
Cost of goods sold				
Raw materials	31,063	32,250	1,187	3.7%
Direct labor	7,860	7,417	−443	−6.0%
Overhead	15,289	13,833	−1,456	−10.5%
Total	54,212	53,500	−712	−1.3%

4 Studying Ratio Analysis

Ratio analysis compares one indicator to another. Ratios can give you significant insight into the performance and relative importance of two indicators.

When to use indicator: Managers and investors can use ratio analysis to understand the health of a company. Ratios lend insight into many critical aspects such as present and future profit potential, expense control, and solvency. For example, the ratio of net income *to* net sales gives substantially different information than examining net income *and* net sales. Assume company A has a net income of $20,000 with net sales of $250,000, and company B has a net income of $18,000 on net sales of $90,000. Company A and company B have net-income-to-net-sales ratios of 8% and 20% respectively. This indicates that although company B generated less income than company A, it operates with much higher profit margins. If company B operates in the same industry as company A, company B is probably better managed.

Example

Net income to net sales = net income / net sales

Net sales = 85,420
Net income = 4,983

Net income to net sales = 4,983 / 85,420 = 0.0583 = 5.83%

CHAPTER TWO

Income Analysis

This chapter details a number of ratios that describe income levels and the quality of income earned. These ratios include income levels such as gross profit, operations income, pretax profit, and net income. When you analyze income levels at each of these discrete levels, you can more readily understand and identify company performance and areas of concern. For example, when gross profit is low relative to that in similar industries, manufacturing expenses may be out of control or sales revenues may be too low to support the manufacturing infrastructure. High gross profit with low pretax income may indicate that expenses are out of line in sales, administration, or research and development.

Income quality is concerned not only with the magnitude of income, but with how sustainable the income stream is and what the levels of return are relative to the investment size. Income quality tends to increase as income returns become larger relative to the capital investments a company makes. Income quality also tends to increase when it is long term rather than coming from one-time orders and when it results from company operations rather than other sources such as investments or financing.

5 Determining Gross Profit

Equation

Gross profit = net sales − cost of goods sold

Gross profit is the profit remaining after you deduct all direct costs from net sales revenue. **Direct costs,** also known as the **cost of goods sold,** include only the costs that are required to produce the product or service directly (i.e., raw materials, direct labor, and direct overhead). You should not account for other costs such as salaries for accountants, product designers, and executives and depreciation of plant equipment when you determine gross profit. The gross profit is thus larger than the operating and net profit amounts because these profit indicators take into account additional expenditures. **Net sales** is total sales minus provisions for returns, discounts, damaged goods, and bad debt. Gross profit is also known as **gross margin.**

When to use indicator: Managers and investors use gross profit to determine the profit potential of a business, product, or service. Because gross profit includes direct costs only, it indicates the amount of margin between the price of a product and the cost to produce the product. This margin does not include all the other expenses required to run a company such as selling and product development costs. When you compare gross profit to the same number in previous years or periods, you can spot positive or negative trends in product pricing and the cost of goods sold.

Meaning of result: Companies usually desire high gross profits because they indicate that more funds remain for indirect costs and net profit. Companies with higher gross profits tend to add more value to the product or service they produce. Companies of all sizes and types should seek to increase gross profits as long as there are no detrimental consequences, such as unacceptable reductions in the quality of goods, delays in delivering goods to the customer, or assumption of unacceptable risk levels. Companies that produce small amounts of goods typically require high gross profits whereas high-volume companies can remain profitable with lower gross profits. This is because high-volume companies have more opportunities to make profit and increase the total amount of gross profit. For example, grocers can be profitable with lower gross profits per item because they sell a very large number of items; however, a manufacturer of an expensive item such as a supercomputer must make a large gross profit since they will sell a relatively small number.

Ways to improve the indicator: Managers can increase gross profits by increasing the volume and/or price of the goods sold and by reducing the costs necessary to produce the goods. Volume increases not only generate larger gross profits as net sales increase, but they can provide reduced costs of goods. This is because operational efficiencies typically increase with increasing volume.

Sector	Mid to large cap	Gross Profit	Small to mid cap	Gross Profit	Micro to small cap	Gross Profit
Manufacturing	General Motors	48,146,000	Toro	388,037	Encad	70,782
Retail	Wal-Mart Stores	24,520,000	Bed Bath & Beyond	441,016	TCBY Enterprises	30,179
Food	McDonald's	4,759,200	Applebee's Int'l	128,329	Garden Fresh Restaurant	66,755
Technology	Microsoft	13,287,000	Cypress Semiconductor	187,437	Jmar Technologies	8,830
Finance	Morgan-Stanley Dean Witter	9,847,000	Franklin Resources	1,003,778	AmeriTrade Holding	54,627
Healthcare	Columbia/HCA Healthcare	10,414,000	Novacare	260,086	National Home Health Care	12,165
Service	Manpower	1,310,196	Air & Water Technologies	70,802	Market Facts	43,672
Media/Publishing	McGraw Hill	1,894,718	Scholastic	521,600	Thomas Nelson	114,569

Price increases must be acceptable to the marketplace. Inflationary effects aside, you typically cannot change prices at will without making commensurate changes to the goods or services offered. You should not increases prices to the point that reductions in sales more than offset the positive effects of the price increases and cause a decrease in net income.

You can reduce the cost of goods sold by purchasing less expensive materials, increasing production efficiency, using cheaper labor, and decreasing overhead. Typically you should not reduce the cost of goods sold to the detriment of the goods offered. For example, charging more for a product that uses cheaper, less reliable raw materials will decrease the cost of goods sold and increase gross profit in the short run, but the market will probably reject the product and leave you with drastically lower sales volumes and gross profit in the long run.

Example

Gross profit = net sales − cost of goods sold

Net sales = 85,420
Cost of goods sold = 54,212

Gross profit = 85,420 − 54,212 = 31,208

6 Examining the Gross Profit Ratio

Equation

Gross profit ratio = gross profit / net sales

where

Gross profit = net sales − cost of goods sold

You can use the **gross profit ratio** to find out the size of the margin between your company's revenue and the direct costs associated with producing your product or service. Direct costs, also known as the cost of goods sold, include only the costs that are required directly to produce the product or service (i.e., raw materials, direct labor, and direct overhead). The gross profit ratio is also known as the **gross margin ratio**.

When to use indicator: With this ratio managers and investors can quickly ascertain the degree of profit potential for a business, product, or service. When you compare this ratio over time, you will notice trends in product pricing and the cost of goods sold. The ratio varies between zero and one, with higher ratios indicating higher, or more profitable, margins.

Meaning of result: The gross profit ratio is a convenient method to determine the profit potential for an entire industry, a company, or a product line within a company. The ratio indicates the percentage of every dollar of sales revenue that remains after you deduct all operations expenses. As gross profit ratios become higher and approach the value of one, profit potential increases. For example, a gross profit ratio of 0.36 indicates that, for every dollar of net sales revenue, 36¢ of gross profit remains after deducting all direct expenses.

Ways to improve the indicator: You can increase gross profit ratios by increasing the volume and/or price of the goods sold and by reducing the costs necessary to produce the goods. Volume increases not only generate larger gross profits as net sales increase. They can also reduce the costs of goods sold because operational efficiencies typically increase with increasing volume.

The marketplace must accept price increases, therefore, inflationary effects aside, typically a manager should not generally change prices at will without making commensurate changes to the goods or services offered. Generally, you should not increase prices to the point that reductions in sales more than offset the positive effects of the price increases and cause a decrease in net income.

You can reduce the cost of goods sold by purchasing less expensive materials, increasing production efficiency, using cheaper labor, and decreasing overhead. Typically you should not reduce the cost of goods sold to the detriment of the goods offered. For example, if you charge more for a product that uses cheaper, less reliable raw materials, you will decrease the cost of goods sold and increase gross profit in the short run. However, the market is like-

Sector	Mid to large cap	Gross Profit Ratio	Small to mid cap	Gross Profit Ratio	Micro to small cap	Gross Profit Ratio
Manufacturing	General Motors	27.0%	Toro	36.9%	Encad	47.5%
Retail	Wal-Mart Stores	20.8%	Bed Bath & Beyond	41.3%	TCBY Enterprises	33.3%
Food	McDonald's	41.7%	Applebee's Int'l	24.9%	Garden Fresh Restaurant	74.0%
Technology	Microsoft	91.7%	Cypress Semiconductor	34.4%	Jmar Technologies	41.1%
Finance	Morgan-Stanley Dean Witter	36.3%	Franklin Resources	46.4%	AmeriTrade Holding	57.1%
Healthcare	Columbia/HCA Healthcare	55.3%	Novacare	24.4%	National Home Health Care	34.7%
Service	Manpower	18.1%	Air & Water Technologies	15.5%	Market Facts	43.6%
Media/Publishing	McGraw Hill	53.6%	Scholastic	49.3%	Thomas Nelson	45.3%

ly to reject the product and cause drastically lower sales volumes and gross profit in the long run.

Example

Gross profit ratio = gross profit / net sales

Gross profit = net sales − cost of goods sold = 85,420 − 54,212 = 31,208

Net sales = 85,420

Gross profit ratio = 31,208 / 85,420 = .365 = 36.5%

7 Calculating Income from Operations

Equation

Income from operations = Net sales − cost of goods sold − R&D expenses − selling expenses − G&A expenses − depreciation − amortization − other operational expenses

Income from operations is the amount of income a company generates after it accounts for all direct and indirect operational costs. These costs include only those expenses which relate to the product or service. Do not include nonoperational expenses such as income on noncompany investments and income taxes. **Direct costs,** also known as the cost of goods sold, include the costs that are required to produce the product or service (i.e., raw materials, direct labor, and direct overhead). **Indirect costs** include all other expenses a company must incur in order to deliver a product or service to the customer (i.e., product development, selling, advertising, accounting, office rent, and utilities).

When to use indicator: Managers and investors use this indicator to determine the profit potential from operations and to examine whether profit trends are positive or negative. Since this ratio takes all operational costs into account, it furnishes a broad picture of the overall health of the business.

Meaning of result: To survive, companies must ultimately deliver positive operations income. Operations are the heart of a business and, in the long run, must provide cash and profit. Positive indications include high and preferably increasing operations income over a number of reporting periods. Companies can survive with no operations income by taking on debt or by selling company equity. These actions are necessary in many start-up, high growth, and turn-around companies. However, all for-profit companies must ultimately provide positive operations income to remain solvent.

Ways to improve the indicator: You can improve income from operations by selling more products or services, increasing the prices of the products or services, or reducing the direct or indirect costs of producing the goods or services.

Volume increases may generate larger operational profits as net sales increase. They can also reduce costs of goods sold because operational efficiencies typically increase as volume increases.

Price increases must be acceptable to the marketplace, and inflationary effects aside, you typically should not change prices at will without making commensurate changes to the goods or services offered. Generally, you should not increase prices to the point that volume reductions more than offset the positive effects of the price increases and cause a decrease in net income.

You can reduce the direct costs, or cost of goods sold, by purchasing less expensive materials, increasing production efficiency, using cheaper labor, and decreasing overhead. Typically you should not reduce the cost of goods sold to the

Sector	Mid to large cap	Income from Operations	Small to mid cap	Income from Operations	Micro to small cap	Income from Operations
Manufacturing	General Motors	15,338,000	Toro	72,347	Encad	26,493
Retail	Wal-Mart Stores	5,162,000	Bed Bath & Beyond	118,914	TCBY Enterprises	−795
Food	McDonald's	2,694,800	Applebee's Int'l	72,492	Garden Fresh Restaurant	7,970
Technology	Microsoft	6,940,000	Cypress Semiconductor	18,313	Jmar Technologies	1,527
Finance	Morgan-Stanley Dean Witter	4,274,000	Franklin Resources	591,460	AmeriTrade Holding	21,788
Healthcare	Columbia/HCA Healthcare	1,545,000	Novacare	94,089	National Home Health Care	3,300
Service	Manpower	255,387	Air & Water Technologies	−21,814	Market Facts	10,281
Media/Publishing	McGraw Hill	484,985	Scholastic	48,200	Thomas Nelson	24,780

detriment of the goods offered. For example, if you charge more for a product that uses cheaper, less reliable raw materials, you will increase your gross profit; however, the market will probably reject the product and cause drastically lower sales volumes.

At first glance, it appears that you can reduce indirect costs by cutting back on R&D (research and development), selling, G&A (general and administrative), and/or depreciation expenses. While this is usually true in the short term, you can suffer catastrophic long-term results if you reduce expenses such as advertising or product development. In fact, it is not unusual to *increase* such expenditures to generate larger future sales and increase operations profit in the long run. Managers should seek to streamline costs where true fat exists and to maintain or increase expenses in areas in which they can realize longer term returns.

Example

Income from operations = net sales − cost of goods sold − R&D expenses − selling expenses − G&A expenses − depreciation − amortization − other operational expenses

Net sales = 85,420
Cost of goods sold = 54,212
R&D expenses = 4,578
Selling and G&A expenses = 15,993
Depreciation & amortization = 1,204
Other operational expenses = 0

Income from operations = 85,420 − 54,212 − 4,578 − 15,993 − 1,204 − 0 = 9,433

Examining the Operations Income Ratio

Equation

Operations income ratio = income from operations / net sales

or

Operations income ratio = (net sales revenue − cost of goods sold − R&D expenses − selling expenses − G&A expenses − depreciation − amortization − other operational expenses) / net sales

The **operations income ratio** indicates the margin between the revenue a company generates and all of the direct and indirect costs associated with producing the product or service. The ratio accounts for only those expenses which relate to the product or service. Do not include nonoperational expenses such as income on noncompany investments and income taxes. Direct costs, also known as the cost of goods sold, include the costs required to produce the product or service (i.e., raw materials, direct labor, and direct overhead). Indirect costs include all other expenses a company incurs in delivering a product or service to the customer (i.e., product development, selling, advertising, accounting, office rent, and utilities).

When to use indicator: Managers and investors use this ratio to ascertain the operational profit potential for a business, product, or service. By comparing this indicator over time, you can spot trends in product pricing, direct costs, and indirect costs. The ratio varies between zero and one, with higher ratios indicating higher, or more profitable operations margins.

Meaning of result: You can use operations income profit ratios to determine quickly the profitability of a company's operations. The ratio indicates the percentage of every dollar of sales revenue that remains after you deduct all operations expenses. For example, an operations income ratio of 0.11 indicates that 11¢ remains as operations profit for every dollar of net sales revenue.

To survive, companies must ultimately deliver positive operations income ratios. Operations are the heart of a business and, in the long run, must provide cash and profit. Positive indications include high and preferably increasing operations income ratios over a number of reporting periods. Companies can survive with no operations income by taking on debt or selling company equity. Many start-up, high growth, or turn-around companies require these measures. However, all companies must ultimately provide positive operations income ratios to remain solvent.

Ways to improve the indicator: You can improve the operations income ratio by selling more products or services, increasing the prices of the products or services, or reducing the direct and indirect costs of producing the goods or services.

Sector	Mid to large cap	Operations Income Ratio	Small to mid cap	Operations Income Ratio	Micro to small cap	Operations Income Ratio
Manufacturing	General Motors	8.6%	Toro	6.9%	Encad	17.8%
Retail	Wal-Mart Stores	4.4%	Bed Bath & Beyond	11.1%	TCBY Enterprises	−0.9%
Food	McDonald's	23.6%	Applebee's Int'l	14.1%	Garden Fresh Restaurant	8.8%
Technology	Microsoft	47.9%	Cypress Semiconductor	3.4%	Jmar Technologies	7.1%
Finance	Morgan-Stanley Dean Witter	15.8%	Franklin Resources	27.3%	AmeriTrade Holding	22.8%
Healthcare	Columbia/HCA Healthcare	8.2%	Novacare	8.8%	National Home Health Care	9.4%
Service	Manpower	3.5%	Air & Water Technologies	−4.8%	Market Facts	10.3%
Media/Publishing	McGraw Hill	13.7%	Scholastic	4.6%	Thomas Nelson	9.8%

Volume increases may generate larger operational profits as net sales increase; they can also reduce the cost of goods sold since operational efficiencies typically increase with increasing volume.

The marketplace must accept price increases, so, inflationary effects aside, typically you can't change prices at will without making commensurate changes to the goods or services offered. Generally you should not increase prices to the point that reductions in sales more than offset the positive effects of the price increases and cause a decrease in net income.

You can reduce the direct costs, or cost of goods sold, by purchasing less expensive materials, increasing production efficiency, using cheaper labor, and decreasing overhead. You should not generally reduce the cost of goods sold to the detriment of the goods offered. For example, by charging more for a product that uses cheaper, less reliable raw materials, you will increase your gross profit; however, the market may reject the product and drastically lower sales volumes may result.

At first glance, it appears that you can reduce indirect costs by cutting back on R&D, selling, G&A, and/or depreciation expenses. While this is usually true in the short term, the long-term effects of reducing expenses such as advertising or product development can be catastrophic. In fact, it is not unusual to *increase* such expenditures to generate larger future sales and increase operations profit in the long run. Managers should seek to streamline costs where true fat exists and to maintain or increase expenses in areas in which they can realize longer term returns.

Example

Operations income ratio = income from operations / net sales

Income from operations = net sales − cost of goods sold − R&D expenses − selling expenses − G&A expenses − depreciation − amortization − other operational expenses

Net sales = 85,420
Cost of goods sold = 54,212
R&D expenses = 4,578
Selling and G&A expenses = 15,993
Depreciation & amortization = 1,204
Other operational expenses = 0

Income from operations = 85,420 − 54,212 − 4,578 − 15,993 − 1,204 − 0 = 9,433

Operations income ratio = 9,433 / 85,420 = 0.110 = 11.0%

9 Measuring Pretax Profit

Equation

Pretax profit = income from operations + nonoperating income − all other expenses other than taxes

or

Pretax profit = net sales − cost of goods sold − R&D expenses − selling expenses − G&A expenses − depreciation − amortization − other operational expenses + non-operating income − all other expenses other than taxes

Pretax profit is the amount of income a company generates after accounting for all direct operational expenses, indirect operational expenses, and non-operational expenses and income. Direct costs, also known as the cost of goods sold, include the costs required to produce a product or service (i.e., raw materials, direct labor, and direct overhead). Indirect costs include all other expenses a company must incur in delivering a product or service to the customer (i.e., product development, selling, advertising, accounting, office rent, and utilities). Nonoperational items include expenses for interest and income from nonoperating activities.

When to use indicator: Managers and investors use this indicator to determine a company's overall pretax profit and evaluate present-period performance. For example, prior-period tax credits can reduce present-period tax expenses and inflate present-period net income results.

Meaning of result: Companies must ultimately deliver positive pretax profit. Pretax profit is a measure of a company's profit-generating capabilities. Positive indications include high and preferably increasing profit over a number of reporting periods. Companies can survive with no pretax profit by taking on debt or selling company equity. This is required in many start-up, high growth, or turn-around companies. However, all for-profit companies, including companies in these categories, must ultimately provide positive pretax profit income to remain solvent.

Ways to improve the indicator: You can improve pretax profit by selling more products or services, increasing prices, reducing the direct and indirect costs required to produce goods or services, increasing nonoperational profit, and reducing nonoperational expenses.

Volume increases may generate larger pretax profits as net sales increase. They can also reduce the costs of goods sold since operational efficiencies typically increase with increasing volume.

The marketplace must accept price increases. Inflationary effects aside, typically you can't change them at will without making commensurate changes to the goods or services offered. Generally, you should not increase prices to the point that reductions in sales more than offset the positive

Sector	Mid to large cap	Pretax Profit	Small to mid cap	Pretax Profit	Micro to small cap	Pretax Profit
Manufacturing	General Motors	7,714,000	Toro	60,344	Encad	26,528
Retail	Wal-Mart Stores	5,719,000	Bed Bath & Beyond	121,398	TCBY Enterprises	13,556
Food	McDonald's	2,407,300	Applebee's Int'l	71,801	Garden Fresh Restaurant	6,435
Technology	Microsoft	7,117,000	Cypress Semiconductor	24,032	Jmar Technologies	1,450
Finance	Morgan-Stanley Dean Witter	4,274,000	Franklin Resources	615,713	AmeriTrade Holding	21,425
Healthcare	Columbia/HCA Healthcare	538,000	Novacare	66,801	National Home Health Care	3,134
Service	Manpower	249,208	Air & Water Technologies	−51,313	Market Facts	9,535
Media/Publishing	McGraw Hill	471,266	Scholastic	38,100	Thomas Nelson	20,276

effects of the price increase and cause a decrease in net income.

You can reduce the direct costs, or cost of goods sold, by purchasing less expensive materials, increasing production efficiency, using cheaper labor, and decreasing overhead. Generally, do not reduce the cost of goods sold to the detriment of the goods offered. For example, if you charge more for a product that uses cheaper, less reliable raw materials, you will increase your gross profit; however, the market may reject the product and you may end up with drastically lower sales.

At first glance, it appears that you can reduce indirect costs by cutting back on R&D, selling, G&A, and/or depreciation expenses. While this is usually true in the short term, the long-term effects of reducing expenses such as advertising or product development can be catastrophic. In fact, it is not unusual to *increase* such expenditures to generate larger future sales and to increase operations profit in the long run. Managers should seek to streamline costs where true fat exists and to maintain or increase expenses in areas in which they can realize longer term returns.

Increases in nonoperational income and decreases in interest expenses will also increase pretax profit. Since nonoperational income is not typically part of a firm's reason for being in business, it is often best to resist the temptation to seek higher income yields with higher risk investments. Solid financial performance will allow your company to qualify for lower interest rates on debt.

Example

Pretax profit = net sales − cost of goods sold − R&D expenses − selling expenses − G&A expenses − depreciation − amortization − other operational expenses + non-operating income − all other expenses other than taxes

$$\text{Net sales} = 85{,}420$$
$$\text{Cost of goods sold} = 54{,}212$$
$$\text{R\&D expenses} = 4{,}578$$
$$\text{Selling and G\&A expenses} = 15{,}993$$
$$\text{Depreciation \& amortization} = 1{,}204$$
$$\text{Other operational expenses} = 0$$
$$\text{Nonoperating income} = 455$$
$$\text{Interest expense} = 784$$

Pretax profit = 85,420 − 54,212 − 4,578 − 15,993 − 1,204 − 0 + 455 − 784 = 9,104

10 Evaluating the Pretax Profit Ratio

Equation

Pretax profit ratio = pretax profit / net sales

or

Pretax profit ratio = (net sales − cost of goods sold − R&D expenses − selling expenses − G&A expenses − depreciation − amortization − other operational expenses + nonoperating income − all other expenses other than taxes) / net sales

The **pretax profit ratio** indicates the margin between the revenue a company generates and all of the costs—excepting such nonoperational items as taxes, gains/losses on investments, and extraordinary items—associated with producing the product or service. Direct costs, also known as the cost of goods sold, include costs required to produce the product or service (i.e., raw materials, direct labor, and direct overhead). Indirect costs include all other expenses a company must incur in delivering a product or service to the customer (i.e., product development, selling, advertising, accounting, office rent, and utilities). Nonoperational items include expenses for interest and income from non-operating activities.

When to use indicator: Managers and investors use the pretax profit ratio to determine a company's overall pretax profit potential. By evaluating pretax profits, they can weigh present-period performance. For example, prior-period tax credits can reduce present-period tax expenses and inflate present-period net income results. Comparing this indicator over time can show trends in product pricing and operational and nonoperational costs and incomes. The ratio varies between zero and one, with higher ratios indicating higher, or more profitable, pretax profit margins.

Meaning of result: You can use pretax profit ratios to determine the pretax profitability of a product or company. The ratio indicates the percentage of every dollar of sales revenue that remains after you have accounted for all operational and nonoperational expenses, except such items as taxes, gains/losses on investments, and extraordinary items. For example, a pretax profit ratio of 0.107 indicates that a little less than 11¢ remains as pretax profit for every dollar of net sales revenue.

Companies must ultimately deliver positive pretax income ratios. The pretax profit ratio indicates a company's profit-generating capabilities. Positive indications include high and preferably increasing profit over a number of reporting periods. Companies can survive with a negative pretax profit ratio by taking on debt or selling company equity. This is required in many start-up, high growth, or turnaround companies. However, all for-profit companies must ultimately provide positive pretax profit income to remain solvent.

Ways to improve the indicator: You can improve pretax profit ratios by selling more products or ser-

Sector	Mid to large cap	Pretax Profit Ratio	Small to mid cap	Pretax Profit Ratio	Micro to small cap	Pretax Profit Ratio
Manufacturing	General Motors	4.3%	Toro	5.7%	Encad	17.8%
Retail	Wal-Mart Stores	4.8%	Bed Bath & Beyond	11.4%	TCBY Enterprises	15.0%
Food	McDonald's	21.1%	Applebee's Int'l	13.9%	Garden Fresh Restaurant	7.1%
Technology	Microsoft	49.1%	Cypress Semiconductor	4.4%	Jmar Technologies	6.8%
Finance	Morgan-Stanley Dean Witter	15.8%	Franklin Resources	28.5%	AmeriTrade Holding	22.4%
Healthcare	Columbia/HCA Healthcare	2.9%	Novacare	6.3%	National Home Health Care	8.9%
Service	Manpower	3.4%	Air & Water Technologies	−11.2%	Market Facts	9.5%
Media/Publishing	McGraw Hill	13.3%	Scholastic	3.6%	Thomas Nelson	8.0%

vices, increasing prices, reducing the direct and indirect costs of producing your goods or service, increasing nonoperational profit, or reducing nonoperational expenses.

Volume increases may generate larger pretax profits as net sales increase; they can also reduce the cost of goods sold since operational efficiencies typically increase with increasing volume.

The marketplace must accept price increases, so, inflationary effects aside, you typically should not change prices at will without making commensurate changes to the goods or services offered. Generally you should not increase prices to the point that reductions in sales more than offset the positive effects of the price increase and cause a decrease in net income.

You can reduce the direct costs, or cost of goods sold, by purchasing less expensive materials, increasing production efficiency, using cheaper labor, or decreasing overhead. Generally, do not reduce the cost of goods sold to the detriment of the goods offered. For example, if you charge more for a product that uses cheaper, less reliable raw materials you will increase your gross profit, but the market may reject the product and you may end up with drastically lower sales volumes.

At first glance, it appears that you can reduce indirect costs by cutting back on R&D, selling, G&A, and/or depreciation expenses. While this is usually true in the short term, the long-term effects of reducing expenses such as advertising or product development can be catastrophic. In fact, it is not unusual to *increase* such expenditures to generate larger future sales and increase operations profit in the long run. Managers should seek to streamline costs where true fat exists and to maintain or increase expenses in areas in which they can realize longer term returns.

Increases in nonoperational income and decreases in interest expenses can also increase pretax profit. As nonoperational income accounts are not typically part of a firm's reason for being in business, it is often best to resist the temptation to seek higher income yields with higher risk investments. Solid financial performance can help you obtain lower interest rates for debts.

Example

Pretax profit ratio = pretax profit / net sales

or

Pretax profit ratio = (net sales − cost of goods sold − R&D expenses − selling expenses − G&A expenses − depreciation − amortization − other operational expenses + nonoperating income − all other expenses other than taxes) / net sales

Net sales = 85,420
Cost of goods sold = 54,212
R&D expenses = 4,578
Selling and G&A expenses = 15,993
Depreciation & amortization = 1,204
Other operational expenses = 0
Non-operating income = 455
Interest expense = 784

Pretax profit = 85,420 − 54,212 − 4,578 − 15,993 − 1,204 − 0 + 455 − 784 = 9,104

Pretax profit ratio = 9,104 / 85,420 = 0.107 = 10.7%

11 Calculating Net Income

Equation

Net income = pretax profit − taxes + extraordinary items

or

Net income = net sales − cost of goods sold − R&D expenses − selling expenses − G&A expenses − depreciation − amortization − other operational expenses + nonoperating income − all other expenses other than taxes − taxes + extraordinary items

Net income is the amount of money remaining after you account for all sources of income and all expenses. It is called the **bottom line** because it literally exists on the last line of the income statement. Income sources include net sales, nonoperational sources, and gains on investments. Expenses include direct and indirect expenses from operations and nonoperational expenses such as interest, losses on investments, and extraordinary items.

Direct costs, also known as the cost of goods sold, include the costs required to produce your product or service (i.e., raw materials, direct labor, and direct overhead). Indirect costs include all other expenses a company incurs in delivering a product or service to the customer (i.e., product development, selling, advertising, accounting, office rent, and utilities). Nonoperational items include expenses for interest, taxes, and investment losses. Nonoperational income-related items include investment gains and income provided by nonoperating activities. Extraordinary items include expenses or income from non-typical events such as the purchase of another company or sale of substantial company assets.

When to use indicator: Managers and investors use this indicator to determine a company's profit potential after they consider all sources of income and expenses. This figure gives a feel for the overall health of a company. Besides sales revenue, it is one of the most commonly reported indicators.

Meaning of result: Companies must ultimately deliver positive net income. Net income is a measure of company's profit-generating capabilities. Positive indications include high and preferably increasing net income over a number of reporting periods. Companies can survive with negative net income by taking on debt or selling company equity. Many start-up, high growth, or turn-around companies must use these measures. However, all for-profit companies, including those in these categories, must ultimately provide positive net income to remain solvent.

Ways to improve the indicator: You can improve net income by selling more products or services, increasing prices, reducing the direct and indirect costs of producing your goods or service, increasing nonoperational profit, or reducing nonoperational expenses.

INCOME ANALYSIS

Sector	Mid to large cap	Net Income	Small to mid cap	Net Income	Micro to small cap	Net Income
Manufacturing	General Motors	6,698,000	Toro	34,845	Encad	17,429
Retail	Wal-Mart Stores	3,526,000	Bed Bath & Beyond	73,142	TCBY Enterprises	8,879
Food	McDonald's	1,642,500	Applebee's Int'l	45,091	Garden Fresh Restaurant	3,887
Technology	Microsoft	4,490,000	Cypress Semiconductor	18,419	Jmar Technologies	1,795
Finance	Morgan-Stanley Dean Witter	2,586,000	Franklin Resources	434,063	AmeriTrade Holding	13,822
Healthcare	Columbia/HCA Healthcare	−305,000	Novacare	38,910	National Home Health Care	1,856
Service	Manpower	163,880	Air & Water Technologies	−160,581	Market Facts	5,822
Media/Publishing	McGraw Hill	290,675	Scholastic	23,600	Thomas Nelson	12,673

Volume increases may generate larger net income as net sales increase, and they can reduce the costs of goods sold since operational efficiencies typically increase with increasing volume.

The market must accept price increases, so, inflationary effects aside, you typically can't change prices at will without making commensurate changes to the goods or services offered. Generally you should not increase prices to the point that reductions in sales more than offset the positive effects of the increase and cause a decrease in net income.

You can reduce the direct costs, or cost of goods sold, by purchasing less expensive materials, increasing production efficiency, using cheaper labor, or decreasing overhead. Generally do not reduce the cost of goods sold to the detriment of the goods offered. For example, if you charge more for a product that uses cheaper, less reliable raw materials, you will increase your gross profit; however, the market may reject the product and drastically lower sales volumes can result.

At first glance, it appears that you can reduce indirect costs by cutting back on R&D, selling, G&A, and/or depreciation expenses. While this is usually true in the short term, the long-term effects of reducing expenses such as advertising or product development can be catastrophic. In fact, it is not unusual to *increase* such expenditures to generate larger future sales and increase operations profit in the long run. Managers should seek to streamline costs where true fat exists and to maintain or increase expenses in areas in which they can realize longer term returns.

Increases in nonoperational income and decreases in interest expenses will also increase pretax profit. As nonoperational income accounts are not typically part of a firm's reason for being in business, it is often best to resist the temptation to seek higher income yields with higher risk investments. Solid financial performance can make lower interest rates available to you.

Example

Net income = net sales − cost of goods sold − R&D expenses − selling expenses − G&A expenses − depreciation − amortization − other operational expenses + non-operating income − all other expenses other than taxes − taxes + extraordinary items

Net sales = 85,420
Cost of goods sold = 54,212
R&D expenses = 4,578
Selling and G&A expenses = 15,993
Depreciation & amortization = 1,204
Other operational expenses = 0
Non-operating income = 455
Interest expense = 784
Income taxes = 3,529
Extraordinary items = −592

Net income = 85,420 − 54,212 − 4,578 − 15,993 − 1,204 − 0 + 455 − 784 − 3,529 − 592 = 4,983

12 Comparing Net Income to Sales

Equation

Net income to sales = net income / net sales

or

Net income to sales = (net sales − cost of goods sold − R&D expenses − selling expenses − G&A expenses − depreciation − amortization − other operational expenses + nonoperating income − all other expenses other than taxes − taxes + extraordinary items) / net sales

The **net income-to-sales ratio** indicates the margin between the revenues a company generates and all of the expenses required to provide the goods or service. Revenues include those generated by operations as well as nonoperational sources such as interest earned on investments. Expenses include direct costs, indirect costs, and nonoperational items such as interest payments and tax payments.

Direct costs, also known as the cost of goods sold, include the costs required to produce your product or service (i.e., raw materials, direct labor, and direct overhead). Indirect costs include all other expenses your company incurs in delivering your product or service to the customer (i.e., product development, selling, advertising, accounting, office rent, and utilities). Nonoperational items include expenses for interest, taxes, and investment losses. Nonoperational income-related items include investment gains and income provided by nonoperating activities. Extraordinary items include expenses or income from non-typical events such as the purchase of another company or sale of substantial company assets.

When to use indicator: Managers and investors use this ratio to determine a company's overall profit potential. You can understand present-period performance by evaluating the net-income-to-sales ratio. When you compare this indicator over time, you can spot trends in product pricing and operational and nonoperations costs and incomes. The ratio varies between zero and one, with higher ratios indicating higher, or more profitable, net income margins.

Meaning of result: You can use net income ratios to determine the profitability of a product or company. The ratio indicates the percentage of every dollar of sales revenue that remains after you account for all expenses and other sources of revenue. For example, a net income ratio of 0.058 indicates that a bit less than 6¢ remains as net income for every dollar of net sales revenue.

Ways to improve the indicator: You can improve net income-to-sales ratios by selling more products or services, increasing prices, reducing the direct and indirect costs required to produce the goods or service, increasing nonoperational profit, or reducing nonoperational expenses.

Volume increases may generate larger net income as net sales increase, but they can also reduce the

Sector	Mid to large cap	Net Income to Sales	Small to mid cap	Net Income to Sales	Micro to small cap	Net Income to Sales
Manufacturing	General Motors	3.76%	Toro	3.31%	Encad	11.69%
Retail	Wal-Mart Stores	2.99%	Bed Bath & Beyond	6.86%	TCBY Enterprises	9.80%
Food	McDonald's	14.40%	Applebee's Int'l	8.74%	Garden Fresh Restaurant	4.31%
Technology	Microsoft	31.00%	Cypress Semiconductor	3.38%	Jmar Technologies	8.37%
Finance	Morgan-Stanley Dean Witter	9.53%	Franklin Resources	20.07%	AmeriTrade Holding	14.45%
Healthcare	Columbia/HCA Healthcare	−1.62%	Novacare	3.65%	National Home Health Care	5.29%
Service	Manpower	2.26%	Air & Water Technologies	−35.19%	Market Facts	5.82%
Media/Publishing	McGraw Hill	8.22%	Scholastic	2.23%	Thomas Nelson	5.01%

cost of goods sold since operational efficiencies typically increase with increasing volume.

The market must accept price increases, so, inflationary effects aside, you typically can't change prices at will without making commensurate changes to the goods or services offered. Generally you should not increase prices to the point that reductions in sales more than offset the positive effects of the increase and cause a decrease in net income.

You can reduce the direct costs, or cost of goods sold, by purchasing less expensive materials, increasing production efficiency, using cheaper labor, or decreasing overhead. Generally do not reduce the cost of goods sold to the detriment of the goods offered. For example, if you charge more for a product that uses cheaper, less reliable raw materials you will increase your gross profit; however, the market may reject the product and drastically lower sales volumes may result.

At first glance, it appears that you can reduce indirect costs by cutting back on R&D, selling, G&A, and/or depreciation expenses. While this is usually true in the short term, the long-term effects of reducing expenses such as advertising or product development can be catastrophic. In fact, it is not unusual to *increase* such expenditures to generate larger future sales and increase operations profit in the long run. Managers should seek to streamline costs where true fat exists, and to maintain or increase expenses in areas in which they can realize longer term returns.

Increases in nonoperational income and decreases in interest expenses will also increase pretax profit. As nonoperational income accounts are not typically part of a firm's reason for being in business, it is often best to resist the temptation to seek higher income yields with higher risk investments. Solid financial performance can make lower interest rates available to you for debt.

Example

Net income to sales = net income / net sales

or

Net income to sales = (net sales − cost of goods sold − R&D expenses − selling expenses − G&A expenses − depreciation − amortization − other operational expenses + non-operating income − all other expenses other than taxes − taxes + extraordinary items) / net sales

$$\begin{aligned}
\text{Net sales} &= 85{,}420 \\
\text{Cost of goods sold} &= 54{,}212 \\
\text{R\&D expenses} &= 4{,}578 \\
\text{Selling and G\&A expenses} &= 15{,}993 \\
\text{Depreciation \& amortization} &= 1{,}204 \\
\text{Other operational expenses} &= 0 \\
\text{Nonoperating income} &= 455 \\
\text{Interest expense} &= 784 \\
\text{Income taxes} &= 3{,}529 \\
\text{Extraordinary items} &= -592
\end{aligned}$$

Net income = 85,420 − 54,212 − 4,578 − 15,993 − 1,204 − 0 + 455 − 784 − 3,529 − 592 = 4,983

Net income to sales = 4,983 / 85,420 = 0.058 = 5.8%

13 Finding the Percentage of Net Sales and Net Income that are Domestic

Equation

Percentage of domestic net sales = net domestic sales / total net sales

and

Percentage of domestic net income = net domestic income / total net income

The percentage of net domestic sales and income indicates the degree to which a company conducts its business domestically.

When to use indicator: Managers and investors can use this indicator to determine the size and, when compared to past performance periods, the rate of change of a company's domestic sales and income.

Meaning of result: Managers often want to ascertain the effect of strategic actions on both domestic and foreign income and sales results. Knowing the amount of domestic revenue and profit is essential in monitoring sales results and planning appropriate future strategies. It is typically beneficial to break down domestic sales and profits even further into more refined regions, such as by sales territory or state.

Example

Percentage of domestic net sales = net domestic sales / total net sales

Net domestic sales = 62,151
Total net sales = 85,420

Percentage of domestic net sales = 62,151 / 85,420 = .728 = 72.8%

14 Finding the Percentage of Sales and Net Income that are Foreign

Equation

Percentage of foreign net sales = net foreign sales / total net sales

and

Percentage of foreign net income = net foreign income / total net income

The percentage of net foreign sales and income indicates the degree to which the company conducts its business in foreign countries.

When to use indicator: Managers and investors can use this indicator to determine the size and, when compared to past performance periods, the rate of change of a company's foreign sales and income.

Meaning of result: Managers often want to ascertain the effect of strategic actions on both domestic and foreign income and sales results. Knowing the degree of foreign revenue and profit is essential in monitoring sales penetration results and planning appropriate future strategies. It is typically beneficial to break down foreign sales and profits even further to more refined regions, such as by sales territory, geographic area or country.

Example

Percentage of foreign net sales = net foreign sales / total net sales

Net foreign sales = 23,269
   Total net sales = 85,420

Percentage of foreign net sales = 23,269 / 85,420 = .272 = 27.2%

15 Determining the Cost of Capital

Equation

Cost of capital = (equity / [debt + equity]) × equity interest rate + (debt / [debt + equity]) × debt interest rate × (1 − tax rate)

The **cost of capital** is a weighted average of the interest a company must pay on both its equity and its debt. Although a company doesn't physically pay interest to shareholders for equity, that interest is considered a real cost because shareholders expect a return on their investment. The equity interest rate is also called the **required equity dividend**. Interest on a company's debt is also a component of the cost of capital, and, as shown in the formula above, it is tax deductible.

When to use indicator: The cost of capital allows managers to determine the overall costs associated with financing an operation such as a project or a new division. You can determine other indicators such as economic value added, EVA (tip #16), and residual income (tip #18) when you know the cost of capital.

Meaning of result: The cost of capital indicates a company's total funding costs. For example, consider a company in a 40% tax bracket which has $5 million in equity capital at 14% and $3.2 million in debt capital at 9% interest. The cost of capital is 10.6% as determined by the following:

Cost of capital = ($5,000,000/[$5,000,000 + $3,200,000]) × 0.14 + ($3,200,000/[$5,000,000 + $3,200,000]) × 0.09 × (1 − 0.40) = 0.106 = 10.6%

Ways to improve the indicator: You can reduce the cost of capital by lowering your debt and equity interest rates. In many cases, you can reduce your debt interest rates with increasingly sound financial performance. Signs of performance improvements are increasingly high net incomes, cash flows, and debt coverage and increasingly lower debt-to-equity ratios. You can reduce equity interest rates with positive, consistent, nonvolatile rates of return.

Example

Cost of capital = (equity / [debt + equity]) × equity interest rate + (debt / [debt + equity]) × debt interest rate × (1 − tax rate)

Equity = market value of equity = shares outstanding × share price = 3,600,000 × 22.5 = $81,000,000 = $81,000 thousands

Debt = interest-bearing debt = notes payable + current portion of long-term debt and capital leases + long-term debt = 1,000 + 650 + 12,513 = $14,163

Equity interest rate = risk-free, inflation-adjusted interest rate (long-term government bond) + risk premium = 7% + 6.9% = 13.9%

Debt interest rate = 8%

Tax rate = 40%

Cost of capital = (81,000 / [14,163 + 81,000]) × .139 + (14,163 / [14,163 + 81,000]) × .08 × (1 − 0.40) = 0.1255 = 12.55%

16 Measuring Economic Value Added (EVA)

Equation

EVA = after-tax operating profit − (cost of capital × capital employed)

Economic value added (EVA) is an overall profitability indicator that considers the costs of conducting an operation when determining profitability. Operations add value only when they provide profit in excess of the cost of the money required to capitalize the operation. The cost of capital is the weighted average of debt and equity financing (see tip #15). **Capital employed items** include all factors which cost money and which a company requires to generate income such as property, machinery, floor space, and working capital.

When to use indicator: You can use EVA to determine the profit potential of a project, person, department or company. EVA calculations indicate whether you should initiate or scrub projects, whether you should purchase or pass over companies, and whether you should purchase or sell a company's stock. Generally, positive EVA results are a good sign and negative EVA results indicate you should not consider or should terminate the project or company. As always, you should weigh return potentials against risk levels. At times, less profitable operations are preferable when they offer significantly reduced risks.

Meaning of result: Positive EVA values indicate successful projects and companies. A project adds value when there is profit left over after a company pays all project or company expenses. It is possible to show positive net income even with unsuccessful projects or companies. This is not so with EVA; since this measurement takes all costs into consideration, EVA is positive only when operations are successful.

For example, assume a given project yields an annual after-tax operating income of $125,000. Let's also assume that the total project cost is $920,000 and the company's cost of capital is 9.5%. The total cost of capital is the product of the total cost and the cost of capital or $87,400 ($920,000 × .095). Figure the EVA by subtracting the total cost of capital from the operating profit. The result is $37,600 ($125,000 − $87,400). Since the EVA is positive, the project is viable, unless the manager could apply the money allocated to the project to another project at no greater risk and, thereby, generate an even larger EVA. If, in this example, the cost of capital were increased to 16%, then you should decline the project because it would cost $147,200, which is more than the $125,000 return.

Ways to improve the indicator: There are many ways to improve EVA. You can develop improved products or services, enhance sales and marketing efforts to increase sales volumes, or increase operations efficiencies to drive down product costs. You can also purchase or develop highly profitable projects or companies, reduce the cost of capital, eliminate redundancy and waste throughout the company, ensure that all expensive capital-intensive equipment is fully utilized, or sell assets that don't generate positive EVA.

Example

EVA = after-tax operating profit − (cost of capital × capital employed)

After-tax operating profit = 9,433 × (1 − tax rate) = 9,433 × (1 − 0.40) = 5,660

Cost of capital = 12.55%

Capital employed = net of property, plant, and equipment + current assets − current liabilities = 10,018 + 44,135 − 12,032 = 42,121

EVA = 5,660 − (0.1255 × 42,121) = 374

17 Comparing Economic Value Added (EVA) to Net Income

Equation

EVA to net income = EVA / net income

Comparing EVA to net income indicates the degree to which EVA contributes to net income. EVA is an overall profitability indicator that takes into account the costs of conducting an operation when determining profitability. Operations add value only when they provide profit in excess of the cost of the money required to capitalize the operation.

When to use indicator: Managers and investors can use this ratio to determine how much value a company or project provides above minimum expected returns.

Meaning of result: Higher EVA-to-net-income ratios indicate better company performance. As this ratio increases, a larger percentage of the company's net income exceeds the company's cost of capital. An operation is breaking even with the cost of capital when this ratio is zero. Since one of a company's primary financial goals is to maximize return to shareholders, this ratio is highly indicative of such performance. When a company has a positive net income and a negative EVA, this ratio is less than one and indicates that the company currently is earning income at a rate less than its cost of capital. If the company cannot improve that level of performance, the company and its shareholders would be better off financially if they dissolved the company and invested the proceeds to achieve a better rate of return.

Ways to improve the indicator: There are many ways to improve EVA-to-net-income ratios. A manager can develop improved products or services, enhance sales and marketing efforts to increase sales volumes, or increase operations efficiencies to drive down product costs. She also can purchase or develop highly profitable projects or companies, reduce the cost of capital, eliminate redundancy and waste throughout the company, ensure that all expensive capital-intensive equipment is fully utilized, or sell assets that don't generate positive EVA.

Example

EVA to net income = EVA / net income

EVA = 374
Net income = 4,983

EVA to net income = 374 / 4,983 = 0.0751 = 7.51%

18 Examining the Size of Residual Income

Equation

Residual income = net income − (cost of capital × capital employed)

Residual income indicates overall profitability by considering the costs of conducting an operation when determining profitability. Operations add value only when they provide net income over the cost of the money required to capitalize the operation. The cost of capital is the weighted average of debt and equity financing (see tip #15). Capital employed items include all factors which cost money and are necessary for a company to generate income such as property, machinery, floor space, and working capital.

When to use indicator: Similar to economic value added (EVA), you use residual income to determine the profit potential of a project, person, department or company. This indicator shows whether you should initiate or scrub projects, whether you should purchase or pass over companies, and whether you should purchase or sell a company's stock. Generally, positive residual income results are a good sign while negative results indicate that you should not consider or should terminate the project or company. As always, you should weigh return potentials against risk levels. At times, less profitable operations are preferable when they offer significantly reduced risks.

The difference between residual income and EVA is that residual income considers net income and EVA considers after-tax operating income. When you are determining net income, you must subtract current-year interest expenses from operating income. To determine residual income, subtract the annual cost of assets from net income. In this manner it is possible to count twice the interest required to pay for assets—first to calculate net income and second to find the residual income. Thus, although EVA and residual income are similar, residual income can be a more stringent or conservative method to determine the viability of a project or company.

Meaning of result: Positive residual income values indicate successful projects and companies. A company adds value only when profit is left over after the company pays all project or company expenses. It is possible to show positive net income even with an unsuccessful project or company. This is not so with residual income; since residual income considers all costs, it is positive only when operations are successful.

For example, assume a given project yields an annual net income of $125,000. Let's also assume that the total project cost is $920,000 and the company's cost of capital is 9.5%. The total cost of capital is the product of the total cost and the cost of capital or $87,400 ($920,000 × .095). Figure the residual income by subtracting the total cost of capital from the net income. The result is $37,600 ($125,000 − $87,400). Since there is a positive residual income, the project is viable unless management could apply the money allocated to the project to another project that has no greater risk and that generates an even larger residual income. If, in this example, the cost of capital were increased to 16%, then management should decline the project because it would cost $147,200, an amount more than the $125,000 return.

Ways to improve the indicator: You can improve residual income in many ways. You can develop improved products or services, enhance sales and marketing efforts to increase sales volumes, and increase operations efficiencies to drive down product costs. You can also purchase or develop highly profitable projects or companies, reduce the cost of capital, eliminate redundancy and waste throughout the company, ensure that all expensive capital-intensive equipment is fully utilized, or sell assets that don't generate positive residual income.

Example

Residual income = net income − (cost of capital × capital employed)

Net income = 4,983

Cost of capital = 12.55%

Capital employed = net of property, plant, and equipment + current assets − current liabilities = 10,018 + 44,135 − 12,032 = 42,121

Residual income = 4,983 − (0.1255 × 42,121) = −303

19 Comparing Residual Income to Net Income

Equation

Residual income to net income = residual income / net income

Comparing residual income to net income indicates the degree to which residual income contributes to net income. Residual income indicates overall profitability by considering the costs of conducting an operation when determining profitability. Operations add value only when they provide profit over the cost of the money required to capitalize the operation.

When to use indicator: Managers and investors can use this ratio to determine how much value a company or project provides over minimum expected returns.

Meaning of result: Higher residual-income-to-net-income ratios indicate better company performance. As this ratio increases, a larger percentage of the company's net income exceeds the company's cost of capital. The company is breaking even with the cost of capital when this ratio is zero. One of a company's primary financial goals is to maximize return to shareholders, and this ratio is highly indicative of such performance. When a company has a positive net income and a negative residual income, this ratio is less than one and indicates that the company currently is earning income at a rate less than its cost of capital. If management cannot improve that level of performance, the company and its shareholders would be better off to dissolve the company and invest the proceeds so that they can achieve acceptable rates of return.

Ways to improve the indicator: There are many ways to improve the ratio of residual income to net income. A company can develop improved products or services, enhance sales and marketing efforts to increase sales volumes, or increase operations efficiencies to drive down product costs. Companies also can purchase or develop highly profitable projects or companies, reduce the cost of capital, eliminate redundancy and waste throughout the company, ensure that all expensive capital-intensive equipment is fully utilized, and sell assets that don't generate positive residual income.

Example

Residual income to net income = residual income / net income

Residual income = –303
Net income = 4,983

Residual income to net income = –303 / 4,983 = –0.0608 = –6.08%

20 Determining the Return on Equity (ROE)

Equation

ROE = net income / shareholder equity

or

ROE = (net income/net sales) × (net sales/total assets) × (total assets/shareholder equity)

Also known as ROE = (profitability) × (asset turnover) × (financial leverage)

or

ROE = (net income / net sales) × (net sales / shareholder equity)

Also known as ROE = (profitability) × (equity turnover)

Return on equity (ROE) is a measure of return a company generates on shareholder equity. **Shareholder equity** includes all balance sheet shareholder equity items such as common stock, additional paid-in capital, and retained earnings.

When to use indicator: Investors can use this ratio to determine how productively a company employs shareholders' equity to generate income.

Meaning of result: The first formula shows that, for a given amount of shareholder equity, ROE increases as net income increases. In other words, the more income a company earns from an equity investment, the better. Shareholders like to see very large ROEs. High ROEs typically drive up share prices since the company is efficiently earning money with its equity capital. The relationship between ROE and net income is apparent from the first formula; however, that formula does not appreciably help management decide what to change to improve the ROE.

Although the second formula yields the identical result for ROE, it helps the manager more than the first. In the second formula, ROE is equivalent to profitability multiplied by asset turnover multiplied by financial leverage. By increasing any of these factors, management can enhance ROE.

High ROE values generally indicate good performance although it is important for you to understand the reasons for a higher or lower trending ROE. Higher ROEs may not be desirable if the company must assume too high a risk in its product offering or degree of debt leverage. Higher ROEs indicate that net profit, and/or asset turnover, and/or financial leverage are increasing. Increases in net profit are good to the extent that a company does not sacrifice growth potential, sales levels, and quality. Increases in asset turnover are good to the extent that a company retains sufficient assets to optimize operations efficiencies. Increases in financial leverage can be positive to the extent that the company has not acquired so much debt for the purchase of assets that the company is at risk of default.

Sector	Mid to large cap	Return on Equity	Small to mid cap	Return on Equity	Micro to small cap	Return on Equity
Manufacturing	General Motors	38.26%	Toro	14.45%	Encad	26.93%
Retail	Wal-Mart Stores	19.06%	Bed Bath & Beyond	24.76%	TCBY Enterprises	11.47%
Food	McDonald's	18.56%	Applebee's Int'l	15.52%	Garden Fresh Restaurant	11.38%
Technology	Microsoft	27.00%	Cypress Semiconductor	2.86%	Jmar Technologies	14.38%
Finance	Morgan-Stanley Dean Witter	18.53%	Franklin Resources	23.41%	AmeriTrade Holding	20.63%
Healthcare	Columbia/HCA Healthcare	–4.21%	Novacare	7.66%	National Home Health Care	7.95%
Service	Manpower	26.54%	Air & Water Technologies	146.97%	Market Facts	10.87%
Media/Publishing	McGraw Hill	20.26%	Scholastic	7.42%	Thomas Nelson	8.10%

When a company pays preferred dividends, ROE is sometimes expressed as the following:

ROE = (net income − preferred dividends) / shareholder equity.

Preferred dividends are subtracted from net income since equity shareholders don't realize a return from preferred dividends.

Ways to improve the indicator: ROE can be increased with increasing profitability, asset turnover, financial leverage, and/or equity turnover. Typically a company can maximize profitability by delivering a desired and properly priced product or service with controlled operating costs. It can maximize asset turnover by fully utilizing company assets. Generation of income requires assets, but they should be purchased only to the extent that they contribute positively to net sales and net income. Financial leverage details what percentage of a company's total funding equity holders provide. The lower the equity position in relationship to total funding, the higher the financial leverage and ROE. A company can increase equity turnover by generating larger net sales for a given amount of equity investment.

Example

ROE = net income / shareholder equity

Net income = 4,983
Shareholder equity = 31,088

ROE = 4,983 / 31,088 = 0.1603 = 16.03%

21 Finding the Return on Assets (ROA)

Equation

ROA = net income / total assets

or

ROA = (net income / net sales) × (net sales / total assets)

or

ROA = profitability × asset turnover

Return on assets (ROA) is a measure of the return a company generates on its assets. Total assets include all balance sheet asset items such as cash, inventory, property, buildings, and machinery.

When to use indicator: Managers and investors can use this ratio to determine how productively the company uses its assets to generate income.

Meaning of result: The first formula shows that, for a given amount of total assets, ROA increases as net income increases. In other words, the more income a company earns with its assets, the better. Managers and shareholders like to see very large ROAs. This typically indicates efficient management and use of company assets. The relationship of ROA and net income is apparent from the first formula; however, it does not offer much help for management in deciding what to change to improve the ROA.

Although the second formula yields the identical result for ROA, it helps the manager more. In the second formula, ROA is equivalent to profitability multiplied by asset turnover. By increasing either one of these factors, management can enhance ROA.

High ROA values generally indicate good performance although management should understand the reasons for a higher or lower trending ROA. A company may not want higher ROAs if the company must assume too high a risk in its product offering. Higher ROAs indicate that net profit and/or asset turnover are increasing. Increases in net profit are good to the extent that a company has not sacrificed growth potential, sales levels, and quality. Increases in asset turnover are good to the extent that sufficient resources remain available to handle orders and optimize efficiencies.

Instead of using net income for the return portion when determining ROA, some managers and investors prefer to use net income plus after-tax interest expense

(net income + (interest × [1 − tax rate]).

Some feel that adding back this interest expense to net income gives a more realistic indication of the return on assets. However, because interest payments are often an integral part of many asset investments, others prefer to include such payments. Since both arguments are reasonable, the latter may be the best choice since the formula is less complex.

Sector	Mid to large cap	Return on Assets	Small to mid cap	Return on Assets	Micro to small cap	Return on Assets
Manufacturing	General Motors	2.93%	Toro	5.27%	Encad	19.30%
Retail	Wal-Mart Stores	7.77%	Bed Bath & Beyond	15.96%	TCBY Enterprises	8.95%
Food	McDonald's	9.00%	Applebee's Int'l	11.95%	Garden Fresh Restaurant	6.23%
Technology	Microsoft	20.08%	Cypress Semiconductor	1.93%	Jmar Technologies	10.40%
Finance	Morgan-Stanley Dean Witter	0.86%	Franklin Resources	14.02%	AmeriTrade Holding	1.83%
Healthcare	Columbia/HCA Healthcare	−1.39%	Novacare	3.84%	National Home Health Care	7.36%
Service	Manpower	8.01%	Air & Water Technologies	−41.92%	Market Facts	6.70%
Media/Publishing	McGraw Hill	7.80%	Scholastic	3.08%	Thomas Nelson	4.44%

Ways to improve the indicator: Increasing profitability and/or asset turnover can increase ROA. Often a company can maximize profitability by delivering a desired and properly priced product or service with controlled operating costs. A company can maximize asset turnover by fully using company assets. Generating income requires assets but they should be purchased only to the extent that they contribute positively to net sales and net income.

Example

ROA = net income / total assets

Net income = 4,983
Total assets = 56,268

ROA = 4,983 / 56,268 = 0.0886 = 8.86%

22 Determining the Return on Invested Capital (ROIC)

Equation

ROIC = (net income) / (long-term liabilities + equity)

or

ROIC = (net income / net sales) × [net sales / (long-term liabilities + equity)]

or

ROIC = profitability × invested capital turnover

Return on invested capital (ROIC) is a measure of return a company generates on all of its invested capital. Invested capital is equivalent to long-term investments plus equity. Using the basic balance sheet relationship of assets equaling liabilities plus equity, this is also equivalent to current assets minus current liabilities (working capital) plus long-term assets. This latter expression is often easier to understand. Companies use investment capital to purchase long-term assets such as machinery and buildings and to provide working capital such as cash and inventory.

Assets = liabilities + equity

where

Assets = current assets + long-term assets
Liabilities = current liabilities + long-term liabilities

Current assets + long-term assets = current liabilities + long-term liabilities + equity

Long-term liabilities + equity = current assets − current liabilities + long-term assets

When to use indicator: Managers and investors can use this ratio to determine how productively the company utilizes *all* of the capital invested in the company whereas ROA provides return information relative to total assets and ROE considers returns on equity only.

Meaning of result: ROIC increases as net income increases for a fixed amount of invested capital. In other words, the more income a company earns with its invested capital, the better, assuming acceptable risk levels. Managers and shareholders like to see large ROIC values. This typically indicates efficient management and use of the capital entrusted to the company.

Although the second formula yields the identical result for ROIC, it helps the manager more. In the second formula, ROIC is equivalent to profitability multiplied by invested capital turnover. By increasing either one of these factors, management can enhance ROIC.

High ROIC values generally indicate good performance although management should understand the reasons for a higher or lower trending ROIC. Higher ROICs may not be desirable if the company

Sector	Mid to large cap	Return on Invested Capital	Small to mid cap	Return on Invested Capital	Micro to small cap	Return on Invested Capital
Manufacturing	General Motors	3.16%	Toro	8.22%	Encad	26.41%
Retail	Wal-Mart Stores	12.16%	Bed Bath & Beyond	23.75%	TCBY Enterprises	10.14%
Food	McDonald's	10.77%	Applebee's Int'l	14.32%	Garden Fresh Restaurant	8.01%
Technology	Microsoft	27.00%	Cypress Semiconductor	2.13%	Jmar Technologies	13.40%
Finance	Morgan-Stanley Dean Witter	6.51%	Franklin Resources	18.20%	AmeriTrade Holding	20.63%
Healthcare	Columbia/HCA Healthcare	−1.66%	Novacare	4.55%	National Home Health Care	7.84%
Service	Manpower	15.72%	Air & Water Technologies	−80.86%	Market Facts	9.10%
Media/Publishing	McGraw Hill	11.54%	Scholastic	4.04%	Thomas Nelson	5.27%

must assume too high a risk in its product offering. Higher ROICs indicate that net profit and/or invested capital turnover are increasing. Increases in net profit are good to the extent that a company does not sacrifice growth potential, sales levels, and quality. Increases in invested capital turnover are good to the extent that the company still has sufficient assets (purchased with invested capital) to optimize operations efficiencies.

Instead of using net income for the return portion when determining ROIC, some managers and investors prefer to use net income plus after-tax interest expense.

Net income + (interest × [1 − tax rate]).

Some feel that adding back this interest expense to net income gives a more realistic indication of the return on invested capital. However, because interest payments are often an integral part of most capital investments, others prefer to include such payments. Since both arguments are reasonable, management may opt for the latter formula since it is less complex.

Ways to improve the indicator: Increasing either profitability or invested capital turnover can increase ROIC. A company can maximize profitability by delivering a desired and properly priced product or service with controlled operating costs. A company can maximize invested capital turnover by fully utilizing its working capital and long-term assets. Generation of income requires assets, but they should be purchased only to the extent that they contribute positively to net sales and net income.

Example

ROIC = (net income) / (long-term liabilities + equity)

Net income = 4,983

Long-term liabilities = Total liabilities − Current liabilities = 25,180 − 12,032 = 13,148

Equity = 31,088

ROIC = 4,983 / (13,148 + 31,088) = 0.1126 = 11.26%

23 Comparing Cash Provided by Operations to Net Income

Equation

Operations cash flow to net income = cash flow from operations / |net income|

The ratio of cash flow from operations to net income measures the quality of a company's income flow.

When to use indicator: Managers and investors can use this indicator to determine the amount of net income that is generated by operations. Comparing this ratio over time can show income quality trends.

Meaning of result: Higher quality companies tend to generate a high percentage of cash flow from operations. By comparing operating cash flow to net income, a manager can understand the quality of the net income. Higher ratios indicate that operations cash flow is generating increasingly large percentages of net income instead of its being generated from such sources as the sale of assets or external financing. Start-up and poorer performing companies typically generate much smaller operations cash flows.

Note that the absolute value of net income is used for this comparison. This gives a better indication of the relative sizes of operating cash flow and net income, particularly when either value is less than zero.

Ways to improve the indicator: You can increase operational cash flow by providing properly priced, highly demanded products while simultaneously controlling direct and indirect costs.

Example

Operations cash flow to net income = cash flow from operations / |net income|

Cash flow from operations = 4,820
Net income = 4,983

Operations cash flow to net income = 4,820 / 4,983 = 0.9673 = 96.7%

Sector	Mid to large cap	Operations Cash Flow to Net Income	Small to mid cap	Operations Cash Flow to Net Income	Micro to small cap	Operations Cash Flow to Net Income
Manufacturing	General Motors	245.66%	Toro	240.70%	Encad	−17.07%
Retail	Wal-Mart Stores	202.01%	Bed Bath & Beyond	65.50%	TCBY Enterprises	192.51%
Food	McDonald's	148.69%	Applebee's Int'l	193.78%	Garden Fresh Restaurant	310.42%
Technology	Microsoft	153.23%	Cypress Semiconductor	445.36%	Jmar Technologies	*
Finance	Morgan-Stanley Dean Witter	−22.74%	Franklin Resources	98.73%	AmeriTrade Holding	171.88%
Healthcare	Columbia/HCA Healthcare	486.23%	Novacare	121.41%	National Home Health Care	129.20%
Service	Manpower	22.03%	Air & Water Technologies	9.34%	Market Facts	175.93%
Media/Publishing	McGraw Hill	128.35%	Scholastic	498.73%	Thomas Nelson	63.79%

* Cash flow data not reported for this company.

24 Comparing Short-Lived Income to Net Income

Equation

Short-lived income to net income = short-lived income / net income

This ratio indicates the percentage of net income that is not repetitive. **Short-lived income** includes sources such as one-time contracts and income generated from short-term fads. Because this type of income is not repeatable, it is of a lower quality than normal, repetitive income.

When to use indicator: Managers and investors can use this measure to determine the quality and seasonality of a firm's income.

Meaning of result: Lower ratios typically indicate higher quality income streams since this means that little net income is of a short-term, or transitory, nature. Higher quality income streams are preferable because they are predictable and cost effective. Predictability allows management to efficiently allocate resources such as direct labor, raw materials, and advertising.

Ways to improve the indicator: Pursuing business and customer bases that are recurrent can decrease the ratio of short-lived income to net income. Since repeat customers are generally the most cost-effective type of customer, you can increase income quality by enlarging that customer base. However, if your company is not fully using its production capacity and revenue generated by a short-term contract more than covers variable costs, the company should accept short-term contracts.

Example

Short-lived income to net income = short-lived income / net income

Short-lived income = 172
Net income = 4,983

Short-lived income to net income = 172 / 4983 = 0.0345 = 3.45%

25 Determining the Significance of Short-Lived Sales to Net Sales

Equation

Short-lived sales to net sales = short-lived sales / net sales

This ratio indicates the percentage of net sales that are not repetitive. **Short-lived sales** include sources such as one-time contracts and sales generated from short-term fads. Because these types of sales are not repeatable, they are of a lower quality than normal, repetitive sales.

When to use indicator: Managers and investors can use this measure to determine the quality and seasonality of a firm's sales.

Meaning of result: Lower ratios typically indicate higher quality sales streams since this means that few net sales are of a short-term, or transitory, nature. Higher quality sales streams are preferable because they are predictable and cost effective. Predictability allows management to allocate efficiently resources such as direct labor, raw materials, and advertising.

Ways to improve the indicator: Pursuing business and customer bases that are recurrent can decrease the percentage of short-lived sales compared to net sales. Pursue business and customer bases that are recurrent. Since repeat customers are generally the most cost-effective type, you can increase sales income quality by enlarging that customer base. However, if a company is not fully using its production capacity, and revenue generated by a short-term contract more than covers variable costs, the company should accept short-term contracts.

Example

Short-lived sales to net sales = short-lived sales / net sales

Short-lived sales = 3,622
Net sales = 85,420

Short-lived sales to net sales = 3,622 / 85,420 = 0.0424 = 4.24%

26 Comparing Cash Flow from Operations to Total Cash Flow

Equation

Cash flow from operations to total cash flow = operating cash flow / |total cash flow|

Operating cash flow, one of the three sources of cash flow (together with investing and financing cash flow), is one of the more important indicators of a company's financial health. This indicator compares the relative sizes of operating and total cash flow.

When to use indicator: Managers and investors can use this indicator to determine how big a part operations plays in generating cash flow. The three manners in which a company uses or generates cash are through its operations, its investments, and its financing activities. It is most desirable to generate cash through operations since this is the intent of forming an organization. Operating cash flow is a direct indication of how much cash is generated from activities core to the company. Examples include a car manufacturer producing and selling cars or a restaurant producing and selling meals. Investment activities include the purchase or sale of machinery for plant use and the buying or selling of securities. Financing activities include the issuance or purchase of additional stock and the issuance or payment of additional debt.

Meaning of result: High percentages of operating cash flows are what companies generally desire. Regardless of how promising the short- and long-term potential for any given firm may be, it needs positive operating cash flows in the long term to keep its doors open. Start-up and growth companies may subsist for a time with low or negative operating cash percentages by generating cash flow from other sources such as by issuing more stock for cash or by taking on additional debt.

Note that the absolute value of total cash flow is used for this comparison. This gives a better indication of the relative sizes of operating and total cash flow, particularly when either cash flow value is less than zero.

Ways to improve the indicator: The main contributors to operating cash flow are often net income and depreciation. Other factors which affect operating cash flow include changes in assets and liabilities such as inventory, accounts receivable, and accounts payable. Improving net income is generally the most desirable method of improving operating cash flow. You can improve net income by providing properly priced, highly demanded products or services while maintaining good cost control. Operating cash flow also increases as the depreciation account increases. However, this amount is not

Sector	Mid to large cap	Cash Flow from Operations to Total Cash Flow	Small to mid cap	Cash Flow from Operations to Total Cash Flow	Micro to small cap	Cash Flow from Operations to Total Cash Flow
Manufacturing	General Motors	5.87	Toro	1,446.09	Encad	–0.52
Retail	Wal-Mart Stores	12.63	Bed Bath & Beyond	3.30	TCBY Enterprises	3.58
Food	McDonald's	212.37	Applebee's Int'l	10.36	Garden Fresh Restaurant	6.97
Technology	Microsoft	51.73	Cypress Semiconductor	0.62	Jmar Technologies	*
Finance	Morgan-Stanley Dean Witter	–0.34	Franklin Resources	7.21	AmeriTrade Holding	0.63
Healthcare	Columbia/HCA Healthcare	494.33	Novacare	0.65	National Home Health Care	6.07
Service	Manpower	0.94	Air & Water Technologies	25.94	Market Facts	0.28
Media/Publishing	McGraw Hill	278.83	Scholastic	588.50	Thomas Nelson	2.15

* Cash flow data not reported for this company.

simply found money. Income statements count depreciation as an expense in the current period. Since you previously purchased the depreciable item with cash, no additional cash is required in the current period, so you add that amount of money back to net income to show a more accurate account of the current-period operating cash flow. Depreciation expenses are, in effect, accounting placeholders.

Example

Cash flow from operations to total cash flow = operating cash flow / |total cash flow|

Operating cash flow = 4,820
Total cash flow = 1,017

Cash flow from operations to total cash flow = 4,820 / 1,017 = 4.739 = 474%

27 Comparsing Cash Flow from Investing Activities to Total Cash Flow

Equation

Cash flow from investing activities to total cash flow = investment-related cash flow / |total cash flow|

When to use indicator: Managers and investors can use this indicator to determine how big a part investment plays in generating cash flow. Investment cash flow is often negative because firms usually purchase more investments than they sell. This is particularly true for growing companies that require additional machinery or are acquiring smaller companies. The main items contained within the investing cash flow group are purchases or sales of property, plant, and equipment; acquisitions or sales of subsidiaries; and purchases or sales of securities.

Meaning of result: Negative amounts of investment cash flow can indicate that the company is plowing money into investments. This is generally a good indication since investments such as new machinery, plants, and subsidiaries may allow the company to increase future earnings. Large amounts of investment can be suspect, however, when, for example, investments are made in plants that already have excess capacity or when other companies are purchased at prices so high that investment return rates suffer.

Positive amounts of investment cash flow usually indicate the company is selling either property, plants, equipment, subsidiaries, or securities investments. Periodically, such sales may be good management moves. However, when investment cash flows remain high over the long run, the company may liquidate so many assets that it can no longer remain a viable concern.

Note that the absolute value of total cash flow is used for this comparison. This gives a better indication of the relative sizes of investing and total cash flow, particularly when either cash flow value is less than zero.

Ways to improve the indicator: Successful companies generally invest cash wisely to ensure promising futures. When plants and equipment are no longer competitive, you should explore investments in more efficient machinery. Similarly, when you identify a subsidiary that can add value to your company, don't hesitate to consider an acquisition. Alternatively, scrutinize divisions that no longer create value and consider selling them if you can use the cash generated from the sale more productively.

Example

Cash flow from investing activities to total cash flow = investment-related cash flow / |total cash flow|

Investment cash flow = −6,594
Total cash flow = 1,017

Cash flow from investing activities to total cash flow = −6,594 / 1,017 = −6.484 = −648%

Sector	Mid to large cap	Cash Flow from Investing Activities to Total Cash Flow	Small to mid cap	Cash Flow from Investing Activities to Total Cash Flow	Micro to small cap	Cash Flow from Investing Activities to Total Cash Flow
Manufacturing	General Motors	−7.48	Toro	−2,873.69	Encad	−1.35
Retail	Wal-Mart Stores	−7.84	Bed Bath & Beyond	−2.84	TCBY Enterprises	0.32
Food	McDonald's	−192.80	Applebee's Int'l	−11.34	Garden Fresh Restaurant	−10.88
Technology	Microsoft	−54.68	Cypress Semiconductor	−0.69	Jmar Technologies	*
Finance	Morgan-Stanley Dean Witter	−1.48	Franklin Resources	−9.98	AmeriTrade Holding	−0.10
Healthcare	Columbia/HCA Healthcare	−915.33	Novacare	−2.57	National Home Health Care	−5.07
Service	Manpower	−2.93	Air & Water Technologies	−21.09	Market Facts	−0.18
Media/Publishing	McGraw Hill	−168.00	Scholastic	−396.00	Thomas Nelson	−1.24

* Cash flow data not reported for this company.

28 Comparing Cash Flow from Financing Activities to Total Cash Flow

Equation

Cash flow from financing activities to total cash flow = finance-related cash flow / |total cash flow|

When to use indicator: Managers and investors can use this indicator to determine how big a part financing plays in generating total cash flow. The main items within the finance cash flow group are issuance or purchases of equity (company stock), issuance or repayment of debt, and dividend payments.

Meaning of result: Low or negative percentages of finance-related cash flow can indicate that the company is not taking in cash flow in the form of additional debt, stock issuance, or related activities. Negative finance cash flows typically arise when companies pay off debt or repurchase equity. Mature, healthy companies often take these actions when productive operations sources supply their cash flow needs.

Higher percentages of finance-related cash flow can indicate a company is raising money via financial means such as issuing stock or taking on more debt. Start-up and growth companies often require finance-related cash to fuel growth for items such as new equipment or larger inventories. Another reason for needing cash from financial activities might be that operations-related activities are not generating sufficient cash.

Note that the absolute value of total cash flow is used for this comparison. This gives a better indication of the relative sizes of financing and total cash flow, particularly when either cash flow value is less than zero.

Ways to improve the indicator: You should maintain finance-related cash flow levels that ensure the most promising future and that are commensurate with the state of the health of the industry in which the company operates and the maturity level of the company. To improve this indicator, you can increase financial cash flow percentages for one company and decrease them for another. For example, a growing company that has shown there is a substantial, and currently undersupplied, market for its products or services could justify increasing finance-related cash flow in order to invest in items that will allow the company to serve the market better. Alternatively, reductions in finance-related cash flow ratios could justify a company's operating in a saturated market when it has not identified any other manners or markets in which to invest its cash.

Example

Cash flow from financing activities to total cash flow = finance-related cash flow / |total cash flow|

Finance cash flow = 2,791
Total cash flow = 1,017

Cash flow from financing activities to total cash flow = 2,791 / 1,017 = 2.744 = 274%

Sector	Mid to large cap	Cash Flow from Financing Activities to Total Cash Flow	Small to mid cap	Cash Flow from Financing Activities to Total Cash Flow	Micro to small cap	Cash Flow from Financing Activities to Total Cash Flow
Manufacturing	General Motors	0.79	Toro	1,504.55	Encad	0.87
Retail	Wal-Mart Stores	–3.79	Bed Bath & Beyond	0.54	TCBY Enterprises	–2.90
Food	McDonald's	–18.57	Applebee's Int'l	–0.01	Garden Fresh Restaurant	4.91
Technology	Microsoft	4.17	Cypress Semiconductor	1.06	Jmar Technologies	*
Finance	Morgan-Stanley Dean Witter	3.50	Franklin Resources	1.77	AmeriTrade Holding	0.47
Healthcare	Columbia/HCA Healthcare	420.00	Novacare	0.92	National Home Health Care	0.00
Service	Manpower	1.10	Air & Water Technologies	–5.85	Market Facts	0.90
Media/Publishing	McGraw Hill	–108.71	Scholastic	–192.00	Thomas Nelson	–1.91

* Cash flow data not reported for this company.

CHAPTER THREE

Investment Analysis

This chapter presents a number of ratios that help describe the investment quality of publicly traded companies, such as earnings per share, earnings growth rates, and cash flow per share. These ratios should help you make more informed investment decisions and help you monitor and compare your company's performance with that of other companies.

29 Determining Revenues Earned Per Share of Stock

Equation

Revenues per share = net sales / weighted average of issued and outstanding shares of common stock

Revenues per share describe the amount of net sales a company achieves per share of stock issued and outstanding. All common stock held by shareholders is considered issued and outstanding. Stock authorized but never sold by the company as well as stock repurchased by the company is not considered issued and outstanding; therefore, you do not use it in most per-share indicators.

When to use indicator: Investors can use revenue per share rates to determine how effectively companies generate revenue. By comparing the revenue per share rate with historical and forecasted results, investors can determine if stocks are appropriately priced.

Meaning of result: Generally, managers prefer higher revenue per share values because they indicate the company is selling a larger dollar amount of products or services per share of stock. Most successful companies seek to generate increasing sales revenues per share, especially companies that sell commodity-type, or low profit margin, products as do supermarkets and service stations. Such companies typically must generate a greater amount of revenue per share than other types of companies since the income generated from each share of stock is lower than that of higher profit margin companies. Although higher revenues per share are desirable, a company with lower revenue per share and higher profit margins may be more desirable than a company with higher revenues per share and lower profit margins. For example, suppose company A generates $100 per share in revenues with a 15% profit margin, and company B generates $200 per share with a 6% profit margin. Company A earns $15 net profit versus $12 net profit for company B.

Ways to improve the indicator: Increasing sales prices and volumes can directly increase net sales earned per share. You can do this by providing highly demanded products or services or by increasing sales efforts with additional promotions, advertising, sales personnel, and new distribution channels.

Companies can also improve their revenues per share by repurchasing outstanding stock. This will decrease the amount of stock outstanding and, for a fixed amount of revenue, inflate the revenue earned on a per-share basis. If a company sells additional stock, dilution occurs and the opposite effect results; revenue per share figures decline.

Example

Revenues per share = net sales / weighted average of issued and outstanding shares of common stock

Net sales = 85,420
Weighted average of issued and outstanding shares of common stock = 3,600

Revenues per share = 85,420 / 3,600 = $23.73

Sector	Mid to large cap	Revenues Per Share	Small to mid cap	Revenues Per Share	Micro to small cap	Revenues Per Share
Manufacturing	General Motors	256.94	Toro	86.24	Encad	12.96
Retail	Wal-Mart Stores	52.64	Bed Bath & Beyond	7.72	TCBY Enterprises	3.84
Food	McDonald's	16.64	Applebee's Int'l	16.38	Garden Fresh Restaurant	21.16
Technology	Microsoft	5.86	Cypress Semiconductor	6.00	Jmar Technologies	1.20
Finance	Morgan-Stanley Dean Witter	45.84	Franklin Resources	8.58	AmeriTrade Holding	3.29
Healthcare	Columbia/HCA Healthcare	29.34	Novacare	17.47	National Home Health Care	6.68
Service	Manpower	90.34	Air & Water Technologies	14.21	Market Facts	11.33
Media/Publishing	McGraw Hill	35.66	Scholastic	68.55	Thomas Nelson	15.81

30 Finding the Amount of Earnings Per Share of Common Stock

Equation

Earnings per share of common stock = net income applicable to common stock / weighted average of issued and outstanding shares of common stock

Earnings per share describe the amount of net sales a company achieves per share of common stock issued and outstanding. All common stock held by shareholders is considered issued and outstanding. Stock authorized but never sold by the company as well as stock repurchased by the company is not considered issued and outstanding; therefore it is not part of most per-share indicators. When a company has issued preferred stock, you can determine the net income applicable to common stock by subtracting preferred dividends from net income.

When to use indicator: Investors use earnings per share rates to determine how effectively companies generate income per share of stock. By comparing the earnings per share rate with historical and forecasted results, you can determine if stocks are appropriately priced.

Meaning of result: Earnings per share is perhaps the most fundamental of all stock-related ratios. This indicator describes how much money the company earns for each share of common stock issued and outstanding. Most managers strive for higher earnings per share since this indicates more profit generated per share of stock. All companies, except unique firms such as nonprofit organizations, seek to generate increasing earnings per share. Higher earnings per share indicate the firm is generating more income for every dollar invested by its shareholders. This can lead to higher share prices because investors are generally willing to pay more for higher earnings.

Ways to improve the indicator: Increasing net income can directly increase earnings per share. You can achieve this by providing highly demanded products or services in a cost-effective manner. Highly demanded products or services can increase net sales by causing sales of larger volumes of products or services at premium prices. By producing the product or service in a cost-effective manner, you can increase profit margins to strengthen earnings.

Companies can also improve their earnings per share figures by repurchasing outstanding stock. This will decrease the amount of stock outstanding and, for a fixed amount of earnings, inflate earnings on a per-share basis. If a company sells additional stock, dilution occurs and the opposite effect results; earnings per share decline.

Example

Earnings per share of common stock = net income applicable to common stock / weighted average of issued and outstanding shares of common stock

Net income applicable to common stock = 4,953
Weighted average of issued and outstanding shares of common stock = 3,600

Earnings per share of common stock = 4,953 / 3,600 = $1.38

Sector	Mid to large cap	Earnings Per Share	Small to mid cap	Earnings Per Share	Micro to small cap	Earnings Per Share
Manufacturing	General Motors	9.52	Toro	2.86	Encad	1.52
Retail	Wal-Mart Stores	1.57	Bed Bath & Beyond	0.53	TCBY Enterprises	0.38
Food	McDonald's	2.40	Applebee's Int'l	1.43	Garden Fresh Restaurant	0.91
Technology	Microsoft	1.81	Cypress Semiconductor	0.20	Jmar Technologies	0.10
Finance	Morgan-Stanley Dean Witter	4.26	Franklin Resources	1.72	AmeriTrade Holding	0.48
Healthcare	Columbia/HCA Healthcare	−0.48	Novacare	0.64	National Home Health Care	0.35
Service	Manpower	2.04	Air & Water Technologies	−5.10	Market Facts	0.66
Media/Publishing	McGraw Hill	2.93	Scholastic	1.53	Thomas Nelson	0.79

31 Examining Dividends Per Common Share

Equation

Dividends per common share = dividend dollar amount for common shares / weighted average of issued and outstanding shares of common stock

Dividends per common share describe the amount of money distributed to shareholders per share of common stock issued and outstanding. All common stock held by shareholders is considered issued and outstanding. Stock authorized but never sold by the company as well as stock repurchased by the company is not considered issued and outstanding; therefore, you will not use it in most per-share indicators.

When to use indicator: Investors use dividends per share to determine how much money a company distributes to shareholders. This ratio is particularly important for those investors who seek steady income, as opposed to share price growth, from their investments. By comparing the dividends per share with historical and forecasted results, an investor can determine if stocks are appropriately priced.

Meaning of result: In addition to relaying current dividend payment amounts, the dividend per share ratio allows the investor to determine two fundamental dividend-related indicators—the dividend return ratio and the dividend payout ratio. These ratios allow investors to evaluate the risks and rewards of income-producing stocks. The dividend ratio suggests potential investment rewards while the dividend payout ratio indicates future dividend payment risk.

Ways to improve the indicator: Increasing dividends can directly increase dividends per share. You can achieve this by either earning more net income or distributing a larger portion of net income to shareholders in the form of dividends. Generally the best method of increasing dividend is to increase net income by providing highly demanded products or services in a cost-effective manner. Distributing larger portions of net income can be unwise because if too large a portion of income is given to shareholders, adequate capital may not remain to reinvest in the company to ensure future growth and sales.

Companies can also improve their dividends per share by repurchasing outstanding stock. This will decrease the amount of stock outstanding and, for a fixed amount of dividend distributions, inflate dividends on a per-share basis. If a company sells additional stock, dilution occurs and the opposite effect results; dividends per share decline.

Example

Dividends per share values are typically already calculated and stated in financial statements. It is uncommon to need to perform the following calculation:

Sector	Mid to large cap	Dividends Per Common Share	Small to mid cap	Dividends Per Common Share	Micro to small cap	Dividends Per Common Share
Manufacturing	General Motors	2.00	Toro	0.48	Encad	0.00
Retail	Wal-Mart Stores	0.27	Bed Bath & Beyond	0.00	TCBY Enterprises	0.20
Food	McDonald's	0.32	Applebee's Int'l	0.08	Garden Fresh Restaurant	0.00
Technology	Microsoft	0.00	Cypress Semiconductor	0.00	Jmar Technologies	0.00
Finance	Morgan-Stanley Dean Witter	0.56	Franklin Resources	0.17	AmeriTrade Holding	0.00
Healthcare	Columbia/HCA Healthcare	0.07	Novacare	0.00	National Home Health Care	0.00
Service	Manpower	0.17	Air & Water Technologies	0.00	Market Facts	0.00
Media/Publishing	McGraw Hill	1.44	Scholastic	0.00	Thomas Nelson	0.16

Dividends per common share = dividend dollar amount for common shares / weighted average of issued and outstanding shares of common stock

Dividend dollar amount = 972
Issued and outstanding shares of common stock = 3600

Dividends per common share = 972 / 3,600 = $0.27

32 Calculating the Growth Rate of Revenues

Equation

Growth rate of revenues = [(net sales, present year / net sales, n years ago) ^ (1/n)] − 1

and

Growth rate of revenues/share = [(net sales/share, present year / net sales/share, n years ago) ^ (1/n)] − 1

The **growth rate of revenues** describes the compounded annual growth rate of net sales growth a company has achieved for any given historical period. The growth rate of revenues per share determines revenue growth rates on a per-share basis. The two growth rates will differ when the number of outstanding shares changes over time.

When to use indicator: Managers use revenue growth rates to determine the effectiveness of their strategies targeted to generate new sales. Investors use revenue growth rates on a per-share basis to help ascertain the value of a company's stock.

Meaning of result: Investors generally expect higher revenue growth rates from growth companies. In assessing growth companies, look for strong rates of both revenue and income growth since stock value in large part depends on these two key indicators.

Stocks which are selected for income such as utility companies and high-dividend-rate blue chips are generally not as dependent on high revenue growth rates for adequate returns because their worth comes primarily through dividend disbursements. These companies typically achieve steady dividends with consistent net sales and income. Simultaneously, dividend payouts should not take too large a percentage of net income because a company needs capital available to plow back into such items as machinery upgrades and advertising.

When determining growth rates on a per-share basis, determine whether stock splits, or any other significant events that affect stock volume, have occurred. Such events may affect growth rate calculations. For example, when a stock is split two for one, revenue on a per-share basis is halved. If you do not know this, the revenue growth rate may mislead you.

Ways to improve the indicator: Achieve higher present-year revenue growth by providing properly priced, highly demanded products or services.

Companies can also improve their growth rates on a per-share basis by repurchasing outstanding stock. This will decrease the amount of stock outstanding and, for a fixed amount of revenue growth, inflate the growth rate on a per-share basis. If a company sells additional stock, dilution occurs and the opposite effect results; per share revenue growth rates decline.

Sector	Mid to large cap	Growth Rate of Revenues	Small to mid cap	Growth Rate of Revenues	Micro to small cap	Growth Rate of Revenues
Manufacturing	General Motors	5.44%	Toro	6.15%	Encad	50.79%
Retail	Wal-Mart Stores	12.24%	Bed Bath & Beyond	33.19%	TCBY Enterprises	−9.18%
Food	McDonald's	7.93%	Applebee's Int'l	22.53%	Garden Fresh Restaurant	21.32%
Technology	Microsoft	29.24%	Cypress Semiconductor	−4.44%	Jmar Technologies	32.58%
Finance	Morgan-Stanley Dean Witter	20.35%	Franklin Resources	31.38%	AmeriTrade Holding	65.28%
Healthcare	Columbia/HCA Healthcare	4.81%	Novacare	8.53%	National Home Health Care	19.51%
Service	Manpower	15.05%	Air & Water Technologies	6.99%	Market Facts	24.45%
Media/Publishing	McGraw Hill	9.73%	Scholastic	6.76%	Thomas Nelson	7.27%

Example

Growth rate of revenues = [(net sales, present year / net sales, n years ago) ^ (1/n)] − 1

Net sales, 1996 = 85,420
Net sales, 1994 (2 years ago) = 63,204
n = 2

Annual growth rate of revenues over the last two years = [(85,420 / 63,204) ^ (1/2)] − 1 = 1.1625 − 1 = 0.1625 = 16.25%

Growth rate of revenues/share = [(net sales/share, present year / net sales/share, n years ago) ^ (1/n)] − 1

Net sales/share, 1996 = 85,420 / 3,600 = 23.73
Net sales/share, 1994 (2 years ago) = 63,204/3,420 = 18.48
n = 2

Annual per share revenue growth rate over the last two years = [(23.73/18.48) ^ (1/2)] − 1 = 1.1332 − 1 = 0.1332 = 13.32% increase

In this example, the per-share revenue growth rate is less than the overall revenue growth rate because there was dilution on company stock. Shares outstanding rose from 3,420 to 3,600.

33 Calculating the Growth Rate of Earnings

Equation

Growth rate of earnings = [(net income applicable to common stock, present year / net income applicable to common stock, n years ago) ^ (1/n)] – 1

and

Growth rate of earnings/share = [(net income per common share, present year / net income per common share, n years ago) ^ (1/n)] – 1

The **earnings growth rate** describes the compounded annual growth rate of net income a company has achieved over any given historical period. The growth rate of net income per share determines income, or earnings, growth rates on a per-share basis. The two growth rates will differ when the number of outstanding shares changes over time.

When to use indicator: Managers use earnings growth rates to determine the effectiveness of their strategies targeted to generate new sales and maintain profit margins. Investors use earnings growth rates on a per-share basis to help ascertain the value of a company's stock.

Meaning of result: Investors generally expect higher earnings growth rates from growth companies. In assessing growth companies, look for strong rates of both revenue and income growth since stock value in large part depends on these two key indicators.

Stocks which are selected for income such as utility companies and high-dividend-rate blue chips are generally not as dependent on high earnings growth rates for adequate returns because their worth generally comes through dividend disbursements. These companies often achieve steady dividends with consistent net sales and income. Simultaneously, dividend payouts should not take too large a percentage of net income (dividend payout ratio) because a company needs adequate capital to plow back into such items as machinery upgrades and advertising.

When determining growth rates on a per-share basis, determine whether stock splits or any other significant stock volume events have affected growth rate calculations. For example, when a stock is split two for one, earnings on a per-share basis are halved. If you do not know about this, the earnings growth rate may be misleading.

Ways to improve the indicator: Achieve higher present-year earnings growth by providing properly priced, highly demanded products or services while using cost controls to maintain profit margins.

Companies can also improve their earnings growth rates on a per-share basis by repurchasing outstanding stock. This will decrease the amount of stock outstanding and, for a fixed amount of earnings growth, inflate the growth rate on a per-share basis. If a company sells additional stock, dilution occurs and the opposite effect results; per-share earnings growth rates decline.

Sector	Mid to large cap	Annual Growth Rate of Earnings over the Last Two Years	Small to mid cap	Annual Growth Rate of Earnings over the Last Two Years	Micro to small cap	Annual Growth Rate of Earnings over the Last Two Years
Manufacturing	General Motors	–1.34%	Toro	–2.52%	Encad	48.94%
Retail	Wal-Mart Stores	13.44%	Bed Bath & Beyond	36.15%	TCBY Enterprises	n/a *
Food	McDonald's	7.27%	Applebee's Int'l	28.24%	Garden Fresh Restaurant	0.81%
Technology	Microsoft	43.02%	Cypress Semiconductor	–57.60%	Jmar Technologies	385.18%
Finance	Morgan-Stanley Dean Witter	32.86%	Franklin Resources	27.04%	AmeriTrade Holding	40.21%
Healthcare	Columbia/HCA Healthcare	n/a *	Novacare	–20.73%	National Home Health Care	14.1%
Service	Manpower	13.13%	Air & Water Technologies	348.45%	Market Facts	61.72%
Media/Publishing	McGraw Hill	13.13%	Scholastic	–13.99%	Thomas Nelson	n/a *

* Negative earnings two years ago render equation unusable.

Example

Growth rate of earnings = [(net income applicable to common stock, present year / net income applicable to common stock, n years ago) ^ (1/n)] − 1

Net income applicable to common stock, 1996 = 4,953
Net income applicable to common stock, 1994 (2 years ago) = 2,852
n = 2

Annual earnings growth rate over the last two years = [(4,953 / 2,852) ^ (1 / 2)] − 1 = 1.3178 − 1 = 0.3178 = 31.78%

Growth rate of earnings per share = [(net income per common share, present year / net income per common share, n years ago) ^ (1/n)] − 1

Net income per common share, 1996 = 4,953/3,600 = 1.376
Net income per common share, 1994 (2 years ago) = 2,852/3,420 = 0.8339
n = 2

Annual per-share earnings growth rate over the last two years = [(1.376/0.8339) ^ (1/2)] − 1 = 1.2846 − 1 = 0.2846 = 28.46% increase

In this example, the per-share earnings growth rate is less than the overall revenue growth rate because there was dilution on company stock. Shares outstanding rose from 3,420 to 3,600.

34 Finding the Common Stock Dividend Growth Rate

Equation

Growth rate of common stock dividends per share = [(common stock dividends per share, present year / common stock dividends per share, n years ago) ^ (1/n)] – 1

The **common stock dividend growth rate per share** describes the compounded annual growth rate of common stock dividends on a per-share basis over any given historical period.

When to use indicator: Investors use dividend growth rates on a per-share basis to help ascertain the value of the company's stock.

Meaning of result: Stocks which are selected for income such as utility companies and high-dividend-rate blue chips should provide steady dividend streams that preferably increase over time. You can use the dividend growth rate to determine how effectively companies have performed to this end. Consistent net sales and income typically produce steady dividends. Dividend payouts should not take too large a percentage of net income (dividend payout ratio) since companies need adequate capital to plow back into such items as machinery upgrades and advertising. Smaller percentage dividend payouts, typically less than 50% of earnings, often indicate a higher likelihood of continuing dividend payouts.

When determining dividend growth rates on a per-share basis, you should determine whether stock splits or any other significant stock volume events have affected growth rate calculations. For example, when a stock is split two for one, dividends on a per-share basis are halved. If you do not know this, the dividend growth rate may mislead you.

Ways to improve the indicator: Achieving higher earnings and income by providing properly priced, highly demanded products or services while controlling costs to maintain profit margins should allow higher dividend growth rates.

Companies can also improve their dividend growth rates on a per-share basis by repurchasing outstanding stock. This will decrease the amount of stock outstanding and, for a fixed amount of dividend capital slated for distribution to shareholders, will inflate the dividend payout and growth rate on a per-share basis. If a company sells additional stock, dilution occurs and the opposite effect results; per-share dividend payouts and growth rates decline.

Example

Growth rate of common stock dividends per share = [(common stock dividends per share, present year / common stock dividends per share, n years ago) ^ (1/n)] – 1

Common stock dividends per share, 1996 = 0.27
Common stock dividends per share, 1994 (2 years ago) = 0.24
n = 2

Annual common stock dividend growth rate over the last two years = [(0.27 / 0.24) ^ (1 / 2)] – 1 = 1.061 – 1 = 0.061 = 6.1%

Sector	Mid to large cap	Annual Growth Rate of Dividends Per Share over the Last Two Years	Small to mid cap	Annual Growth Rate of Dividends Per Share over the Last Two Years	Micro to small cap	Annual Growth Rate of Dividends Per Share over the Last Two Years
Manufacturing	General Motors	34.84%	Toro	100.00%	Encad	*
Retail	Wal-Mart Stores	16.19%	Bed Bath & Beyond	*	TCBY Enterprises	0.00%
Food	McDonald's	10.94%	Applebee's Int'l	15.47%	Garden Fresh Restaurant	*
Technology	Microsoft	*	Cypress Semiconductor	*	Jmar Technologies	*
Finance	Morgan-Stanley Dean Witter	32.29%	Franklin Resources	13.06%	AmeriTrade Holding	*
Healthcare	Columbia/HCA Healthcare	–6.46%	Novacare	*	National Home Health Care	*
Service	Manpower	14.35%	Air & Water Technologies	*	Market Facts	–100.00%
Media/Publishing	McGraw Hill	9.54%	Scholastic	*	Thomas Nelson	0.00%

* No dividends reported by these companies.

35 Determining the Price-to-Earnings (P/E) Ratio

Equation

Price-to-earnings ratio = P/E = (share price of common stock × weighted average of issued and outstanding shares of common stock) / net income applicable to common stock

and

Price to earnings ratio = P/E = share price of common stock / earnings per share of common stock

The **price-to-earnings (P/E) ratio** indicates the degree to which investors value a company. When investors pay a high price for a given amount of corporate earnings, they increase the company's P/E ratio.

When to use indicator: The P/E ratio is one of the fundamental indicators investors use to determine how the stock markets value a company.

Meaning of result: The higher a company's P/E ratio, the more potential investors typically see in the particular company. Generally, companies with higher P/E ratios tend to have higher growth rates and deliver products or services that will probably be in demand for a significant time into the future. Because of such positive projections, investors are willing to pay a higher share price in the hope that sales and earnings growth will fuel further increases in share price.

Ways to improve the indicator: You can increase P/E ratios by increasing net sales and net income growth rates. Increasingly larger profit margins also tend to increase P/E ratios. You can increase profit margins by controlling costs and by maintaining optimum pricing by offering competitive, highly desirable products or services.

Example

Price-to-earnings ratio = P/E = (share price of common stock × weighted average of issued and outstanding shares of common stock) / net income applicable to common stock

Share price = $22.5 per share
Number of common shares issued and outstanding = 3,600,000
Net income applicable to common stock = 4,953,000

Price-to-earnings ratio = (22.5 × 3,600,000) / 4,953,000 = 16.4

Sector	Mid to large cap	P/E Ratio	Small to mid cap	P/E Ratio	Micro to small cap	P/E Ratio
Manufacturing	General Motors	7.13	Toro	11.87	Encad	8.50
Retail	Wal-Mart Stores	38.45	Bed Bath & Beyond	50.62	TCBY Enterprises	24.56
Food	McDonald's	29.64	Applebee's Int'l	15.88	Garden Fresh Restaurant	19.89
Technology	Microsoft	59.00	Cypress Semiconductor	40.62	Jmar Technologies	26.21
Finance	Morgan-Stanley Dean Witter	20.64	Franklin Resources	31.10	AmeriTrade Holding	30.46
Healthcare	Columbia/HCA Healthcare	* n/a	Novacare	17.74	National Home Health Care	14.15
Service	Manpower	13.61	Air & Water Technologies	* n/a	Market Facts	31.88
Media/Publishing	McGraw Hill	27.77	Scholastic	25.93	Thomas Nelson	17.36

* Negative earnings render equation unusable.

36 Measuring the Price-to-Earnings-to-Growth-Rate Ratio (PEG)

Equation

Price to earnings to growth rate = PEG = (share price of common stock × weighted average of issued and outstanding shares of common stock) / (net income applicable to common stock × earnings growth rate)

The **price to earnings to growth rate (PEG)** compares how investors value a company, the P/E ratio, with the company's growth rate.

When to use indicator: Since investors value growth stocks primarily by the degree of their growth, the PEG ratio gives investors a quick indication of the sensibility of current share prices.

Meaning of result: A general, and not always reliable, stock market rule of thumb is that stocks are undervalued, or good buys, when their PEGs are less than 1.0 and overvalued otherwise. For example, many investors generally look to buy a stock when its P/E ratio is less than its earnings growth rate and choose to sell or pass on stocks when their P/E ratios exceed their growth rates. As a company's PEG moves more to the extreme side of 1.0 in either direction, this general rule becomes more reliable. However, as with all general rules, there are many exceptions. At times, high-flying stocks with very high PEG ratios continue to climb while other stocks with low PEGs plummet even further. This latter scenario can occur with growth companies that fail to continue to meet historically high growth rates because of reduced demand or increased competition. Investors note such trends and force share prices down to levels that are more in line with the projected lower growth rates. Since published growth rate values are older and may not consider recent events, very low PEGs can result, giving false buy indications.

Example

Price to earnings to growth rate = PEG = (share price of common stock × weighted average of issued and outstanding shares of common stock) / (net income applicable to common stock × earnings growth rate)

Share price = $22.50 per share
Weighted average of issued and outstanding shares of common stock = 3,600,000
Net income applicable to common stock = 4,953,000
Growth rate (1 year) = 4,953/3,558 − 1 = 1.3921 − 1 = 0.3921 = 39.21%

Price to earnings to growth rate = (22.5 × 3,600,000) / (4,953,000 × 39.21) = 0.417

Sector	Mid to large cap	PEG	Small to mid cap	PEG	Micro to small cap	PEG
Manufacturing	General Motors	0.20	Toro	−2.76	Encad	0.24
Retail	Wal-Mart Stores	2.50	Bed Bath & Beyond	1.54	TCBY Enterprises	0.69
Food	McDonald's	6.67	Applebee's Int'l	0.85	Garden Fresh Restaurant	0.67
Technology	Microsoft	1.93	Cypress Semiconductor	−0.62	Jmar Technologies	0.20
Finance	Morgan-Stanley Dean Witter	0.67	Franklin Resources	0.82	AmeriTrade Holding	0.03
Healthcare	Columbia/HCA Healthcare	* n/a	Novacare	0.11	National Home Health Care	−0.32
Service	Manpower	13.96	Air & Water Technologies	* n/a	Market Facts	0.88
Media/Publishing	McGraw Hill	−0.67	Scholastic	0.00	Thomas Nelson	−0.34

* Negative earnings render equation unusable.

37 Examining the Earnings Yield

Equation

Per share calculation

Earnings yield = net income per share of common stock / share price of common stock

or

Dollar amount calculation

Earnings yield = net income applicable to common stock / (share price of common stock × weighted average number of common stock shares issued and outstanding)

The **earnings yield** describes the percentage return a company generates on its equity investments. It is similar to the return on investment (ROE) but describes return rates as a function of the market value of a company's stock rather than the book value of its shareholders' equity. Companies with promising futures generally exhibit much higher market versus book values of shareholders' equity. This ratio is the inverse of the price-to-earnings (P/E) ratio.

When to use indicator: Investors can use this indicator to determine the percentage return a company supplies for a given investment of capital at market rates.

Meaning of result: This indicator details the market rate of return on stock investments. The difficulty in using this ratio is that higher ratios don't necessarily indicate better performing, or more promising, companies and investments. When investors see a large degree of future earnings potential in a stock, they tend to purchase stock and drive stock prices up. This then causes earnings yields to decrease in the present per the definition shown above. Alternatively, when companies begin to slow down and show less growth, share prices slip and earnings yields rise. This could give the false indication that when companies begin to slow down, it is time to buy.

Ways to improve the indicator: Increasing net income can help improve earnings yield. You can achieve this by cost effectively providing highly demanded goods or services. However, when earnings rise, investors are willing to pay more for stock, so it is plausible that increases in earnings can lower the earnings yield because the market price of a company's stock may outpace any increase in earnings.

Example

Earnings yield = net income per share of common stock / share price of common stock

Net income per share of common stock = 4,983 / 3,600 = $1.38
Share price of common stock = $22.50

Earnings yield = 1.38 / 22.5 = 0.0613 = 6.13%

Sector	Mid to large cap	Earnings Yield	Small to mid cap	Earnings Yield	Micro to small cap	Earnings Yield
Manufacturing	General Motors	13.82%	Toro	8.42%	Encad	11.77%
Retail	Wal-Mart Stores	2.60%	Bed Bath & Beyond	1.98%	TCBY Enterprises	4.07%
Food	McDonald's	3.37%	Applebee's Int'l	6.30%	Garden Fresh Restaurant	5.03%
Technology	Microsoft	1.68%	Cypress Semiconductor	2.46%	Jmar Technologies	3.82%
Finance	Morgan-Stanley Dean Witter	4.72%	Franklin Resources	3.22%	AmeriTrade Holding	3.28%
Healthcare	Columbia/HCA Healthcare	-1.59%	Novacare	5.64%	National Home Health Care	7.07%
Service	Manpower	7.35%	Air & Water Technologies	-177.22%	Market Facts	3.14%
Media/Publishing	McGraw Hill	3.60%	Scholastic	3.86%	Thomas Nelson	5.76%

38 Determining the Market Price Return Ratio

Equation

Market price return = (sale price/purchase price) ^ (1/time period held) – 1

The **market price return ratio** describes the percentage return an investor generates from market price appreciation/depreciation of purchased stock. Compute the annualized two-year return for the benchmark-tabled values by comparing the 1998 midyear share price with the average 1996 share price.

When to use indicator: Investors can use this indicator to determine the percentage return or loss they would realize in selling a stock that they purchased at a given price at a given time period in the past. This information can help them determine whether the rate of return on the investment is appropriate for the investment risk.

Meaning of result: Higher ratios indicate that the investment achieved higher rates of return. Note that this indicator, market price return, and dividend return comprise total investment return.

Example

Market price return = (sale price/purchase price)^(1/time period held) – 1

Sale price = $22.50
Purchase price = $17.00
Time period held (years) = 2

Market price return = (22.5/17)^(1/2) - 1 = 1.1504 - 1 = 0.1504 = 15.04%

Sector	Mid to large cap	Market Price Return Ratio	Small to mid cap	Market Price Return Ratio	Micro to small cap	Market Price Return Ratio
Manufacturing	General Motors	14.48%	Toro	1.03%	Encad	−31.17%
Retail	Wal-Mart Stores	59.87%	Bed Bath & Beyond	49.69%	TCBY Enterprises	45.41%
Food	McDonald's	22.10%	Applebee's Int'l	−6.46%	Garden Fresh Restaurant	44.48%
Technology	Microsoft	84.49%	Cypress Semiconductor	−19.94%	Jmar Technologies	−1.85%
Finance	Morgan-Stanley Dean Witter	77.89%	Franklin Resources	62.91%	AmeriTrade Holding	*
Healthcare	Columbia/HCA Healthcare	−9.85%	Novacare	17.12%	National Home Health Care	−5.55%
Service	Manpower	8.39%	Air & Water Technologies	−36.89%	Market Facts	78.51%
Media/Publishing	McGraw Hill	37.22%	Scholastic	−24.15%	Thomas Nelson	2.61%

*1996 share price information not available.

INVESTMENT ANALYSIS

39 Determining the Common Stock Dividend Return Ratio

Equation

Common stock dividend return = dividend per share of common stock / share price of common stock

The **dividend return ratio** describes the rate of return that common stock dividend disbursements yield.

When to use indicator: Investors can use this ratio to determine the dividend return rate offered by a particular investment. Investors often compare this return rate with the investment risk level to determine the desirability of the investment.

Meaning of result: Investors who seek income streams from their investments often use the common stock dividend return ratio, or percentage earned on investment from dividends. Stocks selected for income often include utility companies and high-dividend-rate blue chips. The dividend return ratio allows the investor to determine if the rate of dividend return is congruent with the risk level of the investment. Investors generally expect higher dividend return ratios when there is a greater risk associated with the investment.

Ways to improve the indicator: You can achieve larger dividend returns by achieving higher present-year net income. You do this by providing properly priced, highly demanded products or services while controlling costs to maintain profit margins. By earning higher income, the company may be able to distribute larger dividend payments. However, when dividend payouts rise, investors are typically willing to pay more for a stock, assuming risk levels have not risen. This can lead to commensurate increases in the market price of a company's stock, thus maintaining dividend return ratios at relatively constant levels.

Companies can also improve their dividend return rates by repurchasing outstanding stock. This will decrease the amount of stock outstanding and, for a fixed amount of dividend capital slated for distribution to shareholders, will inflate the dividend return on a per-share basis. If a company sells additional stock, dilution occurs and the opposite effect results; dividend return rates decline.

Example

Common stock dividend return = dividend per share of common stock / share price of common stock

Dividend per share of common stock = $0.27
Share price of common stock = $22.50

Common stock dividend return = 0.27 / 22.50 = 0.012 = 1.2%

Sector	Mid to large cap	Common Stock Dividend Return Ratio	Small to mid cap	Common Stock Dividend Return Ratio	Micro to small cap	Common Stock Dividend Return Ratio
Manufacturing	General Motors	2.9%	Toro	1.4%	Encad	0.0%
Retail	Wal-Mart Stores	0.4%	Bed Bath & Beyond	0.0%	TCBY Enterprises	2.2%
Food	McDonald's	0.5%	Applebee's Int'l	0.4%	Garden Fresh Restaurant	0.0%
Technology	Microsoft	0.0%	Cypress Semiconductor	0.0%	Jmar Technologies	0.0%
Finance	Morgan-Stanley Dean Witter	0.6%	Franklin Resources	0.3%	AmeriTrade Holding	0.0%
Healthcare	Columbia/HCA Healthcare	0.2%	Novacare	0.0%	National Home Health Care	0.0%
Service	Manpower	0.6%	Air & Water Technologies	0.0%	Market Facts	0.0%
Media/Publishing	McGraw Hill	1.8%	Scholastic	0.0%	Thomas Nelson	1.2%

40 Determining the Size of the Common Stock Dividend Payout

Equation

Common stock dividend payout = dividends declared per share of common stock issued and outstanding / net income per share of common stock

The **common stock dividend payout ratio** describes the percentage of net income that is given back to common stock shareholders in the form of dividends.

When to use indicator: Investors can use this ratio to determine whether dividend payouts are sustainable.

Meaning of result: The dividend payout ratio indicates the degree of risk in present and future dividend payments. Smaller dividend payout ratios are preferred and indicate a higher likelihood of continuing, and potentially increasing, dividend payouts since the company has substantial earning income in excess of dividend disbursements. Higher ratios indicate the company may soon have difficulty in meeting its future dividend obligations. As a company pays out a larger percentage of net income to its shareholders in the form of dividends, it keeps less capital to be reinvested in items such as higher efficiency machinery and advertising campaigns to launch new revenue-producing services or products. This can lead to declining net income, and if dividend payments are maintained, progressively higher dividend payout ratios. If this cycle continues, one of two undesirable situations can occur: the company could declare a lower dividend per share or drive itself into bankruptcy by distributing more cash than it earns. However, higher ratios are more acceptable for mature companies operating in slow-changing industries, where there is less need for significant capital reinvestment.

Ways to improve the indicator: A manager can decrease the ratio by either decreasing the dividend payout or by increasing the amount of company earnings. The second alternative is generally the preferred way to decrease the payout ratio. A company can achieve higher earnings by providing properly priced, highly demanded products or services while using cost controls to maintain profit margins.

Companies can also improve their dividend payout ratios by repurchasing outstanding stock. This will decrease the amount of stock outstanding, increase earnings on a per-share basis, and thus lower the dividend payout ratio. If a company sells additional stock, dilution occurs and the opposite effect results; dividend payout ratios increase.

Example

Common stock dividend payout = dividends declared per share of common stock issued and outstanding / net income per share of common stock

Dividends declared per share = 0.27
Net income per share of common stock = 1.38

Common stock dividend payout = 0.27 / 1.38 = 0.20 = 20.0%

Sector	Mid to large cap	Common Stock Dividend Payout Ratio	Small to mid cap	Common Stock Dividend Payout Ratio	Micro to small cap	Common Stock Dividend Payout Ratio
Manufacturing	General Motors	21.0%	Toro	16.8%	Encad	0.0%
Retail	Wal-Mart Stores	17.2%	Bed Bath & Beyond	0.0%	TCBY Enterprises	53.1%
Food	McDonald's	13.4%	Applebee's Int'l	5.6%	Garden Fresh Restaurant	0.0%
Technology	Microsoft	0.0%	Cypress Semiconductor	0.0%	Jmar Technologies	0.0%
Finance	Morgan-Stanley Dean Witter	13.2%	Franklin Resources	9.9%	AmeriTrade Holding	0.0%
Healthcare	Columbia/HCA Healthcare	−14.7%	Novacare	0.0%	National Home Health Care	0.0%
Service	Manpower	8.3%	Air & Water Technologies	0.0%	Market Facts	0.0%
Media/Publishing	McGraw Hill	49.1%	Scholastic	0.0%	Thomas Nelson	20.2%

Determining the Size of the Dividend Payout in Relation to Operations Cash Flow

Equation

Operations cash flow dividend payout = dividends declared per share of common stock issued and outstanding / operations cash flow per share of common stock

The **operations cash flow dividend payout ratio** describes the percentage of operations cash flow that is given back to common stock shareholders in the form of dividends. This ratio is similar to the common stock dividend payout ratio but is based on operating cash flow rather than net income. At times, operating cash flow can give a more accurate indication of the health of a business since net income can include unusual or extraordinary items that skew current-year financial performance.

When to use indicator: Investors use this ratio to determine whether dividend payouts are sustainable.

Meaning of result: The operations cash flow dividend payout ratio indicates the degree of risk in present and future dividend payments. Investors prefer smaller dividend payout ratios. These indicate a higher likelihood of continuing, and potentially increasing, dividend payouts. Higher ratios indicate the company may soon have difficulty in meeting its future dividend obligations. As a company pays out a larger percentage of operations cash flow to its shareholders in the form of dividends, it keeps less capital to be reinvested in items such as higher efficiency machinery and advertising campaigns to launch new revenue-producing services or products. This can lead to declining operations cash flow, and if dividend payments remain static, progressively higher dividend payout ratios result. If this cycle continues, one of two undesirable situations can occur: the company could declare a lower dividend per share or drive itself into bankruptcy by distributing more cash than it earns.

Ways to improve the indicator: You can decrease the ratio by either decreasing the operations cash flow dividend payout or by increasing the amount of company earnings. The second alternative is generally the preferred way to decrease the payout ratio. You can achieve higher earnings by providing properly priced, highly demanded products or services while using cost controls to maintain profit margins.

Companies can also improve their operations cash flow dividend payout ratios by repurchasing outstanding stock. This will decrease the amount of stock outstanding, increase operations cash flow on a per-share basis, and thus lower the operations cash flow dividend payout ratio. If a company sells additional stock, dilution occurs and the opposite effect results; operations cash flow dividend payout ratios increase.

Sector	Mid to large cap	Operations Cash Flow Dividend Payout Ratio	Small to mid cap	Operations Cash Flow Dividend Payout Ratio	Micro to small cap	Operations Cash Flow Dividend Payout Ratio
Manufacturing	General Motors	8.43%	Toro	6.98%	Encad	0.00%
Retail	Wal-Mart Stores	8.49%	Bed Bath & Beyond	0.00%	TCBY Enterprises	27.59%
Food	McDonald's	8.98%	Applebee's Int'l	2.88%	Garden Fresh Restaurant	0.00%
Technology	Microsoft	0.00%	Cypress Semiconductor	0.00%	Jmar Technologies	0.09%
Finance	Morgan-Stanley Dean Witter	−56.37%	Franklin Resources	10.0%	AmeriTrade Holding	0.00%
Healthcare	Columbia/HCA Healthcare	3.03%	Novacare	0.00%	National Home Health Care	0.00%
Service	Manpower	37.84%	Air & Water Technologies	0.00%	Market Facts	0.00%
Media/Publishing	McGraw Hill	38.25%	Scholastic	0.00%	Thomas Nelson	31.67%

Example

Operations cash flow dividend payout = dividends declared per share of common stock issued and outstanding / operations cash flow per share of common stock

Dividends declared per share = 0.27
Operations cash flow per share = 4,820 / 3,600 = 1.34

Operations cash flow dividend payout = 0.27 / 1.34 = 0.202 = 20.2%

42 Determining the Preferred Dividend Return Ratio

Equation

Preferred dividend return = dividends per share of preferred stock / share price of preferred stock

The **preferred dividend return ratio** describes the rate of return that preferred dividend disbursements yield.

When to use indicator: Investors use this ratio to determine the return rate offered by a particular preferred stock investment. Investors will then typically compare this return rate with the investment risk level to determine the desirability of the investment.

Meaning of result: Investors who seek income streams from their investments often use the preferred dividend return ratio, or percentage earned on investment from preferred dividends. Stocks selected for income include utility companies and high-dividend-rate blue chips. The preferred dividend return ratio allows the investor to determine if the rate of preferred dividend return is congruent with the risk level of the investment. Investors should expect higher dividend return ratios when there is a greater risk associated with the investment.

Ways to improve the indicator: You can realize higher preferred dividend returns by purchasing preferred stock at lower market prices for a given dividend per preferred share.

Example

Preferred dividend return = dividend per share of preferred stock / share price of preferred stock

Dividend per share of preferred stock = $2.00
Share price of preferred stock = $25.00

Preferred dividend return = 2.00 / 25.00 = 0.080 = 8.0%

43 Determining the Size of the Preferred Dividend Payout

Equation

Preferred dividend payout = dividends per preferred share / net income per preferred share

The **preferred dividend payout ratio** describes the percentage of net income that shareholders earn in the form of preferred dividends.

When to use indicator: Investors use this ratio to determine whether preferred dividend payouts are sustainable.

Meaning of result: The preferred dividend payout ratio indicates the degree of risk in present and future preferred dividend payments. Smaller preferred dividend payout ratios are generally desirable and indicate a higher likelihood of continuing preferred dividend payouts because the company is earning income in excess of disbursements.

Higher ratios indicate the company may soon have difficulty in meeting its future preferred dividend obligations. As a company pays out a larger percentage of net income to its preferred shareholders in the form of dividends, it keeps less capital to be reinvested in items such as higher efficiency machinery and advertising campaigns to launch new revenue-producing services or products. This can lead to declining net income, and if preferred dividend payments remain static, progressively higher preferred dividend payout ratios result. If this cycle continues, one of two undesirable situations can occur: the company could declare a lower dividend per share or drive itself into bankruptcy by distributing more cash than it earns. However, higher ratios are more acceptable for mature companies operating in slow-changing industries where there is less need for significant capital reinvestment.

Ways to improve the indicator: You can reduce the ratio by increasing the amount of company earnings. A company can achieve higher earnings by providing properly priced, highly demanded products or services while using cost controls to maintain profit margins.

Example

Preferred dividend payout = dividends per preferred share / net income per preferred share

Dividends per preferred share = 2.00
Net income per preferred share = net income/preferred shares = 4,983/15 = 332.2

Preferred dividend payout = 2.00 / 332.2 = 0.006 = 0.60%

44 Determining the Size of the Preferred Dividend Payout in Relation to Operations Cash Flow

Equation

Operations cash flow preferred dividend payout = preferred dividends per share / operations cash flow per preferred share

The **operations cash flow preferred dividend payout ratio** describes the percentage of operations cash flow that shareholders receive in the form of preferred dividends. This ratio is similar to the preferred dividend payout ratio but is based on operating cash flow rather than net income. At times, operating cash flow can give a more accurate indication of the health of a business because net income can include unusual or extraordinary items that skew current-year financial performance.

When to use indicator: Investors use this ratio to determine whether preferred dividend payouts are sustainable.

Meaning of result: The operations cash flow preferred dividend payout ratio indicates the degree of risk in present and future preferred dividend payments. Smaller preferred dividend payout ratios are generally desirable and indicate a higher likelihood of continuing preferred dividend payouts.

Higher ratios indicate the company may soon have difficulty in meeting its future preferred dividend obligations. When a company pays out a larger percentage of operations cash flow to its shareholders in the form of preferred dividends, it keeps less capital to be reinvested in items such as higher efficiency machinery and advertising campaigns to launch new revenue-producing services or products. This can lead to declining operations cash flow and progressively higher preferred dividend payout ratios. If this cycle continues, one of two undesirable situations can occur: the company could declare a lower dividend per share or drive itself into bankruptcy by distributing more cash than it earns. However, higher ratios are more acceptable for mature companies operating in slow-changing industries where there is less need for significant capital reinvestment.

Ways to improve the indicator: A company can decrease the ratio by increasing operations cash flow. A company can achieve higher cash flow by providing properly priced, highly demanded products or services while controlling costs to maintain profit margins.

Example

Operations cash flow preferred dividend payout = preferred dividends per share / operations cash flow per preferred share

Preferred dividends per share = 2.00
Operations cash flow per preferred share = 4,820 / 15 = 321.3

Operations cash flow preferred dividend payout = 2.00 / 321.3 = 0.0062 = 0.62%

45 Determining the Size of the Total Return on Common Stock

Equation

Total return on common stock = market price return + common stock dividend return

where

Market price return = (market price/purchase price) ^ (1/time period held) −1
Common stock dividend return = Common stock dividend per share of stock / market price of common stock

This ratio describes the total annual percentage return an investor generates from ownership of common stock. Total return includes price appreciation/depreciation and dividend returns. Compute the two-year annualized market price return component for the benchmark-tabled values by comparing the 1998 midyear share price with the average 1996 share price.

When to use indicator: Investors use this ratio to determine whether the rate of return on an investment is appropriate for the investment risk level.

Meaning of result: Higher ratios indicate larger returns on common stock investment. Investors should compare return rates with the risk associated with a particular investment. Stocks that offer the potential for higher return rates generally present a greater risk of loss of capital.

Ways to improve indicator: A company can increase total common stock return with increasing price and dividend return yields. Price return increases are generally the result of increasing current and forecasted sales and income. Dividend return increases are often the result of similar increases in financial performance.

Example

Total return on common stock = market price return + common stock dividend return

Market price return = (market price/purchase price) ^ (1/time period held) − 1

Market price of common stock = 22.50
Purchase price of common stock = 17.00
Time period held (years) = 2

Market price return = (22.5/17)^(1/2) − 1 = 1.1504 −1 = 0.1504 = 15.04%

Common stock dividend return = dividend per share of common stock / Market price of common stock

Dividend per share of common stock = 0.27
Market price of common stock = 22.50

Common stock dividend return = 0.27 / 22.50 = 0.012 = 1.2%

Total return on common stock = 15.04% + 1.2% = 16.24%

Sector	Mid to large cap	Total Return on Common Stock	Small to mid cap	Total Return on Common Stock	Micro to small cap	Total Return on Common Stock
Manufacturing	General Motors	17.38%	Toro	2.45%	Encad	−31.17%
Retail	Wal-Mart Stores	60.32%	Bed Bath & Beyond	49.69%	TCBY Enterprises	47.57%
Food	McDonald's	22.55%	Applebee's Int'l	−6.11%	Garden Fresh Restaurant	44.48%
Technology	Microsoft	84.49%	Cypress Semiconductor	−19.94%	Jmar Technologies	−1.85%
Finance	Morgan-Stanley Dean Witter	78.51%	Franklin Resources	63.23%	AmeriTrade Holding	*
Healthcare	Columbia/HCA Healthcare	−9.61%	Novacare	17.12%	National Home Health Care	−5.55%
Service	Manpower	9.00%	Air & Water Technologies	−36.89%	Market Facts	78.51%
Media/Publishing	McGraw Hill	38.99%	Scholastic	−24.15%	Thomas Nelson	3.77%

* Two-year-old market price data not available.

46 Computing the Cash Flow Per Share of Outstanding Common Stock

Equation

Cash flow per share of common stock = cash flow / number of shares of issued and outstanding common stock

Cash flow is one of the most important indicators of the financial health of a company. This indicator relates how much cash flow is available per share of common stock.

When to use indicator: Managers and investors can use this indicator to determine whether the company is generating adequate cash. The three primary areas in which a company uses or generates cash are through its operations, investments, and financing activities. It is most desirable to generate cash through operations because this is the intent of forming an organization. Investment activities include the purchase or sale of machinery for plant use and the buying or selling of securities. Financing activities include the issuance or purchase of additional stock and the issuance or payment of additional debt.

Meaning of result: High positive cash flows are what companies generally desire to achieve. Regardless of how promising the short- and long-term potential for any given firm may be, positive cash flow is a continual requirement to keep a firm's doors open. At times companies operate with negative cash flows and must tap into cash reserves. This is acceptable to the point that the reserves don't become so depleted that insolvency results.

It is possible to operate with a positive net income, or profit, and nevertheless have a negative cash flow. When such situations remain unchecked, bankruptcy can occur. This special situation often arises with growing companies that require a lot of cash for items such as new capital equipment and the need to maintain larger inventories.

Ways to improve the indicator: A company improves cash flow when all forms of revenue exceed all forms of expenses in increasing quantities. Increasing revenue, whether from operations, investing, or financing, can help improve this indicator. Revenue enhancements include the generation of higher operating profits, the sale of obsolete machinery, and the issuance of new stock or debt. Decreasing expenses again—whether from operations, investing, or financing—can also increase the cash flow. Expense reductions include lowering operating expenses such as labor and raw material costs, reducing investing expenses by actions such as retiring debt and lowering interest payments (however, such an action would likely increase financing expense), and reducing financing expenses by actions such as issuing smaller dividend distributions.

Sector	Mid to large cap	Cash Flow Per Share of Outstanding Common Stock	Small to mid cap	Cash Flow Per Share of Outstanding Common Stock	Micro to small cap	Cash Flow Per Share of Outstanding Common Stock
Manufacturing	General Motors	–4.04	Toro	–0.00	Encad	–0.49
Retail	Wal-Mart Stores	0.25	Bed Bath & Beyond	0.11	TCBY Enterprises	0.20
Food	McDonald's	0.02	Applebee's Int'l	–0.27	Garden Fresh Restaurant	0.41
Technology	Microsoft	0.05	Cypress Semiconductor	1.45	Jmar Technologies	*
Finance	Morgan-Stanley Dean Witter	2.89	Franklin Resources	–0.24	AmeriTrade Holding	1.30
Healthcare	Columbia/HCA Healthcare	–0.00	Novacare	–1.20	National Home Health Care	0.08
Service	Manpower	–0.48	Air & Water Technologies	–0.02	Market Facts	4.11
Media/Publishing	McGraw Hill	0.01	Scholastic	0.01	Thomas Nelson	–0.23

* Cash flow data not reported for this company.

Example

Cash flow per share of common stock = cash flow / number of shares of issued and outstanding common stock

Cash flow = 1,017
Number of issued and outstanding shares of common stock = 3,600

Cash per flow per share of common stock = 1,017 / 3,600 = 0.2825 = $0.28 per share

47 Computing the Operating Cash Flow Per Share of Outstanding Common Stock

Equation

Operating cash flow per share of common stock = operating cash flow / number of shares of issued and outstanding common stock

Operating cash flow, one of the three sources of cash flow (together with investing and financing cash flow), is one of the more important indicators of a company's financial health. This indicator relates how much operating cash flow is generated per share of common stock.

When to use indicator: Managers and investors can use this indicator to determine whether a company is generating positive operating cash flow. The three areas in which a company uses or generates cash are through its operations, investments, and financing activities. It is generally most desirable to generate cash through operations since this is the intent of forming an organization. Operating cash flow is a direct indication of how much cash a company is generating from activities basic to the company. Examples include a car manufacturer producing and selling cars or a restaurant producing and selling meals. Investment activities include the purchase or sale of machinery for plant use and the buying or selling of securities. Financing activities include the issuance or purchase of additional stock and the issuance or payment of additional debt.

Meaning of result: High positive operating cash flows are what companies generally desire to achieve. Regardless of how promising the short- and long-term potential for any given firm may be, a company needs positive operating cash flows in the long term to remain open for business. Start-up and growth companies may subsist for a time with negative operating cash flows by generating cash flow from other sources such as by issuing more stock for cash or by taking on additional debt.

Ways to improve the indicator: The main contributors to operating cash flow are often net income and depreciation. Other factors which affect operating cash flow are changes in assets and liabilities such as inventory, accounts receivable, and accounts payable. Improving net income is generally the most desirable method of improving operating cash flow. A company can improve net income by providing properly priced, highly demanded products or services while maintaining good cost control. Operating cash flow also increases as the depreciation account increases. However, this is not simply found money. The income statement counts depreciation as an expense in the current period. Since you previously purchased the depreciable item with cash, you do not need additional cash in the current period, so add that amount of money back to net income to show a more accurate account of the current-period operating cash flow. Thus, you can think of depreciation expenses as accounting placeholders.

Sector	Mid to large cap	Operating Cash Flow Per Share of Outstanding Common Stock	Small to mid cap	Operating Cash Flow Per Share of Outstanding Common Stock	Micro to small cap	Operating Cash Flow Per Share of Outstanding Common Stock
Manufacturing	General Motors	23.73	Toro	6.88	Encad	−0.26
Retail	Wal-Mart Stores	3.18	Bed Bath & Beyond	0.35	TCBY Enterprises	0.72
Food	McDonald's	3.56	Applebee's Int'l	2.78	Garden Fresh Restaurant	2.83
Technology	Microsoft	2.79	Cypress Semiconductor	0.90	Jmar Technologies	*
Finance	Morgan-Stanley Dean Witter	−0.99	Franklin Resources	1.70	AmeriTrade Holding	0.82
Healthcare	Columbia/HCA Healthcare	2.31	Novacare	0.77	National Home Health Care	0.46
Service	Manpower	0.45	Air & Water Technologies	0.47	Market Facts	1.16
Media/Publishing	McGraw Hill	3.76	Scholastic	7.62	Thomas Nelson	0.51

* Cash flow data not reported for this company.

Example

Operating cash flow per share of common stock = operating cash flow / number of shares of issued and outstanding common stock

Operating cash flow = 4,820
Number of issued and outstanding shares of common stock = 3,600

Operating cash flow per share of common stock = 4,820 / 3,600 = 1.3389 = $1.34 per share

48 Determining the Volatility, or Beta, of a Stock

Equation

The beta of a stock is published by sources such as Valueline, Standard & Poor's, and Morningstar.

Beta is a measure of a stock's volatility. Investors consider stocks which exhibit larger price changes than the S&P 500 average, on both the up and down sides, as more volatile and they are assigned larger beta values.

When to use indicator: Investors use the beta indicator to determine the relative volatility of investments. Depending upon the investor's goals and the potential return a stock selection may offer, either low or high volatility stocks may be desirable.

Meaning of result: Beta values are tied to the performance of one of the primary stock indexes, such as the S&P 500. When a stock's price changes are generally equivalent to the average price changes found in the S&P 500, the stock has a beta of 1.0. For example, suppose an investor holds a stock with a beta of 1.0 and the S&P 500 index rises 15%. The investor could anticipate a rise of 15% in the value of his stock.

Higher beta values indicate higher volatility. Investors who seek high returns and are confident in the direction the markets are headed often seek higher beta stocks. Stock with high beta values will rise at a greater rate than the S&P 500 during market upswings and drop at faster rates during market corrections. For example, an investor holds another stock with a beta of 1.4 and the S&P 500 index rises 15%. This investor can anticipate his stock will rise at a rate of 21%, or 1.4 times the rate of the S&P 500. During market downswings, the same investor can anticipate losses at a rate 1.4 times that of the S&P 500.

Lower beta values indicate lower volatility and are the preference of investors who don't want to risk capital losses or are concerned with the direction of the market. With these stocks, gains are generally smaller than the S&P 500 during market upswings and losses are generally lower than the S&P 500 during downswings.

Negative beta values indicate that the stock tends to move in the opposite direction of the S&P 500.

Example
See published beta values.

CHAPTER FOUR

Product and Factory Costs

This chapter discusses ratios that describe the costs associated with producing a company's products or services such as labor costs, variable costs, and fixed costs. Other topics include important benchmarks such as the break-even volume and the break-even plant capacity.

49 Calculating the Total Amount of Direct Costs Per Production Unit

Equation

Direct costs per production unit = cost of goods sold / number of production units produced

Direct costs per unit indicate the level of direct costs associated with the production of the average company unit. Direct costs are expenses incurred to manufacture a product or supply a service and include labor, raw materials, and overhead. Direct labor includes machine operators and assemblers in manufacturing firms, hair cutters in salons, and draftspersons in architectural firms. Overhead includes floor space rent for manufacturing or service areas, machinery utilities, and the benefit package given to direct labor employees.

When to use indicator: Managers can use this indicator to gain a general sense of the level of manufacturing efficiencies and the cost associated with providing products or services.

Meaning of result: Comparing this indicator with historical and forecasted levels can indicate positive or negative trends. Higher ratios indicate there may be one or more direct expenses which are trending out of control. Managers prefer lower ratios, which are often the result of improved operations.

Ways to improve the indicator: A manager can reduce the cost of goods sold by investigating the expenses associated with producing a product or service. He can reduce raw material expenses with supplier competitive bidding and by redesigning product or service lines with more cost-effective components. He can reduce direct labor costs by improving the efficiency in which products are built. Employee training, increased employee motivation, improvements in production line setups, and the use of more efficient equipment can improve efficiency. Ways to reduce direct overhead expenses include negotiating lower plant leases, equipment leases, or health insurance rates and designing more efficient plant layouts to reduce the need for floor space.

Example

Direct costs per production unit = cost of goods sold / number of production units produced

Cost of goods sold = 54,212
Number of production units produced = 654

Direct costs per production unit = 54,212 / 654 = 82.89 = $82.89 per production unit

50 Determining the Total Labor Cost Per Production Unit

Equation

Total labor cost per production unit = total labor costs / number of production units produced

Total labor cost per unit describes one of the more costly company expenses—labor—and how it is associated with the production of the average company unit. Total labor costs include salaries and hourly wages for all company employees.

When to use indicator: Managers can use this indicator to gain a sense of labor costs and productivity levels.

Meaning of result: Comparing this indicator with historical and forecasted levels can indicate labor expense trends. Higher ratios can indicate labor expenses are trending out of control, changes to higher labor content product or service lines, or reductions in the number of units produced. Managers generally desire lower ratios, which are often the result of improved operations.

Ways to improve the indicator: Maintain a motivated, well-trained, and cooperative staff. Leadership from all employees, line workers to top executives, in each of these areas is critical to improving productivity. Eliminate redundancies. Encourage employees to suggest and develop methods of improving productivity, generating more sales, and reducing costs associated with producing products or services.

Example

Total labor cost per production unit = total labor costs / number of production units produced

Total labor costs = 18,871
Number of production units produced = 654

Total labor cost per production unit = 18,871 / 654 = 28.85 = $28.85 per production unit

51 Calculating the Total Cost Per Production Unit

Equation

Total cost per production unit = (cost of goods sold + indirect expenses) / number of production units produced

Total cost per unit indicates all direct and indirect costs associated with the production of the average company unit. Cost of goods sold includes all direct operations expenses such as raw materials and the labor and overhead used to manufacture the product. Indirect expenses include charges not directly involved with the manufacture of products such as salaries of office workers, office building rents, utilities, insurance, travel, and product development costs. The only factors not considered are interest expenses, taxes, and extraordinary items.

When to use indicator: Managers can use this indicator to gain a general sense of the overall costs of producing goods and trends in expense control and productivity levels.

Meaning of result: Managers generally desire lower trending ratios which can indicate increasing sales levels, increasing labor productivity, reduced raw material costs, or eliminated waste in discretionary spending. They may also indicate changes in product or service line offerings to more or less costly lines.

Higher ratios can indicate slowing or declining sales growth, lower labor productivity, higher raw material costs, or increases in discretionary spending.

Ways to improve the indicator: Maintain a motivated, well-trained, and cooperative staff. Leadership from all employees, line workers to top executives, in each of these areas is critical to improving productivity. Eliminate redundancies. Encourage employees to suggest and develop methods of improving productivity, generating more sales, and reducing costs associated with producing products or services.

Seek to reduce all of the expenses associated with the cost of goods sold. Reduce raw material expenses with supplier competitive bidding and by redesigning product lines with more cost-effective components. Reduce direct labor costs by improving manufacturing or assembly efficiencies. You can improve efficiencies with employee training, increased employee motivation, improvements in production line set-ups, and the use of more efficient equipment. You can reduce direct overhead expenses by negotiating lower plant and equipment leases and by designing more efficient plant layouts.

Example

Total cost per production unit = (cost of goods sold + indirect expenses) / number of production units produced

Cost of goods sold = 54,212
Indirect expenses = gross profit − pretax income + non-operating income = 31,208 − 9,104 + 455 = 22,559
Number of production units produced = 654

Total cost per production unit = (54,212 + 22,559) / 654 = 117.39 = $117.39 per production unit

52 Examining Variable Costs

Equation

Variable cost = costs that are dependent on the number of goods or services produced

The total cost to produce a product or service consists of variable and fixed costs. **Variable costs** are those costs that change with the quantity of goods or services produced while **fixed costs** remain relatively constant regardless of the quantity produced. Variable costs include raw materials, direct labor, and the fuel used to operate machinery. Fixed costs include building rent, interest payments, and salaries for nonmanufacturing employees such as engineers and accountants.

When to use indicator: Managers can use this indicator to determine the degree to which the costs of goods and services produced are variable in nature.

Meaning of result: Higher variable costs indicate that the costs to produce a product or service are very dependent on the volume of products or services produced. There is generally less financial risk with variable costs since a company incurs the costs only when it produces products or services. If there is a business downturn with lower volumes of output required, a company can more readily reduce variable costs than fixed costs. For example, raw material purchase quantities are generally much easier to reduce than the size and lease expense of a building.

However, higher variable costs are not always desirable since they may lead to higher total costs. Management should determine the optimal mix of variable and fixed costs which controls expenses and minimizes risk. This mix is dependent on the company and the industry in which it operates. For example, suppose a company purchases a high-cost fixed asset such as an automated piece of factory equipment. The equipment helps the company produce a product at a much lower total cost but with lower variable costs and higher fixed costs. If management is confident the product produced with the equipment will be in demand for a long time, the company can likely justify the machine cost. However, if demand for the product drops sharply, the company cannot easily reduce the fixed costs associated with the machinery and it could suffer greater losses than if it had not made the purchase.

Ways to improve the indicator: When you desire higher variable costs, shift expenses from fixed to variable costs. You can do this by producing more labor- and material-dependent products or services. You can also achieve this with outsourcing, that is, using contractors for design work, manufacturing, sales and marketing, etc. Outsourcing is typically more variable in nature than the use of in-house, salaried employees since contracts are more readily initiated and terminated than full-time positions.

Example

Variable cost = costs that are dependent on the number of goods or services produced

Total cost of goods sold = 54,212
Raw material cost = 31,063
Direct labor = 7,860
Overhead cost = 15,164
Other direct costs = 125
R&D costs = 4,578
SG&A costs = 15,993
Depreciation & amortization = 1,204
Interest = 784

Variable cost = raw material cost + direct labor cost = 31,063 + 7,860 = 38,923

53 Comparing Variable Costs with Total Costs

Equation

Variable cost to total cost = variable cost / total cost

The total cost to produce a product or service consists of variable and fixed costs. The **variable-to-total-cost ratio** indicates the percentage of all product or service costs which are variable in nature. Variable costs are those costs that change with the quantity of goods or services produced while fixed costs remain relatively constant regardless of the quantity produced. Variable costs include raw materials, direct labor, and the fuel used to operate machinery. Fixed costs include building rent, interest payments, and salaries for nonmanufacturing employees such as engineers and accountants.

When to use indicator: Managers can use this indicator to determine the cost makeup and risk level associated with its products or services.

Meaning of result: Higher variable cost ratios indicate that the costs to produce a product or service are largely dependent on the volume of products or services produced. There is generally less financial risk with higher variable cost ratios since a company incurs variable costs only when it produces products or services. If there is a business downturn with lower volumes of output, you can more readily reduce variable costs than fixed costs. For example, raw material purchase quantities are generally much easier to reduce than the size and lease cost of a building.

However, higher variable cost ratios are not always desirable since they may lead to higher total costs. Management should determine the optimal mix of variable and fixed costs which controls expenses and minimizes risk. This mix is dependent on the company and the industry in which it operates. For example, suppose a company purchases a high-cost fixed asset such as an automated piece of factory equipment. The equipment helps the company produce a product at a much lower total cost but with lower variable costs and higher fixed costs. If management is confident the product produced with the equipment will be in demand for a long time, it can likely justify the machine cost. However, if demand for the product drops sharply, the company cannot easily reduce the fixed costs associated with the machinery and the company could suffer greater losses than if it had not made the purchase.

Ways to improve the indicator: When you desire higher variable cost ratios, seek to shift expenses from fixed to variable costs. You can do this by producing more labor- and material-dependent products or services. You can also outsource or use contractors for design work, manufacturing, sales and marketing, etc. Contractor use is typically more variable in nature than the use of in-house, fixed-cost expertise.

Example

Variable cost to total cost = variable cost / total cost

Total cost of goods sold = 54,212
Raw material cost = 31,063
    Direct labor = 7,860
    Overhead cost = 15,164
Other direct costs = 125
R&D costs = 4,578
SG&A costs = 15,993
Depreciation & amortization = 1,204
Interest = 784
Variable cost = raw material cost + direct labor cost = 31,063 + 7,860 = 38,923
Total cost = total cost of goods sold + R&D costs + SG&A costs + depreciation + interest expense = 54,212 + 4,578 + 15,993 + 1,204 + 784 = 76,771

Variable cost to total cost = 38,923 / 76,771 = .5070 = 50.70%

54 Examining Variable Costs Per Production Unit

Equation

Variable cost per production unit = costs that are dependent on the number of goods or services produced / number of production units produced

The total cost to produce a product or service consists of variable and fixed costs. The **variable-cost-per-unit ratio** describes the variable cost per average production unit. Variable costs are those costs that change with the quantity of goods or services produced while fixed costs remain relatively constant regardless of the quantity produced. Variable costs include raw materials, direct labor, and the fuel used to operate machinery. Fixed costs include building rent, interest payments, and salaries for nonmanufacturing employees such as engineers and accountants.

When to use indicator: Managers can use this indicator to determine the degree to which the costs of goods and services produced are variable in nature.

Meaning of result: Higher variable costs indicate the costs to produce a product or service are very dependent on the volume of products or services produced. There is generally less financial risk with variable costs since the costs are incurred only when the company produces products or services. If there is a business downturn with lower volumes of output required, you can reduce variable costs more readily than fixed costs. For example, raw material purchase quantities are generally much easier to reduce than the size and lease expense of a building.

However, higher variable costs are not always desirable because they may lead to higher total costs. Management should determine the optimal mix of variable and fixed costs which controls expenses and minimizes risk. This mix is dependent on the company and the industry in which it operates. For example, suppose a company purchases a high-cost fixed asset such as an automated piece of factory equipment. The equipment helps the company produce a product at a much lower total cost but with lower variable costs and higher fixed costs. If management is confident the product produced with the equipment will be in demand for a long time, the company can likely justify the machine cost. However, if demand for the product drops sharply, the company cannot easily reduce the fixed costs associated with the machinery and it could suffer greater losses than if it had not made the purchase.

Ways to improve the indicator: When you desire higher variable costs, shift expenses from fixed to variable costs. You can do this by producing more labor- and material-dependent products or services. You can also achieve this with outsourcing, using contractors for design work, manufacturing, sales and marketing, etc. Contractor use is typically more variable in nature than the use of in-house, fixed-cost expertise.

Example

Variable cost per production unit = costs that are dependent on the number of goods or services produced / number of production units produced

Total cost of goods sold = 54,212
Raw material cost = 31,063
    Direct labor = 7,860
    Overhead cost = 15,164
 Other direct costs = 125
R&D costs = 4,578
SG&A costs = 15,993
Depreciation & amortization = 1,204
Interest = 784
Variable cost = raw material cost + direct labor cost = 31,063 + 7,860 = 38,923
Number of production units produced = 654

Variable cost per production unit = 38,923 / 654 = 59.52

55 Examining Fixed Costs

Equation

Fixed cost = costs that are independent of the number of goods or services produced

The total cost to produce a product or service consists of variable and fixed costs. Fixed costs are those costs that remain relatively constant regardless of the quantity of goods or services produced while variable costs are those costs that change with volume. Fixed costs include building rent, interest payments, and salaries for nonmanufacturing employees such as engineers and accountants. Variable costs include raw materials, direct labor, and the fuel used to operate machinery.

When to use indicator: Managers can use this indicator to determine the degree to which the costs of goods and services produced are fixed in nature.

Meaning of result: Higher fixed costs indicate that the costs to produce a product or service are very independent of the volume of products or services produced. There is generally more financial risk with higher fixed costs since a company incurs fixed costs regardless of the volume of products or services produced. If there is a business downturn with lower volumes of output required, a company can reduce variable costs more readily than fixed costs. For example, it is easier to reduce raw material purchase quantities than the size and lease cost of a building.

However, lower fixed costs are not always desirable since they may lead to higher total costs. Management should determine the optimal mix of variable and fixed costs which controls expenses and minimizes risk. This mix is dependent on the company and the industry in which it operates. For example, suppose a company purchases a high-cost fixed asset such as an automated piece of factory equipment. The equipment helps the company produce a product at a much lower total cost but with lower variable costs and higher fixed costs. If management is confident the product produced with the equipment will be in demand for a long time, the company can likely justify the machine cost. However, if demand for the product drops sharply, the company cannot easily reduce the fixed costs associated with the machinery and it could suffer greater losses than if it had not made the purchase.

Ways to improve the indicator: When you desire lower fixed costs, shift expenses from fixed to variable costs. You can do this by producing more labor- and material-dependent products or services. You can also achieve this with outsourcing, using contractors for design work, manufacturing, sales and marketing, etc. Contractor use is typically more variable in nature than the use of in-house, fixed-cost expertise.

Sector	Mid to large cap	Fixed Costs	Small to mid cap	Fixed Costs	Micro to small cap	Fixed Costs
Manufacturing	General Motors	38,921,000	Toro	335,590	Encad	44,289
Retail	Wal-Mart Stores	20,142,000	Bed Bath & Beyond	322,102	TCBY Enterprises	31,734
Food	McDonald's	2,428,800	Applebee's Int'l	57,542	Garden Fresh Restaurant	60,364
Technology	Microsoft	6,347,000	Cypress Semiconductor	176,321	Jmar Technologies	7,303
Finance	Morgan-Stanley Dean Witter	5,573,000	Franklin Resources	437,651	AmeriTrade Holding	32,839
Healthcare	Columbia/HCA Healthcare	9,362,000	Novacare	181,241	National Home Health Care	8,865
Service	Manpower	1,054,809	Air & Water Technologies	116,972	Market Facts	34,522
Media/Publishing	McGraw Hill	1,462,275	Scholastic	493,500	Thomas Nelson	95,862

Example

Fixed cost = costs that are independent of the number of goods or services produced

Total cost of goods sold = 54,212
Raw material cost = 31,063
Direct labor = 7,860
Overhead cost = 15,164
Other direct costs = 125
R&D costs = 4,578
SG&A costs = 15,993
Depreciation & amortization = 1,204
Interest = 784

Fixed cost = overhead cost + other direct costs + R&D cost + SG&A cost + depreciation + interest
= 15,164 + 125 + 4,578 + 15,993 + 1,204 + 784
= 37,848

56 Comparing Fixed Costs to Total Costs

Equation

Fixed cost to total cost = fixed cost / total cost

The total cost to produce a product or service consists of variable and fixed costs. The **fixed-to-total-cost ratio** indicates the percentage of all product or service costs which are fixed in nature. Fixed costs are those costs that remain relatively constant regardless of the quantity of goods or services produced while variable costs are those costs that change with volume. Fixed costs include building rent, interest payments, and salaries for nonmanufacturing employees such as engineers and accountants. Variable costs include raw materials, direct labor, and the fuel used to operate machinery.

When to use indicator: Managers can use this indicator to determine the cost makeup and risk level associated with its products or services.

Meaning of result: Higher fixed cost ratios indicate the costs to produce a product or service are independent of the volume of products or services produced. There is generally more financial risk with higher fixed costs since a company incurs fixed costs regardless of the volume of products or services produced. If there is a business downturn with lower volumes of output required, a company can more readily reduce variable costs than fixed costs. For example, raw material purchase quantities are generally much easier to reduce than the size and lease cost of a building.

However, lower fixed cost ratios are not always desirable since they may lead to higher total costs. Management should determine the optimal mix of variable and fixed costs which controls expenses and minimizes risk. This mix is dependent on the company and the industry in which it operates. For example, suppose a company purchases a high-cost fixed asset such as an automated piece of factory equipment. The equipment helps the company produce a product at a much lower total cost but with lower variable costs and higher fixed costs. If management is confident the product produced with the equipment will be in demand for a long time, the company can likely justify the machine cost. However, if demand for the product drops sharply, the company cannot easily reduce the fixed costs associated with the machinery and it could suffer greater losses than if it had not made the purchase.

Ways to improve the indicator: When you desire lower fixed costs, shift expenses from fixed to variable costs. You can do this by producing more labor- and material-dependent products or services. You can also achieve this with outsourcing, using contractors for design work, manufacturing, sales and marketing, etc. Contractor use is typically more variable in nature than the use of in-house, fixed-cost expertise.

Sector	Mid to large cap	Fixed-to-Total-Cost Ratio	Small to mid cap	Fixed-to-Total-Cost Ratio	Micro to small cap	Fixed-to-Total-Cost Ratio
Manufacturing	General Motors	23.04%	Toro	33.60%	Encad	36.14%
Retail	Wal-Mart Stores	17.73%	Bed Bath & Beyond	33.99%	TCBY Enterprises	34.44%
Food	McDonald's	26.75%	Applebee's Int'l	12.93%	Garden Fresh Restaurant	71.98%
Technology	Microsoft	84.13%	Cypress Semiconductor	33.07%	Jmar Technologies	36.64%
Finance	Morgan-Stanley Dean Witter	24.38%	Franklin Resources	27.04%	AmeriTrade Holding	44.45%
Healthcare	Columbia/HCA Healthcare	52.69%	Novacare	18.35%	National Home Health Care	27.90%
Service	Manpower	15.06%	Air & Water Technologies	23.28%	Market Facts	37.97%
Media/Publishing	McGraw Hill	47.15%	Scholastic	47.90%	Thomas Nelson	40.92%

Example

Fixed cost to total cost = fixed cost / total cost

Total cost of goods sold = 54,212
Raw material cost = 31,063
    Direct labor = 7,860
    Overhead cost = 15,164
 Other direct costs = 125
R&D costs = 4,578
SG&A costs = 15,993
Depreciation & amortization = 1,204
Interest = 784

Fixed cost = overhead cost + other direct costs + R&D cost + SG&A cost + depreciation + interest
= 15,164 + 125 + 4,578 + 15,993 + 1,204 + 784
= 37,848

Total cost = total cost of goods sold + R&D costs + SG&A costs + depreciation + interest expense
= 54,212 + 4,578 + 15,993 + 1,204 + 784 = 76,771

Fixed cost to total cost = 37,848 / 76,771 = .4930 = 49.30%

57 Finding the Fixed Cost Per Unit

Equation

Fixed cost per unit = costs that are independent of the number of goods or services produced / number of units produced

The total cost to produce a product or service consists of variable and fixed costs. The **fixed-cost-per-unit ratio** describes the fixed cost per average production unit. Fixed costs are those costs that remain relatively constant regardless of the quantity of goods or services produced while variable costs are those that change with volume. Fixed costs include building rent, interest payments, and salaries for nonmanufacturing employees such as engineers and accountants. Variable costs include raw materials, direct labor, and the fuel used to operate machinery.

When to use indicator: Managers can use this indicator to determine the degree to which the costs of goods and services produced are fixed in nature.

Meaning of result: Higher fixed cost ratios indicate that the costs to produce a product or service are independent of the volume of products or services produced. There is generally more financial risk with higher fixed costs since a company incurs fixed costs regardless of the volume of products or services produced. If there is a business downturn with lower volumes of output required, a company can reduce variable costs more readily than fixed costs. For example, raw material purchase quantities are generally much easier to reduce than the size and lease cost of a building.

However, lower fixed cost ratios are not always desirable since they may lead to higher total costs. Management should determine the optimal mix of variable and fixed costs which controls expenses and minimizes risk. This mix is dependent on the company and the industry in which it operates. For example, suppose a company purchases a high-cost fixed asset such as an automated piece of factory equipment. The equipment helps the company produce a product at a much lower total cost but with lower variable costs and higher fixed costs. If management is confident the product produced with the equipment will be in demand for a long time, the company can likely justify the machine cost. However, if demand for the product drops sharply, the company cannot easily reduce the fixed costs associated with the machinery and it could suffer greater losses than if it had not made the purchase.

Ways to improve the indicator: When you desire lower fixed costs per unit, shift expenses from fixed to variable costs. You can do this by producing more labor- and material-dependent products or services. You can also achieve this with outsourcing, using contractors for design work, manufacturing, sales and marketing, etc. Contractor use is typically more variable in nature than the use of in-house, fixed-cost expertise.

Example

Fixed cost per unit = costs that are independent of the number of goods or services produced / number of units produced

Total cost of goods sold = 54,212
Raw material cost = 31,063
    Direct labor = 7,860
    Overhead cost = 15,164
Other direct costs = 125
R&D costs = 4,578
SG&A costs = 15,993
Depreciation & amortization = 1,204
Interest = 784
Fixed cost = overhead cost + other direct costs + R&D costs + SG&A costs + depreciation + interest = 15,164 + 125 + 4,578 + 15,993 + 1,204 + 784 = 37,848
Number of production units produced = 654

Fixed cost per unit = 37,848 / 654 = 57.87

58 Finding the Contribution Margin

Equation

Contribution margin = net sales − variable costs

Contribution margin percentage = (net sales − variable costs) / net sales

The **contribution margin** is the amount of revenue that remains after you have accounted for all variable costs. Managers often determine contribution margins for individual products, but they can sometimes describe total company performance. Variable costs are those costs that change with the quantity of goods or services produced while fixed costs remain relatively constant regardless of the quantity produced. Variable costs include raw materials, direct labor, and the fuel used to operate machinery. Fixed costs include building rent, interest payments, and salaries for nondirect manufacturing employees such as supervisors, engineers, and accountants.

When to use indicator: Managers can use these ratios to determine the degree of income available to pay fixed costs and, when those costs are paid in full, to return a profit. Contribution margin determinations also allow the manager to figure how many units must be sold to break even, the point at which sales revenues equal total costs.

Meaning of result: Higher contribution margin percentages indicate the company's variable costs are low and a larger amount of revenue remains to defray fixed costs. When the fixed costs are fully paid for, the remaining revenue remains as profit.

Ways to improve the indicator: Reducing variable costs and increasing sales prices can increase contribution margins. The primary variable cost components for manufacturing and service companies are often raw materials and direct labor. For retailers the primary variable cost is often purchased merchandise. Negotiating lower purchase prices with existing suppliers and finding new, lower cost suppliers of raw materials and merchandise can increase contribution margins. Increasing direct labor productivity to reduce the labor content per unit produced can also increase contribution margins.

Although increasing sales prices will increase contribution margins, such price increases can also reduce sales volumes, potentially reducing overall profit. Price increases are thus generally acceptable only to the point that overall company profit is maximized.

Example

Contribution margin = net sales − variable costs

Contribution margin percentage = (net sales − variable costs) / net sales

Individual product

Contribution margin = sales price − variable costs

Sales price per unit = 88
Variable costs per unit = 27

Contribution margin = 88 − 27 = 61

Contribution margin percentage = (sales price − variable costs) / sales price

Sales price per unit = 88
Variable costs per unit = 27

Contribution margin percentage = (88 − 27) / 88 = 0.6932 = 69.32%

Companywide

Contribution margin = net sales − variable costs

Net sales = 85,420
Variable costs = costs that are dependent on the number of goods or services produced
Variable costs = raw material cost + direct labor cost = 31,063 + 7,860 = 38,923

Contribution margin = 85,420 − 38,923 = 46,497

Contribution margin percentage = (net sales − variable costs) / net sales

Net sales = 85,420
Variable costs = costs that are dependent on the number of goods or services produced
Variable costs = raw material cost + direct labor cost = 31,063 + 7,860 = 38,923

Contribution margin percentage = (85,420 − 38,923) / 85,420 = 0.5443 = 54.43%

Determining the Break-Even Point in Sales Volume

Equation

Break-even volume = total fixed costs / contribution margin per unit

= total fixed costs / (net sales price per unit − variable costs per unit)

The **break-even volume** is the volume of products that must be sold to pay for all variable and fixed costs. It is the point at which total sales equal total costs. Sales volume levels above the break-even volume will achieve an operating profit while sales volume levels below that point will not. The contribution margin is the amount of revenue that remains after you have accounted for all variable costs. Variable costs are those costs that change with the quantity of goods or services produced while fixed costs remain relatively constant regardless of the quantity produced. Variable costs include raw materials, direct labor, and the fuel used to operate machinery. Fixed costs include building rent, interest payments, and salaries for nondirect manufacturing employees such as supervisors, engineers, and accountants.

When to use indicator: This ratio is useful for managers in determining the desirability of offering a product for sale given sales pricing, sales volume estimates, and product cost information.

Meaning of result: As the sales volume estimates become much higher than the break-even volume, the offering of the particular product becomes more desirable. This is particularly true for higher priced and higher contribution margin products because each additional unit sold generates a substantial stream of operating income.

When the sales volume estimates are lower than the break-even volume, the product or service will not return an operating profit. Generally this indicates that the company should not sell the product because it will cost the company more money than it generates. However, when the offering of such a product will generate additional sales and/or prevent losses in the sales of other company products, it may be beneficial to offer the product. Consider total company performance in such cases in addition to particular product performance. Also if idle plant or personnel capacity exists, it may be beneficial to offer the product or service when sales volumes are projected at below break-even levels as long as the projected sales volumes allow the coverage of all variable costs. You can use revenue remaining after you pay the variable costs to defray existing fixed cost expenses.

Ways to improve the indicator: You can lower break-even volumes by increasing contribution margins and reducing fixed costs. Reducing variable costs and increasing sales prices can increase contribution margins. The primary variable cost components are often raw materials and direct labor for manufacturing and service companies and purchased merchandise for retailers. Negotiating lower purchase prices with existing suppliers and finding new, lower cost suppliers of raw materials and merchandise can increase contribution margins. Increasing direct labor productivity to reduce the labor content per unit produced can also increase contribution margins.

Although increasing sales prices will increase contribution margins, such price increases can also reduce sales volumes, potentially reducing overall profit. Price increases are thus generally acceptable only to the point that they maximize overall company profit.

Example

Break-even volume

= total fixed costs / contribution margin per unit

= total fixed costs / (net sales price per unit − variable costs per unit)

Individual product

Break-even volume = total fixed costs / contribution margin per unit

Sales price per unit = 88
Variable costs per unit = 27
Total fixed costs required to produce the unit (machinery, rent, supervision, insurance, etc.) = 91,000
Contribution margin per unit = net sales price per unit − variable costs per unit = 88 − 27 = 61

Break-even volume = 91,000 / 61 = 1,492

Companywide

Break-even volume = total fixed costs / average contribution margin per unit

Net sales = 85,420
Total cost of goods sold = 54,212
 Raw material cost = 31,063
  Direct labor = 7,860
  Overhead cost = 15,164
 Other direct costs = 125
R&D costs = 4,578
SG&A costs = 15,993
Depreciation & amortization = 1,204
Interest = 784

Variable costs = costs that are dependent on the number of goods or services produced
Variable costs = raw material cost + direct labor cost = 31,063 + 7,860 = 38,923

Fixed costs = costs that are independent of the number of goods or services produced
Fixed costs = overhead cost + other direct costs + R&D costs + SG&A costs + depreciation + interest = 15,164 + 125 + 4,578 + 15,993 + 1,204 + 784 = 37,848
Number of production units produced = 654

Average contribution margin per unit = (net sales − variable costs) / number of units produced = (85,420 − 38,923) / 654 = 71.1

Break-even volume = 37,848 / 71.1 = 532

60 Determining the Break-Even Point in Sales Dollars

Equation

Break-even sales level = total fixed costs / contribution margin percentage per unit

= Total fixed costs / ([net sales price per unit − variable costs per unit] / net sales per unit)

The **break-even sales level** describes the point at which net sales equal total costs. Total costs include all variable and fixed costs. Sales volume levels above the break-even sales volume will achieve an operating profit while sales volume levels below that point will not. The contribution margin is the amount of revenue that remains after you have accounted for all variable costs. The contribution margin percentage is the contribution margin divided by net sales. It describes the size of the contribution margin on a percentage basis. Variable costs are those costs that change with the quantity of goods or services produced while fixed costs remain relatively constant regardless of the quantity produced. Variable costs include raw materials, direct labor, and the fuel used to operate machinery. Fixed costs include building rent, interest payments, and salaries for nondirect manufacturing employees such as supervisors, engineers, and accountants.

When to use indicator: This ratio is useful for managers in determining the desirability of offering for sale a particular product given sales pricing, sales volume estimates, and product cost information.

Meaning of result: As the sales level estimates become much higher than the break-even sales level, the offering of the particular product or service becomes more and more desirable. When the sales level estimates are less than the break-even sales level, the product or service will not return an operating profit. Generally this suggests that a company should not sell the product since it will cost the company more money than it generates. However, when the offering of such a product or service will generate additional sales and/or prevent losses in the sales of other company products, it may be beneficial to offer the product. Consider total company performance in such cases in addition to particular product performance. Also, if idle plant or personnel capacity exists, it may be beneficial to offer the product or service when sales levels are projected at below break-even levels as long as the projected sales levels cover all variable costs. You can use revenue remaining after the variable costs are paid to defray existing fixed cost expenses.

Ways to improve the indicator: You can lower break-even sales levels by increasing contribution margins and reducing fixed costs. Reducing variable costs and increasing sales prices can increase contribution margins. The primary variable cost components are often raw materials and direct labor for manufacturing and service companies and purchased merchandise for retailers. Negotiating lower purchase prices with existing suppliers and finding new, lower cost suppliers of raw materials and merchandise can increase contribution margins. Increasing direct labor productivity to reduce the labor content per unit produced can also increase contribution margins.

Although increasing sales prices will increase contribution margins, such price increases can also reduce sales levels, potentially reducing overall profit. Price increases are thus generally acceptable only to the point that they maximize overall company profit.

Example

Break-even sales level

= Total fixed costs / contribution margin percentage per unit

= Total fixed costs / ([net sales price per unit − variable costs per unit] / net sales per unit)

Individual product

Break-even sales level = total fixed costs / contribution margin percentage per unit

Sales price per unit = 88
Variable costs per unit = 27
Total fixed costs required to produce the unit (machinery, rent, supervision, insurance, etc.) = 91,000
Contribution margin percentage per unit = (net sales price per unit − variable costs per unit) / net sales price per unit = (88 − 27) / 88 = 0.693

Break-even sales level = 91,000 / 0.693 = 131,279

Companywide

Break-even sales level = total fixed costs / average contribution margin percentage per unit

Net sales = 85,420
Total cost of goods sold = 54,212

Raw material cost = 31,063
Direct labor = 7,860
Overhead cost = 15,164
Other direct costs = 125

R&D costs = 4,578
SG&A costs = 15,993
Depreciation & amortization = 1,204
Interest = 784

Variable costs = costs that are dependent on the number of goods or services produced
Variable costs = raw material cost + direct labor cost = 31,063 + 7,860 = 38,923

Fixed costs = costs that are independent of the number of goods or services produced

Fixed costs = overhead cost + other direct costs + R&D costs + SG&A costs + depreciation + interest = 15,164 + 125 + 4,578 + 15,993 + 1,204 + 784 = 37,848

Average contribution margin percentage per unit = (net sales − variable costs) / net sales = (85,420 − 38,923) / 85,420 = 0.544

Break-even sales level = 37,848 / 0.544 = 69,574

61 Finding the Sales Volume Necessary to Generate a Desired Operating Income

Equation

Volume required to generate a desired operating income

= (total fixed costs + desired operating income) / contribution margin per unit

= (total fixed costs + desired operating income) / (net sales price per unit − variable costs per unit)

This ratio describes the volume of goods or services that must be sold to achieve a desired level of operating income. The ratio is identical to the break-even ratio with the exception of the addition of the desired operating income variable. The contribution margin is the amount of revenue that remains after you have accounted for all variable costs. Variable costs are those costs that change with the quantity of goods or services produced while fixed costs remain relatively constant regardless of the quantity produced. Variable costs include raw materials, direct labor, and the fuel used to operate machinery. Fixed costs include building rent, interest payments, and salaries for nondirect manufacturing employees such as supervisors, engineers, and accountants.

When to use indicator: This ratio is useful for managers in determining the desirability of offering a product for sale given sales pricing, sales volume estimates, and product cost information.

Meaning of result: When the projected sales volume estimate is greater than the sales volume required to achieve a desired operating income, the product or service will return an amount of operating income equal to or greater than the desired figure. When this is not the case, operating income projections will fall short of desired levels. However, as long as the projected sales volumes cover total fixed costs, the product or service will generate positive operating income. When operating income projections are positive but fall short of desired profit level, a company may or may not decide to offer the particular product or service, depending upon a number of factors such as the strategic importance and growth potential of the product line. For example, if the offering of such a product will generate additional tagalong sales or prevent losses in the sales of other company products, it may be beneficial to offer the product even in light of lower profit projections. You should consider total company performance when evaluating the desirability of individual product or service offerings. Also, if idle plant or personnel capacity exists, it may be beneficial to offer the product or service when you project sales levels to be well below desired levels as long as the projected sales levels cover all variable costs. You can use revenue remaining after you pay variable costs to defray existing fixed cost expenses.

Ways to improve the indicator: You can lower the sales volumes required to achieve a desired operating income by increasing contribution margins and reducing fixed costs. Reducing variable costs and increasing sales prices can increase contribution margins. The primary variable cost components are often raw materials and direct labor for manufacturing and service companies and purchased merchandise for retailers. Negotiating lower purchase prices with existing suppliers and finding new, lower cost suppliers of raw materials and merchandise can increase contribution margins. Increasing direct labor productivity to reduce the labor content per unit produced can also increase contribution margins.

Although increasing sales prices will increase contribution margins, such price increases can also reduce sales volumes, potentially reducing overall profit. Price increases are thus generally acceptable only to the point that they maximize overall company profit.

Example

Volume required to generate a desired operating income

= (total fixed costs + desired operating income) / contribution margin per unit
= (total fixed costs + desired operating income) / net sales price per unit − variable costs per unit

Individual product

Volume required to generate a desired operating income = (total fixed costs + desired operating income) / contribution margin per unit

Desired operating income = 44,500
Sales price per unit = 88
Variable costs per unit = 27
Total fixed costs required to produce the unit (machinery, rent, supervision, insurance, etc.) = 91,000
Contribution margin per unit = net sales price per unit − variable costs per unit = 88 − 27 = 61

Volume required to generate a desired operating income = (91,000 + 44,500) / 61 = 2,221

Companywide

Volume required to generate a desired operating income = (total fixed costs + desired operating income) / average contribution margin per unit

Desired operating income = 12,000
Net sales = 85,420
Total cost of goods sold = 54,212
 Raw material cost = 31,063
  Direct labor = 7,860
  Overhead cost = 15,164
 Other direct costs = 125
R&D costs = 4,578
SG&A costs = 15,993
Depreciation & amortization = 1,204
Interest = 784

Variable costs = costs that are dependent on the number of goods or services produced
Variable costs = raw material cost + direct labor cost = 31,063 + 7,860 = 38,923
Fixed costs = costs that are independent of the number of goods or services produced
Fixed costs = overhead cost + other direct costs + R&D costs + SG&A costs + Depreciation + interest = 15,164 + 125 + 4,578 + 15,993 + 1,204 + 784 = 37,848
Number of production units produced = 654
Average contribution margin per unit = (net sales − variable costs) / number of units produced = (85,420 − 38,923) / 654 = 71.1

Volume required to generate a desired operating income = (37,848 + 12,000) / 71.1 = 701

62 Finding the Sales Dollars Necessary to Generate a Desired Operating Income

Equation

Sales level required to generate a desired operating income

= (total fixed costs + desired operating income) / contribution margin percentage per unit

= (total fixed costs + desired operating income) / ([net sales price per unit − variable costs per unit] / net sales per unit)

This ratio describes the sales levels required to achieve a desired level of operating income. The ratio is identical to the break-even sales level with the exception of the addition of the desired operating income variable. The contribution margin is the amount of revenue that remains after you have accounted for all variable costs. The contribution margin percentage is the contribution margin divided by net sales and describes the size of the contribution margin on a percentage basis. Variable costs are those costs that change with the quantity of goods or services produced while fixed costs remain relatively constant regardless of the quantity produced. Variable costs include such costs as raw materials, direct labor, and the fuel used to operate machinery. Fixed costs include such costs as building rent, interest payments, and salaries for nondirect manufacturing employees such as supervisors, engineers, and accountants.

When to use indicator: This ratio is useful for managers in determining the desirability of offering a product for sale given sales pricing, sales volume estimates, and product cost information.

Meaning of result: When the projected sales level estimate is greater than the sales level required to achieve a desired operating income, the product or service will return an amount of operating income equal to or greater than the desired figure. When this is not the case, operating income projections will fall short of desired levels. However, as long as the projected sales levels cover total fixed costs, the product or service will generate positive operating income.

When operating income projections are positive but fall short of desired profit level, the company may or may not decide to offer the particular product or service, depending upon a number of factors such as the strategic importance and growth potential of the product line. For example, if the offering of such a product will generate additional tagalong sales or prevent losses in the sales of other company products, it may be beneficial to offer the product even in light of lower profit projections. Consider total company performance when evaluating the desirability of individual product or service offerings. Also, if idle plant or personnel capacity exists, it may be beneficial to offer the product or service when you project sales levels to be well below desired levels as long as the projected sales levels cover all variable costs. You can use revenue remaining after you pay the variable costs to defray existing fixed cost expenses.

Ways to improve the indicator: You can lower the sales levels required to achieve a desired operating income by increasing contribution margins and reducing fixed costs. Reducing variable costs and increasing prices can increase contribution margins. The primary variable cost components are often raw materials and direct labor for manufacturing and service companies and purchased merchandise for retailers. Negotiating lower purchase prices with existing suppliers and finding new, lower cost suppliers of raw materials and merchandise can increase contribution margins. Increasing direct labor productivity to reduce the labor content per unit produced can also increase contribution margins.

Although increasing prices will increase contribution margins, such price increases can also reduce sales levels, potentially reducing overall profit. Price increases are thus generally acceptable only to the point that they maximize overall company profit.

Example

Sales level required to generate a desired operating income

= (total fixed costs + desired operating income) / contribution margin percentage per unit

= (total fixed costs + desired operating income) / ([net sales price per unit − variable costs per unit] / net sales per unit)

Individual product

Sales level required to generate a desired operating income = (total fixed costs + desired operating income) / contribution margin percentage per unit

Desired operating income = 44,500
Sales price per unit = 88
Variable costs per unit = 27
Total fixed costs required to produce the unit (machinery, rent, supervision, insurance, etc.) = 91,000
Contribution margin percentage per unit = (88 − 27) / 88 = 0.693

Sales level required to generate a desired operating income = (91,000 + 44,500) / 0.693 = 195,526

Companywide

Sales level required to generate a desired operating income = (total fixed costs + desired operating income) / average contribution margin percentage per unit

Desired operating income = 12,000
Net sales = 85,420
Total cost of goods sold = 54,212
Raw material cost = 31,063
    Direct labor = 7,860
   Overhead cost = 15,164
Other direct costs = 125
R&D costs = 4,578
SG&A costs = 15,993
Depreciation & amortization = 1,204
Interest = 784

Variable costs = costs that are dependent on the number of goods or services produced

Variable costs = raw material cost + direct labor cost = 31,063 + 7,860 = 38,923
Fixed costs = costs that are independent of the number of goods or services produced
Fixed costs = overhead cost + other direct costs + R&D costs + SG&A costs + depreciation + interest = 15,164 + 125 + 4,578 + 15,993 + 1,204 + 784 = 37,848
Average contribution margin percentage per unit = (net sales − variable costs) / net sales = (85,420 − 38,923) / 85,420 = 0.544

Sales level required to generate a desired operating income = (37,848 + 12,000) / 0.544 = 91,632

63 Finding the Break-Even Plant Capacity

Equation

Break-even plant capacity = (fixed costs × current percentage of plant capacity) / (net sales − variable costs)

This benchmark roughly estimates the percentage of full capacity at which a factory must run to achieve break-even sales. Break-even corresponds to the point at which total sales equal total costs. Sales volumes above the break-even volume will achieve an operating profit while sales volume levels below that point will not. The benchmark assumes a constant relationship between variable costs and sales, and between plant capacity and sales, and assumes that fixed costs are constant with changes in sales levels. Variable costs are those costs that change with the quantity of goods or services produced while fixed costs remain relatively constant regardless of the quantity produced. Variable costs include such costs as raw materials, direct labor, and the fuel used to operate machinery. Fixed costs include such items as building rent, interest payments, and salaries for nondirect manufacturing employees such as supervisors, engineers, and accountants.

When to use indicator: Managers can use this indicator to estimate the level at which plant capacity must be used to break even.

Meaning of result: Lower ratios indicate that a plant produces high-margin products and/or products with low fixed costs. When the break-even point is low, there is greater potential for profit as a plant becomes fully utilized. When the break-even point is high, there is greater risk of poor financial performance since small amounts of idle capacity may lead to unprofitable operations.

Ways to improve indicator: You can reduce break-even plant capacity by increasing contribution margins and lowering fixed costs. Reducing variable costs and increasing sales prices can increase contribution margins. The primary variable cost components are often raw materials and direct labor for manufacturing and service companies and purchased merchandise for retailers. Negotiating lower purchase prices with existing suppliers and finding new, lower cost suppliers of raw materials and merchandise can increase contribution margins. Increasing direct labor productivity to reduce the labor content per unit produced can also increase contribution margins.

Although increasing sales prices will increase contribution margins, such price increases can also reduce sales levels, potentially reducing overall profit. Price increases are thus generally acceptable only to the point that they maximize overall company profit.

Example

Break-even plant capacity = (fixed costs × current percentage of plant capacity) / (net sales − variable costs)

Net sales = 85,420
Current percentage of plant capacity = 80% = 0.80
Total cost of goods sold = 54,212
 Raw material cost = 31,063
     Direct labor = 7,860
    Overhead cost = 15,164
 Other direct costs = 125
R&D costs = 4,578
SG&A costs = 15,993
Depreciation & amortization = 1,204
Interest = 784

Variable costs = costs that are dependent on the number of goods or services produced

Variable costs = raw material cost + direct labor cost = 31,063 + 7,860 = 38,923
Fixed costs = Costs that are independent of the number of goods or services produced
Fixed costs = overhead cost + other direct costs + R&D costs + SG&A costs + depreciation + interest = 15,164 + 125 + 4,578 + 15,993 + 1,204 + 784 = 37,848

Break-even plant capacity = (37,848 × 0.80) / (85,420 − 38,923) = 0.651 = 65.1%

CHAPTER FIVE

Expense Analysis

This chapter details many of the expenses associated with producing a product or service such as direct and indirect labor costs and productivity levels. It presents ratios to help monitor costs such as raw materials, overhead, and the repair and maintenance of fixed assets.

64 Comparing the Cost of Goods Sold to Sales and Net Income

Equation

Cost of goods sold to sales = cost of goods sold / net sales

Cost of goods sold to net income = cost of goods sold / net income

Cost-of-goods-sold ratios are measures of the direct expenses a company has incurred to manufacture products and how such expenses relate to trends in sales and profit indicators. Cost-of-goods-sold items are all direct operational expenses including raw materials and the labor and overhead used to manufacture a product.

When to use indicator: Managers and investors can use these ratios to track the total direct expenses associated with the manufacture of products.

Meaning of result: To maintain or increase a company's performance, it is typically useful to maintain expense control and tracking of the costs associated with the manufacture of products. It is often desirable to reduce the cost of goods sold because this will tend to maximize profit. Exceptions to this approach include initiating items that reduce customer or employee goodwill. For example, suppose a company uses a new and cheaper raw material and that this is noticed and disliked by its customers. Although the cost-of-goods-sold ratios would decrease, sales volumes would likely suffer and net profit may be reduced.

Industries will exhibit ratios unique to their markets. It is most helpful to compare cost-of-goods-sold indicators with companies operating in similar industries and markets. For example, software companies tend to show low cost-of-goods-sold ratios since there is not a lot of money tied up in physically producing manuals and CD-ROMs. With these types of companies, more expenses are tied up in nondirect costs such as software development. On the other hand, car manufacturers have a tremendous amount of expense associated with raw materials, purchased parts, and the labor and overhead required to manufacture vehicles.

Ways to improve the indicator: By seeking to reduce all of the expenses associated with cost-of-goods-sold items, you may reduce total cost-of-goods-sold expenses. You can reduce raw material expenses with supplier competitive bidding and by redesigning products in a manner which requires less expensive materials. You can reduce direct labor costs by improving the efficiency with which you produce products. Employee training, increased employee motivation, improvements in production line setups, and the use of more efficient equipment can improve efficiencies. You can reduce direct overhead expenses by negotiating lower plant and equipment leases and by designing more efficient plant layouts.

Sector	Mid to large cap	Cost-of-Goods-Sold Ratio	Small to mid cap	Cost-of-Goods-Sold Ratio	Micro to small cap	Cost-of-Goods-Sold Ratio
Manufacturing	General Motors	0.73	Toro	0.63	Encad	0.53
Retail	Wal-Mart Stores	0.79	Bed Bath & Beyond	0.59	TCBY Enterprises	0.67
Food	McDonald's	0.58	Applebee's Int'l	0.75	Garden Fresh Restaurant	0.26
Technology	Microsoft	0.08	Cypress Semiconductor	0.66	Jmar Technologies	0.59
Finance	Morgan-Stanley Dean Witter	0.64	Franklin Resources	0.54	AmeriTrade Holding	0.43
Healthcare	Columbia/HCA Healthcare	0.45	Novacare	0.76	National Home Health Care	0.65
Service	Manpower	0.82	Air & Water Technologies	0.84	Market Facts	0.56
Media/Publishing	McGraw Hill	0.46	Scholastic	0.51	Thomas Nelson	0.55

Example

Cost of goods sold to sales = cost of goods sold / net sales

Cost of goods sold = 54,212
Net sales = 85,420

Cost of goods sold to sales = 54,212 / 85,420 = 0.6347 = 63.47%

65 Calculating the Amount of Sales and Cost of Goods Sold Per Employee

Equation:

Sales per employee = net sales / number of employees

Cost of goods sold per employee = cost of goods sold / number of employees

Ratios of sales and cost of goods sold per employee are measures of employee productivity and the revenue-generating and expense-controlling state of the business.

When to use indicator: Investors and managers can use this indicator to determine a number of important issues. First, the sales per employee ratio provides a general sense of the company's sales-generating capability and trends. This ratio can also indicate employee productivity levels. The costs-of-goods-sold ratio can indicate expense control effectiveness. You can also anticipate required staffing levels through sales level forecasts.

Meaning of result: Higher trending sales per employee are often the pleasant indication of either higher sales levels or improving employee productivity. You can improve productivity with increased morale, incentives, education, expertise, teamwork, and the use of tools such as computers to perform more work in less time. Watch that increases in sales per employee are not the result of excessive overtime, which could lead to excessive attrition or a lowering of morale. Lower trending sales per employee ratios are often the result of opposite causes—reduced sales levels or decreased employee productivity.

Lower ratios of cost of goods sold per employee are typically desirable and can indicate falling raw materials prices; lower direct labor costs; lower direct overhead costs; the manufacture of new, higher margin products; and increased employee productivity. Higher ratios are generally undesirable and can indicate the opposite causes.

Ways to improve the indicator: Maintain a motivated, well-trained, and cooperative staff. Leadership from all employees, line workers to top executives, in each of these areas is critical to improve productivity. Eliminate redundancies. Encourage employees to suggest and develop methods of improving productivity, generating more sales, and reducing costs associated with producing products or services.

Example

Sales per employee = net sales / number of employees

Net sales = 85,420
Number of employees = 836

Sales per employee = 85,420 / 836 = $102.2 (this is in thousands of dollars)

66 Determining Sales, Net Income, and the Cost of Goods Sold Per Direct Labor Employee

Equation

Sales per direct labor employee = net sales / number of direct labor employees

Net income per direct labor employee = net income / number of direct labor employees

Cost of goods sold per direct labor employee = cost of goods sold / number of direct labor employees

You can determine companywide performance and direct labor employee productivity with ratios of sales, income, and cost of goods per direct labor employee. **Direct labor employees** are those employees directly involved in the production of the product or service such as machine operators and assemblers in manufacturing firms, hair cutters in salons, and draftspersons in architectural firms. For manufacturing firms, direct labor is one of the three primary constituents of the costs of goods sold expenses. The other two items are raw material and direct overhead expenses.

These ratios can also be used to track the performance of indirect and other nondirect employees by substituting the appropriate labor group information. **Indirect employees** are those operations employees not directly involved in the production of the product or service such as warehouse receiving employees, production supervisors, and maintenance personnel. **Other nondirect employees** are employees fully removed from work that is directly associated with or in direct support of producing a company's primary product or service such as employees in human resources, accounting, computer services, R&D, sales, marketing, and customer service.

When to use indicator: Managers can use these indicators to ascertain if the levels of direct laborers are at historic and/or budgeted levels relative to sales, income, and total direct costs. Management can also use this indicator to anticipate required staffing levels according to forecasted sales levels.

Meaning of result: Companies generally seek to maximize the amount of sales per direct employee. Management should investigate direct labor expense factors when these ratios are trending high or low. When ratio levels are trending higher, this indicates that production efficiencies could be rising due to factors such as increased throughput, increased morale or incentives, reduced production line downtime, improved equipment, or production layouts. Watch that increased levels of sales per direct employee are not at the cost of excessive overtime since this could lead to decreased profit and morale.

Industries will exhibit ratios unique to their markets. It is typically most beneficial to compare direct labor cost indicators with companies operating in similar industries and markets. Companies which produce high labor content products will tend to exhibit higher ratios than those with lower labor needs. For example, a manufacturer of custom, handmade wooden furniture would likely have higher direct labor ratios than a manufacturer of plastic patio furniture that is primarily made with machines.

Ways to improve the indicator: You can reduce direct labor costs by improving the efficiency with which your company builds products or renders services. You can improve efficiencies with employee training, increased employee motivation and morale, improvements in production line setups, and the use of more efficient equipment. Eliminate redundancies in direct labor tasks. Ensure that employees minimize slack time; all direct employees should have productive tasks to complete at all times.

Example

Sales per direct employee = net sales / number of direct employees

Net sales = 85,420
Number of direct employees = 512

Sales per direct employee = 85,420 / 512 = $166.84 (this is in thousands)

Comparing the Cost of Direct Labor and Direct Labor Hours Worked to Sales, Net Income, and the Cost of Goods Sold

Equation

Direct labor cost to sales = direct labor cost / net sales

Direct labor cost to net income = direct labor cost / net income

Direct labor cost to cost of goods sold = direct labor cost / cost of goods sold

Direct labor hours worked to sales = direct labor hours worked / net sales

Direct labor hours worked to net income = direct labor hours worked / net income

Direct labor hours worked to cost of goods sold = direct labor hours worked / cost of goods sold

Direct labor cost ratios are measures of the direct labor expenses and labor hours used to manufacture products or provide services and of how such labor investments relate to trends in sales and profit indicators. Direct labor employees are those employees directly involved in the production of the product or service such as machine operators and assemblers in manufacturing firms, hair cutters in salons, and draftspersons in architectural firms.

These ratios can also be used to track the performance of indirect and other nondirect employees by substituting the appropriate labor group information. Indirect employees are those operations employees not directly involved in the production of the product or service such as warehouse receiving employees, production supervisors, and maintenance personnel. Other nondirect employees are employees fully removed from work that is directly associated with or in direct support of producing a company's primary product or service. Examples include employees in human resources, accounting, computer services, R&D, sales, marketing, and customer service.

When to use indicator: Managers can use these indicators to ascertain if direct labor costs and uses are at historic and/or budgeted levels relative to sales, income, and total direct costs. Management can also use these indicators to anticipate required staffing needs according to forecasted sales levels.

Meaning of result: Higher trending ratios can be the result of unusually high direct labor use and cost, downturns in sales and net income, or reductions in the cost of goods sold. Excessive overtime and direct labor inefficiencies can cause higher direct labor costs and labor use. Downturns in sales and net income can indicate there are too many direct employees on hand for new, lower sales levels. Conversely, increasing sales generally require immediate additional direct labor costs to produce more products or deliver additional services. Reductions in the costs of goods sold can be the result of a variety of causes such as improved raw material purchase prices, lowered building lease costs, or the development of new products or services that are less dependent on direct costs.

Industries will exhibit ratios unique to their markets. It is most beneficial to compare direct labor cost and use indicators with companies operating in similar industries and markets. Companies which produce products with a high labor content will tend to exhibit higher ratios than those with lower labor needs. For example, a manufacturer of custom, handmade wooden furniture would likely have higher direct labor ratios than a manufacturer of plastic patio furniture that is primarily made with machines.

Ways to improve the indicator: You can reduce the ratios of direct labor costs and hours worked by improving the efficiency with which you build products or render services. You can improve efficiencies with employee training, increased employee motivation and morale, improvements in production line setups, and the use of more efficient equipment. Eliminate redundancies in direct labor tasks. Ensure that slack time is kept to a minimum; all direct employees should have productive tasks to complete at all times.

When sales levels have changed dramatically and will likely remain at the new level for some time and the direct labor hour ratios have changed accordingly, it may be necessary to adjust the amount of direct labor staff. Increases in the ratios of direct labor hours to sales can indicate too many direct employees are on staff while reductions may indicate the need for further hiring. When there is excessive use of overtime, the hiring of additional direct labor employees can lower the ratios of cost and hours worked.

You can increase the ratios of direct labor cost and hours worked to cost of goods sold by reducing the cost-of-goods-sold ratio. Some ways to do this are by purchasing raw materials at lower prices, lowering building lease costs, or developing new products or services that use less raw materials.

Example

Direct labor cost to sales = direct labor cost / net sales

Direct labor cost = 7,860
Net sales = 85,420

Direct labor cost to sales = 7,860 / 85,420 = 0.092 = 9.20%

68 Comparing Direct Labor Costs, Direct Labor Employees, and Direct Labor Hours Worked to the Cost of All Labor

Equation

Direct labor cost to total labor cost = direct labor cost / total labor cost

Direct labor employees to total labor cost = direct labor employees / total labor cost

Direct labor hours worked to total labor cost = direct labor hours worked / total labor cost

These indicators compare the costs and availability of direct labor with a company's total labor expenditures. The hours-worked ratio is useful in determining the level of direct labor available as a percentage of total labor costs. Think of this ratio as the measure of the hours of direct labor available, or the time degree of direct labor horsepower purchased, for every dollar spent on all labor. The inverse of this indicator conveys the amount of money spent on all labor per hour of direct labor. Direct labor employees are those employees directly involved in the production of a product or service such as machine operators and assemblers in manufacturing firms, hair cutters in salons, and draftspersons in architectural firms.

You can also use these ratios to track the performance of indirect and other nondirect employees by substituting the appropriate labor group information. Indirect employees are those operations employees not directly involved in the production of the product or service such as warehouse receiving employees, production supervisors, and maintenance personnel. Other nondirect employees are employees fully removed from work that is directly associated with or in direct support of producing a company's primary product or service. Examples include employees in human resources, accounting, computer services, R&D, sales, marketing, and customer service.

When to use indicator: Managers and investors use these ratios to track direct labor expenses and uses. When the ratio of direct labor to total labor cost is trending too low or high, this indicator can alert management to investigate direct labor cost factors. Management can also use this ratio to track the change in direct labor expenses because of additional direct employee training, experience level, overtime requirements, new product lines, and the installation of new manufacturing equipment. Direct labor is one of the three primary constituents of the cost of goods sold expenses. The other two items are raw materials and direct overhead expenses.

Meaning of result: Higher ratios can be the result of higher than usual direct labor hour use or reductions in the use of nondirect labor. Higher use of direct labor can arise because of increasing sales, increasing direct labor inefficiencies, a wave of new hires, or changes in product or service offerings. Labor inefficiencies can occur from issues such as inadequate training, poor morale, and problematic equipment. You can reduce the percentage use of nondirect labor through staff streamlining and increased sales levels. Increasing sales generally require immediate additional direct labor costs to produce more products or deliver additional services.

Industries will exhibit ratios unique to their markets, so it is best to compare direct labor cost indicators with companies operating in similar industries and markets. Companies which produce products with a high labor content will tend to exhibit higher ratios than those that have a lower labor content. For example, a manufacturer of custom, handmade wooden furniture would likely have higher direct-labor-hour ratios than a manufacturer of plastic patio furniture that is primarily made with machines.

Ways to improve the indicator: You can reduce direct labor cost ratios by improving the efficiency with which you build products or render services. You can improve efficiencies with employee training, increased motivation and morale, improvements in production line setups, and the use of more efficient equipment. Eliminate redundancies in direct labor tasks. Ensure that slack time is kept to a minimum; all direct employees should have productive tasks to complete at all times.

When sales levels have changed dramatically and will likely remain at the new level for some time and the direct labor hour ratios have changed accordingly, it may be necessary to adjust the amount of direct labor staff. Increases in the ratios of direct labor hours to sales can indicate too many direct employees are on staff while reductions may indicate the need to hire additional direct labor staff. If there is simply excess direct labor capacity and the extra employees cannot be retrained or relocated for other positions, management may face the uncomfortable choice between layoffs and maintaining inefficient operations.

Example

Direct labor cost to total labor cost = direct labor cost / total labor cost

Direct labor cost = 7,860
Total labor cost = 18,871

Direct labor cost to total labor cost = 7,860 / 18,871 = 0.4165 = 41.65%

69 Finding the Labor Cost and Hours Worked Per Direct Employee

Equation

Labor cost per direct employee = direct labor cost / direct labor employees

Hours worked per direct labor employee = direct labor hours / direct labor employees

These ratios allow you to determine the average yearly salary and hours worked per direct labor employee. Direct labor employees are those employees directly involved in the production of the product or service such as machine operators and assemblers in manufacturing firms, hair cutters in salons, and draftspersons in architectural firms.

You can also use these ratios to track the performance of indirect and other nondirect employees by substituting the appropriate labor group information. Indirect employees are those operations employees not directly involved in the production of the product or service such as warehouse receiving employees, production supervisors, and maintenance personnel. Other nondirect employees are employees fully removed from work that is directly associated with or in direct support of producing a company's primary product or service. Examples include employees in human resources, accounting, computer services, R&D, sales, marketing, and customer service.

When to use indicator: Managers can use these ratios to determine direct labor salary trends and the manner in which the company is using direct labor. The hours worked ratio can indicate the level of direct labor capacity available, the degree to which the company uses full-time employees, and the extent to which absences affect direct labor availability. You can also use this ratio for long-term direct labor planning purposes since it can give an accurate portrayal of the actual hours worked per direct employee.

Meaning of result: Higher cost ratios indicate increasing direct labor costs per employee. A number of factors can cause such increases including excessive overtime, rising wage rates, more labor-intensive work processes, increases in direct labor inefficiencies, and increases in the use of part-time direct staff.

Higher hours worked ratios generally indicate that a company uses direct labor employees on a full-time basis, potentially using a high degree of overtime. Lower ratios can indicate significant use of part-time employees, increases in direct labor absences, and reductions in direct labor requirements because of factors such as decreasing sales levels or increasing production efficiencies.

Ways to improve the indicator: You can reduce ratios of direct labor cost and hours worked by improving the efficiency with which you build products or render services. You can improve efficiencies with employee training, increased employee motivation and morale, improvements in production line setups, the use of more efficient equipment, or reengineering products and services to minimize direct labor requirements. Eliminate redundancies in direct labor tasks. Ensure that slack time is kept to a minimum; all direct employees should have productive tasks to complete at all times.

When there is excessive use of overtime, it is often beneficial to hire additional direct employees to lower the labor cost per employee. This is particularly true when overtime requirements are not seasonal in nature and when you project overtime requirements to remain steady or increase in the future.

When a company decreases part-time staffing, there are more employees working full-time, which increases the labor cost per direct employee. However, since these employees contribute more by working additional hours, there is essentially no increased cost on an hourly basis, only on a per-employee basis. However, there may be hidden cost differences when comparing part- and full-time employees such as variability in productivity, wage rates, and benefit costs.

Example

Labor cost per direct employee = direct labor cost / direct labor employees

Direct labor cost = 7,860,000
Direct labor employees = 512
Direct labor hours = 768,000

Labor cost per direct employee = 7,860,000 / 512 = $15,351 per direct labor employee

Labor cost per hour per direct employee = 7,860,000 / 768,000 = $10.23

Determining the Percentage of All Employees Who Are Direct Laborers

Equation

Direct labor employee percentage = direct labor employees / total employees

You can use this ratio to find the percentage of the total work force that represents direct labor employees. Direct labor employees are those employees directly involved in the production of the product or service such as machine operators and assemblers in manufacturing firms, hair cutters in salons, and draftspersons in architectural firms.

You can also use this ratio to track the performance of indirect and other nondirect employees by substituting the appropriate labor group information. Indirect employees are those operations employees not directly involved in the production of the product or service such as warehouse receiving employees, production supervisors, and maintenance personnel. Other nondirect employees are employees fully removed from work that is directly associated with or in direct support of producing a company's primary product or service. Examples include employees in human resources, accounting, computer services, R&D, sales, marketing, and customer service.

When to use indicator: Managers can use this ratio to determine trends in use of direct labor and to be sure an appropriate amount of direct employees are on the payroll. They can also use this ratio to track how the number of direct labor employees varies with changes such as additional training, experience levels, or the installation of new and more productive manufacturing equipment.

Meaning of result: Higher ratios indicate growing percentages of direct labor employees. This can occur when there are increasing direct labor requirements or reductions in nondirect employees. Increasing direct labor requirements often result from rising sales levels because increasing demand requires additional labor. Higher trends may also indicate decreased direct employee productivity. This could be a result of a morale problem, a training issue, or existing machinery that is becoming more troublesome with age and requires replacing. Management may also identify events that justify the higher trending ratios. For example, higher trends could be the result of a wave of new hires who have less experience and lower productivity levels; a new, more labor-intensive product line; or indirect labor productivity increases that have reduced the need for indirect employees.

Reductions in the amount of nondirect employees can arise from improvements in nondirect employee efficiencies, cost-cutting measures, and changes in business strategies. When you reduce the number of nondirect employees as a cost-cutting measure, investigate further to be sure such short-term cost-cutting gains are not at the cost of long-term revenue and income losses. For example, reductions in sales and R&D staffing can surely save money in the short term but could cripple the potential for future sales and income growth.

Ways to improve the indicator: Depending upon staff size and business outlook, you may want to increase or decrease the percentage of direct labor employees. Changes from historical norms of the percentage of direct to total employees can alert you to investigate all potential causes. For example, is a significant change due to increasing or decreasing sales? Or excessive or insufficient nondirect employee staffing? Or from changes in direct labor efficiencies?

Before adding additional direct headcount, management should ask whether changing, larger workloads can be handled by improving the efficiency with which the company builds products and provides services? This is typically a more cost-effective way to tackle changing workloads than through the hiring of more people. You can improve efficiencies with employee training, increased employee motivation and morale, improvements in production line or service-related setups and work processes, and the use of more efficient equipment. Eliminate redundancies in direct labor tasks. Ensure that slack time is kept to a minimum; all direct employees should have productive tasks to complete at all times.

Example

Direct labor employee percentage = direct labor employees / total employees

Direct labor employees = 512
Total employees = 836

Direct labor employee percentage = 512 / 836 = 0.612 = 61.2%

71 Determining the Direct Labor Costs Per Production Unit and Other Direct Labor Efficiency Ratios

Equation

Direct labor costs per production unit = direct labor costs / number of units produced

Production units per direct labor employee = number of units produced / direct labor employees

Production units per direct labor hour = number of units produced / direct labor hours worked

These ratios describe the level of direct labor efficiency in producing a product or service. They can also indicate changes in direct labor requirements because of changing product lines or service offerings. Direct labor employees are those employees directly involved in the production of the product or service such as machine operators and assemblers in manufacturing firms, hair cutters in salons, and draftspersons in architectural firms.

You can also use these ratios to track the performance of indirect and other nondirect employees by substituting the appropriate labor group information. Indirect employees are those operations employees not directly involved in the production of the product or service such as warehouse receiving employees, production supervisors, and maintenance personnel. Other nondirect employees are employees fully removed from work that is directly associated with or in direct support of producing a company's primary product or service. Examples include employees in human resources, accounting, computer services, R&D, sales, marketing, and customer service.

When to use indicator: Managers can use this ratio to determine trends in the efficiency and costs in fabricating products or delivering services. You can use this indicator for distinct product lines and services as well as for determining overall company trends.

Meaning of result: Higher costs per unit and lower units per employee or hour can indicate decreases in direct labor efficiency, increases in wages, or changes in the type of product or service offered. New products or service offerings may require more or less direct labor per unit, depending upon the relative complexity of the new process. These ratios will tend to change temporarily during the initial rollout of new products or services. This can occur because of extra time required for training and skills development.

Ways to improve the indicator: You can improve direct labor ratios by increasing the efficiency with which your company builds products or renders services. You can improve efficiencies with employee training, increased employee motivation and morale, improvements in production line or service-related setups, and the use of more efficient equipment. Eliminate redundancies in direct labor tasks. Ensure that slack time is kept to a minimum; all direct employees should have productive tasks to complete at all times.

Example

Direct labor costs per production unit = direct labor costs / number of units produced

Direct labor costs = 7,860
Number of units produced = 654

Direct labor costs per production unit = 7,860 / 654 = $12.02

72 Comparing the Direct Overhead Cost to Sales, Net Income, and the Cost of Goods Sold

Equation

Direct overhead cost to sales = direct overhead cost / net sales

Direct overhead cost to net income = direct overhead cost / net income

Direct overhead cost to cost of goods sold = direct overhead cost / cost of goods sold

Direct overhead cost ratios are measures of the direct overhead expenses a company incurs to manufacture products and of how such expenses relate to trends in sales, profit, and expense indicators.

When to use indicator: Managers can use these ratios to track the direct overhead expenses associated with the manufacture of products. Management can then investigate direct overhead expense factors when these ratios trend high or low. Direct overhead is one of the three primary constituents of the cost of goods sold. The other two items are raw materials and direct labor expenses.

Meaning of result: To maintain or increase a company's performance, you must maintain expense control and tracking of the costs associated with the manufacture of products. Direct overhead costs are the overhead expenses allocated to the portion of the company involved with the actual manufacture of products. Examples include salaries for direct labor management, leases and maintenance costs for buildings and equipment, utilities expenses, and insurance.

It is almost always desirable to reduce the cost of goods sold, of which direct overhead costs are a main component, since this will tend to maximize profit. However, more effective managers also consider factors such as the safety and productivity that overhead expenses provide. For example, reducing the amount of lighting will cut overhead expenses but will likely reduce labor output due to reduced vision. Even worse, employee morale and/or safety issues could arise from such a move. In this example, it may be more cost-effective to *increase* lighting to improve profit.

Industries will exhibit ratios unique to their markets, so it is best to compare direct overhead cost indicators to companies operating in similar industries and markets. Companies which produce products in high cost of living locations tend to exhibit higher ratios than those located in other areas. For example, a manufacturer located in San Francisco will likely pay higher overhead ratios than one in a less expensive area.

Ways to improve the indicator: You can reduce direct overhead costs by lowering equipment and building lease expenses and by installing more efficient equipment. You can reduce lease costs by designing more efficient floor space manufacturing layouts or simply by negotiating better lease terms. More efficient equipment may lower electric, water, and even insurance costs.

Example

Direct overhead cost to sales = direct overhead cost / net sales

Direct overhead cost = 15,164
Net sales = 85,420

Direct overhead cost to sales = 15,164 / 85,420 = 0.1775 = 17.75%

73 Comparing Raw Materials Costs to Sales, Net Income, and the Cost of Goods Sold

Equation

Raw materials costs to sales = raw materials costs / net sales

Raw materials costs to net income = raw materials costs / net income

Raw materials costs to cost of goods sold = raw materials costs / cost of goods sold

Raw materials cost ratios are measures of the raw materials expenses a company incurs to manufacture products and of how such expenses relate to trends in sales, profit, and expense indicators.

When to use indicator: Managers can use these ratios to track the raw materials expenses associated with the manufacture of products. These ratios can alert management to investigate raw materials expense factors when these ratios trend high or low. Raw materials are one of the three primary constituents of the cost of goods sold. The other two items are direct labor and direct overhead expenses.

Meaning of result: To maintain or increase a company's performance, a manager must maintain expense control and track the costs associated with the manufacture of products. Raw materials costs are the overhead expenses allocated to the purchased parts, assemblies, and raw materials required to fabricate a company's products.

Usually you will want to reduce the cost of goods sold, of which raw materials are a main component, because this will tend to maximize profit. However, more effective managers also consider factors such as the quality, dependability, and responsiveness of raw material suppliers. For example, using a less expensive raw material will cut expenses, but it may reduce finished product quality to the point that customers become dissatisfied. Or a supplier might provide a superior quality product at a great price but, because of continually late shipments, cause the manufacturer to stop production lines and lose customers who can't wait until they start up again.

Industries will exhibit ratios unique to their markets, so it is best to compare raw material cost indicators with companies operating in similar industries and markets. Companies which produce products with a large degree of purchased parts will tend to exhibit higher raw materials ratios than those that use simple commodity-type raw materials. For example, a computer manufacturer that purchases microprocessors and other sophisticated parts for its product line will likely have higher raw materials ratios than a manufacturer of surfboards, whose raw materials are basic and most of whose costs are associated with the labor required to manufacture the product.

Ways to improve the indicator: You can reduce raw materials costs by lowering piece part costs and by redesigning product lines with more cost-effective components. Good negotiating techniques and additional vendor sourcing may help drive down component costs. Excellent engineering should help with redesign efforts.

Example

Raw materials costs to sales = raw material costs / net sales

Raw materials costs = 31,603
Net sales = 85,420

Raw materials costs to sales = 31,063 / 85,420 = 0.3637 = 36.4%

74 Comparing Other Direct Costs to Sales, Gross Profit, Net Income, and the Cost of Goods Sold

Equation

Other direct costs to sales = other direct costs / net sales

Other direct costs to net income = other direct costs / net income

Other direct costs to cost of goods sold = other direct costs / cost of goods sold

Other direct cost ratios are measures of the miscellaneous direct expenses a company incurs to manufacture products and of how such expenses relate to trends in sales and profit indicators.

When to use indicator: Managers use these ratios to track the miscellaneous direct expenses associated with the manufacture of products. Other direct costs include all costs other than those included in the three primary constituents of the cost of goods sold expenses: raw materials, direct labor, and direct overhead.

Meaning of result: To maintain or increase its performance, a company must maintain expense control and track the costs associated with the manufacture of products. Other direct costs are the overhead expenses allocated to direct expense items which are not related to either raw materials, direct labor, or direct overhead.

Most companies prefer to reduce the cost of goods sold, of which other direct expenses are a component, because this will tend to maximize profit. Industries will exhibit ratios unique to their markets, so it is best to compare other direct cost indicators with companies operating in similar industries and markets.

Ways to improve the indicator: You can reduce other direct costs by lowering or eliminating the miscellaneous expenses associated with cost of goods sold.

Example

Other direct costs to sales = other direct costs / net sales

Other direct costs = 125
Net sales = 85,420

Other direct costs to sales = 125 / 85,420 = 0.0015 = 0.15%

Comparing R&D Costs to Sales and Net Income

Equation

R&D costs to sales = R&D costs / net sales

R&D costs to net income = R&D costs / net income

R&D cost ratios are measures of the R&D expenditures a company incurs to develop new products and of how such expenditures relate to trends in sales and profit indicators. R&D expenses include salaries, raw material, and equipment for development efforts, travel, and training.

When to use indicator: Managers and investors use these ratios to determine whether a company is spending proper amounts of money on R&D.

Meaning of result: R&D expenditures are forward looking. Money invested in R&D in the present may not turn into profit-generating products for years, if ever. However, most firms that sell products must make R&D expenditures to remain competitive. This is particularly true for those companies operating in fast-paced industries where continual product updates are demanded, such as in the electronics and computer industries.

When this ratio is trending lower, management could be cutting R&D expenses in the near term to increase net income. This could have an adverse long-term effect on company growth and net income since new products developed by R&D may not be ready when needed. Lower trends could also indicate the company is entering a phase which does not require new products because of lack of competition or reduced demand for new products.

Higher trending R&D ratios could indicate the development of more product offerings or more complex products for a given amount of present-day sales. If you can realize commensurate increases in future sales with this additional R&D outlay, you can justify the increasing trend. Higher ratios can also indicate R&D expenses are out of control if the company does not generate additional R&D output. If this is the case, management should determine the cause of the lowered R&D productivity levels.

Ways to improve the indicator: Management should compare future product needs with current R&D expenditure levels. When product needs are at typical levels, historical R&D expenditure levels are likely appropriate. When product needs are greater in either volume or complexity, you can expect R&D expense levels to increase, and vice versa. For example, suppose R&D costs to sales have historically averaged 8%, and sales from products developed in the last year are 20%. If you desire higher rates of new products, you will likely need larger R&D expenses. In this case, if sales from products developed in the coming year must increase to 30%, then R&D ratios should likely increase by a commensurate amount to 12% [8% × (30/20)].

Sector	Mid to large cap	R&D Costs to Sales Levels	Small to mid cap	R&D Costs to Sales Levels	Micro to small cap	R&D Costs to Sales Levels
Manufacturing	General Motors	0.0%	Toro	0.0%	Encad	0.0%
Retail	Wal-Mart Stores	0.0%	Bed Bath & Beyond	0.0%	TCBY Enterprises	0.0%
Food	McDonald's	0.0%	Applebee's Int'l	0.0%	Garden Fresh Restaurant	7.1%
Technology	Microsoft	17.3%	Cypress Semiconductor	0.0%	Jmar Technologies	0.0%
Finance	Morgan-Stanley Dean Witter	0.0%	Franklin Resources	17.2%	AmeriTrade Holding	0.0%
Healthcare	Columbia/HCA Healthcare	0.0%	Novacare	0.0%	National Home Health Care	0.0%
Service	Manpower	0.0%	Air & Water Technologies	0.0%	Market Facts	0.0%
Media/Publishing	McGraw Hill	0.0%	Scholastic	0.0%	Thomas Nelson	0.0%

Many of the R&D costs to sales levels shown in the table above are zero. Some of these companies did have R&D expenditures (and commensurate R&D costs to sales ratios) but elected not to itemize R&D expenditures on their financial statements.

Increases in R&D productivity may allow the reduction of historic spending levels. A company can realize productivity increases by using new, more efficient, computer-based design and management tools; offering additional experience, training and education; adding incentive programs; and creating work environments which maximize motivation.

Example

R&D costs to sales = R&D costs / net sales

R&D costs = 4,578
 Net sales = 85,420

R&D costs to sales = 4,578 / 85,420 = 0.0536 = 5.36%

76 Comparing Selling, General, and Administrative Costs (SG&A) to Sales and Net Income

Equation

SG&A costs to sales = SG&A costs / net sales

SG&A costs to net income = SG&A costs / net income

Selling, general, and administrative costs (SG&A) ratios are measures of the expenditures a company incurs to sell and support its product lines and of how such expenditures relate to trends in sales and profit indicators. Selling expenses include the costs for sales personnel salaries and sales-related expenses such as travel and advertising. General and administrative expenses include salaries for executives, accountants, human resource personnel, and most other indirect employees and for items such as office leases, utilities, and insurance. Many companies will report selling expenses and G&A expenses as separate line items.

When to use indicator: Managers and investors use these ratios to determine whether a company is spending proper amounts of money on SG&A.

Meaning of result: Lower SG&A expenditure ratios indicate less money being spent, on a percentage basis, for sales, general, and administrative items. This could be the result of more efficient and effectively run operations or the result of cost-cutting measures designed to increase near-term profit. The latter possibility could have adverse short- to long-term effects on company growth and net income when a company reduces income-generating items such as advertising programs and the number of salespeople. Longer term adverse effects could result if, for example, expense reduction took the form of eliminating all executive level sales and marketing positions. With no forward-looking strategic planning and coordination—tasks typically performed by such senior level management—future sales-generating capability would likely suffer.

Higher trending SG&A ratios can indicate SG&A expenses are out of control. Examples could include excessive discretionary expenses such as travel and executive perks. Higher ratios could also indicate overstaffing in one or more departments. Overstaffing can result during business downturns and from ineffective management. When company revenue and earning levels decrease with no change in staffing levels, expense ratios rise. Such situations are usually sustainable for short periods, but not typically in the long run. Either revenues must increase or staff levels must decrease to a level suitable for the new size of the company.

Ways to improve the indicator: Management should assess current SG&A expenditure levels and determine in what areas waste or redundancy exists and take appropriate action to improve efficiencies. Developing expense budgets should help to identify and correct expenses that are out of control.

Example

SG&A costs to sales = SG&A costs / net sales

SG&A costs = 15,993

Net sales = 85,420

SG&A costs to sales = 15,993 / 85,420 = 0.1872 = 18.72%

Sector	Mid to large cap	SG&A Ratio	Small to mid cap	SG&A Ratio	Micro to small cap	SG&A Ratio
Manufacturing	General Motors	9.1%	Toro	30.0%	Encad	22.6%
Retail	Wal-Mart Stores	16.4%	Bed Bath & Beyond	30.2%	TCBY Enterprises	34.2%
Food	McDonald's	18.1%	Applebee's Int'l	10.2%	Garden Fresh Restaurant	58.3%
Technology	Microsoft	26.5%	Cypress Semiconductor	13.8%	Jmar Technologies	34.0%
Finance	Morgan-Stanley Dean Witter	20.5%	Franklin Resources	17.5%	AmeriTrade Holding	34.3%
Healthcare	Columbia/HCA Healthcare	40.5%	Novacare	15.6%	National Home Health Care	24.6%
Service	Manpower	14.5%	Air & Water Technologies	16.6%	Market Facts	33.4%
Media/Publishing	McGraw Hill	31.6%	Scholastic	41.6%	Thomas Nelson	34.8%

77 Comparing Individual Overhead Expenses to Total Overhead Expenses and Sales

Equation

Individual expense to total overhead expense = individual expense (i.e., nondirect employee salaries, benefits, travel, entertainment, utilities) / total overhead expense

Individual expense to sales = individual expense (i.e., salaries, benefits, travel, entertainment, utilities) / net sales

These indicators track the size of individual overhead expenses in relation to total overhead expenditures and net sales levels. Overhead expenses include all expenses not directly involved in the fabrication of a product in a manufacturing firm or the rendering of a service in a service-related firm. Examples of individual overhead expenses include nondirect employee salaries, health benefits, retirement plans, travel, entertainment, meals, office rent, and office utilities.

When to use indicator: Managers can use these indicators to determine whether a company is incurring historic and appropriate overhead expenses. By tracking individual overhead expenses, managers can quickly discover unusual expenditure levels and investigate their causes. Individual overhead items can be more than or less than appropriate expenditure levels. For example, too low a travel expense could indicate sales and marketing personnel are not interacting with customers to an appropriate degree whereas too high a travel expense could indicate excessive travel, which may have generated little additional sales or goodwill.

Meaning of result: Lower ratios of individual overhead to sales are generally desirable and are often the result of rapidly increasing sales levels or lowered expense costs. Expense control is the process of determining what expense levels will offer the greatest benefit. At times, this means curbing or cutting expenses which generate little gain. At other times, this can mean increasing spending in areas where the benefits outweigh the costs. In other words, expense control does not always mean expense reduction. For example, since nondirect personnel are typically one of the most costly overhead expenses, you can exercise considerable overhead control keeping nondirect staff numbers at levels where there is no redundancy or waste. However, it is important that management not trim nondirect labor costs to levels so low that critical functions can no longer operate smoothly. For example, eliminating all sales positions would certainly cut the amount of nondirect salaries but would also likely cripple sales income, forcing the company into an early bankruptcy. It may even be possible that additional salespeople should be added to the staff if this allows increases in net sales and profit far in excess of the costs.

Ways to improve the indicator: You can lower expenses by negotiating lower individual expenses with the appropriate supplier of the overhead item. For example, negotiations with landlords, travel companies, advertising agencies, janitorial services, and healthcare companies may yield lower expense outlays.

Increasing sales levels will often lower ratios of individual overhead to sales because many overhead expenses lag behind changes in sales levels. For example, an increase in sales does not typically immediately translate into significant increases in utility, insurance, or building rental rates. And as a company continues to grow with increasing sales levels, many overhead items can become less expensive since the company purchases higher volumes. For instance, negotiating optimal health plan options and costs can be much easier for the 500-employee company than for a sole proprietorship.

Example

Health benefit to total overhead expense = health benefit expense / total overhead expense

Health benefit expense = 1,440
Total overhead expense = gross profit − pretax income = 31,208 − 9,104 = 22,104
Net sales = 85,420

Health benefit to total overhead expense = 1,440 / 22,104 = 0.0651 = 6.51%

and

Health benefit expense to sales = health benefit expense / net sales

Health benefit expense to sales = 1,440 / 85,420 = 0.0169 = 1.69%

78 Finding Plant Equipment Costs Per Hour

Equation

Plant equipment cost per hour = total costs to maintain and operate plant equipment / hours of fixed asset operation

This ratio details the hourly costs of using and maintaining plant equipment. Costs include all expenses incurred to operate plant equipment such as the labor expense for machinery maintenance, replacement parts, and utility costs. Plant equipment, one type of fixed asset, includes items such as machinery and tooling. Fixed assets (also referred to on the balance sheet as property, plant, and equipment) include items with lifetimes of greater than three years such as land, buildings, machinery, tooling, leasehold improvements, office equipment, and vehicles.

When to use indicator: Managers and creditors can use this indicator to determine the costs associated with using plant equipment. This information can give insight into plant equipment maintenance trends, age, and the type of machinery employed. Cost-per-hour data can indicate expense trends that warrant further management investigation. For example, some product or service lines may be found to be too costly to sell at current price points because of higher than anticipated costs of production. You can also use this ratio to justify the purchase of replacement equipment. This ratio can describe any lot of equipment from individual tools to the entire plant-wide inventory of machinery.

Meaning of result: Higher ratios indicate higher costs to maintain and operate plant equipment. This can result from a number of factors such as using obsolete machinery, producing equipment-intensive products or services, or using improperly maintained machinery that requires frequent repairs.

When machinery downtime for breakage or maintenance increases, plant-equipment-per-hour costs rise. This is due to two factors. First, there are costs associated with repair efforts and replacement parts. Second, since the machinery is not being used during repairs and maintenance, equipment operation hours decline and costs per hour increase.

Ways to improve the indicator: Properly maintaining equipment to increase useful life and limit downtime for repairs can improve plant equipment costs per hour. You can also reduce plant equipment run costs by using high quality, contemporary equipment that can operate with a minimum of downtime and at high efficiency levels.

Example

Machinery cost per hour = total costs to maintain and operate machinery / hours of machinery operation

Maintenance costs = 165
Depreciation expense = 855
Floor space costs = 132
Utility costs = 327
Insurance costs = 94
Other costs = 24
Hours of operation = 1,654

Machinery cost per hour = (165 + 855 + 132 + 327 + 94 + 24)/1,654 = 1,597 / 1,654 = 0.9655 = $966/hour

79 Comparing the Cost of Fixed Asset Maintenance to Sales

Equation:

Fixed asset maintenance to sales = fixed asset maintenance cost / net sales

You should maintain fixed assets properly to maximize useful life and minimize downtime. This ratio can be used to determine trends in fixed asset maintenance. Fixed assets include machinery, tooling, and facilities such as buildings and improvements to properties.

When to use indicator: Managers, investors, and creditors can use this indicator to ascertain whether a company is performing appropriate amounts of maintenance.

Meaning of result: Ratios of fixed asset maintenance to sales are highly dependent upon the type of fixed assets employed and in what industry the business competes. For a given business, decreasing fixed asset maintenance ratios may indicate the company is not performing necessary maintenance possibly, as a cost-saving measure to increase short-term profit. Such action can have longer term detrimental effects because proper maintenance typically enhances greatly the useful life and productivity of fixed assets. However, lower fixed asset maintenance costs can also indicate the company is using newer, less maintenance-intensive equipment or that fewer fixed asset-intensive sources are generating sales.

When ratios are increasing with time, this can indicate improved, more costly maintenance procedures. It can also indicate the company is using fixed assets past their useful lives, which has driven up maintenance costs. Another possibility is that the company is using new types of equipment that are more maintenance intensive.

Ways to improve the indicator: It is generally desirable to maintain fixed assets according to prescribed procedures and at indicated time intervals. Any cutbacks in maintenance can have adverse long-term financial impacts.

Example

Fixed asset maintenance to sales = fixed asset maintenance cost / net sales

Fixed asset maintenance cost = 245
Net sales = 85,420

Fixed asset maintenance to sales = 245 / 85,420 = 0.0028 = 0.28%

Comparing the Cost of Fixed Asset Maintenance to the Value of Fixed Assets

Equation

Fixed asset maintenance to fixed asset value = fixed asset maintenance cost / fixed asset book value

A company must properly maintain fixed assets to maximize useful life and minimize downtime. You can use this ratio to determine trends in fixed asset maintenance. Fixed assets include machinery, tooling, and facilities such as buildings and improvements to properties.

When to use indicator: Managers, investors, and creditors can use this indicator to ascertain if a company is performing appropriate amounts of maintenance.

Meaning of result: Ratios of fixed asset maintenance to value are highly dependent upon the type of fixed assets employed and in what industry the business competes. For a given business, when fixed asset maintenance ratios are decreasing with time, it may indicate the company is not performing necessary maintenance, possibly as a cost-saving measure to increase short-term profit. Such action can have longer term detrimental effects since proper maintenance typically enhances greatly the useful life and productivity of fixed assets.

However, lower fixed asset maintenance costs can also indicate the company is using newer, less maintenance-intensive equipment or that fewer fixed asset-intensive sources are generating sales.

When ratios are increasing with time, this can indicate improved, more costly maintenance procedures. It can also indicate a company is using fixed assets past their useful lives, which has driven up maintenance costs. Another possibility is that the company is using new types of equipment that are more maintenance intensive.

Ways to improve the indicator: It is generally desirable to maintain fixed assets according to prescribed procedures and at indicated time intervals. Any cutbacks in maintenance can have adverse long-term financial impacts.

Example

Fixed asset maintenance to fixed asset value = fixed asset maintenance cost / fixed asset book value

Fixed asset maintenance cost = 245
Fixed asset book value = 10,018

Fixed asset maintenance to fixed asset value = 245 / 10,018 = 0.0245 = 2.45%

81 Relating Insurance Costs to Sales Revenue

Equation

Insurance costs to sales revenue = insurance costs / net sales

This ratio compares insurance costs, a significant portion of operational expenses, to company size. Insurance costs protect company assets from partial or total losses arising from events such as fires, floods, and machinery breakdowns.

When to use indicator: Managers and creditors can use this indicator to determine if insurance levels are proper given the size of the company.

Meaning of result: Lower ratios can indicate inadequate asset coverage. Creditors will typically want to ensure that insurance levels fully cover assets to reduce the risk associated with the extension of credit for those assets. High insurance cost ratios can indicate companies with large amounts of fixed assets, companies with extensive asset coverage, and companies that pay higher insurance rates, possibly because of a high number of insurance claims.

Ways to improve the indicator: It is generally desirable to maintain proper insurance of company assets, particularly when the uninsured asset losses would severely strain financial resources.

Example

Insurance costs to sales revenue = insurance costs / net sales

Insurance costs = 1,322
Net sales = 85,420

Insurance costs to sales revenue = 1,322 / 85,420 = 0.0155 = 1.55%

EXPENSE ANALYSIS

82 Relating Insurance Expenses to the Value of Fixed Assets

Equation

Insurance costs to fixed assets = insurance costs / fixed assets

This ratio compares insurance costs, a significant portion of operational expenses, to fixed assets. Insurance costs protect company assets from partial or total losses arising from events such as fires, floods, and machinery breakdowns. Fixed assets (also referred to on the balance sheet as property, plant, and equipment) include tangible items with lifetimes of greater than three years such as land, buildings, machinery, tooling, vehicles, leasehold improvements, furniture, and office equipment.

When to use indicator: Managers and creditors can use this indicator to determine if insurance levels are proper given the amount of fixed assets.

Lower ratios can indicate inadequate asset coverage. Creditors will typically want to ensure that insurance levels fully cover assets to reduce the risk associated with the extension of credit for those assets. High insurance cost ratios can indicate companies with extensive asset coverage and companies that pay higher insurance rates, possibly because of a high number of insurance claims.

Ways to improve the indicator: It is generally desirable to maintain proper insurance of company assets, particularly when the uninsured asset losses would severely strain financial resources.

Example

Insurance costs to fixed assets = insurance costs / fixed assets

Insurance costs = 1,322
Fixed assets = 10,018

Insurance costs to fixed assets = 1,322 / 10,018 = 0.1320 = 13.2%

83 Examining Book Depreciation

Equation

Book depreciation = depreciation method used in financial reports

Depreciation is used to amortize the purchase price of assets over their useful lifetimes. When you use this technique for financial reporting, it is called **book depreciation,** and it is often different from the depreciation amounts used for tax returns. In the United States it is common to depreciate assets more quickly on tax returns using accelerated depreciation schedules. This has the effect of lowering current-year tax expenses.

Depreciation allows companies to demonstrate that assets typically decrease in value as they age and as they are used. Companies do this by converting a portion of balance sheet assets to current-year expenses shown on the income statement. When a company has fully depreciated an asset, it is not necessarily worthless. Further, the book value of assets is not necessarily similar to market values. This is especially true for assets such as factories and buildings for which actual lifetimes are often greater than depreciation schedule lifetimes and market values are often larger than book values.

When to use indicator: Companies use depreciation methods to account for the gradual consumption of assets. Investors can compare asset values to depreciation expenses to determine the rate at which the company depreciates assets.

Meaning of result: A company generally depreciates, or uses up, longer lived assets over longer periods of time. The depreciation per year thus tends to be a smaller portion of the purchase price for long-lived assets. Companies that depreciate assets over longer periods will tend to show lower rates of depreciation expense relative to asset book value.

Example

Current year book depreciation (depreciation method used in financial reports) = 1,204

Sector	Mid to large cap	Book Depreciation	Small to mid cap	Book Depreciation	Micro to small cap	Book Depreciation
Manufacturing	General Motors	16,616,000	Toro	-	Encad	-
Retail	Wal-Mart Stores	-	Bed Bath & Beyond	-	TCBY Enterprises	-
Food	McDonald's	-	Applebee's Int'l	3,258	Garden Fresh Restaurant	6,147
Technology	Microsoft	-	Cypress Semiconductor	-	Jmar Technologies	-
Finance	Morgan-Stanley Dean Witter	-	Franklin Resources	34,294	AmeriTrade Holding	-
Healthcare	Columbia/HCA Healthcare	1,238,000	Novacare	-	National Home Health Care	245
Service	Manpower	-	Air & Water Technologies	16,861	Market Facts	-
Media/Publishing	McGraw Hill	293,518	Scholastic	33,100	Thomas Nelson	1,839

84 Examining Tax Return Depreciation

Equation

Tax return depreciation = depreciation method used in tax returns

Companies use depreciation to amortize the purchase price of assets over their useful lifetimes. Depreciation used for financial reporting, called book depreciation, is often different from the depreciation amounts used for tax returns. In the United States it is common to depreciate assets more quickly on tax returns using accelerated depreciation schedules. This has the effect of lowering current-year tax expenses.

Depreciation allows companies to demonstrate that assets typically decrease in value as they age and as they are used. Depreciation allows companies to convert a portion of balance sheet assets to current-year expenses shown on the income statement. When a company has fully depreciated an asset, it is not necessarily worthless. Further, the book value of assets is not necessarily similar to market values. This is especially true for assets such as factories and buildings for which actual lifetimes are often greater than depreciation schedule lifetimes and market values are often larger than book values.

When to use indicator: Companies use depreciation methods to account for the gradual consumption of assets. Firms will often use accelerated depreciation schedules to maximize current-year depreciation expense deductions and minimize current-year taxes.

Meaning of result: When tax return depreciation varies from book value depreciation, you use different asset lifetime schedules. Higher rates of depreciation correspond to shorter lifetimes and reduce current-year tax liabilities.

Example

Tax return depreciation = depreciation method used in tax returns

85 Relating Book Depreciation Expenses to Sales Revenue

Equation

Book depreciation to sales revenue = book depreciation / net sales

Companies use depreciation to amortize the purchase price of assets over their useful lifetimes. When you use this technique for financial reporting, it is called book depreciation. Comparing book depreciation with sales levels allows you to determine that the company is incurring expected levels of depreciation.

When to use indicator: Creditors and investors can use this indicator to determine trends in asset purchase and depreciation rates relative to the sales level or company size.

Meaning of result: Higher levels of depreciation to sales can indicate higher levels of fixed asset investment, reductions in depreciation time schedules, and reductions in sales levels.

Lower rates of depreciation to sales can indicate reduced or inadequate asset replacement and acquisition, possibly as a short-term, cost-saving measure. When you use assets beyond their useful lifetimes, you may compromise operations productivity and efficiency, and long-term growth and income can suffer. Lower ratios can also indicate that you are using longer term depreciation schedules, which may also indicate the use of obsolete assets.

Example

Book depreciation to sales revenue = book depreciation / net sales

Book depreciation = 1,204
Net sales = 85,420

Book depreciation to sales revenue = 1,204 / 85,420 = 0.0141 = 1.41%

Sector	Mid to large cap	Book Depreciation Expenses to Sales Revenue	Small to mid cap	Book Depreciation Expenses to Sales Revenue	Micro to small cap	Book Depreciation Expenses to Sales Revenue
Manufacturing	General Motors	9.33%	Toro	0.00%	Encad	0.00%
Retail	Wal-Mart Stores	0.00%	Bed Bath & Beyond	0.00%	TCBY Enterprises	0.00%
Food	McDonald's	0.00%	Applebee's Int'l	0.63%	Garden Fresh Restaurant	6.81%
Technology	Microsoft	0.00%	Cypress Semiconductor	0.00%	Jmar Technologies	0.00%
Finance	Morgan-Stanley Dean Witter	0.00%	Franklin Resources	1.59%	AmeriTrade Holding	0.00%
Healthcare	Columbia/HCA Healthcare	6.58%	Novacare	0.00%	National Home Health Care	0.70%
Service	Manpower	0.00%	Air & Water Technologies	3.69%	Market Facts	0.00%
Media/Publishing	McGraw Hill	8.31%	Scholastic	3.13%	Thomas Nelson	0.73%

86 Comparing Book Depreciation Expenses to the Value of Fixed Assets

Equation

Book depreciation to fixed assets = book depreciation / fixed assets

Companies use depreciation to amortize the purchase price of assets over their useful lifetimes. When you use this technique for financial reporting, it is called book depreciation. Comparing book depreciation to fixed assets allows you to determine that the company is incurring expected levels of depreciation.

When to use indicator: Creditors and investors can use this indicator to determine trends in asset purchase and depreciation rates relative to asset levels.

Meaning of result: Higher levels of depreciation to fixed assets can indicate higher levels of fixed asset investment and reductions in depreciation time schedules.

Lower rates of depreciation to fixed assets can indicate reduced or inadequate asset replacement and acquisition, possibly as a short-term, cost-saving measure. When you use assets beyond their useful lifetimes, you may compromise operations productivity and efficiency, and long-term growth and income can suffer. Lower ratios can also indicate a company is using longer term depreciation schedules, which may also indicate the use of obsolete assets.

Example

Book depreciation to fixed assets = book depreciation / fixed assets

Book depreciation = 1,204
Fixed assets = 10,018

Book depreciation to fixed assets = 1,204 / 10,018 = 0.1202 = 12.02%

Sector	Mid to large cap	Book Depreciation to Fixed Assets	Small to mid cap	Book Depreciation to Fixed Assets	Micro to small cap	Book Depreciation to Fixed Assets
Manufacturing	General Motors	24.48%	Toro	0.0%	Encad	0.0%
Retail	Wal-Mart Stores	0.0%	Bed Bath & Beyond	0.0%	TCBY Enterprises	0.0%
Food	McDonald's	0.0%	Applebee's Int'l	1.18%	Garden Fresh Restaurant	11.33%
Technology	Microsoft	0.0%	Cypress Semiconductor	0.0%	Jmar Technologies	0.0%
Finance	Morgan-Stanley Dean Witter	0.0%	Franklin Resources	15.80%	AmeriTrade Holding	0.0%
Healthcare	Columbia/HCA Healthcare	12.10%	Novacare	0.0%	National Home Health Care	64.81%
Service	Manpower	0.0%	Air & Water Technologies	125.94%	Market Facts	0.0%
Media/Publishing	McGraw Hill	107.27%	Scholastic	24.20%	Thomas Nelson	5.73%

CHAPTER SIX

Assets

Most companies use assets to produce a product or service. Manufacturers obviously require a great deal of machinery and factory floor space to produce goods, but even service-related companies tend to use many assets such as automobiles, computers, and trade-specific equipment. This chapter explores intangible assets such as patent rights and trademarks since many service and product-related firms use them. Also described are a number of ratios that help determine the degree of asset productivity, age, risk level, and quality.

87 Determining the Size of Fixed Assets

Equation

Fixed assets = tangible and long-lived assets

This indicator describes the level of fixed assets a business employs. Fixed assets (also referred to on the balance sheet as property, plant, and equipment) include tangible items with lifetimes of greater than three years such as land, buildings, machinery, tooling, vehicles, leasehold improvements, furniture, and office equipment.

When to use indicator: Managers and investors can use this indicator to determine the level of fixed asset investments employed to operate the business and how these investment levels have changed with time.

Meaning of result: High fixed asset levels indicate the company is capital intensive; that is, the company requires a lot of fixed assets to operate the business. When a company uses fixed assets ineffectively or at less than full capacity, this indicator will creep to higher levels. Manufacturing companies tend to have higher ratios than service-related companies since they typically require greater amounts of fixed assets.

When fixed asset investments are trending higher, the manager should determine the cause of the increase to ensure that events justify the increase. Possible reasons for increasingly higher fixed investments include the release of new products or services that require more than usual, or more costly, amounts of fixed assets; an infrequent purchase of a building or piece of property; and management that has anticipated higher sales levels and has made early fixed asset purchases.

Low ratios indicate the company is not capital intensive; that is, the company requires few fixed assets to operate the business. When ratios are trending lower, management should determine the cause of the decrease to ensure that events justify the decrease. Possible reasons for increasingly lower fixed asset investment include required asset updating and replacement to increase short-term profit; the release of new, lower fixed asset-intensive products or services; and reductions in fixed asset investment in anticipation of reduced sales levels.

Ways to improve the indicator: Depending on the state of the business, it may be desirable to increase, decrease, or hold steady the investment level in fixed assets. See previous section for examples.

Example

Fixed assets = tangible and long-lived assets

Net property, plant, and equipment = 10,018

Fixed assets = 10,018

Sector	Mid to large cap	Size of Fixed Assets	Small to mid cap	Size of Fixed Assets	Micro to small cap	Size of Fixed Assets
Manufacturing	General Motors	67,869,000	Toro	116,852	Encad	14,825
Retail	Wal-Mart Stores	23,606,000	Bed Bath & Beyond	111,381	TCBY Enterprises	40,341
Food	McDonald's	14,961,400	Applebee's Int'l	276,082	Garden Fresh Restaurant	54,257
Technology	Microsoft	1,505,000	Cypress Semiconductor	442,661	Jmar Technologies	2,500
Finance	Morgan-Stanley Dean Witter	1,705,000	Franklin Resources	217,085	AmeriTrade Holding	8,710
Healthcare	Columbia/HCA Healthcare	10,230,000	Novacare	69,740	National Home Health Care	378
Service	Manpower	136,376	Air & Water Technologies	13,388	Market Facts	17,081
Media/Publishing	McGraw Hill	273,630	Scholastic	136,800	Thomas Nelson	32,103

88 Examining the Relationship Between Fixed Assets and Sales

Equation

Fixed assets to sales = fixed assets / net sales

This indicator describes the level of fixed assets employed to generate a given amount of net sales. It also indicates trends in fixed asset age and procurement practices. Fixed assets (also referred to on the balance sheet as property, plant, and equipment) include items with lifetimes of greater than three years such as land, buildings, machinery, tooling, leasehold improvements, office equipment, and vehicles.

The inverse of the equation, net sales divided by fixed assets, is an indicator known as fixed asset turnover. **Fixed asset turnover** also describes the relative size of net sales and fixed assets, but more specifically, how many times a company achieves, or turns over, the book value of fixed assets in net sales.

When to use indicator: Managers and investors can use this indicator to determine the level of fixed asset investment required to generate every dollar of net sales and how these investment levels have changed with time. You can use the ratio as a forecasting tool to estimate fixed asset requirements given assumed net sales levels.

Meaning of result: High ratios indicate the company is capital intensive; that is, to achieve sales levels, the company uses a great deal of fixed assets. When a company uses fixed assets ineffectively or at less than full capacity, this ratio will creep to higher levels. Manufacturing companies tend to have higher ratios than service-related companies since they typically require greater amounts of fixed assets.

When ratios are trending higher, management should determine the cause of the increase to ensure that events justify the increase. Possible reasons for increasingly higher ratios include the release of new products or services that require more than usual, or more costly, amounts of fixed assets; a drop in sales levels; an infrequent purchase of a building or piece of property; and management that has anticipated higher sales levels and has made early fixed asset purchases.

Low ratios indicate the company is not capital intensive; that is, that to generate sales, the company requires few fixed assets. When ratios are trending lower, management should determine the cause of the decrease to ensure that events justify the decrease. Possible reasons for increasingly lower ratios include required asset updating and replacement to increase short-term profit; the release of new, lower fixed asset-intensive products or services; an increase in sales levels; or reductions in fixed asset investment in anticipation of reduced sales levels.

Ways to improve the indicator: Depending on the state of the business, it may be desirable to increase, decrease, or hold steady the ratio of fixed assets to sales. See previous section for examples.

Example

Fixed assets to sales = fixed assets / net sales

Fixed assets = 10,018
Net sales = 85,420

Fixed assets to sales = 10,018 / 85,420 = 0.1173 = 11.73

Sector	Mid to large cap	Fixed Assets to Sales	Small to mid cap	Fixed Assets to Sales	Micro to small cap	Fixed Assets to Sales
Manufacturing	General Motors	38.09%	Toro	11.12%	Encad	9.95%
Retail	Wal-Mart Stores	20.01%	Bed Bath & Beyond	10.44%	TCBY Enterprises	44.54%
Food	McDonald's	131.14%	Applebee's Int'l	53.52%	Garden Fresh Restaurant	60.12%
Technology	Microsoft	10.39%	Cypress Semiconductor	81.32%	Jmar Technologies	11.65%
Finance	Morgan-Stanley Dean Witter	6.28%	Franklin Resources	10.04%	AmeriTrade Holding	9.10%
Healthcare	Columbia/HCA Healthcare	54.36%	Novacare	6.54%	National Home Health Care	1.08%
Service	Manpower	1.88%	Air & Water Technologies	2.93%	Market Facts	17.07%
Media/Publishing	McGraw Hill	7.74%	Scholastic	12.93%	Thomas Nelson	12.69%

89 Examining the Relationship Between Fixed Assets and Net Income

Equation

Fixed assets to net income = fixed assets / net income

This indicator describes the level of fixed assets employed to generate a given amount of net income. It also indicates trends in fixed asset age and procurement practices. Fixed assets (also referred to on the balance sheet as property, plant, and equipment) include items with lifetimes of greater than three years such as land, buildings, machinery, tooling, leasehold improvements, office equipment, and vehicles.

When to use indicator: Managers and investors can use this indicator to determine the level of fixed asset investment required to generate every dollar of net income and to learn how these investment levels have changed with time.

Meaning of result: High ratios indicate the company is capital intensive; that is, to achieve net income levels, the company uses a great deal of fixed assets. When a company uses fixed assets ineffectively or at less than full capacity, this ratio will creep to higher levels. Manufacturing companies tend to have higher ratios than service-related companies since they typically require greater amounts of fixed assets. When net income levels are very low or negative, this ratio loses meaning since small changes in net income will have dramatic effects on the fixed asset to net income indicator.

When ratios are trending higher, management should determine the cause of the increase to ensure that events justify the increase. Possible reasons for increasingly higher ratios include the release of new products or services that require more than usual, or more costly, amounts of fixed assets; a drop in sales levels; a reduction in profit margins; an infrequent purchase of a building or piece of property; and management that has anticipated higher sales levels and has made early fixed asset purchases.

Low ratios indicate the company is not capital intensive or that the company generates its net income stream with smaller fixed asset requirements. When a company uses fixed assets effectively and at full capacity, this ratio will trend toward lower levels. Service-related companies tend to have lower ratios than manufacturers since there is typically less need for fixed assets.

When ratios are trending lower, management should determine the cause of the decrease to ensure that events justify the decrease. Possible reasons for decreasing ratios include required asset updating and replacement to increase short-term profit; the release of new, lower fixed asset-intensive products or services; an increase in sales levels; an increase in profit margins; or reductions in fixed asset investment in anticipation of reduced sales levels.

Sector	Mid to large cap	Fixed Assets to Net Income	Small to mid cap	Fixed Assets to Net Income	Micro to small cap	Fixed Assets to Net Income
Manufacturing	General Motors	1013.27%	Toro	335.35%	Encad	85.06%
Retail	Wal-Mart Stores	669.48%	Bed Bath & Beyond	152.28%	TCBY Enterprises	454.33%
Food	McDonald's	910.89%	Applebee's Int'l	612.28%	Garden Fresh Restaurant	1395.86%
Technology	Microsoft	33.52%	Cypress Semiconductor	2403.28%	Jmar Technologies	139.28%
Finance	Morgan-Stanley Dean Witter	65.93%	Franklin Resources	50.01%	AmeriTrade Holding	63.01%
Healthcare	Columbia/HCA Healthcare	–3354.10%	Novacare	179.23%	National Home Health Care	20.37%
Service	Manpower	83.22%	Air & Water Technologies	–8.34%	Market Facts	293.39%
Media/Publishing	McGraw Hill	94.14%	Scholastic	579.66%	Thomas Nelson	253.32%

Ways to improve the indicator: Depending on the state of the business, it may be desirable to increase, decrease, or hold steady the ratio of fixed assets to net income. See previous section for examples.

Example

Fixed assets to net income = fixed assets / net income

Fixed assets = 10,018
Net income = 4,983

Fixed assets to net income = 10,018 / 4,983 = 2.01 = 201%

90 Examining the Relationship Between Fixed Assets and Operations Cash Flow

Equation

Fixed assets to operations cash flow = fixed assets / cash from operations

This indicator describes the level of fixed assets a company employs to generate a given amount of cash from operations. It also indicates trends in fixed asset age and procurement practices. Fixed assets (also referred to on the balance sheet as property, plant, and equipment) include items with lifetimes of greater than three years such as land, buildings, machinery, tooling, leasehold improvements, office equipment, and vehicles.

When to use indicator: Managers and investors can use this indicator to determine the level of fixed asset investment required to generate cash from operations and to learn how these investment levels have changed with time.

Meaning of result: Low ratios indicate companies that generate a substantial amount of cash with a relatively small fixed asset investment. This is common for service-oriented rather than manufacturing-intensive companies since fixed asset investments of service companies are generally lower.

When ratios of fixed assets to operations cash flow are trending lower, it could be an indication that a company is using fixed assets more productively or with less idle or downtime or that sales levels have risen, thereby increasing cash generated from operations. Another possibility is that operations cash flow has increased by reducing inventory levels or working capital requirements. It could also indicate that a company has not purchased any new fixed assets for some time and has reduced the book value of those fixed assets with depreciation.

When ratios of fixed assets to operations cash flow are trending higher, it could indicate excess fixed asset capacity, either because of reduced sales levels or because the company has recently made a new fixed asset investment.

Ways to improve the indicator: You can reduce ratios of fixed assets to operations cash flow by using existing fixed assets to their fullest extent in the most productive manner possible. When this is not possible because, for example, sales levels don't warrant additional production, excess fixed asset capacity exists and it may be beneficial to sell or lease the unwanted fixed assets.

When rates of return justify new fixed asset investment, you may improve this indicator by updating older fixed assets with newer, more productive fixed assets. New machinery may increase productivity and substantially reduce the costs associated with producing a product, thereby significantly increasing cash from operations.

Example

Fixed assets to operations cash flow = fixed assets / cash from operations

Fixed assets = 10,018

Cash from operations = 4,820

Fixed assets to operations cash flow = 10,018 / 4,820 = 2.078 = 207.8%

Sector	Mid to large cap	Fixed Assets to Operations Cash Flow	Small to mid cap	Fixed Assets to Operations Cash Flow	Micro to small cap	Fixed Assets to Operations Cash Flow
Manufacturing	General Motors	412.48%	Toro	139.32%	Encad	–498.32%
Retail	Wal-Mart Stores	331.41%	Bed Bath & Beyond	232.49%	TCBY Enterprises	236.01%
Food	McDonald's	612.59%	Applebee's Int'l	315.96%	Garden Fresh Restaurant	449.67%
Technology	Microsoft	21.88%	Cypress Semiconductor	539.63%	Jmar Technologies	*
Finance	Morgan-Stanley Dean Witter	–289.97%	Franklin Resources	50.66%	AmeriTrade Holding	36.66%
Healthcare	Columbia/HCA Healthcare	689.82%	Novacare	147.63%	National Home Health Care	15.76%
Service	Manpower	377.78%	Air & Water Technologies	89.29%	Market Facts	166.77%
Media/Publishing	McGraw Hill	73.34%	Scholastic	116.23%	Thomas Nelson	397.12%

* Cash flow data not reported for this company.

91 Comparing Fixed Assets to Total Assets

Equation

Fixed assets to total assets = fixed assets / total assets

This indicator describes the portion of all of a company's assets that are fixed assets. It also indicates trends in fixed asset age and procurement practices. Fixed assets (also referred to on the balance sheet as property, plant, and equipment) include items with lifetimes of greater than three years such as land, buildings, machinery, tooling, leasehold improvements, office equipment, and vehicles. Total assets include fixed assets, current assets, intangible assets, long-term security investments, and other noncurrent assets.

When to use indicator: Managers and investors can use this indicator to determine the level of fixed assets to total asset investments employed to operate the business and to learn how these investment levels have changed with time. They can also use the ratio as a forecasting tool to estimate fixed asset requirements given assumed total asset levels.

Meaning of result: Companies with high ratios of fixed assets to total assets employ large amounts of land, buildings, equipment, and other types of fixed assets. This is typical of manufacturing companies which require a great deal of component fabrication and assembly, such as in the automobile industry. Alternatively, an architectural consulting firm may exhibit a low ratio of fixed assets to total assets. It is likely to require few fixed assets to operate because it primarily supplies noncapital-intensive products such as guidance, reports, and drawings.

Look for changes in ratios of fixed assets to total assets over time and seek to understand the reasons for such changes. Are lower ratios due to cost-cutting measures in which needed fixed asset replacements were passed over? If this is the case, the company could be entering a severe business downturn. Or are the lower ratios due to the use of newer, less costly equipment? Or has the business begun to offer different lines of products or services that require different fixed asset investments?

Ways to improve the indicator: Depending on the state of the business, it may be desirable to increase, decrease, or hold steady the ratio of fixed assets to total assets. See previous section for examples.

Example

Fixed assets to total assets = fixed assets / total assets

Fixed assets = 10,018
Total assets = 56,268

Fixed assets to total assets = 10,018 / 56,268 = 0.1780 = 17.80%

Sector	Mid to large cap	Fixed Assets to Total Assets	Small to mid cap	Fixed Assets to Total Assets	Micro to small cap	Fixed Assets to Total Assets
Manufacturing	General Motors	29.65%	Toro	17.66%	Encad	16.42%
Retail	Wal-Mart Stores	52.01%	Bed Bath & Beyond	24.30%	TCBY Enterprises	40.64%
Food	McDonald's	82.02%	Applebee's Int'l	73.14%	Garden Fresh Restaurant	86.94%
Technology	Microsoft	6.73%	Cypress Semiconductor	46.29%	Jmar Technologies	14.48%
Finance	Morgan-Stanley Dean Witter	0.56%	Franklin Resources	7.01%	AmeriTrade Holding	1.15%
Healthcare	Columbia/HCA Healthcare	46.50%	Novacare	6.88%	National Home Health Care	1.50%
Service	Manpower	6.66%	Air & Water Technologies	3.49%	Market Facts	19.66%
Media/Publishing	McGraw Hill	7.35%	Scholastic	17.88%	Thomas Nelson	11.25%

92 Assessing the Fixed-Asset-to-Equity Ratio

Equation

Fixed assets to equity = fixed assets / total shareholder equity

This indicator compares the relative level of fixed asset investment with investor investment. You can think of it as the portion of shareholders' equity used for fixed assets. Fixed assets (also referred to on the balance sheet as property, plant, and equipment) include items with lifetimes of greater than three years such as land, buildings, machinery, tooling, leasehold improvements, office equipment, and vehicles. Total shareholder equity includes all equity balance sheet items, typically the most significant of which are additional paid-in capital for stock purchases and retained earnings (income generated that the company has reinvested in the company).

When to use indicator: Investors can use this indicator to gain a sense of how a company employs its equity.

Meaning of result: Higher ratios indicate that fixed asset investments account for a great deal of equity. This is common for capital-intensive companies such as in the automobile industry. Lower ratios indicate small levels of fixed asset investment typically found in service-related companies such as brokerage firms or temporary help companies.

Look for changes in ratios of fixed assets to total equity over time and seek to understand the reasons for such changes. Are lower ratios due to cost-cutting measures in which needed fixed asset replacements were passed over? If this is the case, the company in question could be entering a severe business downturn. Or are the lower ratios due to the use of newer, less costly equipment? Or has the business begun to offer different lines of products or services that require different fixed asset investments?

Ways to improve the indicator: Depending on the state of the business, it may be desirable to increase, decrease, or hold steady the ratio of fixed assets to shareholder equity. See previous section for examples.

Example

Fixed assets to equity = fixed assets / total shareholder equity

Fixed assets = 10,018
Total shareholder equity = 31,088

Fixed assets to equity = 10,018 / 31,088 = 0.3222 = 32.22%

Sector	Mid to large cap	Fixed-Asset-to-Equity Ratio	Small to mid cap	Fixed-Asset-to-Equity Ratio	Micro to small cap	Fixed-Asset-to-Equity Ratio
Manufacturing	General Motors	387.69%	Toro	48.45%	Encad	22.91%
Retail	Wal-Mart Stores	127.58%	Bed Bath & Beyond	37.71%	TCBY Enterprises	52.10%
Food	McDonald's	169.02%	Applebee's Int'l	95.06%	Garden Fresh Restaurant	158.79%
Technology	Microsoft	9.05%	Cypress Semiconductor	68.79%	Jmar Technologies	20.02%
Finance	Morgan-Stanley Dean Witter	12.22%	Franklin Resources	11.71%	AmeriTrade Holding	13.00%
Healthcare	Columbia/HCA Healthcare	141.10%	Novacare	13.73%	National Home Health Care	1.62%
Service	Manpower	22.08%	Air & Water Technologies	−12.25%	Market Facts	31.90%
Media/Publishing	McGraw Hill	19.07%	Scholastic	43.01%	Thomas Nelson	20.53%

93 Determining the Relationship Between Fixed Assets and Long-Term Debt

Equation

Fixed assets to long-term debt = fixed assets / long-term debt

The relative level of the book value of fixed assets and long-term debt describes the degree of a company's fixed asset financial leverage. Fixed assets (also referred to on the balance sheet as property, plant, and equipment) include items with lifetimes of greater than three years such as land, buildings, machinery, tooling, leasehold improvements, office equipment, and vehicles. Long-term debt is debt that is due in more than 12 months.

When to use indicator: Creditors and managers use this indicator to determine the risk level associated with long-term debt.

Meaning of result: Lower ratios indicate potential credit or solvency problems and could preclude the issuance of further debt. This ratio has less meaning for service-related companies and those companies that use few fixed assets. Such companies will tend to have lower fixed asset-to-debt ratios simply because they use fewer fixed asset items such as factories and equipment.

Higher ratios are typical of profitable companies that exhibit little or no long-term debt and that finance fixed asset acquisitions with operating income.

Ways to improve the indicator: Paying down long-term debt levels to industry standards can reduce the fixed asset-to-long-term debt ratio.

Example

Fixed assets to long-term debt = fixed assets / long-term debt

Fixed assets = 10,018
Long-term debt = 13,148

Fixed assets to long-term debt = 10,018 / 13,148 = 0.7619 = 76.19%

Sector	Mid to large cap	Fixed Assets to Long-Term Debt	Small to mid cap	Fixed Assets to Long-Term Debt	Micro to small cap	Fixed Assets to Long-Term Debt
Manufacturing	General Motors	34.87%	Toro	63.98%	Encad	1164.57%
Retail	Wal-Mart Stores	225.18%	Bed Bath & Beyond	884.68%	TCBY Enterprises	397.65%
Food	McDonald's	233.57%	Applebee's Int'l	1124.89%	Garden Fresh Restaurant	377.78%
Technology	Microsoft	*	Cypress Semiconductor	201.45%	Jmar Technologies	275.61%
Finance	Morgan-Stanley Dean Witter	6.61%	Franklin Resources	40.88%	AmeriTrade Holding	*
Healthcare	Columbia/HCA Healthcare	91.81%	Novacare	20.14%	National Home Health Care	119.62%
Service	Manpower	32.10%	Air & Water Technologies	4.35%	Market Facts	164.10%
Media/Publishing	McGraw Hill	25.25%	Scholastic	51.53%	Thomas Nelson	38.16%

* Companies with no long-term debt reported.

94 Comparing Fixed Assets to Short-Term Debt

Equation

Fixed assets to short-term debt = fixed assets / short-term debt

This indicator compares the relative size of the book value of fixed assets to the size of short-term debt. You can think of it as the portion of fixed assets that is financed with short-term debt. Fixed assets (also referred to on the balance sheet as property, plant, and equipment) include items with lifetimes of greater than three years such as land, buildings, machinery, tooling, leasehold improvements, office equipment, and vehicles. Short-term debt, referred to as current liabilities on the balance sheet, is debt that is due in less than one year. It includes notes payable, accounts payable, and accrued expenses such as payroll and property taxes.

When to use indicator: Creditors and managers use this indicator to determine the risk level associated with short-term debt.

Meaning of result: When companies use short-term debt to finance fixed assets, banks require higher payments to service the loans since the loans must be paid more quickly. Higher payments could put a company into a precarious financial position. It is generally desirable to finance fixed assets with loans that last about as long as the life of the fixed asset, typically at least three years. Since payments will be lower, this will put less pressure on company cash flow.

Lower fixed asset-to-short-term debt ratios indicate potential credit or solvency problems and could preclude the issuance of further short-term debt. This ratio has less meaning for service-related companies and those companies that use few fixed assets. Such companies will tend to have lower ratios simply because they use few fixed asset items such as factories and equipment.

Higher ratios are typical of profitable companies that exhibit little or no short-term debt and finance fixed asset acquisitions with operating income or long-term debt.

Ways to improve the indicator: Paying down short-term debt levels to industry standards can reduce the fixed-asset-to-short-term-debt ratio.

Example

Fixed assets to short-term debt = fixed assets / short-term debt

Fixed assets = 10,018
Short-term debt = current liabilities = 12,032

Fixed assets to short-term debt = 10,018 / 12,032 = 0.8326 = 83.26%

Sector	Mid to large cap	Fixed Assets to Short-Term Debt	Small to mid cap	Fixed Assets to Short-Term Debt	Micro to small cap	Fixed Assets to Short-Term Debt
Manufacturing	General Motors	430.04%	Toro	49.13%	Encad	61.01%
Retail	Wal-Mart Stores	163.25%	Bed Bath & Beyond	74.08%	TCBY Enterprises	344.97%
Food	McDonald's	501.30%	Applebee's Int'l	441.82%	Garden Fresh Restaurant	390.93%
Technology	Microsoft	26.27%	Cypress Semiconductor	475.71%	Jmar Technologies	64.55%
Finance	Morgan-Stanley Dean Witter	0.65%	Franklin Resources	30.58%	AmeriTrade Holding	1.26%
Healthcare	Columbia/HCA Healthcare	368.91%	Novacare	44.61%	National Home Health Care	24.42%
Service	Manpower	13.57%	Air & Water Technologies	7.32%	Market Facts	74.47%
Media/Publishing	McGraw Hill	22.68%	Scholastic	75.29%	Thomas Nelson	71.72%

95 Examining Fixed Asset Turnover

Equation

Fixed asset turnover = net sales / fixed assets

Fixed asset turnover describes the relative size of net sales and fixed assets and, more specifically, how many times a company achieves, or turns over, the book value of fixed assets in net sales. Fixed assets (also referred to on the balance sheet as property, plant, and equipment) include items with lifetimes of greater than three years such as land, buildings, machinery, tooling, leasehold improvements, office equipment, and vehicles.

When to use indicator: Managers and investors can use this indicator to determine the level of fixed asset investment required to generate every dollar of net sales and to learn how these investment levels have changed with time. You can also use this indicator to forecast fixed asset requirements based on expected future net sales levels.

Meaning of result: Low ratios indicate the company is capital intensive or that the company requires a lot of fixed assets to generate a given amount of sales. When ratios are trending lower, management should determine the cause of the increase to ensure that events justify the increase. Possible reasons for increasingly lower ratios include the release of new products or services that require more than usual, or more costly, amounts of fixed assets; a drop in sales levels; an infrequent purchase of a building or piece of property; and management that has anticipated higher sales levels and has made early fixed asset purchases.

Higher ratios indicate the company is not capital intensive; that is, the company requires few fixed assets to generate a given amount of sales. When ratios are trending higher, management should determine the cause of the increase to ensure that events justify the increase. Possible reasons for increasingly higher ratios include required asset updating and replacement (short-term profit is enhanced by foregoing asset replacement); the release of new, less fixed asset-intensive products or services; an increase in sales levels; or reductions in fixed asset investment in anticipation of reduced sales levels.

Ways to improve the indicator: Depending on the state of the business, it may be desirable to increase, decrease, or hold steady fixed asset turnover. See previous section for examples.

Example

Fixed asset turnover = net sales / fixed assets

Net sales = 85,420
Fixed assets = 10,018

Fixed asset turnover = 85,420 / 10,018 = 8.53

Sector	Mid to large cap	Fixed Asset Turnover	Small to mid cap	Fixed Asset Turnover	Micro to small cap	Fixed Asset Turnover
Manufacturing	General Motors	2.63	Toro	9.00	Encad	10.05
Retail	Wal-Mart Stores	5.00	Bed Bath & Beyond	9.58	TCBY Enterprises	2.25
Food	McDonald's	0.76	Applebee's Int'l	1.87	Garden Fresh Restaurant	1.66
Technology	Microsoft	9.62	Cypress Semiconductor	1.23	Jmar Technologies	8.58
Finance	Morgan-Stanley Dean Witter	15.91	Franklin Resources	9.97	AmeriTrade Holding	10.98
Healthcare	Columbia/HCA Healthcare	1.84	Novacare	15.29	National Home Health Care	92.78
Service	Manpower	53.22	Air & Water Technologies	34.09	Market Facts	5.86
Media/Publishing	McGraw Hill	12.92	Scholastic	7.74	Thomas Nelson	7.88

96 Assessing the Age of Fixed Assets

Equation

Fixed asset acquisitions to total fixed assets = newly purchased fixed assets / fixed assets

This indicator describes the age of fixed assets. Fixed assets (also referred to on the balance sheet as property, plant, and equipment) include items with lifetimes of greater than three years such as land, buildings, machinery, tooling, leasehold improvements, office equipment, and vehicles.

When to use indicator: Investors and managers can use this indicator to gain a sense of the age of fixed assets and the degree to which fixed asset reinvestment is occurring.

Meaning of result: Higher ratios indicate the quicker replacement of obsolete or worn out fixed assets with new fixed assets or that the company is growing at such a fast rate that the company readily purchases additional fixed assets to keep pace with sales levels. By using fixed assets that allow the most productive fabrication of products or delivery of services, you can minimize production costs. In rapidly changing industries, this typically means the regular updating of fixed assets. This ratio has less meaning for those companies operating in slow-changing industries, such as service or manufacturing companies, that warrant less rapid fixed asset replacement.

Ways to improve the indicator: When you can justify fixed asset replacement costs, or when you need additional fixed assets to meet sales demand, you want higher ratios and can achieve them with the purchase of new fixed assets.

Example

Fixed asset acquisitions to total fixed assets = newly purchased assets / fixed assets

Newly purchased fixed assets = change in book value of fixed assets = 12,065 − 5,790 = 6,275
Fixed assets = 10,018

Fixed asset acquisitions to total fixed assets = 6,275 / 10,018 = 0.6274 = 62.74%

Sector	Mid to large cap	Fixed Asset Acquisitions to Total Fixed Assets	Small to mid cap	Fixed Asset Acquisitions to Total Fixed Assets	Micro to small cap	Fixed Asset Acquisitions to Total Fixed Assets
Manufacturing	General Motors	62.13%	Toro	58.84%	Encad	26.60%
Retail	Wal-Mart Stores	18.86%	Bed Bath & Beyond	20.69%	TCBY Enterprises	2.97%
Food	McDonald's	6.38%	Applebee's Int'l	28.66%	Garden Fresh Restaurant	23.42%
Technology	Microsoft	2.66%	Cypress Semiconductor	1.15%	Jmar Technologies	−8.16%
Finance	Morgan-Stanley Dean Witter	14.25%	Franklin Resources	25.55%	AmeriTrade Holding	75.28%
Healthcare	Columbia/HCA Healthcare	5.54%	Novacare	9.21%	National Home Health Care	15.61%
Service	Manpower	16.30%	Air & Water Technologies	−115.79%	Market Facts	12.28%
Media/Publishing	McGraw Hill	0.93%	Scholastic	10.16%	Thomas Nelson	−2.31%

97 Determining the Turnover Rate of Total Assets

Equation

Total asset turnover = net sales / total assets

Total asset turnover describes the relative size of net sales and total company assets and, more specifically, how many times a company achieves, or turns over, the book value of all assets in net sales. Total assets include all current and long-term assets such as cash, inventory, accounts receivable, property, plants, equipment, patents, goodwill, and investments.

When to use indicator: Managers and investors can use this indicator to determine the level of asset investment required to generate every dollar of net sales and to learn how these investment levels have changed with time.

Meaning of result: Low ratios indicate the company is asset-intensive or that, to achieve sales levels, the company uses a great deal of assets. When a company uses assets ineffectively or in less-than-optimum capacity, this indicator will creep to higher levels. Generating sales requires assets, and it is the manager's responsibility to employ assets in an optimum mix that allows the greatest sales and income levels attainable.

Ways to improve the indicator: Optimal use of assets will tend to improve, or increase, the total asset turnover ratio. Improved use of current assets such as cash, inventories, and accounts receivable will enhance asset turnover. It is desirable to keep cash and inventory balances at levels that allow payment of short-term debt and the delivery of customer orders, but not so high that there is any degree of excess cash or inventory. This is because rates of return on cash are generally much lower than the returns that longer term investments, such as fixed assets, can achieve. The return on excess inventory is even less because idle inventory does not earn a return and could be depreciating if the product is in a rapidly changing industry. Similarly, by maintaining accounts receivable balances at levels which allow credit purchases, but not so high as to attract deadbeat customers, you can achieve optimal asset use.

Good long-term asset investments will tend to increase total asset turnover. You should purchase fixed assets when you can realize a suitable return from the product or service produced with the fixed assets. Optimizing total asset turnover can be achieved by using fixed assets at full capacity and in productive manners. Purchasing additional long-term assets such as subsidiaries and patent rights can generate substantial sales and income streams that may also tend to increase asset turnover.

Example

Total asset turnover = net sales / total assets

Net sales = 85,420
Total assets = 56,268

Total asset turnover = 85,420 / 56,268 = 1.52

Sector	Mid to large cap	Total Asset Turnover Rate	Small to mid cap	Total Asset Turnover Rate	Micro to small cap	Total Asset Turnover Rate
Manufacturing	General Motors	0.78	Toro	1.59	Encad	1.65
Retail	Wal-Mart Stores	2.60	Bed Bath & Beyond	2.33	TCBY Enterprises	0.91
Food	McDonald's	0.63	Applebee's Int'l	1.37	Garden Fresh Restaurant	1.45
Technology	Microsoft	0.65	Cypress Semiconductor	0.57	Jmar Technologies	1.24
Finance	Morgan-Stanley Dean Witter	0.09	Franklin Resources	0.70	AmeriTrade Holding	0.13
Healthcare	Columbia/HCA Healthcare	0.86	Novacare	1.05	National Home Health Care	1.39
Service	Manpower	3.55	Air & Water Technologies	1.19	Market Facts	1.15
Media/Publishing	McGraw Hill	0.95	Scholastic	1.38	Thomas Nelson	0.89

98 Finding the Total Asset Coverage Ratio

Equation

Total asset coverage ratio = total assets / long-term debt

The relative level of the book value of total assets and long-term debt describes the degree of a company's financial leverage. Total assets include all current and long-term assets such as cash, inventory, accounts receivable, property, plants, equipment, patents, goodwill, and investments. Long-term debt is debt that is due in more than 12 months.

When to use indicator: Creditors and managers use this indicator to determine the risk level associated with long-term debt.

Meaning of result: Lower ratios indicate potential credit or solvency problems and could preclude the issuance of further debt. Higher ratios are typical of profitable companies that exhibit little or no long-term debt and that finance current and long-term assets with operating income.

Ways to improve the indicator: Paying down debt levels can increase the total asset coverage ratio.

Example

Total asset coverage ratio = total assets / long-term debt

Total assets = 56,268
Long-term debt = 25,180 − 12,032 = 13,148

Total asset coverage ratio = 56,268 / 13,148 = 4.28

Sector	Mid to large cap	Total Asset Coverage Ratio	Small to mid cap	Total Asset Coverage Ratio	Micro to small cap	Total Asset Coverage Ratio
Manufacturing	General Motors	1.18	Toro	3.62	Encad	70.93
Retail	Wal-Mart Stores	4.33	Bed Bath & Beyond	36.40	TCBY Enterprises	9.78
Food	McDonald's	2.85	Applebee's Int'l	15.38	Garden Fresh Restaurant	4.35
Technology	Microsoft	*	Cypress Semiconductor	4.35	Jmar Technologies	19.03
Finance	Morgan-Stanley Dean Witter	11.72	Franklin Resources	5.83	AmeriTrade Holding	*
Healthcare	Columbia/HCA Healthcare	1.97	Novacare	2.93	National Home Health Care	79.82
Service	Manpower	4.82	Air & Water Technologies	1.24	Market Facts	8.35
Media/Publishing	McGraw Hill	3.44	Scholastic	2.88	Thomas Nelson	3.39

* Companies with no reported long-term debt.

99 Comparing Intangible Assets to Sales Revenue

Equation

Intangible assets to sales = intangible assets / net sales

This indicator describes the level of intangible assets a company employs to generate a given amount of net sales. Intangible assets are nonphysical items that have value to the company such as goodwill associated with brand names, trademarks, skilled employees, loyal customers, patents, copyrights, permits, investments, deferred charges, and leasehold improvements.

When to use indicator: Managers and investors can use this indicator to determine the level of intangible assets a company uses to generate every dollar of net sales and to learn how these investment levels have changed with time.

Meaning of result: High ratios indicate the company employs a significant level of intangible assets as a percentage of sales. Since intangible assets are harder to liquidate than tangible assets such as land, buildings, or equipment, the investor should be concerned if the level of intangible assets is so high that the intangible assets may be overstated. However, intangible assets can provide significant sales and income streams when properly marketed. For example, patents for a highly demanded new product or well-known trademarks can provide returns far in excess of machinery or plant equipment.

When ratios are trending higher, management should determine the cause of the increase to ensure that events justify the increase. A possible reason for increasingly higher ratios is the purchase of other companies at prices in excess of their book value. The difference is considered goodwill, an intangible asset, and includes items that justify the excess price paid such as highly regarded products, brand names and trademarks, patents, and skilled employees. Typically you should record intangibles such as goodwill, patents, and copyrights on the balance sheet only when you purchase them from another company. For example, there is enormous goodwill associated with the Coca-Cola trademark, but this goodwill is not recorded as an asset by Coca-Cola. However, if another company purchased Coca-Cola, the purchasing company would likely pay an amount far in excess of the fair market value of Coca-Cola's tangible assets, and this excess would be recorded on the purchasing company's balance sheet as goodwill.

Low ratios indicate the company has not declared a significant amount of intangible assets, and there is thus little risk of intangible asset overstatement.

Ways to improve the indicator: Depending on the state of, and opportunities presented to, a business, it may be desirable to increase, decrease, or hold steady the ratio of intangible assets to sales. See previous section for examples.

Example

Intangible assets to sales = intangible assets / net sales

Intangible assets = 435
Net sales = 85,420

Intangible assets to sales = 435 / 85,420 = 0.0051 = 0.51%

Sector	Mid to large cap	Intangible Assets to Sales	Small to mid cap	Intangible Assets to Sales	Micro to small cap	Intangible Assets to Sales
Manufacturing	General Motors	6.44%	Toro	0.00%	Encad	0.00%
Retail	Wal-Mart Stores	0.00%	Bed Bath & Beyond	0.00%	TCBY Enterprises	4.78%
Food	McDonald's	7.25%	Applebee's Int'l	10.22%	Garden Fresh Restaurant	1.63%
Technology	Microsoft	0.00%	Cypress Semiconductor	0.00%	Jmar Technologies	1.81%
Finance	Morgan-Stanley Dean Witter	0.00%	Franklin Resources	56.58%	AmeriTrade Holding	6.63%
Healthcare	Columbia/HCA Healthcare	18.71%	Novacare	53.26%	National Home Health Care	12.25%
Service	Manpower	0.00%	Air & Water Technologies	36.01%	Market Facts	4.96%
Media/Publishing	McGraw Hill	37.02%	Scholastic	6.30%	Thomas Nelson	22.35%

100 Comparing Intangible Assets to Net Income

Equation

Intangible assets to net income = intangible assets / net income

This indicator describes the level of intangible assets employed to generate a given amount of net income. Intangible assets are nonphysical items that have value to a company such as goodwill associated with brand names, trademarks, skilled employees, loyal customers, patents, copyrights, permits, investments, deferred charges, and leasehold improvements.

When to use indicator: Managers and investors can use this indicator to determine the level of intangible assets used to generate every dollar of net income and to learn how these investment levels have changed with time.

Meaning of result: High ratios indicate the company has employed a significant level of intangible assets as a percentage of net income. Since intangible assets are harder to liquidate than tangible assets such as land, buildings, or equipment, the investor should be concerned if the level of intangible assets is so high that the intangible assets may be overstated. However, intangible assets can provide significant sales and income streams when properly marketed. For example, patents for a highly demanded new product or well-known trademarks can provide returns far in excess of machinery or plant equipment. When net income levels are very low or negative, this ratio loses meaning since small changes in net income will have dramatic effects on the intangible asset-to-net income indicator.

When ratios are trending higher, management should determine the cause of the increase to ensure that events justify the increase. A possible reason for increasingly higher ratios is the purchase of other companies at prices in excess of book value. The difference is considered goodwill, an intangible asset, and includes items that justify the excess price paid for the company such as highly regarded products, brand names and trademarks, patents, and skilled employees. Typically you should record intangibles such as goodwill, patents, and copyrights on the balance sheet only when you purchase them from another company. For example, there is enormous goodwill associated with the Coca-Cola trademark, but Coca-Cola does not record this goodwill as an asset. However, if another company purchased Coca-Cola, the purchasing company would likely pay an amount far in excess of the fair market value of Coca-Cola's tangible assets, and the purchasing company would record this excess on its balance sheet as goodwill.

Low ratios indicate the company has not declared a significant amount of intangible assets, and there is thus little risk of intangible asset overstatement.

Sector	Mid to large cap	Intangible Assets to Net Income	Small to mid cap	Intangible Assets to Net Income	Micro to small cap	Intangible Assets to Net Income
Manufacturing	General Motors	171.23%	Toro	0.00%	Encad	0.00%
Retail	Wal-Mart Stores	0.00%	Bed Bath & Beyond	0.00%	TCBY Enterprises	48.72%
Food	McDonald's	50.38%	Applebee's Int'l	116.95%	Garden Fresh Restaurant	37.87%
Technology	Microsoft	0.00%	Cypress Semiconductor	0.00%	Jmar Technologies	21.62%
Finance	Morgan-Stanley Dean Witter	0.00%	Franklin Resources	281.99%	AmeriTrade Holding	45.92%
Healthcare	Columbia/HCA Healthcare	−1154.43%	Novacare	1459.85%	National Home Health Care	231.52%
Service	Manpower	0.00%	Air & Water Technologies	−102.34%	Market Facts	85.19%
Media/Publishing	McGraw Hill	450.08%	Scholastic	282.63%	Thomas Nelson	446.11%

Ways to improve the indicator: Depending on the state of, and opportunities presented to, a business, it may be desirable to increase, decrease, or hold steady the ratio of intangible assets to net income. See previous section for examples.

Example

Intangible assets to net income = intangible assets / net income

Intangible assets = 435
Net income = 4,983

Intangible assets to net income = 435 / 4,983 = 0.0873 = 8.73%

101 Comparing Intangible Assets to Total Assets

Equation

Intangible assets to total assets = intangible assets / total assets

This indicator describes the portion of all of a company's assets that are intangible assets. It also indicates trends in intangible asset age and procurement practices. Intangible assets are nonphysical items that have value to the company such as goodwill associated with brand names, trademarks, skilled employees, loyal customers, patents, copyrights, permits, investments, deferred charges, and leasehold improvements. Total assets include fixed assets, current assets, intangible assets, long-term security investments, and other noncurrent assets.

When to use indicator: Managers and investors can use this indicator to determine the level of intangible asset to total asset investments employed to operate the business and to learn how these investment levels have changed with time.

Meaning of result: High ratios indicate the company has employed a significant level of intangible assets as a percentage of all assets available to the company. Since intangible assets are harder to liquidate than tangible assets such as land, buildings, or equipment, the investor should be concerned if the level of intangible assets is so high that the intangible assets may be overstated. However, intangible assets can provide significant sales and income streams when properly marketed. For example, patents for a highly demanded new product or well-known trademarks can provide returns far in excess of machinery or plant equipment. When net income levels are very low or negative, this ratio loses meaning since small changes in net income will have dramatic effects on the intangible asset-to-net income indicator.

Low ratios indicate the company has not declared a significant amount of intangible assets, and there is thus little risk of intangible asset overstatement.

Look for changes in intangible asset-to-total asset ratios over time and understand their causes. Are higher ratios due to the overstatement of intangible assets' worth? If this is the case, the company in question could be entering a severe business downturn. Or are the higher ratios due to purchased intangible goodwill assets such as patents, brand names, and trademarks? When a company purchases another for a price in excess of its book value, the difference is considered goodwill, an intangible asset. This asset includes intangible items that generate excess profit such as highly regarded customer knowledge of the company's products or services, brand names, and trademarks. Such intangible assets may provide handsome returns.

Sector	Mid to large cap	Intangible Assets to Total Assets	Small to mid cap	Intangible Assets to Total Assets	Micro to small cap	Intangible Assets to Total Assets
Manufacturing	General Motors	5.01%	Toro	0.00%	Encad	0.00%
Retail	Wal-Mart Stores	0.00%	Bed Bath & Beyond	0.00%	TCBY Enterprises	4.36%
Food	McDonald's	4.54%	Applebee's Int'l	13.97%	Garden Fresh Restaurant	2.36%
Technology	Microsoft	0.00%	Cypress Semiconductor	0.00%	Jmar Technologies	2.25%
Finance	Morgan-Stanley Dean Witter	0.00%	Franklin Resources	39.55%	AmeriTrade Holding	0.84%
Healthcare	Columbia/HCA Healthcare	16.00%	Novacare	56.00%	National Home Health Care	17.04%
Service	Manpower	0.00%	Air & Water Technologies	42.90%	Market Facts	5.71%
Media/Publishing	McGraw Hill	35.13%	Scholastic	8.72%	Thomas Nelson	19.82%

Ways to improve indicator: Depending on the state of the business, it may be desirable to increase, decrease, or hold steady the ratio of intangible assets to total assets. See previous section for examples.

Example

Intangible assets to total assets = intangible assets / total assets

Intangible assets = 435
Total assets = 56,268

Intangible assets to total assets = 435 / 56,268 = 0.0077 = 0.77%

102 Comparing Intangible Assets to Owner's Equity

Equation

Intangible assets to equity = intangible assets / total shareholder equity

This indicator compares the relative level of intangible asset investment to investor investment. You can think of it as the portion of shareholders' equity that the company uses for intangible assets. Intangible assets are nonphysical items that have value to the company such as goodwill associated with brand names, trademarks, skilled employees, loyal customers, patents, copyrights, permits, investments, deferred charges, and leasehold improvements. Total shareholder equity includes all equity balance sheet items. Typically the most significant of these are additional paid-in capital for stock purchases and retained earnings (income generated that the company has reinvested in itself).

When to use indicator: Investors can use this indicator to gain a sense of how the company has employed the equity invested in the company.

Meaning of result: Higher ratios indicate that the company uses a great deal of equity for intangible asset investments. Since intangible assets are harder to liquidate than tangible assets such as land, buildings, or equipment, the investor should be concerned if the level of intangible assets is so high that the intangible assets may be overstated. However, intangible assets can provide significant sales and income streams when properly marketed. For example, patents for a highly demanded new product or well-known trademarks can provide returns far in excess of machinery or plant equipment.

Low ratios indicate the company has not declared a significant amount of intangible assets, and there is thus little risk of intangible asset overstatement.

Look for changes in intangible asset-to-total asset ratios over time and understand their causes. Are higher ratios due to the overstatement of intangible assets' worth? If this is the case, the company in question could be entering a severe business downturn. Or are the higher ratios due to purchased intangible goodwill assets such as patents, brand names, and trademarks? When a company purchases another for a price in excess of its book value, the difference is considered goodwill, an intangible asset. This asset includes intangible items that generate excess profit such as highly regarded customer knowledge of the company's products or services, patents, brand names, and trademarks. Such intangible assets may provide handsome returns.

Ways to improve the indicator: Depending on the state of the business, it may be desirable to increase, decrease, or hold steady the ratio of intangible assets to shareholder equity. See previous section for examples.

Example

Intangible assets to equity = intangible assets / total shareholder equity

Intangible assets = 435
Total shareholder equity = 31,088

Intangible assets to equity = 435 / 31,088 = 0.0140 = 1.40%

Sector	Mid to large cap	Intangible Assets to Owner's Equity	Small to mid cap	Intangible Assets to Owner's Equity	Micro to small cap	Intangible Assets to Owner's Equity
Manufacturing	General Motors	65.51%	Toro	0.00%	Encad	0.00%
Retail	Wal-Mart Stores	0.00%	Bed Bath & Beyond	0.00%	TCBY Enterprises	5.59%
Food	McDonald's	9.35%	Applebee's Int'l	18.16%	Garden Fresh Restaurant	4.31%
Technology	Microsoft	0.00%	Cypress Semiconductor	0.00%	Jmar Technologies	3.11%
Finance	Morgan-Stanley Dean Witter	0.00%	Franklin Resources	66.01%	AmeriTrade Holding	9.47%
Healthcare	Columbia/HCA Healthcare	48.57%	Novacare	111.82%	National Home Health Care	18.39%
Service	Manpower	0.00%	Air & Water Technologies	−150.41%	Market Facts	9.26%
Media/Publishing	McGraw Hill	91.19%	Scholastic	20.97%	Thomas Nelson	36.15%

103 Comparing Changes in Intangible Assets to Changes in Net Income

Equation

Changes in value of intangible assets to changes in net income = change in value of intangible assets / change in net income

This indicator describes the extent to which changes in intangible assets provide commensurate changes in net income. Intangible assets are non-physical items that have value to the company such as goodwill associated with brand names, trademarks, skilled employees, loyal customers, patents, copyrights, permits, investments, deferred charges, and leasehold improvements.

When to use indicator: Managers and investors can use this indicator to determine if newly acquired intangible assets are providing reasonable returns. Similarly, this indicator can reveal the effect to net income when a company sells intangible assets. When changes in net income levels are very low or negative, this ratio loses meaning since small changes in net income will have dramatic effects on the ratio of change in intangible asset to change in net income.

Meaning of result: When a company purchases intangible assets, management usually desires lower ratios which indicate positive and significant changes in net income occurred at the time of the asset acquisition. When a company sells intangible assets, investors expect higher ratios which indicate the sale of those assets had little effect on net income. As it is difficult to allocate increases in net income to specific asset pools, investors must be careful when ascertaining what degree of the income change was due to asset change. Part of the change could have been coincidental or because of other changes in operations.

Ways to improve the indicator: You can improve this ratio with the acquisition of intangible assets that positively affect the bottom line, net income, at rates of return that justify the acquisition. Investigate the liquidation of intangible assets which generate few returns.

Example

Change in value of intangible assets to changes in net income = change in value of intangible assets / change in net income

Change in value of intangible assets = 435 − 500 = −65
Change in net income = 4,983 − 3,588 = 1,395

Change in value of intangible assets to changes in net income = −65 / 1,395 = −0.0466 = −4.66%

This indicator has little meaning when a company has acquired no new income-producing intangible assets. Since in the example above the company did not acquire any intangible assets, the result is of negligible significance. The change in intangible asset value is negative because of amortization of existing intangible assets.

Sector	Mid to large cap	Changes in Intangible Assets to Changes in Net Income	Small to mid cap	Changes in Intangible Assets to Changes in Net Income	Micro to small cap	Changes in Intangible Assets to Changes in Net Income
Manufacturing	General Motors	−70.43%	Toro	0.00%	Encad	0.00%
Retail	Wal-Mart Stores	0.00%	Bed Bath & Beyond	0.00%	TCBY Enterprises	−6.84%
Food	McDonald's	115.16%	Applebee's Int'l	351.69%	Garden Fresh Restaurant	−11.29%
Technology	Microsoft	0.00%	Cypress Semiconductor	0.00%	Jmar Technologies	−71.26%
Finance	Morgan-Stanley Dean Witter	0.00%	Franklin Resources	487.74%	AmeriTrade Holding	−2.87%
Healthcare	Columbia/HCA Healthcare	3.37%	Novacare	905.29%	National Home Health Care	−270.15%
Service	Manpower	0.00%	Air & Water Technologies	3.37%	Market Facts	286.43%
Media/Publishing	McGraw Hill	−0.96%	Scholastic	−4.74%	Thomas Nelson	11.66%

104 Comparing Individual Intangible Assets to Sales

Equation

Individual intangible assets to sales = individual intangible assets (i.e., goodwill, patents, leasehold improvements) / net sales

These indicators track the size of individual intangible assets in relation to net sales levels. Intangible assets are nonphysical items that have value to the company such as goodwill associated with brand names, trademarks, skilled employees, loyal customers, patents, copyrights, permits, investments, deferred charges, and leasehold improvements.

When to use indicator: Managers and investors can use these indicators to determine the mix of intangible assets and how the investment levels in specific intangible assets relative to sales levels have changed with time. By tracking individual intangible assets, investors can quickly identify unusual intangible expenditure levels and investigate reasons for such investments.

It may be difficult for the investor to get enough information from resources such as annual reports to get the entire breakdown of individual intangible assets. Companies often lump all intangible assets in a balance sheet group called "other assets" or "intangible assets." Sometimes the footnotes following the financial reports disclose useful detailed intangible asset information.

Meaning of result: Lower individual intangible asset-to-sales ratios are often the result of rapidly increasing sales levels or reduced investment in a specific intangible asset, either due to the sale or amortization of the intangible asset. Amortization is the process of writing off a portion of the intangible asset as an expense in the current year. For example, if a purchased patent had five years of useful life remaining, the company would amortize, or write off, 20%, or one fifth, of the cost of the patent as an operating expense each year.

Higher individual intangible asset-to-sales ratios indicate decreasing sales levels or an investment in an individual intangible asset. Since intangible assets are harder to liquidate than tangible assets such as land, buildings, or equipment, the investor should be concerned if the level of the individual intangible asset is so high that it may be overstated or that the investment may not realize an adequate return. However, individual intangible assets can provide significant sales and income streams. For example, a purchased patent for a highly demanded new product can provide returns far in excess of machinery or plant equipment.

Ways to improve the indicator: Depending on the state of the business, it may be desirable to increase, decrease, or hold steady the ratio of individual intangible assets to net sales. See previous section for examples.

Example

Goodwill to sales = goodwill / net sales

Goodwill = 339
Net sales = 85,420

Goodwill to sales = 339 / 85,420 = 0.0040 = 0.40%

105 Comparing Individual Intangible Assets to Net Income

Equation

Individual intangible assets to net income = individual intangible assets (i.e., goodwill, patents, leasehold improvements) / net income

These indicators track the size of individual intangible assets in relation to net income levels. Intangible assets are nonphysical items that have value to the company such as goodwill associated with brand names, trademarks, skilled employees, loyal customers, patents, copyrights, permits, investments, deferred charges, and leasehold improvements.

When to use indicator: Managers and investors can use this indicator to determine the ratio of specific intangible asset investments to investments in all of the company assets employed to operate the business and to learn how these ratios have changed with time. When net income levels are very low or negative, this ratio loses meaning since small changes in net income will have dramatic effects on the specific intangible asset-to-net income indicator.

It may be difficult for the investor to get enough information from resources such as annual reports to get the entire breakdown of individual intangible assets. Companies often lump all intangible assets in a balance sheet group called "other assets" or "intangible assets." Sometimes the footnotes folowing the financial reports disclose useful detailed intangible asset information.

Meaning of result: Lower specific individual intangible asset-to-net income ratios are often the result of increasing net income levels or reduced investments in intangible assets. Liquidation or amortization reduces the value of specific intangible asset accounts. Liquidation is simply the sale of an intangible asset such as a patent or a brand name. Amortization is the process of writing off a portion of the intangible asset as an expense in the current year. For example, if a purchased patent had five years of useful life remaining, the company would amortize, or write off, 20%, or one fifth, of the cost of the patent as an operating expense each year.

Higher individual intangible asset-to-net income ratios indicate decreasing net income levels or an investment in an individual intangible asset. Since intangible assets are harder to liquidate than tangible assets such as land, buildings, or equipment, the investor should be concerned if the level of the individual intangible asset is so high that it may be overstated or that the investment may not realize an adequate return. However, individual intangible assets can provide significant sales and income streams. For example, a purchased patent for a highly demanded new product can provide returns far in excess of fixed assets such as machinery or plant equipment.

Ways to improve the indicator: Depending on the state of the business, it may be desirable to increase, decrease, or hold steady the ratio of individual intangible assets to net income. See previous section for examples.

Example

Goodwill to net income = goodwill / net income

Goodwill = 339
Net income = 4,983

Goodwill to net income = 339 / 4,983 = 0.0680 = 6.80%

106 Comparing Individual Intangible Assets to Total Assets

Equation

Individual intangible assets to total assets = individual intangible assets (i.e., goodwill, patents, leasehold improvements) / total assets

These indicators track the size of individual intangible assets in relation to total asset levels. Intangible assets are nonphysical items that have value to the company such as goodwill associated with brand names, trademarks, skilled employees, loyal customers, patents, copyrights, permits, investments, deferred charges, and leasehold improvements. Total assets include fixed assets, current assets, intangible assets, long-term security investments, and other noncurrent assets.

When to use indicator: Managers and investors can use this indicator to determine the ratio of specific intangible asset investments to investments in all of the company assets employed to operate the business and to learn how these ratios have changed with time. By tracking individual intangible assets, investors can quickly identify unusual intangible expenditure levels and investigate reasons for such investments.

It may be difficult for the investor to get enough information from resources such as annual reports to get the entire breakdown of individual intangible assets. Companies often lump all intangible assets in a balance sheet group called "other assets" or "intangible assets." Sometimes the footnotes following the financial reports disclose useful detailed intangible asset information.

Meaning of result: Lower individual intangible asset-to-total asset ratios are the result of increasing total asset levels or lowered investment in a specific intangible asset. Increasing total asset levels indicate businesses that are generating excess cash, either through operations, financing, or investments. Ideally, total asset levels are increasing because the company's operations are providing excess net income and the company is plowing that profit back into additional long-term assets to fuel future growth.

Liquidation or amortization reduces the value of specific intangible asset accounts. Liquidation is simply the sale of an intangible asset such as a patent or a brand name. Amortization is the process of writing off a portion of the intangible asset as an expense in the current year. For example, if a purchased patent had five years of useful life remaining, the company would amortize, or write off, 20%, or one fifth, of the cost of the patent as an operating expense each year.

Higher ratios of individual intangible assets to total assets indicate decreasing total asset levels or increased investment in an individual intangible asset. Decreasing total asset levels indicate businesses in decline or businesses that have sold assets and distributed the proceeds to shareholders.

Since intangible assets are harder to liquidate than tangible assets such as land, buildings, or equipment, the investor should be concerned if the level of the individual intangible asset is so high that it may be overstated or that the investment may not realize an adequate return. However, individual intangible assets can provide significant sales and income streams when properly marketed. For example, a purchased patent for a highly demanded new product can provide returns far in excess of machinery or plant equipment.

Ways to improve the indicator: Depending on the state of the business and the risk/return benefit ratio for the specific intangible asset investment, it may be desirable to increase, decrease, or hold steady the ratio of individual intangible assets to total assets. See previous section for examples.

Example

Goodwill to total assets = goodwill / total assets

Goodwill = 339
Total assets = 56,268

Goodwill to total assets = 339 / 56,268 = 0.0060 = 0.60%

107 Measuring the Rate of Fixed Asset Reinvestment

Equation

Fixed asset reinvestment rate = fixed asset investments / (depreciation + proceeds from sale of fixed assets)

This indicator describes the rate at which a company replaces old and liquidated fixed assets with new fixed assets. Fixed assets (also referred to on the balance sheet as property, plant, and equipment) include items with lifetimes of greater than three years such as land, buildings, machinery, tooling, leasehold improvements, office equipment, and vehicles.

You can also use this indicator for the equipment portion of fixed assets to gain insight into equipment reinvestment rates. As equipment is often the most rapidly changing of the fixed assets, tracking the equipment reinvestment rate is a useful management and investment tool.

When to use indicator: Managers and investors can use this indicator to determine the age of fixed assets and to determine whether the company has made changes in replacement trends.

Meaning of result: Higher ratios indicate that the procurement of new fixed assets has outpaced the liquidation or obsoletion of older fixed assets. This is generally a good sign because it indicates the company is investing in its future. Lower ratios could indicate that the company is not making needed fixed asset investments, possibly to increase near-term net income figures. If this is the case, the tactic could adversely affect longer term income streams since plant equipment or facilities might not continue to be competitive.

Ways to improve the indicator: You can improve this indicator by making needed investments in fixed assets to ensure products or services can be provided in the most cost-effective manner possible.

Example

Fixed asset reinvestment rate = fixed asset investments / (depreciation + proceeds from sale of fixed assets)

Fixed asset investments = 6,275
Depreciation = 1,139
Proceeds from sale of fixed assets = 0

Fixed asset reinvestment rate = 6,275 / 1,139 = 5.509 = 551%

108 Determining the Productivity of Fixed Assets

Equation

Fixed asset productivity = cash from operations / fixed assets

Fixed asset productivity is a measure of how much income a company derives from investments in fixed assets such as plant equipment, tooling, machinery, land, and buildings.

When to use indicator: Managers and investors can use this indicator to determine the extent to which a company uses fixed assets and how effectively those assets return profit.

Meaning of result: High ratios indicate companies that generate substantial amounts of cash with small amounts of fixed asset investment. This is common for service-oriented, rather than manufacturing-intensive, companies since service companies' fixed asset investments are generally lower.

When fixed asset productivity is climbing higher, it could indicate that the company is using fixed assets more productively, with less idle or downtime, or alternatively that sales levels have risen, thereby increasing cash generated from operations. It could also indicate that the company has not purchased any new fixed assets for some time and depreciation has reduced the book value of those fixed assets.

When fixed asset productivity is dropping, it could be an indication of excess fixed asset capacity, either because of reduced sales levels or because a new fixed asset investment has recently been made and is not yet fully utilized.

Ways to improve the indicator: You can increase fixed asset productivity by using existing fixed assets to their fullest extent in the most productive manner possible. When this is not possible because, for example, sales levels don't warrant additional production, excess fixed asset capacity exists and it may be beneficial to sell or lease the unwanted fixed assets.

When rates of return justify new fixed asset investment, you can improve this indicator by updating older fixed assets with newer, more productive fixed assets. New machinery may increase productivity to a point that reduces the costs associated with producing a product, thereby significantly increasing cash from operations.

Example

Fixed asset productivity = cash from operations / fixed assets

Cash from operations = 4,820
Fixed assets = 10,018

Fixed asset productivity = 4,820 / 10,018 = 0.4811 = 48.11%

Sector	Mid to large cap	Fixed Assets Productivity	Small to mid cap	Fixed Assets Productivity	Micro to small cap	Fixed Assets Productivity
Manufacturing	General Motors	24.24%	Toro	71.78%	Encad	−20.07%
Retail	Wal-Mart Stores	30.17%	Bed Bath & Beyond	43.01%	TCBY Enterprises	42.37%
Food	McDonald's	16.32%	Applebee's Int'l	31.65%	Garden Fresh Restaurant	22.24%
Technology	Microsoft	457.14%	Cypress Semiconductor	18.53%	Jmar Technologies	0.00%
Finance	Morgan-Stanley Dean Witter	−34.49%	Franklin Resources	197.40%	AmeriTrade Holding	272.76%
Healthcare	Columbia/HCA Healthcare	14.50%	Novacare	67.74%	National Home Health Care	634.39%
Service	Manpower	26.47%	Air & Water Technologies	112.00%	Market Facts	59.96%
Media/Publishing	McGraw Hill	136.34%	Scholastic	86.04%	Thomas Nelson	25.18%

109 Comparing Fixed Asset Replacement Cost and Book Value

Equation

Fixed asset replacement cost to book value = fixed asset replacement cost / fixed asset book value

The ratio of fixed asset replacement costs to book value indicates the degree to which fixed asset book values are similar to market values. **Replacement cost** is the price one must pay to purchase similar fixed assets at market rates. **Book value** is the net value of the fixed assets shown on the balance sheet. You determine this value by deducting all depreciation taken to date for the fixed asset from the purchase price. Fixed assets (also referred to on the balance sheet as property, plant, and equipment) include items with lifetimes of greater than three years such as land, buildings, machinery, tooling, leasehold improvements, office equipment, and vehicles.

When to use indicator: Investors and managers can use this indicator to determine the true, or market, value of fixed assets. At times, fixed asset levels shown in financial reports can vary significantly from market, or replacement cost, values. The fixed asset replacement cost can be difficult for the investor to ascertain since financial reports seldom divulge detailed descriptions of fixed assets.

Meaning of result: Higher ratios indicate that fixed asset book values understate the market price for fixed assets. This can be particularly true for those fixed assets that were purchased long ago and tend to hold their value, or even appreciate, such as land and buildings.

Lower ratios indicate overvaluation of the company's fixed assets, which could also indicate overvaluation of the company and stock price.

Example

Fixed asset replacement cost to book value = fixed asset replacement cost / fixed asset book value

Fixed asset replacement cost = 14,874
Fixed asset book value = 10,018

Fixed asset replacement cost to book value = 14,874 / 10,018 = 1.485 = 148.5%

110 Comparing High-Risk Assets to Sales Revenue

Equation

High-risk assets to sales = high-risk assets / net sales

This indicator describes the level of high-risk assets employed to generate a given amount of net sales. High-risk assets are any assets for which there is substantial risk that the asset investment may not realize a return. For example, many managers consider accounts receivable that have gone uncollected for many months as high risk. Assets that are harder to liquidate tend to be higher risk, such as patents rights or key employees of a purchased company.

When to use indicator: Investors and managers can use this indicator to determine the level of higher risk assets used to generate every dollar of net sales and to learn how these high-risk asset levels have changed with time. The amount of high-risk assets held can be difficult for the investor to ascertain since financial reports seldom divulge detailed descriptions of higher risk assets.

Meaning of result: Higher ratios indicate the company has taken on considerable risk and may not be able to generate the returns necessary to warrant the higher rate of risk. Higher ratios may also indicate overvaluation of the company, especially when the company's value comes from the book value of assets rather than from corporate earning potential.

Ways to improve the indicator: You can improve this indicator by investing in assets in which the rate of return on the asset investment level justifies the risk.

Example

High-risk assets to sales = high-risk assets / net sales

High-risk assets = 520
Net sales = 85,420

High-risk assets to sales = 520 / 85,420 = 0.0061 = 0.61%

111 Relating High-Risk Assets to Total Assets

Equation

High-risk assets to total assets = high-risk assets / total assets

This indicator describes the portion that high-risk assets represent of a company's total assets. High-risk assets are any assets in which there is substantial risk that the asset investment may not realize a return. For example, many managers consider accounts receivable that have gone uncollected for many months as high risk. Assets that are harder to liquidate tend to be higher risk, such as patents rights or key employees of a purchased company.

When to use indicator: Investors and managers can use this indicator to determine the level of higher risk assets to total asset investments employed to operate the business and to learn how these investment levels have changed with time. The amount of high-risk assets held can be difficult for the investor to ascertain because financial reports seldom divulge detailed descriptions of higher risk assets.

Meaning of result: Higher ratios indicate the company has taken on considerable risk and may not be able to generate the returns necessary to warrant the higher rate of risk. Higher ratios may also indicate overvaluation of the company, especially when the company's value comes from the book value of assets rather than from corporate earning potential.

Ways to improve the indicator: You can improve this indicator by investing in assets in which the rate of return on the asset investment justifies the risk level.

Example

High-risk assets to total assets = high-risk assets / total assets

High-risk assets = 520
Total assets = 56,268

High-risk assets to total assets = 520 / 56,268 = 0.0092 = 0.92%

CHAPTER SEVEN

Debt

This chapter details ratios which describe debt levels relative to sales, income, assets, and equity levels. These ratios help give a general indication of the suitability of a company's debt levels and the ability of a company to meet its debt obligations.

112 Comparing Debt to Sales

Equation

Debt to sales = debt / sales

This ratio describes the degree of financial leverage taken on relative to the size of the company.

When to use indicator: Creditors, investors, and managers can use this indicator to determine the risk level associated with a company's debt burden.

Meaning of result: Higher ratios indicate the company has acquired a great deal of debt, which may flag potential difficulty in meeting existing debt payments. As debt-to-sales ratios climb, creditors may require higher interest rates or refuse issuance of additional debt.

Ways to improve the indicator: Paying down debt levels and/or increasing the level of sales revenue can decrease the debt-to-sales ratio.

Example

Debt to sales = debt / sales

Debt = 25,180
Net sales = 85,420

Debt to sales = 25,180 / 85,420 = 0.2948 = 29.48%

Sector	Mid to large cap	Debt to Sales	Small to mid cap	Debt to Sales	Micro to small cap	Debt to Sales
Manufacturing	General Motors	118.11%	Toro	40.00%	Encad	17.16%
Retail	Wal-Mart Stores	21.15%	Bed Bath & Beyond	15.28%	TCBY Enterprises	24.11%
Food	McDonald's	82.30%	Applebee's Int'l	16.87%	Garden Fresh Restaurant	31.29%
Technology	Microsoft	39.56%	Cypress Semiconductor	57.46%	Jmar Technologies	22.28%
Finance	Morgan-Stanley Dean Witter	1062.70%	Franklin Resources	57.37%	AmeriTrade Holding	721.63%
Healthcare	Columbia/HCA Healthcare	73.95%	Novacare	47.13%	National Home Health Care	5.32%
Service	Manpower	19.69%	Air & Water Technologies	107.55%	Market Facts	33.33%
Media/Publishing	McGraw Hill	64.79%	Scholastic	42.25%	Thomas Nelson	50.96%

113 Examining the Debt-to-Operating Income Ratio

Equation

Debt to operating income = total liabilities / operating income

This ratio describes the ability to meet debt requirements with income generated from ongoing operations. Total liabilities include all debt such as loans payable to lenders, accounts payable to suppliers, and income taxes payable to the government.

When to use indicator: Creditors, investors, and managers can use this indicator to determine the risk level associated with a company's debt burden.

Meaning of result: Higher ratios can indicate a potential difficulty in meeting existing debt payments with income generated from operations. Companies often use external financing to service debt when this indicator is at higher levels. Start-up companies and companies experiencing financial difficulties will tend to exhibit higher ratios. As debt-to-operating income ratios climb, creditors may require higher interest rates or refuse to issue additional debt.

Ways to improve the indicator: Paying down debt levels and/or increasing the level of income generated from operations can decrease the debt-to-operating income ratio.

Example

Debt to operating income = total liabilities / operating income

Total liabilities = 25,180
Operating income = 9,433

Debt to operating income = 25,180 / 9,433 = 2.669 = 266.9%

Sector	Mid to large cap	Debt to Operating Income	Small to mid cap	Debt to Operating Income	Micro to small cap	Debt to Operating Income
Manufacturing	General Motors	1371.97%	Toro	581.19%	Encad	96.53%
Retail	Wal-Mart Stores	483.20%	Bed Bath & Beyond	137.02%	TCBY Enterprises	*
Food	McDonald's	348.45%	Applebee's Int'l	120.06%	Garden Fresh Restaurant	354.34%
Technology	Microsoft	82.56%	Cypress Semiconductor	1708.04%	Jmar Technologies	313.09%
Finance	Morgan-Stanley Dean Witter	6746.16%	Franklin Resources	209.82%	AmeriTrade Holding	3168.55%
Healthcare	Columbia/HCA Healthcare	900.71%	Novacare	534.23%	National Home Health Care	56.48%
Service	Manpower	559.73%	Air & Water Technologies	*	Market Facts	324.35%
Media/Publishing	McGraw Hill	472.14%	Scholastic	927.80%	Thomas Nelson	520.16%

* Companies with negative operating income.

114 Examining the Debt-to-Asset Ratio

Equation

Debt to asset = total liabilities / total assets

This ratio describes the degree to which a company has financed assets with debt. Total liabilities include all debt such as loans payable to lenders, accounts payable to suppliers, and income taxes payable to the government.

When to use indicator: Creditors, investors, and managers can use this indicator to determine the risk level associated with a company's debt burden.

Meaning of result: Higher ratios indicate that a company has financed a large portion of assets with debt. As debt-to-asset ratios climb, creditor risk increases because there is less margin available if the company must liquidate assets. Creditors may require higher interest rates or refuse to issue additional debt under these circumstances. However, a certain degree of debt is generally quite acceptable, especially in the view of investors, because the leverage gained with debt financing may yield higher returns on equity investments. You can determine an acceptable level of debt by examining the ratio of interest payments to operating income. In the case of start-ups or companies experiencing special situations, compare all sources of income including additional debt financing with interest payments to ascertain the acceptability of current debt levels.

Ways to improve the indicator: You can decrease the debt-to-asset ratio by paying down debt levels and/or purchasing future assets with income from operations or equity.

Example

Debt to asset = total liabilities / total assets

Total liabilities = 25,180
Total assets = 56,268

Debt to asset = 25,180 / 56,268 = 0.4475 = 44.75%

Sector	Mid to large cap	Debt-to-Asset Ratio	Small to mid cap	Debt-to-Asset Ratio	Micro to small cap	Debt-to-Asset Ratio
Manufacturing	General Motors	91.94%	Toro	63.55%	Encad	28.32%
Retail	Wal-Mart Stores	54.96%	Bed Bath & Beyond	35.55%	TCBY Enterprises	22.00%
Food	McDonald's	51.48%	Applebee's Int'l	23.06%	Garden Fresh Restaurant	45.25%
Technology	Microsoft	25.63%	Cypress Semiconductor	32.71%	Jmar Technologies	27.68%
Finance	Morgan-Stanley Dean Witter	95.38%	Franklin Resources	40.09%	AmeriTrade Holding	91.15%
Healthcare	Columbia/HCA Healthcare	63.25%	Novacare	49.56%	National Home Health Care	7.39%
Service	Manpower	69.83%	Air & Water Technologies	128.14%	Market Facts	38.38%
Media/Publishing	McGraw Hill	61.48%	Scholastic	58.43%	Thomas Nelson	45.18%

115 Examining the Debt-to-Equity Ratio

Equation

Debt to equity = total liabilities / total shareholder equity

This ratio describes the relationship between a company's debt and its equity. Total liabilities include all debt such as loans payable to lenders, accounts payable to suppliers, and income taxes payable to the government. Shareholder equity includes all equity balance sheet items, typically the most significant of which are additional paid-in capital for stock purchases and retained earnings (income generated that the company has reinvested to provide additional assets).

When to use indicator: Creditors, investors, and managers can use this indicator to determine the risk level associated with a company's debt burden and the degree to which a company is leveraged with debt.

Meaning of result: Creditors generally frown upon higher ratios because they indicate the company may be stretched to meet debt interest payments and because creditors like to see a substantial investment by the owners. Investors are more likely to view higher ratios in a positive light since the leverage gained with debt financing may lead to greater returns on equity investment.

Ways to improve the indicator: Paying down debt levels with operating income or owner's equity can reduce the debt-to-equity ratio. Acquiring additional debt can increase the debt-to-equity ratio and thus increase company leverage.

Example

Debt to equity = total liabilities / total shareholder equity

Total liabilities = 25,180
Total shareholder equity = 31,088

Debt to equity = 25,180 / 31,088 = 0.810 = 81.0%

Sector	Mid to large cap	Debt-to-Equity Ratio	Small to mid cap	Debt-to-Equity Ratio	Micro to small cap	Debt-to-Equity Ratio
Manufacturing	General Motors	1202.06%	Toro	174.35%	Encad	39.51%
Retail	Wal-Mart Stores	134.81%	Bed Bath & Beyond	55.16%	TCBY Enterprises	28.21%
Food	McDonald's	106.08%	Applebee's Int'l	29.96%	Garden Fresh Restaurant	82.65%
Technology	Microsoft	34.46%	Cypress Semiconductor	48.61%	Jmar Technologies	38.28%
Finance	Morgan-Stanley Dean Witter	2066.00%	Franklin Resources	66.93%	AmeriTrade Holding	1030.57%
Healthcare	Columbia/HCA Healthcare	191.94%	Novacare	98.95%	National Home Health Care	7.98%
Service	Manpower	231.47%	Air & Water Technologies	−449.23%	Market Facts	62.28%
Media/Publishing	McGraw Hill	159.61%	Scholastic	140.58%	Thomas Nelson	82.42%

116 Comparing Debt to the Market Value of Assets

Equation

Debt to market value of assets = total liabilities / market value of total assets

This ratio describes the degree to which a company's assets are financed with debt. Since the market value of assets can be quite different from the book value of assets, the value shown on the balance sheet, this ratio can give a more accurate portrayal of debt to assets. Total liabilities include all debt such as loans payable to lenders, accounts payable to suppliers, and income taxes payable to the government.

When to use indicator: Creditors, investors, and managers can use this indicator to determine the risk level associated with a company's debt burden.

Meaning of result: Higher ratios indicate that a company has financed a large portion of assets with debt. As debt-to-asset ratios climb, creditor risk increases because there is less margin available if a company must liquidate assets. Creditors may require higher interest rates or refuse to issue additional debt under these circumstances. However, a certain degree of debt is generally quite acceptable, especially in the view of investors, since the leverage gained with debt financing may yield higher returns on equity investments. You can determine an acceptable level of debt by examining the ratio of interest payments to operating income. In the case of start-ups or companies experiencing special situations, you can compare all sources of income including additional debt financing with interest payments to ascertain the acceptability of current debt levels.

Ways to improve the indicator: You can decrease the ratio of debt to the market value of assets by paying down debt levels and/or purchasing future assets with income from operations or equity.

Example

Debt to market value of assets = total liabilities / market value of total assets

Total liabilities = 25,180
Market value of total assets = market value of debt + market value of equity = 25,180 + (3,600 common shares × $22.50/share) + (15 preferred shares × $25.00/share) = 106,555

Debt to market value of assets = 25,180 / 106,555 = 0.2363 = 23.63%

Sector	Mid to large cap	Debt to Market Value of Assets	Small to mid cap	Debt to Market Value of Assets	Micro to small cap	Debt to Market Value of Assets
Manufacturing	General Motors	81.27%	Toro	50.41%	Encad	14.72%
Retail	Wal-Mart Stores	15.54%	Bed Bath & Beyond	4.22%	TCBY Enterprises	9.10%
Food	McDonald's	16.17%	Applebee's Int'l	10.83%	Garden Fresh Restaurant	26.75%
Technology	Microsoft	2.11%	Cypress Semiconductor	29.48%	Jmar Technologies	9.22%
Finance	Morgan-Stanley Dean Witter	84.33%	Franklin Resources	8.42%	AmeriTrade Holding	62.12%
Healthcare	Columbia/HCA Healthcare	42.06%	Novacare	42.13%	National Home Health Care	6.63%
Service	Manpower	39.07%	Air & Water Technologies	84.15%	Market Facts	15.24%
Media/Publishing	McGraw Hill	22.10%	Scholastic	42.23%	Thomas Nelson	36.94%

117 Determining Debt Turnover

Equation

Debt turnover = net sales / total liabilities

This ratio compares the relative size of all debt with sales revenues and gives a general indication of a company's ability to meet its debt obligations. Total liabilities include all debt such as loans payable to lenders, accounts payable to suppliers, and income taxes payable to the government.

When to use indicator: Creditors, investors, and managers can use this indicator to assess the risk associated with current debt levels and with the issuance of additional debt.

Meaning of result: Higher ratios indicate that a company generates a great deal of sales for every dollar of debt. This generally is a financially healthy condition and indicates a higher likelihood that the company can meet debt interest payments particularly if net income levels are high.

Ways to improve the indicator: You can increase debt turnover by increasing sales levels and/or by paying down debt levels with operating income or the issuance of owner's equity (stock).

Example

Debt turnover = net sales / total liabilities

Net sales = 85,420
Total liabilities = 25,180

Debt turnover = 85,420 / 25,180 = 3.392 = 339.2%

Sector	Mid to large cap	Debt Turnover	Small to mid cap	Debt Turnover	Micro to small cap	Debt Turnover
Manufacturing	General Motors	0.85	Toro	2.50	Encad	5.83
Retail	Wal-Mart Stores	4.73	Bed Bath & Beyond	6.55	TCBY Enterprises	4.15
Food	McDonald's	1.22	Applebee's Int'l	5.93	Garden Fresh Restaurant	3.20
Technology	Microsoft	2.53	Cypress Semiconductor	1.74	Jmar Technologies	4.49
Finance	Morgan-Stanley Dean Witter	0.09	Franklin Resources	1.74	AmeriTrade Holding	0.14
Healthcare	Columbia/HCA Healthcare	1.35	Novacare	2.12	National Home Health Care	18.81
Service	Manpower	5.08	Air & Water Technologies	0.93	Market Facts	3.00
Media/Publishing	McGraw Hill	1.54	Scholastic	2.37	Thomas Nelson	1.96

118 Comparing Debt and Total Invested Capital

Equation

Debt to total invested capital = long-term liabilities / (total shareholder equity + long-term liabilities)

This ratio indicates the percentage that debt represents of a company's total invested capital. Invested capital, composed of debt, stock, and retained earnings, is the money used to purchase assets such as inventory, buildings, and machinery. Long-term liabilities are those debts that are payable in full in more than 12 months.

When to use indicator: Creditors, investors, and managers can use this indicator to assess the risk associated with existing debt levels and with the issuance of additional debt.

Meaning of result: Higher ratios indicate that debt comprises a larger portion of the money invested in a company than equity in the form of stock or retained earnings. Since a company must pay debt back with interest, higher ratios can indicate potential leverage problems. Creditors like to see equity as a good portion of invested capital since equity does not require interest payments and this investment tells them there are other stakeholders in the company. Investors are generally not as adverse to higher debt levels as long as the company can readily make the interest payments with income generated from operations. This is because the leverage gained with debt financing may yield a higher return on investment for shareholders.

Ways to improve the indicator: You can reduce debt capitalization by paying down debt levels with operating income and/or by issuing additional stock. Increasing company profitability to allow increased retained earnings also reduces the degree to which a company is capitalized with debt. Opposite actions will tend to increase leverage and debt capitalization.

Example

Debt to total invested capital = long-term liabilities / (total shareholder equity + long-term liabilities)

Long-term liabilities = 25,180 − 12,032 = 13,148

Total shareholder equity = 31,088

Debt to total invested capital = 13,148 / (31,088 + 13,148) = 0.2972 = 29.72%

Sector	Mid to large cap	Debt to Total Invested Capital	Small to mid cap	Debt to Total Invested Capital	Micro to small cap	Debt to Total Invested Capital
Manufacturing	General Motors	91.75%	Toro	43.10%	Encad	1.93%
Retail	Wal-Mart Stores	36.17%	Bed Bath & Beyond	4.09%	TCBY Enterprises	11.58%
Food	McDonald's	41.98%	Applebee's Int'l	7.79%	Garden Fresh Restaurant	29.59%
Technology	Microsoft	0.00%	Cypress Semiconductor	25.46%	Jmar Technologies	6.77%
Finance	Morgan-Stanley Dean Witter	64.89%	Franklin Resources	22.26%	AmeriTrade Holding	0.00%
Healthcare	Columbia/HCA Healthcare	60.58%	Novacare	40.54%	National Home Health Care	1.33%
Service	Manpower	40.75%	Air & Water Technologies	155.02%	Market Facts	16.28%
Media/Publishing	McGraw Hill	43.03%	Scholastic	45.49%	Thomas Nelson	34.98%

119 Relating Short-Term Debt to Long-Term Debt

Equation

Short-term to long-term debt = current liabilities / long-term liabilities

Ratios of short- to long-term debt indicate the degree to which a company finances its debt with short-term debt.

When to use indicator: Creditors, investors, and managers can use this indicator to assess the risk associated with current short-term debt levels and with the issuance of additional debt, either short- or long-term.

Meaning of result: Higher ratios indicate that a large portion of debt is short-term in nature. This can present cash flow problems since short-term debt must be paid off more quickly than long-term debt. Some companies will finance all debt with short-term notes, regardless of the use and useful life of the expense or asset purchased. This practice tends to reduce cash flow and can impair liquidity.

Ways to improve the indicator: Financing assets with terms, or loan time periods, similar to the useful life of the asset will tend to achieve proper ratios of short- to long-term debt. This should shift inappropriate short-term liabilities to a more suitable long term, decrease the short-to-long-term-debt ratio, and increase cash flow.

Highly profitable companies are often not concerned with the potential cash flow problems associated with excessive short-term financing, because they can easily handle the increased level of loan payments with operating income.

Example

Short-term to long-term debt = current liabilities / long-term liabilities

Current liabilities = 12,032
Long-term liabilities = 25,180 − 12,032 = 13,148

Short-term to long-term debt = 12,032 / 13,148 = 0.9151 = 91.51%

Sector	Mid to large cap	Short-Term Debt to Long-Term Debt	Small to mid cap	Short-Term Debt to Long-Term Debt	Micro to small cap	Short-Term Debt to Long-Term Debt
Manufacturing	General Motors	8.11%	Toro	130.22%	Encad	1908.88%
Retail	Wal-Mart Stores	137.94%	Bed Bath & Beyond	1194.15%	TCBY Enterprises	115.27%
Food	McDonald's	46.59%	Applebee's Int'l	254.61%	Garden Fresh Restaurant	96.64%
High Technology	Microsoft	*	Cypress Semiconductor	42.35%	Jmar Technologies	426.95%
Finance	Morgan-Stanley Dean Witter	1017.95%	Franklin Resources	133.67%	AmeriTrade Holding	*
Healthcare	Columbia/HCA Healthcare	24.89%	Novacare	45.14%	National Home Health Care	489.87%
Service	Manpower	236.51%	Air & Water Technologies	59.44%	Market Facts	220.36%
Media/Publishing	McGraw Hill	111.32%	Scholastic	68.44%	Thomas Nelson	53.21%

* Companies with no reported long-term debt.

120 Determining the Cost of Debt Capital

Equation

Cost of debt capital = debt interest paid / debt

The interest rate paid to service debt is known as the **cost of debt capital**. Existing debt includes long-term debt, the current portion of long-term debt, and any other interest-bearing debt such as notes payable.

When to use indicator: Creditors, managers, and investors can use this indicator to determine the interest rate paid for debt capital. You can also use this indicator to be sure that income statement interest expenses correlate with balance sheet debt burdens.

Meaning of result: Lower ratios indicate the company has achieved excellent interest rate terms, probably because of strong financial performance. Creditors view such performance favorably because of reduced chance of loan default.

Ways to improve the indicator: You can reduce debt interest rates with increasingly sound financial performance such as increasingly high sales growth, net incomes, cash flows, and debt coverage and increasingly lower debt-to-equity ratios.

Example

Cost of debt capital = debt interest paid / debt

Debt interest paid = 784

Debt = interest-bearing debt = notes payable + current portion of long-term debt + long-term debt = 1,000 + 650 + 12,513 = $14,163

Cost of debt capital = 784 / 14,163 = 0.0554 = 5.54%

Sector	Mid to large cap	Cost of Debt Capital	Small to mid cap	Cost of Debt Capital	Micro to small cap	Cost of Debt Capital
Manufacturing	General Motors	6.57%	Toro	9.09%	Encad	*
Retail	Wal-Mart Stores	9.53%	Bed Bath & Beyond	*	TCBY Enterprises	8.02%
Food	McDonald's	5.64%	Applebee's Int'l	5.90%	Garden Fresh Restaurant	9.06%
Technology	Microsoft	*	Cypress Semiconductor	*	Jmar Technologies	*
Finance	Morgan-Stanley Dean Witter	*	Franklin Resources	3.57%	AmeriTrade Holding	*
Healthcare	Columbia/HCA Healthcare	5.24%	Novacare	4.45%	National Home Health Care	*
Service	Manpower	*	Air & Water Technologies	7.90%	Market Facts	10.99%
Media/Publishing	McGraw Hill	7.68%	Scholastic	7.93%	Thomas Nelson	7.30%

* Companies with no reported debt or debt interest paid.

CHAPTER EIGHT

Equity

This chapter details ratios which describe equity levels relative to sales, assets, and debt levels. This information gives a general indication of how a company has employed equity and the effectiveness in which the company has used equity to generate sales revenue.

121 Comparing Equity to Sales Revenue

Equation

Equity to sales = total shareholder equity / net sales

Equity to sales is a measure of how effectively a company uses shareholder equity to generate sales revenue. Shareholder equity includes all equity balance sheet items, typically the most significant of which are additional paid-in capital for stock purchases and retained earnings (income generated that a company has reinvested in itself).

When to use indicator: Investors use this indicator to ascertain a company's sales-generating potential for a given amount of equity investment.

Meaning of result: Lower ratios indicate that the company generates a greater amount of sales with a given amount of shareholder equity. This is generally a good indication that management has effectively used the capital provided by equity holders to purchase assets that generate healthy sales levels.

Note that successful companies often generate high levels of retained earnings, which boost total shareholder equity and increase the equity-to-sales ratio.

Ways to improve the indicator: Effective use of the capital provided by shareholders can generate additional sales and increase the equity-to-sales ratio.

Example

Equity to sales = total shareholder equity / net sales

Total shareholder equity = 31,088
Net sales = 85,420

Equity to sales = 31,088 / 85,420 = 0.3639 = 36.39%

Sector	Mid to large cap	Equity to Sales	Small to mid cap	Equity to Sales	Micro to small cap	Equity to Sales
Manufacturing	General Motors	9.83%	Toro	22.94%	Encad	43.43%
Retail	Wal-Mart Stores	15.69%	Bed Bath & Beyond	27.69%	TCBY Enterprises	85.48%
Food	McDonald's	77.59%	Applebee's Int'l	56.31%	Garden Fresh Restaurant	37.86%
Technology	Microsoft	114.80%	Cypress Semiconductor	118.21%	Jmar Technologies	58.19%
Finance	Morgan-Stanley Dean Witter	51.44%	Franklin Resources	85.71%	AmeriTrade Holding	70.02%
Healthcare	Columbia/HCA Healthcare	38.52%	Novacare	47.64%	National Home Health Care	66.61%
Service	Manpower	8.51%	Air & Water Technologies	−23.94%	Market Facts	53.51%
Media/Publishing	McGraw Hill	40.59%	Scholastic	30.05%	Thomas Nelson	61.83%

122 Comparing Equity to Total Assets

Equation

Equity to assets = total shareholder equity / total assets

This indicator compares the relative level of shareholder equity to all company assets. You can think of it as the portion of assets that were purchased with shareholders' equity. Total assets include all current and long-term assets such as cash, inventory, accounts receivable, property, plants, equipment, patents, goodwill, and investments. Shareholder equity includes all equity balance sheet items, typically the most significant of which are additional paid-in capital for stock purchases and retained earnings (income generated that a company has reinvested in itself).

When to use indicator: Creditors and investors can use this indicator to see the percentage of company assets that were purchased with shareholder equity rather than with debt.

Meaning of result: Higher ratios indicate that a company uses a great deal of equity for asset-related investments. This further indicates that the company has likely not acquired much debt since equity has been used for asset purchases. Creditors generally approve of higher ratios since the large shareholder stake reduces creditor risk. This is somewhat analogous to a lender's viewpoint of a homeowner's mortgage. An owner who finances 50% of his home with a mortgage (debt) is much less likely to default on his payments than a similar owner with a 95% mortgage. Creditors also like to see higher ratios since lower debt levels indicate the company is using less money to pay existing interest payments, and thus more operating income remains to service new debt.

Lower ratios indicate the opposite effect—little equity investment and larger debt incurred for asset acquisitions. While creditors generally frown upon large debt levels accompanied by small equity investments for the reason discussed above, investors are more likely to view such lower ratios in a positive light because the leverage gained with debt financing may lead to greater returns on equity investment.

Ways to improve the indicator: Depending on the state of the business, it may be desirable to increase, decrease, or hold steady the ratio of shareholder equity to total assets. See previous section for examples.

Example

Equity to assets = total shareholder equity / total assets

Total shareholder equity = 31,088
Total assets = 56,268

Equity to assets = 31,088 / 56,268 = 0.5525 = 55.25%

Sector	Mid to large cap	Equity to Assets	Small to mid cap	Equity to Assets	Micro to small cap	Equity to Assets
Manufacturing	General Motors	7.65%	Toro	36.45%	Encad	71.68%
Retail	Wal-Mart Stores	40.77%	Bed Bath & Beyond	64.45%	TCBY Enterprises	78.00%
Food	McDonald's	48.52%	Applebee's Int'l	76.94%	Garden Fresh Restaurant	54.75%
Technology	Microsoft	74.37%	Cypress Semiconductor	67.29%	Jmar Technologies	72.32%
Finance	Morgan-Stanley Dean Witter	4.62%	Franklin Resources	59.91%	AmeriTrade Holding	8.85%
Healthcare	Columbia/HCA Healthcare	32.95%	Novacare	50.08%	National Home Health Care	92.61%
Service	Manpower	30.17%	Air & Water Technologies	−28.52%	Market Facts	61.62%
Media/Publishing	McGraw Hill	38.52%	Scholastic	41.57%	Thomas Nelson	54.82%

123 Comparing Equity to Total Debt

Equation

Equity to debt = total shareholder equity / total liabilities

This indicator compares the relative level of shareholder equity to all company debt. Shareholder equity includes all equity balance sheet items, typically the most significant of which are additional paid-in capital for stock purchases and retained earnings (income generated that the company has reinvested in itself). Total liabilities include all debt such as loans payable to lenders, accounts payable to suppliers, and income taxes payable to the government.

When to use indicator: Creditors and investors can use this indicator to gauge the manner in which a company is capitalized. Are the company's assets financed with debt or equity?

Meaning of result: Creditors generally frown upon lower ratios because they indicate the company may be stretched to meet debt interest payments and because creditors like to see a substantial investment by the owners. Investors are more likely to view lower ratios in a positive light since the leverage gained with debt financing may lead to greater returns on equity investment.

Ways to improve the indicator: Paying down debt levels with operating income or owner's equity can increase the equity-to-debt ratio. Acquiring additional debt can reduce the equity-to-debt ratio, and thus increase company leverage.

Example

Equity to debt = total shareholder equity / total liabilities

Total shareholder equity = 31,088
Total liabilities = 25,180

Equity to debt = 31,088 / 25,180 = 1.2346 = 123.5%

Sector	Mid to large cap	Equity to Debt	Small to mid cap	Equity to Debt	Micro to small cap	Equity to Debt
Manufacturing	General Motors	8.32%	Toro	57.36%	Encad	253.09%
Retail	Wal-Mart Stores	74.18%	Bed Bath & Beyond	181.30%	TCBY Enterprises	354.53%
Food	McDonald's	94.27%	Applebee's Int'l	333.72%	Garden Fresh Restaurant	120.99%
Technology	Microsoft	290.17%	Cypress Semiconductor	205.72%	Jmar Technologies	261.22%
Finance	Morgan-Stanley Dean Witter	4.84%	Franklin Resources	149.42%	AmeriTrade Holding	9.70%
Healthcare	Columbia/HCA Healthcare	52.10%	Novacare	101.07%	National Home Health Care	1253.22%
Service	Manpower	43.20%	Air & Water Technologies	−22.26%	Market Facts	160.57%
Media/Publishing	McGraw Hill	62.65%	Scholastic	71.13%	Thomas Nelson	121.34%

124 Determining the Turnover of Equity

Equation:

Equity turnover = net sales / total shareholder equity

This ratio compares the relative size of all shareholder equity to sales revenues and indicates a company's ability to use shareholder equity to generate sales.

When to use indicator: Investors can use this indicator to assess the level of sales return associated with equity investments. Equity turnover multiplied by profit margin yields a particularly important ratio, the return on shareholder equity (ROE).

Meaning of result: Higher ratios indicate that a company generates a great deal of sales for every dollar of equity. Higher and increasing ratios are desirable because they indicate, for a given profit margin level, that returns on equity are also increasing.

Note that successful companies often generate high levels of retained earnings, which boost total shareholder equity and reduce the equity turnover ratio.

Ways to improve the indicator: Increasing sales levels and/or reducing equity levels with stock repurchases can increase the equity turnover ratio.

Example

Equity turnover = net sales / total shareholder equity

$$\text{Net sales} = 85{,}420$$
$$\text{Total shareholder equity} = 31{,}088$$

Equity turnover = 85,420 / 31,088 = 2.7477 = 274.8%

Sector	Mid to large cap	Equity Turnover	Small to mid cap	Equity Turnover	Micro to small cap	Equity Turnover
Manufacturing	General Motors	1017.79%	Toro	435.89%	Encad	230.28%
Retail	Wal-Mart Stores	637.51%	Bed Bath & Beyond	361.08%	TCBY Enterprises	116.99%
Food	McDonald's	128.89%	Applebee's Int'l	177.60%	Garden Fresh Restaurant	264.14%
Technology	Microsoft	87.11%	Cypress Semiconductor	84.60%	Jmar Technologies	171.86%
Finance	Morgan-Stanley Dean Witter	194.41%	Franklin Resources	116.67%	AmeriTrade Holding	142.81%
Healthcare	Columbia/HCA Healthcare	259.57%	Novacare	209.93%	National Home Health Care	150.13%
Service	Manpower	1175.35%	Air & Water Technologies	−417.69%	Market Facts	186.88%
Media/Publishing	McGraw Hill	246.34%	Scholastic	332.73%	Thomas Nelson	161.74%

125 Examining the Turnover of Invested Capital

Equation

Invested capital turnover = net sales / (long-term liabilities + total shareholder equity)

This ratio compares the relative size of invested capital to sales revenues and indicates a company's ability to use invested capital to generate sales.

When to use indicator: Investors can use this indicator to assess the level of sales return associated with capital investments. Invested capital turnover multiplied by profit margin yields a particularly important ratio, the return on invested capital (ROIC).

Meaning of result: Higher ratios indicate that a company generates a great deal of sales for every dollar of invested capital. Higher and increasing ratios are desirable because they indicate, for a given profit margin level, that returns on invested capital are also increasing.

Note that successful companies often generate high levels of retained earnings, which boost total shareholder equity and reduce the invested capital turnover ratio.

Ways to improve the indicator: Increasing sales levels and/or reducing debt and/or reducing equity levels with stock repurchases can increase the invested capital turnover.

Example

Invested capital turnover = net sales / (long-term liabilities + total shareholder equity)

$$\text{Net sales} = 85,420$$
$$\text{Long-term liabilities} = 25,180 - 12,032 = 13,148$$
$$\text{Total shareholder equity} = 31,088$$

Invested capital turnover = 85,420 / (13,148 + 31,088) = 1.931 = 193.1%

Sector	Mid to large cap	Invested Capital Turnover	Small to mid cap	Invested Capital Turnover	Micro to small cap	Invested Capital Turnover
Manufacturing	General Motors	83.98%	Toro	248.04%	Encad	225.84%
Retail	Wal-Mart Stores	406.95%	Bed Bath & Beyond	346.32%	TCBY Enterprises	103.43%
Food	McDonald's	74.78%	Applebee's Int'l	163.76%	Garden Fresh Restaurant	185.97%
Technology	Microsoft	87.11%	Cypress Semiconductor	63.06%	Jmar Technologies	160.22%
Finance	Morgan-Stanley Dean Witter	68.26%	Franklin Resources	90.69%	AmeriTrade Holding	142.81%
Healthcare	Columbia/HCA Healthcare	102.32%	Novacare	124.83%	National Home Health Care	148.12%
Service	Manpower	696.36%	Air & Water Technologies	229.82%	Market Facts	156.46%
Media/Publishing	McGraw Hill	140.34%	Scholastic	181.36%	Thomas Nelson	105.17%

126 Comparing Net Income to Invested Capital

Equation

Net income to invested capital = net income / (long-term liabilities + total shareholder equity)

This ratio describes the ability of a company to generate income with the capital invested in the company.

When to use indicator: Managers and investors can use this indicator to determine the effectiveness with which a company uses invested capital to generate income.

Meaning of result: Higher ratios indicate management has effectively invested its capital in assets that allow the generation of high net income streams.

Ways to improve the indicator: Investing in assets which increase company profitability can increase the net income-to-invested capital ratio.

Example

Net income to invested capital = net income / (long-term liabilities + total shareholder equity)

Net income = 4,983
Long-term liabilities = 25,180 − 12,032 = 13,148
Total shareholder equity = 31,088

Net income to invested capital = 4,983 / (13,148 + 31,088) = 0.1126 = 11.26%

Sector	Mid to large cap	Net Income to Invested Capital	Small to mid cap	Net Income to Invested Capital	Micro to small cap	Net Income to Invested Capital
Manufacturing	General Motors	3.16%	Toro	8.22%	Encad	26.41%
Retail	Wal-Mart Stores	12.16%	Bed Bath & Beyond	23.75%	TCBY Enterprises	10.14%
Food	McDonald's	10.77%	Applebee's Int'l	14.32%	Garden Fresh Restaurant	8.01%
Technology	Microsoft	27.00%	Cypress Semiconductor	2.13%	Jmar Technologies	13.40%
Finance	Morgan-Stanley Dean Witter	6.51%	Franklin Resources	18.20%	AmeriTrade Holding	20.63%
Healthcare	Columbia/HCA Healthcare	−1.66%	Novacare	4.55%	National Home Health Care	7.84%
Service	Manpower	15.72%	Air & Water Technologies	−80.86%	Market Facts	9.10%
Media/Publishing	McGraw Hill	11.54%	Scholastic	4.04%	Thomas Nelson	5.27%

127 Comparing Stock to Invested Capital

Equation

Stock to invested capital = stock / (long-term liabilities + total shareholder equity)

This ratio indicates the percentage that stock represents of a company's total invested capital. Invested capital, composed of long-term liabilities and shareholder equity in the form of stock and retained earnings, is the money used to purchase assets such as inventory, buildings, and machinery.

When to use indicator: Creditors, investors, and managers can use this indicator to assess the manner in which a company has financed its assets.

Meaning of result: Higher ratios indicate that stock comprises a larger portion of the money invested in a company than debt or equity in the form of retained earnings. Creditors like to see that equity represents a good portion of invested capital since equity does not require interest payments and represents other stakeholders in the company.

Investors are generally not as adverse to lower stock-to-invested capital ratios. Such lower ratios either indicate substantial debt financing or retained earnings. Debt is generally acceptable as long as the company can pay interest payments associated with the debt with income generated from operations. This is because the leverage gained with debt financing may yield a higher return on investment for shareholders. Increases in retained earnings, desired by both creditors and shareholders, will tend to lower the stock-to-invested capital ratio.

Ways to improve the indicator: You can increase stock-to-invested capital ratios by issuing additional stock, reducing debt levels, or reducing retained earnings with income generated from operations.

Example

Stock to invested capital = stock / (long-term liabilities + total shareholder equity)

Stock = 300 + 36 + 12,085 − 55 = 12,366
Long-term liabilities = 25,180 − 12,032 = 13,148
Total shareholder equity = 31,088

Stock to invested capital = 12,366 / (13,148 + 31,088) = 0.2795 = 27.95%

Sector	Mid to large cap	Stock to Invested Capital	Small to mid cap	Stock to Invested Capital	Micro to small cap	Stock to Invested Capital
Manufacturing	General Motors	7.79%	Toro	10.28%	Encad	26.65%
Retail	Wal-Mart Stores	2.79%	Bed Bath & Beyond	20.37%	TCBY Enterprises	9.37%
Food	McDonald's	−20.16%	Applebee's Int'l	49.43%	Garden Fresh Restaurant	80.03%
Technology	Microsoft	54.16%	Cypress Semiconductor	35.86%	Jmar Technologies	0.00%
Finance	Morgan-Stanley Dean Witter	11.53%	Franklin Resources	3.89%	AmeriTrade Holding	34.99%
Healthcare	Columbia/HCA Healthcare	18.95%	Novacare	25.24%	National Home Health Care	73.99%
Service	Manpower	144.52%	Air & Water Technologies	215.01%	Market Facts	65.19%
Media/Publishing	McGraw Hill	−0.84%	Scholastic	28.87%	Thomas Nelson	39.98%

128 Comparing Retained Earnings to Invested Capital

Equation

Retained earnings to invested capital = retained earnings / (long-term liabilities + total shareholder equity)

This ratio indicates the percentage that retained earnings represent of a company's total invested capital. Invested capital, composed of debt as well as equity in the form of stock and retained earnings, is the money used to purchase assets such as inventory, buildings, and machinery.

When to use indicator: Creditors, investors, and managers can use this indicator to assess the manner in which a company has financed its assets.

Meaning of result: Higher ratios indicate that retained earnings, a form of equity, represent a larger portion of the money invested in a company than debt or equity in the form of stock. Retained earnings are the excess income generated from operations that a company reinvests in additional assets. High retained earnings-to-invested capital ratios indicate profitable, mature companies that have had a history of generating excellent income and cash flow. Creditors, managers, and investors generally desire higher retained earnings-to-invested capital ratios.

Investors are typically less adverse than creditors to lower retained earnings-to-invested capital ratios. Lower ratios indicate substantial debt financing and/or the issuance of considerable amounts of stock. Debt is generally acceptable as long as a company can readily make the interest payments associated with the debt with income generated from operations. This is because the leverage gained with debt financing may yield a higher return on investment for shareholders. The issuance of stock is acceptable when the company uses the proceeds for assets that offer good rates of return.

Ways to improve the indicator: You can improve retained earnings capitalization by generating higher percentages of retained earnings, paying off debt, and repurchasing stock. You can improve retained earnings generation by providing highly demanded products or services with large profit margins. You can optimize profit margins with excellent marketing, product/service design and quality, cost control, and customer service.

Example

Retained earnings to invested capital = retained earnings / (long-term liabilities + total shareholder equity)

Retained earnings = 18,722
Long-term liabilities = 25,180 − 12,032 = 13,148
Total shareholder equity = 31,088

Retained earnings to invested capital = 18,722 / (13,148 + 31,088) = 0.4232 = 42.32%

Sector	Mid to large cap	Retained Earnings to Invested Capital	Small to mid cap	Retained Earnings to Invested Capital	Micro to small cap	Retained Earnings to Invested Capital
Manufacturing	General Motors	2.55%	Toro	47.82%	Encad	71.42%
Retail	Wal-Mart Stores	62.68%	Bed Bath & Beyond	75.54%	TCBY Enterprises	79.04%
Food	McDonald's	82.38%	Applebee's Int'l	42.75%	Garden Fresh Restaurant	−9.62%
Technology	Microsoft	45.84%	Cypress Semiconductor	38.68%	Jmar Technologies	0.00%
Finance	Morgan-Stanley Dean Witter	23.47%	Franklin Resources	73.68%	AmeriTrade Holding	65.01%
Healthcare	Columbia/HCA Healthcare	19.89%	Novacare	34.22%	National Home Health Care	24.67%
Service	Manpower	−81.37%	Air & Water Technologies	−269.52%	Market Facts	19.81%
Media/Publishing	McGraw Hill	61.27%	Scholastic	26.49%	Thomas Nelson	25.04%

CHAPTER NINE

Liquidity

Liquidity ratios describe the ability of a company to meet current debt obligations with assets that are readily available. Poor liquidity can lead to bankruptcy regardless of the level of revenue and income-producing potential a firm may possess. This chapter describes ratios such as the current ratio, the acid test, and a number of working capital ratios to help determine company liquidity.

129 Finding the Current Ratio

Equation

Current ratio = current assets / current liabilities

The current ratio describes the ability of a company to meet current debt obligations with assets that are readily available. Current assets include cash, marketable securities, accounts receivable, inventory, and notes receivable.

When to use indicator: Creditors, investors, and managers can use this indicator to measure the liquidity of a company.

Meaning of result: Higher ratios indicate an increased ability to pay short-term debt obligations such as accounts payable and interest payments on debt. Lower ratios can indicate an inability to meet short-term debt obligations, which could lead to insolvency and bankruptcy. A historic rule of thumb is that healthy current ratios equal or exceed the value of 2.0. However, very high current ratios, much in excess of 2.0, can indicate a company is not using its assets in an ideal manner. This is because current assets seldom yield returns as large as long-term assets such as investments in equipment and subsidiaries.

Ways to improve the indicator: When ratios are too low, management can look to increase the level of liquid assets and/or decrease the level of short-term debt. When ratios are too high, management can seek to invest a portion of excess liquid assets in longer term assets that will generate higher returns on investment.

Example

Current ratio = current assets / current liabilities

Current assets = 44,135
Current liabilities = 12,032

Current ratio = 44,135 / 12,032 = 3.668

LIQUIDITY

Sector	Mid to large cap	Current Ratio	Small to mid cap	Current Ratio	Micro to small cap	Current Ratio
Manufacturing	General Motors	6.43	Toro	1.98	Encad	2.97
Retail	Wal-Mart Stores	1.34	Bed Bath & Beyond	2.17	TCBY Enterprises	3.95
Food	McDonald's	0.38	Applebee's Int'l	0.70	Garden Fresh Restaurant	0.44
Technology	Microsoft	2.77	Cypress Semiconductor	4.28	Jmar Technologies	3.49
Finance	Morgan-Stanley Dean Witter	1.12	Franklin Resources	1.71	AmeriTrade Holding	1.04
Healthcare	Columbia/HCA Healthcare	1.60	Novacare	2.11	National Home Health Care	11.89
Service	Manpower	1.68	Air & Water Technologies	0.70	Market Facts	2.75
Media/Publishing	McGraw Hill	1.21	Scholastic	2.11	Thomas Nelson	4.13

130 Using the Acid Test

Equation

Acid test = liquid assets / current liabilities

The **acid test** describes the ability of a company to meet current debt obligations with assets that are readily available. Liquid assets include cash, marketable securities, and accounts receivable. Liquid assets are sometimes called **quick assets,** and the acid test is at times called the **quick ratio.** Since the acid test does not include all current assets, it is more conservative than the current ratio and yields lower results.

When to use indicator: Creditors, investors, and managers can use this indicator to measure the liquidity of a company.

Meaning of result: Higher ratios indicate an increased ability to pay short-term debt obligations such as accounts payable and interest payments on debt. Lower ratios can indicate an inability to meet short-term debt obligations, which could lead to insolvency and bankruptcy. A historic rule of thumb is that healthy acid test ratios equal or exceed the value of 1.0. However, very high acid test ratios, much in excess of 1.0, can indicate a company is not using its assets in an ideal manner. This is because liquid assets seldom yield returns as large as long-term assets such as investments in equipment and subsidiaries.

Ways to improve the indicator: When ratios are too low, management can look to increase the level of liquid assets and/or decrease the level of short-term debt. When ratios are too high, management can seek to invest a portion of excess liquid assets in longer term assets that will generate higher returns on investment.

Example

Acid test = liquid assets / current liabilities

Liquid assets = cash + marketable securities + accounts receivable = 4,139 + 524 + 24,878 = 29,541

Current liabilities = 12,032

Acid test = 29,541 / 12,032 = 2.455

Sector	Mid to large cap	Acid Test	Small to mid cap	Acid Test	Micro to small cap	Acid Test
Manufacturing	General Motors	5.66	Toro	1.09	Encad	1.57
Retail	Wal-Mart Stores	0.17	Bed Bath & Beyond	0.35	TCBY Enterprises	2.64
Food	McDonald's	0.28	Applebee's Int'l	0.58	Garden Fresh Restaurant	0.17
Technology	Microsoft	2.69	Cypress Semiconductor	2.90	Jmar Technologies	2.05
Finance	Morgan-Stanley Dean Witter	0.57	Franklin Resources	1.25	AmeriTrade Holding	1.04
Healthcare	Columbia/HCA Healthcare	0.95	Novacare	1.79	National Home Health Care	11.63
Service	Manpower	1.57	Air & Water Technologies	0.49	Market Facts	2.47
Media/Publishing	McGraw Hill	0.82	Scholastic	0.67	Thomas Nelson	2.30

131 Determining the Cash Flow Ratio

Equation

Cash flow ratio = (cash + marketable securities) / current liabilities

The **cash flow ratio** describes the ability of a company to meet current debt obligations with assets that are the most readily available. For the cash flow ratio, readily available assets include only cash and marketable securities. Since the cash flow ratio includes only very liquid current assets, it is more conservative than the current ratio or acid test ratios and yields lower results.

When to use indicator: Creditors, investors, and managers can use this indicator to measure the liquidity of a company.

Meaning of result: Higher ratios indicate a greater ability to pay short-term debt obligations such as accounts payable and interest payments on debt. Lower ratios can indicate an inability to meet short-term debt obligations, which could lead to insolvency and bankruptcy. However, very high cash flow ratios can indicate a company is not using its assets in an ideal manner. This is because liquid assets seldom yield returns as large as long-term assets such as investments in equipment and subsidiaries.

Ways to improve the indicator: When ratios are too low, management can increase the level of liquid assets and/or decrease the level of short-term debt. When ratios are too high, management can invest a portion of excess liquid assets in longer term assets that will generate higher returns on investment.

Example

Cash flow ratio = (cash + marketable securities) / current liabilities

Cash = 4,139
Marketable securities = 524
Current liabilities = 12,032

Cash flow ratio = (4,139 + 524) / 12,032 = 0.3875

LIQUIDITY

Sector	Mid to large cap	Cash Flow Ratio	Small to mid cap	Cash Flow Ratio	Micro to small cap	Cash Flow Ratio
Manufacturing	General Motors	1.46	Toro	0.00	Encad	0.05
Retail	Wal-Mart Stores	0.10	Bed Bath & Beyond	0.35	TCBY Enterprises	1.89
Food	McDonald's	0.11	Applebee's Int'l	0.32	Garden Fresh Restaurant	0.17
Technology	Microsoft	2.43	Cypress Semiconductor	2.17	Jmar Technologies	0.94
Finance	Morgan-Stanley Dean Witter	0.38	Franklin Resources	0.93	AmeriTrade Holding	0.54
Healthcare	Columbia/HCA Healthcare	0.04	Novacare	0.15	National Home Health Care	6.35
Service	Manpower	0.14	Air & Water Technologies	0.06	Market Facts	1.59
Media/Publishing	McGraw Hill	0.00	Scholastic	0.03	Thomas Nelson	0.89

132 Calculating Cash Turnover

Equation

Cash turnover = net sales / cash

Cash turnover describes the relationship between cash balances and sales levels.

When to use indicator: Managers, creditors, and investors can use this indicator to determine if the company holds an appropriate amount of cash.

Meaning of result: Very high ratios can indicate inadequate cash reserves, which may lead to problems in meeting debt obligations such as accounts payable and interest payments. Very low ratios can indicate excessive cash reserves. In this case, a portion of the cash balance would better be invested in other types of assets that yield greater returns such as plant equipment and subsidiaries.

Ways to improve indicator: When ratios are too high, increasing cash reserves by reducing investments in other types of assets can decrease cash turnover. When ratios are trending too low, finding manners in which the excessive cash may be invested where returns are higher and risk levels are acceptable will tend to increase cash turnover.

Example

Cash turnover = net sales / cash

Net sales = 85,420
Cash = 4,139

Cash turnover = 85,420 / 4,139 = 20.64

Sector	Mid to large cap	Cash Turnover	Small to mid cap	Cash Turnover	Micro to small cap	Cash Turnover
Manufacturing	General Motors	15.82	Toro	131,400.50	Encad	117.82
Retail	Wal-Mart Stores	81.52	Bed Bath & Beyond	20.02	TCBY Enterprises	4.60
Food	McDonald's	33.42	Applebee's Int'l	57.91	Garden Fresh Restaurant	38.49
Technology	Microsoft	1.04	Cypress Semiconductor	3.59	Jmar Technologies	5.89
Finance	Morgan-Stanley Dean Witter	1.79	Franklin Resources	4.89	AmeriTrade Holding	0.26
Healthcare	Columbia/HCA Healthcare	171.08	Novacare	46.95	National Home Health Care	3.76
Service	Manpower	51.03	Air & Water Technologies	37.75	Market Facts	2.75
Media/Publishing	McGraw Hill	741.21	Scholastic	207.53	Thomas Nelson	6.37

133 Finding How Many Days of Cash Expenses are Available

Equation

Days of cash expenses = cash / (year's cash expenses/365)

This ratio examines how many days of average daily expenses the company can pay with the existing cash balance. You can approximate the average daily expenses by dividing a full year of expenses by the number of days in a year. Expenses include items such as the cost to produce a product or service, salaries, interest, and taxes.

When to use indicator: Managers, creditors, and investors can use this indicator to determine if the company holds an appropriate amount of cash.

Meaning of result: Very low ratios can indicate inadequate cash reserves, which may lead to problems in meeting debt obligations such as accounts payable and interest payments. Very high ratios can indicate excessive cash reserves. In this case, a portion of the cash balance would better be invested in other types of assets that yield greater returns such as plant equipment and subsidiaries.

Ways to improve indicator: When ratios are too low, increasing cash reserves by reducing investments in other types of assets can increase the days of cash expenses available. When ratios are trending too high, finding manners in which the excessive cash may be invested, where returns are higher and risk levels are acceptable, will tend to decrease the days of cash expenses available.

Example

Days of cash expenses = cash / (year's cash expenses/365)

Cash = 4,139
Year's cash expenses = all expenses − depreciation/amortization = cost of goods sold + R&D + SG&A + interest + taxes − depreciation/amortization = 54,212 + 4,578 + 15,993 + 784 + 3,529 − 1,204 = 77,892

Days of cash expenses = 4,139 / (77,892 / 365) = 19.4 days

LIQUIDITY

Sector	Mid to large cap	Days of Cash Expenses	Small to mid cap	Days of Cash Expenses	Micro to small cap	Days of Cash Expenses
Manufacturing	General Motors	30.05	Toro	0.00	Encad	3.51
Retail	Wal-Mart Stores	4.57	Bed Bath & Beyond	19.53	TCBY Enterprises	74.25
Food	McDonald's	12.66	Applebee's Int'l	6.99	Garden Fresh Restaurant	11.55
Technology	Microsoft	499.79	Cypress Semiconductor	102.77	Jmar Technologies	67.90
Finance	Morgan-Stanley Dean Witter	225.21	Franklin Resources	94.49	AmeriTrade Holding	1,672.14
Healthcare	Columbia/HCA Healthcare	2.59	Novacare	8.16	National Home Health Care	104.53
Service	Manpower	7.32	Air & Water Technologies	9.40	Market Facts	140.57
Media/Publishing	McGraw Hill	0.65	Scholastic	1.90	Thomas Nelson	60.86

134 Examining How Many Days of Sales in Cash are Available

Equation

Days of sales in cash = cash / (net sales/365)

This ratio describes the relationship between cash balances and sales levels and examines how many days of average net sales are available in cash.

When to use indicator: Managers, creditors, and investors can use this indicator to determine if the company holds an appropriate amount of cash.

When to use indicator: Very low ratios can indicate inadequate cash reserves, which may lead to problems in meeting debt obligations such as accounts payable and interest payments. Very high ratios can indicate excessive cash reserves. In this case, a portion of the cash balance would better be invested in other types of assets that yield greater returns such as plant equipment and subsidiaries.

Ways to improve indicator: When ratios are too low, increasing cash reserves by reducing investments in other types of assets can increase the days of sales in cash. When ratios are trending too high, finding manners in which the excessive cash may be invested, where returns are higher and risk levels are acceptable, can decrease the days-of-sales-in-cash ratio.

Example

Days of sales in cash = cash / (net sales/365)

Cash = 4,139
Net sales = 85,420

Days of sales in cash = 4,139 / (85,420/365) = 17.7 days

Sector	Mid to large cap	Days of Sales in Cash	Small to mid cap	Days of Sales in Cash	Micro to small cap	Days of Sales in Cash
Manufacturing	General Motors	23.07	Toro	0.00	Encad	3.10
Retail	Wal-Mart Stores	4.48	Bed Bath & Beyond	18.23	TCBY Enterprises	79.36
Food	McDonald's	10.92	Applebee's Int'l	6.30	Garden Fresh Restaurant	9.48
Technology	Microsoft	350.96	Cypress Semiconductor	101.73	Jmar Technologies	61.98
Finance	Morgan-Stanley Dean Witter	203.74	Franklin Resources	74.70	AmeriTrade Holding	1,424.20
Healthcare	Columbia/HCA Healthcare	2.13	Novacare	7.77	National Home Health Care	97.04
Service	Manpower	7.15	Air & Water Technologies	9.67	Market Facts	132.94
Media/Publishing	McGraw Hill	0.49	Scholastic	1.76	Thomas Nelson	57.30

135 Using Altman's Z-score to Determine the Probability of Bankruptcy

Equation

Altman's Z-score = (1.2 × working capital/total assets) + (1.4 × retained earnings/ total assets) + (3.3 × operating income/total assets) + (0.6 × market value of common and preferred stock / total liabilities) + (1.0 × net sales / total assets)

Altman developed a series of formulas to determine the likelihood of business failure because of low liquidity and inadequate earnings.

When to use indicator: Managers, investors, and creditors can use this formula to determine if a company is likely to fail because of an inappropriate amount of liquid assets or because of ineffective operations which generate little or no income and retained earnings. You should compare Z-scores to companies of similar size and in similar industries because acceptable standards can vary significantly. Altman developed his original Z-score model for smaller sized manufacturers. Several modified formulas have been developed for increased accuracy when analyzing privately held firms or nonmanufacturing companies.

Meaning of result: Lower ratios indicate higher probabilities of bankruptcy. Z-scores tend to trend lower prior to bankruptcy.

Z-score	Probability of bankruptcy
1.80 or less	Very high
1.81 to 2.99	Not sure
3.0 or greater	Very low

Ways to improve the indicator: Increasing short-term assets such as cash and marketable securities can increase the Z-score. Turning around operations to generate positive and healthy operating income and retained earnings can also move the Z-score in a positive direction.

Example

Altman's Z-score = (1.2 × working capital / total assets) + (1.4 × retained earnings / total assets) + (3.3 × operating income / total assets) + (0.6 × market value of common and preferred stock / total liabilities) + (1.0 × net sales / total assets)

Working capital = 44,135 − 12,032 = 32,103
Total assets = 56,268
Retained earnings = 18,722
Operating income = 9,433
Market value of common stock = 3,600 shares × $22.50 / share = 81,000
Market value of preferred stock = 15 shares × $25.00 / share = 375
Total liabilities = 25,180
Net sales = 85,420

Altman's Z-score = (1.2 × 32,103/56,268) + (1.4 × 18,722 / 56,268) + (3.3 × 9,433 / 56,268) + (0.6 × 81,375 / 25,180) + (1.0 × 85,420 / 56,268) = 0.6846 + 0.4658 + 0.5532 + 1.939 + 1.5181 = 5.161

Sector	Mid to large cap	Probability of Bankruptcy	Small to mid cap	Probability of Bankruptcy	Micro to small cap	Probability of Bankruptcy
Manufacturing	General Motors	1.62	Toro	3.39	Encad	7.46
Retail	Wal-Mart Stores	6.93	Bed Bath & Beyond	17.99	TCBY Enterprises	8.27
Food	McDonald's	5.07	Applebee's Int'l	7.38	Garden Fresh Restaurant	3.26
Technology	Microsoft	30.55	Cypress Semiconductor	2.94	Jmar Technologies	8.11
Finance	Morgan-Stanley Dean Witter	0.41	Franklin Resources	8.85	AmeriTrade Holding	0.71
Healthcare	Columbia/HCA Healthcare	2.24	Novacare	2.79	National Home Health Care	11.40
Service	Manpower	4.71	Air & Water Technologies	−1.01	Market Facts	5.64
Media/Publishing	McGraw Hill	4.16	Scholastic	3.01	Thomas Nelson	3.08

136 Comparing Sales to Current Assets

LIQUIDITY

Equation

Sales to current assets = net sales / current assets

This ratio describes the relationship between current assets and sales levels. Current assets include cash, marketable securities, accounts receivable, and inventory.

When to use indicator: Managers, creditors, and investors can use this indicator to determine if the company holds an appropriate amount of current assets.

Meaning of result: Very high ratios can indicate inadequate current assets, which may lead to problems in meeting debt obligations, supplying customers in a timely manner with existing inventory, or providing reasonable amounts of credit to customers. Very low ratios can indicate excessive current assets. In this case, a portion of the cash, inventory, or accounts receivable would better be invested in other types of assets that yield greater returns such as plant equipment and subsidiaries.

Ways to improve indicator: When ratios are too high, increasing current assets by reducing investments in long-term assets can reduce the sales-to-current-assets ratio. When ratios are trending too low, finding manners in which the excessive current assets may be invested where returns are higher and risk levels are acceptable, can increase the sales-to-current-assets ratio.

Example

Sales to current assets = net sales / current assets

Net sales = 85,420
Current assets = 44,135

Sales to current assets = 85,420 / 44,135 = 1.935

Sector	Mid to large cap	Sales to Current Assets	Small to mid cap	Sales to Current Assets	Micro to small cap	Sales to Current Assets
Manufacturing	General Motors	1.76	Toro	2.23	Encad	2.07
Retail	Wal-Mart Stores	6.10	Bed Bath & Beyond	3.27	TCBY Enterprises	1.96
Food	McDonald's	9.99	Applebee's Int'l	11.74	Garden Fresh Restaurant	14.79
Technology	Microsoft	0.91	Cypress Semiconductor	1.37	Jmar Technologies	1.59
Finance	Morgan-Stanley Dean Witter	0.09	Franklin Resources	1.79	AmeriTrade Holding	0.13
Healthcare	Columbia/HCA Healthcare	4.25	Novacare	3.23	National Home Health Care	1.91
Service	Manpower	4.30	Air & Water Technologies	3.55	Market Facts	1.59
Media/Publishing	McGraw Hill	2.41	Scholastic	2.77	Thomas Nelson	1.37

137 Comparing Liquid Assets to Current Liabilities

Equation

Liquid assets to current liabilities = liquid assets / current liabilities

This ratio examines the ability to meet short-term debt with cash-like assets. Liquid assets include cash, marketable securities, and accounts receivable.

When to use indicator: Creditors, managers, and investors can use this indicator to determine if short-term debt obligations can be covered adequately with assets that are readily converted to cash such as cash, easily liquidated stock and bond investments, and accounts receivable.

Meaning of result: Higher ratios indicate the ability to meet short-term debt obligations readily with liquid assets on hand. When ratios are trending too high, however, it may indicate excessive liquid assets on hand that might be better invested in longer term assets that yield greater returns. Lower ratios can indicate inadequate cash-like assets to meet short-term debt obligations.

Ways to improve the indicator: When ratios are too low, increasing liquid assets by reducing investments in longer term assets can increase the liquid-assets-to-current-liabilities ratio. When ratios are trending too high, finding manners in which the excessive liquid assets may be invested where returns are higher and risk levels are acceptable, can reduce this ratio.

Example

Liquid assets to current liabilities = liquid assets / current liabilities

Liquid assets = quick assets = cash + marketable securities + accounts receivable = 4,139 + 524 + 24,878 = 29,541
Current liabilities = 12,032

Liquid assets to current liabilities = 29,541 / 12,032 = 2.455

LIQUIDITY

Sector	Mid to large cap	Liquid Assets to Current Liabilities	Small to mid cap	Liquid Assets to Current Liabilities	Micro to small cap	Liquid Assets to Current Liabilities
Manufacturing	General Motors	5.66	Toro	1.09	Encad	1.57
Retail	Wal-Mart Stores	0.17	Bed Bath & Beyond	0.35	TCBY Enterprises	2.64
Food	McDonald's	0.28	Applebee's Int'l	0.58	Garden Fresh Restaurant	0.17
Technology	Microsoft	2.69	Cypress Semiconductor	2.90	Jmar Technologies	2.05
Finance	Morgan-Stanley Dean Witter	0.57	Franklin Resources	1.25	AmeriTrade Holding	1.04
Healthcare	Columbia/HCA Healthcare	0.95	Novacare	1.79	National Home Health Care	11.63
Service	Manpower	1.57	Air & Water Technologies	0.49	Market Facts	2.47
Media/Publishing	McGraw Hill	0.82	Scholastic	0.67	Thomas Nelson	2.30

138 Relating Liquid Assets to Cash Expenses

Equation

Liquid assets to cash expenses = liquid assets / (year's cash expenses/365)

This ratio determines the ability to meet average daily expenditure levels with cash-like assets. Liquid assets include cash, marketable securities, and accounts receivable.

When to use indicator: Creditors, managers, and investors can use this indicator to determine if typical daily expenditures can be covered adequately with assets that are readily converted to cash such as cash, easily liquidated stock and bond investments, and accounts receivable.

Meaning of result: Higher ratios indicate the ability to meet typical expense requirements readily with liquid assets on hand. When ratios are trending too high, however, it may indicate excessive liquid assets, some percentage of which might be better invested in longer term assets that yield greater returns. Lower ratios can indicate there may be inadequate cash-like assets to meet expense payments.

Ways to improve the indicator: When ratios are too low, increasing liquid assets by reducing investments in longer term assets can increase the liquid-assets-to-cash-expenses ratio. When ratios are trending too high, finding manners in which the excessive liquid assets may be invested, in which returns are higher and risk levels are acceptable, can decrease this ratio.

Example

Liquid assets to cash expenses = liquid assets / (year's cash expenses/365)

Liquid assets = quick assets = cash + marketable securities + accounts receivable = 4,139 + 524 + 24,878 = 29,541

Year's cash expenses = cost of goods sold + R&D + SG&A + interest = 54,212 + 4,578 + 15,993 + 784 = 75,567

Liquid assets to cash expenses = 29,541 / (75,567/365) = 142.7

Sector	Mid to large cap	Liquid Assets to Cash Expenses	Small to mid cap	Liquid Assets to Cash Expenses	Micro to small cap	Liquid Assets to Cash Expenses
Manufacturing	General Motors	214.08	Toro	94.70	Encad	113.37
Retail	Wal-Mart Stores	7.79	Bed Bath & Beyond	20.52	TCBY Enterprises	122.22
Food	McDonald's	33.17	Applebee's Int'l	29.91	Garden Fresh Restaurant	11.01
Technology	Microsoft	744.47	Cypress Semiconductor	184.41	Jmar Technologies	145.62
Finance	Morgan-Stanley Dean Witter	2,393.96	Franklin Resources	207.98	AmeriTrade Holding	3,539.96
Healthcare	Columbia/HCA Healthcare	58.12	Novacare	103.18	National Home Health Care	208.50
Service	Manpower	82.33	Air & Water Technologies	66.71	Market Facts	227.15
Media/Publishing	McGraw Hill	128.25	Scholastic	44.58	Thomas Nelson	161.72

139 Relating Current Debt to Sales

Equation

Current debt to sales = current liabilities / net sales

This ratio indicates whether the level of current debt is suitable for the size of the company and the industry in which it operates. Current liabilities include debt that must be paid in full in less than one year such as accounts payable for suppliers and income taxes payable to the government.

When to use indicator: Creditors, investors, and managers can use this indicator to determine the risk level associated with a company's short-term debt burden.

Meaning of result: Higher ratios indicate a great deal of debt is due in less than one year. This situation is less troublesome for profitable firms than for start-ups or companies that are experiencing cash flow problems.

When current debt to sales is increasing, it can indicate slowing sales or slower repayment of creditor debt.

Ways to improve the indicator: When current debt-to-sales ratios are too high, refinancing shorter term debt with long-term debt, preferably matching loan time periods with the useful life of the assets, can reduce the current-debt-to-sales ratio.

Example

Current debt to sales = current liabilities / net sales

Current liabilities = 12,032
Net sales = 85,420

Current debt to sales = 12,032 / 85,420 = 0.1409 = 14.09%

Sector	Mid to large cap	Current Debt to Sales	Small to mid cap	Current Debt to Sales	Micro to small cap	Current Debt to Sales
Manufacturing	General Motors	8.86%	Toro	22.62%	Encad	16.30%
Retail	Wal-Mart Stores	12.26%	Bed Bath & Beyond	14.10%	TCBY Enterprises	12.91%
Food	McDonald's	26.16%	Applebee's Int'l	12.11%	Garden Fresh Restaurant	15.38%
Technology	Microsoft	39.56%	Cypress Semiconductor	17.09%	Jmar Technologies	18.05%
Finance	Morgan-Stanley Dean Witter	967.64%	Franklin Resources	32.82%	AmeriTrade Holding	721.63%
Healthcare	Columbia/HCA Healthcare	14.74%	Novacare	14.66%	National Home Health Care	4.41%
Service	Manpower	13.84%	Air & Water Technologies	40.10%	Market Facts	22.92%
Media/Publishing	McGraw Hill	34.13%	Scholastic	17.17%	Thomas Nelson	17.70%

Comparing Current Debt to Total Debt

Equation

Current debt to total debt = current liabilities / total liabilities

This ratio indicates the percentage of total debt that is current, or short-term, in nature. Current debt to total debt is also a liquidity indicator since short-term debt repayment requirements are greater because of higher principal repayment demands. Current liabilities include debt that must be paid in full in less than one year such as accounts payable for suppliers and income taxes payable to the government. Total liabilities include all debt such as loans payable to lenders, accounts payable to suppliers, and income taxes payable to the government.

When to use indicator: Creditors, investors, and managers can use this indicator to determine the risk level associated with a company's short-term debt burden.

Meaning of result: Higher ratios indicate large percentages of total debt are due in less than one year. This presents greater demands on the company to generate the additional income necessary to meet the higher payments required of short-term debt. This is less troublesome for profitable firms than for start-ups or companies that are experiencing cash flow problems.

Ways to improve the indicator: When current-debt-to-total-debt ratios are too high, refinancing shorter term debt with long-term debt, preferably matching loan time periods with the useful life of the assets, can reduce the current-debt-to-total-debt ratio.

Example

Current debt to total debt = current liabilities / total liabilities

Current liabilities = 12,032
Total liabilities = 25,180

Current debt to total debt = 12,032 / 25,180 = 0.4778 = 47.78%

Sector	Mid to large cap	Current Debt to Total Debt	Small to mid cap	Current Debt to Total Debt	Micro to small cap	Current Debt to Total Debt
Manufacturing	General Motors	7.50%	Toro	56.56%	Encad	95.02%
Retail	Wal-Mart Stores	57.97%	Bed Bath & Beyond	92.27%	TCBY Enterprises	53.55%
Food	McDonald's	31.78%	Applebee's Int'l	71.80%	Garden Fresh Restaurant	49.14%
Technology	Microsoft	100.00%	Cypress Semiconductor	29.75%	Jmar Technologies	81.02%
Finance	Morgan-Stanley Dean Witter	91.06%	Franklin Resources	57.21%	AmeriTrade Holding	100.00%
Healthcare	Columbia/HCA Healthcare	19.93%	Novacare	31.10%	National Home Health Care	83.05%
Service	Manpower	70.28%	Air & Water Technologies	37.28%	Market Facts	68.79%
Media/Publishing	McGraw Hill	52.68%	Scholastic	40.63%	Thomas Nelson	34.73%

141 Examining Working Capital

Equation

Working capital = current assets − current liabilities

This equation describes the amount of capital used to run day-to-day business operations. **Working capital** is necessary to finance a company's cash conversion cycle. You can think of it as a measure of liquidity. The **cash conversion cycle** describes the process by which a company converts cash into products and then back into cash again. For a manufacturing company, this includes using cash to purchase raw materials; perform the work required to make, inspect, and store the product; sell the product; and ultimately collect cash from the customer. Current assets include cash, marketable securities, accounts receivable, inventory, and all other assets that are likely to be held less than one year. Current liabilities include accounts payable, accrued liabilities such as payroll and property taxes, and all other debts due in less than one year.

When to use indicator: Managers, investors, and creditors use working capital to ensure the company has a proper degree of liquidity.

Meaning of result: Low amounts of working capital can indicate the business is insufficiently liquid and could have problems meeting current debt obligations. Very high working capital accounts could indicate ineffective management since current assets seldom yield returns as great as long-term assets.

Ways to improve the indicator: Firms should seek to maintain working capital levels that provide sufficient current assets to meet short-term debt requirements but in which current asset accounts are not so excessive that overall company profit margins suffer. When working capital is too low, increasing current assets and/or reducing current liabilities can increase working capital. When working capital is trending too high, investing excess current assets in longer term assets, which yield higher rates of return at acceptable risk levels, can decrease working capital levels.

Example

Working capital = current assets − current liabilities

Current assets = 44,135
Current liabilities = 12,032

Working capital = 44,135 − 12,032 = 32,103

LIQUIDITY

Sector	Mid to large cap	Working Capital	Small to mid cap	Working Capital	Micro to small cap	Working Capital
Manufacturing	General Motors	85,667,000	Toro	234,211	Encad	47,818
Retail	Wal-Mart Stores	4,892,000	Bed Bath & Beyond	175,617	TCBY Enterprises	34,532
Food	McDonald's	−1,842,200	Applebee's Int'l	−18,534	Garden Fresh Restaurant	−7,776
Technology	Microsoft	10,159,000	Cypress Semiconductor	305,027	Jmar Technologies	9,635
Finance	Morgan-Stanley Dean Witter	30,664,000	Franklin Resources	500,571	AmeriTrade Holding	26,150
Healthcare	Columbia/HCA Healthcare	1,650,000	Novacare	173,576	National Home Health Care	16,853
Service	Manpower	682,224	Air & Water Technologies	−54,317	Market Facts	40,161
Media/Publishing	McGraw Hill	258,179	Scholastic	201,000	Thomas Nelson	140,256

142 Finding the Turnover of Working Capital

Equation

Working capital turnover = net sales / working capital

where

working capital = current assets − current liabilities

This equation describes the relationship between the size of the company and the amount of working capital used to run day-to-day business operations. Working capital is necessary to finance a company's cash conversion cycle. You can think of it as a measure of liquidity. The cash conversion cycle describes the process by which a company converts cash into products and then back into cash again. For a manufacturing company, this includes using cash to purchase raw materials; perform the work required to make, inspect, and store the product; sell the product; and ultimately collect cash from the customer. Current assets include cash, marketable securities, accounts receivable, inventory, and all other assets that are likely to be held less than one year. Current liabilities include accounts payable, accrued liabilities such as payroll and property taxes, and all other debts due in less than one year.

When to use indicator: Managers, investors, and creditors use working capital turnover to ensure the company has a proper degree of liquidity.

Meaning of result: High working capital turnover can indicate the business is insufficiently liquid and could have problems meeting current debt obligations. Low working capital turnover can indicate ineffective management since current assets seldom yield returns as great as long-term assets.

Ways to improve the indicator: Firms should seek to maintain the turnover of working capital at levels that provide sufficient current assets to meet short-term debt requirements but at which current asset accounts are not so excessive that overall company profit margins suffer. When working capital turnover is too high, increasing current assets and/or reducing current liabilities can decrease working capital turnover levels. When working capital turnover is trending too low, investing excess current assets in longer term assets, which yield higher rates of return at acceptable risk levels, can increase working capital turnover levels.

Example

Working capital turnover = net sales / working capital

Net sales = 85,420
Working capital = 32,103

Working capital turnover = 85,420 / 32,103 = 2.661 = 266.1%

Sector	Mid to large cap	Working Capital Turnover	Small to mid cap	Working Capital Turnover	Micro to small cap	Working Capital Turnover
Manufacturing	General Motors	2.08	Toro	4.49	Encad	3.12
Retail	Wal-Mart Stores	24.11	Bed Bath & Beyond	6.07	TCBY Enterprises	2.62
Food	McDonald's	−6.19	Applebee's Int'l	−27.83	Garden Fresh Restaurant	−11.61
Technology	Microsoft	1.43	Cypress Semiconductor	1.78	Jmar Technologies	2.23
Finance	Morgan-Stanley Dean Witter	0.88	Franklin Resources	4.32	AmeriTrade Holding	3.66
Healthcare	Columbia/HCA Healthcare	11.41	Novacare	6.14	National Home Health Care	2.08
Service	Manpower	10.64	Air & Water Technologies	−8.40	Market Facts	2.49
Media/Publishing	McGraw Hill	13.69	Scholastic	5.27	Thomas Nelson	1.80

143 Comparing Working Capital to Sales

Equation

Working capital to sales = working capital / net sales

where

working capital = current assets − current liabilities

This equation describes the relationship between the size of the company and the amount of working capital used to run day-to-day business operations. Working capital to sales is the inverse of working capital turnover. Working capital is necessary to finance a company's cash conversion cycle and is a measure of liquidity. The cash conversion cycle describes the process by which a company converts cash into products and then back into cash again. For a manufacturing company, this includes using cash to purchase raw materials; perform the work required to make, inspect, and store the product; sell the product; and ultimately collect cash from the customer. Current assets include cash, marketable securities, accounts receivable, inventory, and all other assets that are likely to be held less than one year. Current liabilities include accounts payable, accrued liabilities such as payroll and property taxes, and all other debts due in less than one year.

When to use indicator: Managers, investors, and creditors use working capital to sales to ensure the company has a proper degree of liquidity.

Meaning of result: Low working-capital-to-sales ratios can indicate the business is insufficiently liquid and could have problems meeting current debt obligations. High working-capital-to-sales ratios can indicate ineffective management since current assets seldom yield returns as great as long-term assets.

Ways to improve the indicator: Firms should seek to maintain working-capital-to-sales ratios at levels that provide sufficient current assets to meet short-term debt requirements but at which current asset accounts are not so excessive that overall company profit margins suffer. When working-capital-to-sales ratios are too low, increasing current assets and/or reducing current liabilities can increase the ratios. When working-capital-to-sales ratios are trending too high, investing excess current assets in longer term assets, which yield higher rates of return at acceptable risk levels, can decrease the ratios.

Example

Working capital to sales = working capital / net sales

Working capital = 32,103
Net sales = 85,420

Working capital to sales = 32,103 / 85,420 = 0.3758 = 37.58%

LIQUIDITY

Sector	Mid to large cap	Working Capital to Sales	Small to mid cap	Working Capital to Sales	Micro to small cap	Working Capital to Sales
Manufacturing	General Motors	48.08%	Toro	22.28%	Encad	32.08%
Retail	Wal-Mart Stores	4.15%	Bed Bath & Beyond	16.46%	TCBY Enterprises	38.12%
Food	McDonald's	−16.15%	Applebee's Int'l	−3.59%	Garden Fresh Restaurant	−8.62%
Technology	Microsoft	70.14%	Cypress Semiconductor	56.03%	Jmar Technologies	44.89%
Finance	Morgan-Stanley Dean Witter	113.02%	Franklin Resources	23.14%	AmeriTrade Holding	27.33%
Healthcare	Columbia/HCA Healthcare	8.77%	Novacare	16.28%	National Home Health Care	48.06%
Service	Manpower	9.40%	Air & Water Technologies	−11.90%	Market Facts	40.14%
Media/Publishing	McGraw Hill	7.31%	Scholastic	18.99%	Thomas Nelson	55.45%

144 Comparing Working Capital to Net Income

Equation

Working capital to net income = working capital / net income

where

working capital = current assets − current liabilities

This ratio describes the relationship between the size and earning power of a company and the amount of working capital used to run day-to-day business operations. Working capital is necessary to finance a company's cash conversion cycle. You can think of it as a measure of liquidity. The cash conversion cycle describes the process by which a company converts cash into products and then back into cash again. For a manufacturing company, this includes using cash to purchase raw materials; perform the work required to make, inspect, and store the product; sell the product; and ultimately collect cash from the customer. Current assets include cash, marketable securities, accounts receivable, inventory, and all other assets that are likely to be held less than one year. Current liabilities include accounts payable, accrued liabilities such as payroll and property taxes, and all other debts due in less than one year.

When to use indicator: Since working capital is a cost of operating a business, managers can use this ratio to investigate if that cost is generating an acceptable amount of profit.

Meaning of result: Low working-capital-to-net-income ratios indicate that a given amount of working capital generates a great deal of income. This is indicative of either highly profitable businesses or those companies that operate with little working capital.

High or negative working-capital-to-net-income ratios can indicate poorly performing companies which generate little or no income and/or those businesses that require a great deal of working capital.

Ways to improve the indicator: To maximize the amount of income generated for a given amount of working capital, firms should seek to maintain working capital at levels that provide sufficient current assets to meet short-term debt requirements but at which current asset accounts are not so excessive that overall company profit margins suffer. Seeking to invest excess current assets in longer term assets that can provide additional income at acceptable risk levels tends to optimize the use of a company's assets.

Example

Working capital to net income = working capital / net income

Working capital = 32,103
Net income = 4,983

Working capital to net income = 32,103 / 4,983 = 6.443 = 644.3%

Sector	Mid to large cap	Working Capital to Net Income	Small to mid cap	Working Capital to Net Income	Micro to small cap	Working Capital to Net Income
Manufacturing	General Motors	1278.99%	Toro	672.15%	Encad	274.36%
Retail	Wal-Mart Stores	138.74%	Bed Bath & Beyond	240.10%	TCBY Enterprises	388.91%
Food	McDonald's	−112.16%	Applebee's Int'l	−41.10%	Garden Fresh Restaurant	−200.05%
Technology	Microsoft	226.26%	Cypress Semiconductor	1656.05%	Jmar Technologies	536.66%
Finance	Morgan-Stanley Dean Witter	1185.77%	Franklin Resources	115.32%	AmeriTrade Holding	189.19%
Healthcare	Columbia/HCA Healthcare	−540.98%	Novacare	446.10%	National Home Health Care	908.03%
Service	Manpower	416.29%	Air & Water Technologies	33.83%	Market Facts	689.80%
Media/Publishing	McGraw Hill	88.82%	Scholastic	851.69%	Thomas Nelson	1106.73%

145 Relating Working Capital to Current Debt

Equation

Working capital to current debt = working capital / current liabilities

where

working capital = current assets − current liabilities

This ratio describes the relationship between short-term debt and the amount of capital used to run day-to-day business operations. Working capital is necessary to finance a company's cash conversion cycle. It is a measure of liquidity. The cash conversion cycle describes the process by which a company converts cash into products and then back into cash again. For a manufacturing company, this includes using cash to purchase raw materials; perform the work required to make, inspect, and store the product; sell the product; and ultimately collect cash from the customer. Current assets include cash, marketable securities, accounts receivable, inventory, and all other assets that are likely to be held less than one year. Current liabilities include accounts payable, accrued liabilities such as payroll and property taxes, and all other debts due in less than one year.

When to use indicator: Managers, investors, and creditors use working capital to current liabilities to ensure the company has a proper degree of liquidity to service short-term debt demands. This ratio allows a fast and easy method of directly determining the size of working capital in relation to current liabilities. It is the percentage by which working capital exceeds short-term debt.

Meaning of result: Low working-capital-to-current-debt ratios can indicate the business is insufficiently liquid and could have problems meeting current debt obligations. However, when ratios become too high, it can indicate ineffective management since current assets seldom yield returns as great as long-term assets.

Ways to improve the indicator: Firms should seek to maintain working-capital-to-current-debt ratios at levels that provide sufficient working capital to meet short-term debt requirements but at which current asset accounts are not so excessive that overall company profit margins suffer. When working-capital-to-current-debt ratios are too low, increasing current assets and/or reducing current liabilities can increase the ratios. When working-capital-to-current-debt ratios are trending too high, investing excess current assets in longer term assets, which yield higher rates of return at acceptable risk levels, can lower the ratios.

Example

Working capital to current debt = working capital / current liabilities

Working capital = 32,103
Current liabilities = 12,032

Working capital to current debt = 32,103 / 12,032 = 2.668 = 266.8%

Sector	Mid to large cap	Working Capital to Current Debt	Small to mid cap	Working Capital to Current Debt	Micro to small cap	Working Capital to Current Debt
Manufacturing	General Motors	542.81%	Toro	98.48%	Encad	196.78%
Retail	Wal-Mart Stores	33.83%	Bed Bath & Beyond	116.81%	TCBY Enterprises	295.30%
Food	McDonald's	−61.73%	Applebee's Int'l	−29.66%	Garden Fresh Restaurant	−56.03%
Technology	Microsoft	177.29%	Cypress Semiconductor	327.80%	Jmar Technologies	248.73%
Finance	Morgan-Stanley Dean Witter	11.68%	Franklin Resources	70.51%	AmeriTrade Holding	3.79%
Healthcare	Columbia/HCA Healthcare	59.50%	Novacare	111.04%	National Home Health Care	1088.70%
Service	Manpower	67.90%	Air & Water Technologies	−29.68%	Market Facts	175.09%
Media/Publishing	McGraw Hill	21.40%	Scholastic	110.62%	Thomas Nelson	313.32%

146 Relating Working Capital to Long-Term Debt

Equation

Working capital to long-term debt = working capital / long-term liabilities

where

working capital = current assets − current liabilities

This ratio describes the relationship between long-term debt and the amount of capital used to run day-to-day business operations. Working capital is necessary to finance a company's cash conversion cycle and is a measure of liquidity. The cash conversion cycle describes the process by which a company converts cash into products and then back into cash again. For a manufacturing company, this includes using cash to purchase raw materials; perform the work required to make, inspect, and store the product; sell the product; and ultimately collect cash from the customer. Current assets include cash, marketable securities, accounts receivable, inventory, and all other assets that are likely to be held less than one year. Current liabilities include accounts payable, accrued liabilities such as payroll and property taxes, and all other debts due in less than one year. Long-term liabilities are those debts that are due in full in longer than one year such as with buildings and machinery.

When to use indicator: Managers, investors, and creditors use ratios of working capital to long-term debt to determine the relative amounts of long-term debt and current assets available.

Meaning of result: Low ratios of working capital to long-term debt can indicate highly leveraged businesses, companies that hold substantial amounts of long-term debt. Low ratios can also indicate situations in which there is insufficient liquidity.

High ratios of working capital to long-term debt indicate highly liquid businesses and/or businesses that hold little long-term debt. They also indicate companies that can probably pay off long-term debt balances readily with current assets if so desired.

Ways to improve the indicator: Firms should seek to maintain ratios of working capital to long-term debt at levels which provide sufficient working capital to meet short-term debt requirements. Beyond short-term needs, the relative size of long-term debt and working capital is dependent upon the degree of financial leverage a company can comfortably service. Higher degrees of financial leverage can help improve performance with additional asset procurement, but there is a commensurate increase in risk because of increased levels of long-term debt.

Example

Working capital to long-term debt = working capital / long-term liabilities

Working capital = 32,103
Long-term liabilities = 25,180 − 12,032 = 13,148

Working capital to long-term debt = 32,103 / 13,148 = 2.442 = 244.2%

Sector	Mid to large cap	Working Capital to Long-Term Debt	Small to mid cap	Working Capital to Long-Term Debt	Micro to small cap	Working Capital to Long-Term Debt
Manufacturing	General Motors	44.01%	Toro	128.24%	Encad	3756.32%
Retail	Wal-Mart Stores	46.67%	Bed Bath & Beyond	1394.89%	TCBY Enterprises	340.39%
Food	McDonald's	−28.76%	Applebee's Int'l	−75.52%	Garden Fresh Restaurant	−54.14%
Technology	Microsoft	*	Cypress Semiconductor	138.81%	Jmar Technologies	1061.97%
Finance	Morgan-Stanley Dean Witter	118.89%	Franklin Resources	94.26%	AmeriTrade Holding	*
Healthcare	Columbia/HCA Healthcare	14.81%	Novacare	50.12%	National Home Health Care	5333.23%
Service	Manpower	160.60%	Air & Water Technologies	−17.64%	Market Facts	385.83%
Media/Publishing	McGraw Hill	23.83%	Scholastic	75.71%	Thomas Nelson	166.71%

* Companies with no long-term debt.

147 Relating Working Capital to Total Debt

Equation

Working capital to total debt = working capital / total liabilities

where

working capital = current assets − current liabilities

This ratio describes the relationship between all forms of debt and the amount of capital used to run day-to-day business operations. Working capital is necessary to finance a company's cash conversion cycle and is a measure of liquidity. The cash conversion cycle describes the process by which a company converts cash into products and then back into cash again. For a manufacturing company, this includes using cash to purchase raw materials; perform the work required to make, inspect, and store the product; sell the product; and ultimately collect cash from the customer. Current assets include cash, marketable securities, accounts receivable, inventory, and all other assets that are likely to be held less than one year. Current liabilities include accounts payable, accrued liabilities such as payroll and property taxes, and all other debts due in less than one year. Long-term liabilities are those debts that are payable in full in more than one year such as with buildings and machinery. Total liabilities include both current and long-term liabilities.

When to use indicator: Managers, investors, and creditors use the ratio of working capital to total debt to compare the relative size of a company's debt and current assets available.

Meaning of result: Low ratios of working capital to total debt can indicate highly leveraged businesses, companies that hold substantial amounts of debt. Low ratios can also indicate situations in which there is insufficient liquidity.

High ratios of working capital to total debt indicate highly liquid businesses that can easily service all forms of debt. They also indicate companies that can probably pay off debt balances readily with current assets if so desired.

Ways to improve the indicator: Firms should seek to maintain ratios of working capital to total debt at levels that provide sufficient working capital to meet short-term debt requirements. Beyond short-term needs, the relative size of total debt and working capital is dependent upon the degree of financial leverage a company can comfortably service. Higher degrees of financial leverage can help improve performance with additional asset procurement, but there is a commensurate increase in risk because of the increased levels of debt.

Example

Working capital to total debt = working capital / total liabilities

Working capital = 32,103
Total liabilities = 25,180

Working capital to total debt = 32,103 / 25,180 = 1.275 = 127.5%

Sector	Mid to large cap	Working Capital to Total Debt	Small to mid cap	Working Capital to Total Debt	Micro to small cap	Working Capital to Total Debt
Manufacturing	General Motors	40.71%	Toro	55.70%	Encad	186.99%
Retail	Wal-Mart Stores	19.61%	Bed Bath & Beyond	107.78%	TCBY Enterprises	158.12%
Food	McDonald's	−19.62%	Applebee's Int'l	−21.30%	Garden Fresh Restaurant	−27.53%
Technology	Microsoft	177.29%	Cypress Semiconductor	97.52%	Jmar Technologies	201.53%
Finance	Morgan-Stanley Dean Witter	10.63%	Franklin Resources	40.34%	AmeriTrade Holding	3.79%
Healthcare	Columbia/HCA Healthcare	11.86%	Novacare	34.53%	National Home Health Care	904.13%
Service	Manpower	47.73%	Air & Water Technologies	−11.07%	Market Facts	120.44%
Media/Publishing	McGraw Hill	11.28%	Scholastic	44.95%	Thomas Nelson	108.81%

148 Comparing Working Capital to Current Assets

Equation

Working capital to current assets = working capital / current assets

where

working capital = current assets − current liabilities

This ratio describes the relationship between current assets and the amount of capital used to run day-to-day business operations. Working capital is necessary to finance a company's cash conversion cycle and is a measure of liquidity. The cash conversion cycle describes the process by which a company converts cash into products and then back into cash again. For a manufacturing company, this includes using cash to purchase raw materials; perform the work required to make, inspect, and store the product; sell the product; and ultimately collect cash from the customer. Current assets include cash, marketable securities, accounts receivable, inventory, and all other assets that are likely to be held less than one year. Current liabilities include accounts payable, accrued liabilities such as payroll and property taxes, and all other debts due in less than one year.

When to use indicator: Managers, investors, and creditors use ratios of working capital to current assets to determine if a company is sufficiently liquid. This ratio allows a fast and easy method of determining the size of working capital in relation to current assets. You can think of it as the percentage of current assets available after a company services all short-term debt.

Meaning of result: Low ratios of working capital to current assets can indicate situations with insufficient liquidity.

High ratios of working capital to current assets indicate highly liquid businesses that can easily service all forms of debt. When the ratio becomes excessively high, however, it can indicate that management is not optimally using all assets available since current assets seldom offer returns as great as longer term assets.

Ways to improve the indicator: Firms should seek to maintain ratios of working capital to current assets at levels which provide sufficient working capital to meet short-term debt requirements. Beyond meeting those debt requirements, management should seek to invest excess current assets in longer term vehicles that offer greater rates of return at acceptable risk levels. Such investments might include the purchase of a subsidiary, plant equipment to produce a new product line, or additional retail floor space to generate additional sales.

Example

Working capital to current assets = working capital / current assets

Working capital = 32,103
Current assets = 44,135

Working capital to current assets = 32,103 / 44,135 = 0.7274 = 72.74%

Sector	Mid to large cap	Working Capital to Current Assets	Small to mid cap	Working Capital to Current Assets	Micro to small cap	Working Capital to Current Assets
Manufacturing	General Motors	84.44%	Toro	49.62%	Encad	66.31%
Retail	Wal-Mart Stores	25.28%	Bed Bath & Beyond	53.88%	TCBY Enterprises	74.70%
Food	McDonald's	−161.27%	Applebee's Int'l	−42.17%	Garden Fresh Restaurant	−127.41%
Technology	Microsoft	63.94%	Cypress Semiconductor	76.62%	Jmar Technologies	71.32%
Finance	Morgan-Stanley Dean Witter	10.46%	Franklin Resources	41.35%	AmeriTrade Holding	3.65%
Healthcare	Columbia/HCA Healthcare	37.30%	Novacare	52.62%	National Home Health Care	91.59%
Service	Manpower	40.44%	Air & Water Technologies	−42.21%	Market Facts	63.65%
Media/Publishing	McGraw Hill	17.63%	Scholastic	52.52%	Thomas Nelson	75.81%

149 Comparing Working Capital to Specific Current Assets Such as Cash and Inventory

Equation

Working capital to cash = working capital / cash

Working capital to inventory = working capital / inventory

where

working capital = current assets − current liabilities

This ratio describes the relationship between specific current asset accounts and the amount of capital used to run day-to-day business operations. Working capital is necessary to finance a company's cash conversion cycle and is a measure of liquidity. The cash conversion cycle describes the process by which a company converts cash into products and then back into cash again. For a manufacturing company, this includes using cash to purchase raw materials; perform the work required to make, inspect, and store the product; sell the product; and ultimately collect cash from the customer. Current assets include cash, marketable securities, accounts receivable, inventory, and all other assets that are likely to be held less than one year. Current liabilities include accounts payable, accrued liabilities such as payroll and property taxes, and all other debts due in less than one year.

When to use indicator: Managers, investors, and creditors use the ratio of working capital to specific current asset accounts to determine the liquidity level of working capital.

Meaning of result: Low ratios of working capital to specific current asset accounts indicate that the specific account makes up a considerable portion of working capital. When those current assets are more liquid in nature, then working capital as a whole is more liquid. For example, if there is a large cash balance, working-capital-to-cash ratios are low and the entire working capital account is more liquid. Conversely, low ratios for less liquid current assets such as inventory indicate a high percentage of working capital is tied up in inventory and the entire working capital account is less liquid.

Ways to improve the indicator: Firms should seek to maintain ratios of working capital to specific current assets at levels that provide sufficient liquid working capital to meet short-term debt requirements. Beyond short-term needs, the relative size of specific current asset accounts and working capital is dependent upon the type of business in question. For example, some companies require higher inventories than others because of the additional time required to produce and sell goods.

Example

Working capital to inventory = working capital / inventory

Working capital = 32,103
Inventory = 13,421

Working capital to inventory = 32,103 / 13,421 = 2.392 = 239.2%

Sector	Mid to large cap	Working Capital to Inventory	Small to mid cap	Working Capital to Inventory	Micro to small cap	Working Capital to Inventory
Manufacturing	General Motors	707.87%	Toro	146.27%	Encad	164.01%
Retail	Wal-Mart Stores	29.65%	Bed Bath & Beyond	64.96%	TCBY Enterprises	323.36%
Food	McDonald's	−2613.05%	Applebee's Int'l	−387.09%	Garden Fresh Restaurant	−269.44%
Technology	Microsoft	*	Cypress Semiconductor	396.53%	Jmar Technologies	205.61%
Finance	Morgan-Stanley Dean Witter	34.84%	Franklin Resources	*	AmeriTrade Holding	*
Healthcare	Columbia/HCA Healthcare	365.04%	Novacare	940.79%	National Home Health Care	*
Service	Manpower	*	Air & Water Technologies	−2869.36%	Market Facts	*
Media/Publishing	McGraw Hill	88.88%	Scholastic	100.85%	Thomas Nelson	198.69%

* Companies without any reported inventory.

150 Comparing Working Capital to Total Assets

Equation

Working capital to total assets = working capital / total assets

where

working capital = current assets − current liabilities

This ratio describes the relationship between the size of a company and the amount of capital used to run day-to-day business operations. Working capital is necessary to finance a company's cash conversion cycle and is a measure of liquidity. The cash conversion cycle describes the process by which a company converts cash into products and then back into cash again. For a manufacturing company, this includes using cash to purchase raw materials; perform the work required to make, inspect, and store the product; sell the product; and ultimately collect cash from the customer. Current assets include cash, marketable securities, accounts receivable, inventory, and all other assets that are likely to be held less than one year. Current liabilities include accounts payable, accrued liabilities such as payroll and property taxes, and all other debts due in less than one year. Total assets include current assets such as cash, inventory, and accounts receivable and longer term assets such as plant equipment, buildings, intangible assets, and long-term security investments.

When to use indicator: Managers, investors, and creditors use the ratio of working capital to total assets to determine if there is sufficient and appropriate working capital given the size and type of business.

Meaning of result: Since total assets are an excellent indication of the size of the company in question, comparing working capital with assets allows the manager to determine the appropriateness of the size of the working capital account. Low ratios of working capital to total assets can indicate insufficient liquidity. A manager may want to investigate further when this ratio is declining because the company may soon have difficulty in meeting its debt payments. Note that the degree of liquidity, or working capital, required is dependent upon the type of business and industry in which the business operates.

High ratios of working capital to total assets indicate highly liquid businesses. Although this indicates less financial risk, when the ratio becomes very high, it can indicate that the company is not using excess cash to its fullest extent. Current assets generally do not offer the rates of return that longer term assets can provide.

Ways to improve the indicator: Firms should seek to maintain ratios of working capital to total assets at levels that provide sufficient working capital to meet short-term debt requirements. Beyond short-term needs, the relative size of total debt and working capital is dependent upon the degree of financial leverage a company can comfortably service.

Sector	Mid to large cap	Working Capital to Total Assets	Small to mid cap	Working Capital to Total Assets	Micro to small cap	Working Capital to Total Assets
Manufacturing	General Motors	37.43%	Toro	35.40%	Encad	52.96%
Retail	Wal-Mart Stores	10.78%	Bed Bath & Beyond	38.32%	TCBY Enterprises	34.79%
Food	McDonald's	−10.10%	Applebee's Int'l	−4.91%	Garden Fresh Restaurant	−12.46%
Technology	Microsoft	45.44%	Cypress Semiconductor	31.90%	Jmar Technologies	55.79%
Finance	Morgan-Stanley Dean Witter	10.14%	Franklin Resources	16.17%	AmeriTrade Holding	3.45%
Healthcare	Columbia/HCA Healthcare	7.50%	Novacare	17.11%	National Home Health Care	66.81%
Service	Manpower	33.33%	Air & Water Technologies	−14.18%	Market Facts	46.22%
Media/Publishing	McGraw Hill	6.93%	Scholastic	26.26%	Thomas Nelson	49.16%

Higher degrees of financial leverage can help improve performance with additional asset procurement, but there is a commensurate increase in risk because of the increased levels of debt.

Example

Working capital to total assets = working capital / total assets

Working capital = 32,103
Total assets = 56,268

Working capital to total assets = 32,103 / 56,268 = 0.5705 = 57.05%

151 Relating Liquid Assets to Total Current Assets

Equation

Liquid assets to total current assets = liquid assets / current assets

This ratio describes the portion of current assets that are highly liquid in nature. Liquid assets include cash, marketable securities, and accounts receivable. Current assets include liquid assets and inventory, notes receivable, and other current assets.

When to use indicator: Managers and creditors can use this indicator to determine the composition and degree of liquidity of current assets.

Meaning of result: A high ratio of liquid assets to current assets indicates that very liquid assets such as cash and cash equivalents comprise a large part of the current asset account. Lower ratios indicate that less liquid accounts such as inventory and notes receivable make up a large part of current assets.

Ways to improve the indicator: When you desire higher ratios, shifting current asset accounts from less liquid to more liquid accounts can improve liquidity and allow the more ready payment of expenses.

Example

Liquid assets to total current assets = liquid assets / current assets

Liquid assets = quick assets = cash + marketable securities + accounts receivable = 4,139 + 524 + 24,878 = 29,541
Current assets = 44,135

Liquid assets to total current assets = 29,541 / 44,135 = 0.6693 = 66.93%

Sector	Mid to large cap	Liquid Assets to Total Current Assets	Small to mid cap	Liquid Assets to Total Current Assets	Micro to small cap	Liquid Assets to Total Current Assets
Manufacturing	General Motors	88.07%	Toro	54.90%	Encad	52.78%
Retail	Wal-Mart Stores	12.52%	Bed Bath & Beyond	16.35%	TCBY Enterprises	66.74%
Food	McDonald's	72.21%	Applebee's Int'l	82.37%	Garden Fresh Restaurant	38.42%
Technology	Microsoft	96.84%	Cypress Semiconductor	67.68%	Jmar Technologies	58.88%
Finance	Morgan-Stanley Dean Witter	51.13%	Franklin Resources	73.57%	AmeriTrade Holding	100.00%
Healthcare	Columbia/HCA Healthcare	59.51%	Novacare	84.63%	National Home Health Care	97.86%
Service	Manpower	93.64%	Air & Water Technologies	68.99%	Market Facts	89.67%
Media/Publishing	McGraw Hill	67.38%	Scholastic	31.83%	Thomas Nelson	55.66%

152 Relating Marketable Securities to Total Current Assets

Equation

Marketable securities to total current assets = marketable securities / total current assets

This ratio describes the portion of current assets represented by marketable securities. Marketable securities include investments that are readily turned into cash and are likely to be held less than one year. Companies often park excess cash in marketable securities to earn a higher yield than do simple cash checking accounts.

When to use indicator: Managers and creditors can use this indicator to determine the composition and degree of liquidity of current assets.

Meaning of result: A high ratio of marketable securities to current assets indicates that the current asset account includes a large part of this very liquid asset.

Ways to improve the indicator: When you desire higher ratios, shifting other current asset accounts to the marketable securities account can increase this ratio. Shifting assets from other liquid current asset accounts such as cash and cash equivalents will tend to increase rates of return. Shifting assets from less liquid current asset accounts such as inventory will tend to improve liquidity and allow more ready payment of expenses.

Example

Marketable securities to total current assets = marketable securities / total current assets

Marketable securities = 524
Total current assets = 44,135

Marketable securities to total current assets = 524 / 44,135 = 0.0119 = 1.19%

Sector	Mid to large cap	Marketable Securities to Total Current Assets	Small to mid cap	Marketable Securities to Total Current Assets	Micro to small cap	Marketable Securities to Total Current Assets
Manufacturing	General Motors	11.55%	Toro	0.00%	Encad	0.00%
Retail	Wal-Mart Stores	0.00%	Bed Bath & Beyond	0.00%	TCBY Enterprises	5.20%
Food	McDonald's	0.00%	Applebee's Int'l	24.81%	Garden Fresh Restaurant	0.00%
Technology	Microsoft	0.00%	Cypress Semiconductor	12.52%	Jmar Technologies	0.00%
Finance	Morgan-Stanley Dean Witter	28.82%	Franklin Resources	17.67%	AmeriTrade Holding	0.00%
Healthcare	Columbia/HCA Healthcare	0.00%	Novacare	0.00%	National Home Health Care	2.76%
Service	Manpower	0.00%	Air & Water Technologies	0.00%	Market Facts	0.08%
Media/Publishing	McGraw Hill	0.00%	Scholastic	0.00%	Thomas Nelson	0.00%

153 Comparing Accounts Receivable to Total Current Assets

Equation

Accounts receivable to total current assets = accounts receivable / total current assets

This ratio describes the portion of current assets that accounts receivable represent. Current assets include cash, marketable securities, accounts receivable, inventory, and all other assets that are likely to be held less than one year. Accounts receivable represent cash due to a company for products or services already delivered to a customer.

When to use indicator: Managers and creditors can use this indicator to determine the composition and degree of liquidity of current assets.

Meaning of result: A high ratio of accounts receivable to current assets indicates that accounts receivable comprise a large part of the current asset account. Accounts receivable are generally less liquid than cash and marketable securities and more liquid than inventory and notes receivable.

Ways to improve the indicator: When you desire higher ratios, extending additional credit to customers can increase accounts receivable. This generally increases sales levels but may increase the percentage of unrecoverable accounts receivable because more liberal credit policies tend to increase bad debt levels.

When you desire lower ratios, tightening credit policies and attempting to shorten customer payment time can reduce the levels of accounts receivable. In the short-term, this should shift a portion of accounts receivable to cash and thus increase the liquidity of the total current asset account.

Example

Accounts receivable to total current assets = accounts receivable / total current assets

Accounts receivable = 24,878
Total current assets = 44,135

Accounts receivable to total current assets = 24,878 / 44,135 = 0.5637 = 56.37%

Sector	Mid to large cap	Accounts Receivable to Total Current Assets	Small to mid cap	Accounts Receivable to Total Current Assets	Micro to small cap	Accounts Receivable to Total Current Assets
Manufacturing	General Motors	65.42%	Toro	54.90%	Encad	51.03%
Retail	Wal-Mart Stores	5.04%	Bed Bath & Beyond	0.00%	TCBY Enterprises	18.93%
Food	McDonald's	42.33%	Applebee's Int'l	37.29%	Garden Fresh Restaurant	0.00%
Technology	Microsoft	9.19%	Cypress Semiconductor	17.05%	Jmar Technologies	31.90%
Finance	Morgan-Stanley Dean Witter	17.14%	Franklin Resources	19.32%	AmeriTrade Holding	47.90%
Healthcare	Columbia/HCA Healthcare	57.02%	Novacare	77.75%	National Home Health Care	44.43%
Service	Manpower	85.21%	Air & Water Technologies	59.59%	Market Facts	31.83%
Media/Publishing	McGraw Hill	67.05%	Scholastic	30.49%	Thomas Nelson	34.19%

154 Comparing Inventory to Total Current Assets

Equation

Inventory to total current assets = inventory / total current assets

This ratio describes the portion of current assets that inventory represents. Current assets include cash, marketable securities, accounts receivable, inventory, and all other assets that are likely to be held less than one year.

When to use indicator: Managers and creditors can use this indicator to determine the composition and degree of liquidity of current assets.

Meaning of result: A high ratio of inventory to current assets indicates that inventory represents a large part of the current asset account. Inventory is generally one of the least liquid of the current asset accounts.

Ways to improve the indicator: You can increase liquidity by shifting inventory account levels to more liquid accounts such as cash, marketable securities, and accounts receivable. When you desire increased liquidity, seek to reduce inventory requirements by improving production planning systems, product quality, supplier delivery schedules, and the general manner in which your company produces goods or services.

Example

Inventory to total current assets = inventory / total current assets

Inventory = 13,421
Total current assets = 44,135

Inventory to total current assets = 13,421 / 44,135 = 0.3041 = 30.41%

LIQUIDITY

Sector	Mid to large cap	Inventory to Total Current Assets	Small to mid cap	Inventory to Total Current Assets	Micro to small cap	Inventory to Total Current Assets
Manufacturing	General Motors	11.93%	Toro	33.92%	Encad	40.43%
Retail	Wal-Mart Stores	85.25%	Bed Bath & Beyond	82.94%	TCBY Enterprises	23.10%
Food	McDonald's	6.17%	Applebee's Int'l	10.89%	Garden Fresh Restaurant	47.29%
Technology	Microsoft	0.00%	Cypress Semiconductor	19.32%	Jmar Technologies	34.69%
Finance	Morgan-Stanley Dean Witter	30.02%	Franklin Resources	0.00%	AmeriTrade Holding	0.00%
Healthcare	Columbia/HCA Healthcare	10.22%	Novacare	5.59%	National Home Health Care	0.00%
Service	Manpower	0.00%	Air & Water Technologies	1.47%	Market Facts	0.00%
Media/Publishing	McGraw Hill	19.84%	Scholastic	52.08%	Thomas Nelson	38.15%

155 Comparing Other Specific Current Asset Accounts to Total Current Assets

Equation

Notes receivable to total current assets = notes receivable / total current assets

This ratio describes the portion of current assets that specific assets such as notes receivable represent. Current assets include cash, marketable securities, accounts receivable, notes receivable, inventory, and all other assets that are likely to be held less than one year. Notes receivable are funds due to the company in less than one year from persons or companies other than customers.

When to use indicator: Managers and creditors can use this indicator to determine the composition and degree of liquidity of current assets.

Meaning of result: A high ratio of a specific current asset to total current assets indicates that a specific asset comprises a large part of the current asset account. You can determine the degree of current asset liquidity with these ratios since some current assets are more liquid than others.

Ways to improve the indicator: You can increase liquidity by shifting current assets from less to more liquid accounts such as cash, marketable securities, and accounts receivable. When you want increased liquidity, reduce less liquid accounts such as inventory and notes receivable. You can reduce inventory requirements by improving production planning systems, quality, supplier delivery schedules, and the general manner in which your company produces goods or services. You can reduce notes receivable accounts by selling these accounts for cash or other highly liquid equivalents.

Example

Notes receivable to total current assets = notes receivable / total current assets

Notes receivable = 125
Total current assets = 44,135

Notes receivable to total current assets = 125 / 44,135 = 0.0028 = 0.28%

Sector	Mid to large cap	Notes Receivable to Total Current Assets	Small to mid cap	Notes Receivable to Total Current Assets	Micro to small cap	Notes Receivable to Total Current Assets
Manufacturing	General Motors	0.00%	Toro	0.00%	Encad	0.00%
Retail	Wal-Mart Stores	0.00%	Bed Bath & Beyond	0.00%	TCBY Enterprises	4.60%
Food	McDonald's	0.00%	Applebee's Int'l	0.00%	Garden Fresh Restaurant	0.00%
Technology	Microsoft	0.00%	Cypress Semiconductor	0.00%	Jmar Technologies	0.82%
Finance	Morgan-Stanley Dean Witter	0.00%	Franklin Resources	24.47%	AmeriTrade Holding	0.00%
Healthcare	Columbia/HCA Healthcare	0.00%	Novacare	0.00%	National Home Health Care	0.00%
Service	Manpower	0.00%	Air & Water Technologies	0.00%	Market Facts	0.30%
Media/Publishing	McGraw Hill	0.00%	Scholastic	0.00%	Thomas Nelson	0.00%

156 Comparing Specific Expenses Such as Interest and Taxes to Total Current Assets

Equation

Interest expense to total current assets = interest expense / total current assets

This ratio indicates a company's ability to meet individual expenses with current assets.

When to use indicator: Managers can use this indicator to determine the size of individual expenses relative to total current assets. This information can be useful in ensuring adequate liquid assets are available at times when specific expense payments are due such as with tax and interest payments.

Meaning of result: Higher ratios indicate individual expenses that account for larger portions of current assets and will likely put more strain on the more liquid forms of current assets.

Ways to improve the indicator: When ratios are excessive, shifting assets to current accounts such as cash can lower the ratio of expense to current assets and increase company liquidity.

Example

Interest expense to total current assets = interest expense / total current assets

Interest expense = 784
Total current assets = 44,135

Interest expense to total current assets = 784 / 44,135 = 0.0178 = 1.78%

LIQUIDITY

Sector	Mid to large cap	Interest Expense to Total Current Assets	Small to mid cap	Interest Expense to Total Current Assets	Micro to small cap	Interest Expense to Total Current Assets
Manufacturing	General Motors	6.03%	Toro	4.22%	Encad	0.00%
Retail	Wal-Mart Stores	4.05%	Bed Bath & Beyond	0.00%	TCBY Enterprises	1.64%
Food	McDonald's	31.90%	Applebee's Int'l	3.88%	Garden Fresh Restaurant	25.87%
Technology	Microsoft	0.00%	Cypress Semiconductor	1.81%	Jmar Technologies	0.00%
Finance	Morgan-Stanley Dean Witter	0.00%	Franklin Resources	2.09%	AmeriTrade Holding	0.00%
Healthcare	Columbia/HCA Healthcare	11.15%	Novacare	4.62%	National Home Health Care	0.00%
Service	Manpower	0.00%	Air & Water Technologies	18.93%	Market Facts	1.79%
Media/Publishing	McGraw Hill	3.59%	Scholastic	5.25%	Thomas Nelson	3.28%

CHAPTER TEN

Solvency

Solvency ratios describe the ability of a company to meet long-term debt obligations such as loans and leases. The ratios detailed in this chapter describe the ability of a company to meet such debt obligations with operations-related cash flow and income.

157 Determining How Many Times Interest Expense is Earned

Equation

Times interest expense earned = operating income / interest expense

Times interest earned is a measure of how readily a company can meet interest payments with income earned from operations.

When to use indicator: Managers, investors, and creditors can use this indicator to determine the solvency and profitability of a company.

Meaning of result: Higher ratios indicate healthy companies that generate high income streams from operations and/or companies that employ little or no debt. As the times interest earned ratios increase, there is typically less risk to creditors that debt payment schedules will not be met.

Lower ratios indicate highly leveraged firms with significant interest expense and/or those firms that generate small income streams from operations. While creditor risk increases as times interest earned ratios decrease, there is the potential that the leverage gained with the financed debt may allow enhanced future returns. Less mature companies, especially start-ups, will tend to exhibit lower ratios. This is because these companies typically require larger amounts of debt because income generation has not yet reached optimum levels and because growth generally requires cash investments for assets such as inventories and accounts receivable.

Ways to improve the indicator: You can achieve higher ratios by paying off debt and reducing interest expense and/or increasing operations profitability.

Example

Times interest expense earned = operating income / interest expense

Operating income = 9,433
Interest expense = 784

Times interest expense earned = 9,433 / 784 = 12.03 = 1203%

SOLVENCY

Sector	Mid to large cap	Times Interest Expense Earned	Small to mid cap	Times Interest Expense Earned	Micro to small cap	Times Interest Expense Earned
Manufacturing	General Motors	2.51	Toro	3.64	Encad	*
Retail	Wal-Mart Stores	6.58	Bed Bath & Beyond	*	TCBY Enterprises	–1.05
Food	McDonald's	7.40	Applebee's Int'l	42.52	Garden Fresh Restaurant	5.05
Technology	Microsoft	*	Cypress Semiconductor	2.54	Jmar Technologies	*
Finance	Morgan-Stanley Dean Witter	*	Franklin Resources	23.35	AmeriTrade Holding	*
Healthcare	Columbia/HCA Healthcare	3.13	Novacare	6.17	National Home Health Care	*
Service	Manpower	*	Air & Water Technologies	–0.90	Market Facts	9.08
Media/Publishing	McGraw Hill	9.23	Scholastic	2.40	Thomas Nelson	4.08

* Companies without any reported interest expense.

158 Comparing Operations Cash Flow Plus Interest to Interest

Equation

Operations cash flow plus interest to interest = (operations cash flow + interest expense) / interest expense

The ratio of operations cash flow plus interest to interest is a measure of how readily a company can meet interest payments with cash flow generated from operations. Operations cash flow and operating income can vary significantly because a number of factors affect operations cash flow. These factors include operations income, depreciation, and changes in a number of other asset and liability levels such as inventory, accounts receivable, and accounts payable.

When to use indicator: Managers, investors, and creditors can use this indicator to determine the solvency and profitability of a company.

Meaning of result: Higher ratios indicate healthy companies that generate high cash flows from operations and/or companies that employ little or no debt. As the ratio of operations cash flow plus interest to interest increases, there is generally less risk to creditors that debt payment schedules will not be met.

Lower ratios indicate highly leveraged firms with significant interest expense and/or those firms that generate small cash flows from operations. While creditor risk typically increases as the ratio of operations cash flow plus interest to interest decreases, there is the potential that the leverage gained with the financed debt may allow enhanced future returns. Less mature companies, especially start-ups, will tend to exhibit lower ratios because these companies typically require larger amounts of debt. This is because income generation has not yet reached optimum levels and growth generally requires cash investments for assets such as inventories and accounts receivable.

Ways to improve the indicator: You can achieve higher ratios by paying off debt, reducing interest expense levels, and/or increasing operations cash flow.

Example

Operations cash flow plus interest to interest = (operations cash flow + interest expense) / interest expense

Operations cash flow = 4,820
Interest expense = 784

Operations cash flow plus interest to interest = (4,820 + 784) / 784 = 7.148 = 714.8%

Sector	Mid to large cap	Operations Cash Flow Plus Interest to Interest	Small to mid cap	Operations Cash Flow Plus Interest to Interest	Micro to small cap	Operations Cash Flow Plus Interest to Interest
Manufacturing	General Motors	369%	Toro	521%	Encad	*
Retail	Wal-Mart Stores	1009%	Bed Bath & Beyond	*	TCBY Enterprises	2350%
Food	McDonald's	770%	Applebee's Int'l	5225%	Garden Fresh Restaurant	864%
Technology	Microsoft	*	Cypress Semiconductor	1240%	Jmar Technologies	*
Finance	Morgan-Stanley Dean Witter	*	Franklin Resources	1792%	AmeriTrade Holding	*
Healthcare	Columbia/HCA Healthcare	401%	Novacare	410%	National Home Health Care	*
Service	Manpower	*	Air & Water Technologies	162%	Market Facts	1005%
Media/Publishing	McGraw Hill	810%	Scholastic	686%	Thomas Nelson	233%

* Companies without any reported interest expense.

159 Finding How Many Times Debt Expenses are Covered

Equation

Times debt expenses covered = operating income / debt expenses

Times debt expenses covered is a measure of how readily a company can meet interest and principal payments with income earned from operations.

When to use indicator: Managers, investors, and creditors can use this indicator to determine the solvency and profitability of a company.

Meaning of result: Higher ratios indicate healthy companies that generate high income streams from operations and/or companies that employ little or no debt. As the times debt expenses ratios increase, there is typically less risk to creditors that debt payment schedules will not be met.

Lower ratios indicate highly leveraged firms with significant principal and interest expense and/or those firms that generate small income streams from operations. While creditor risk increases as times debt expenses covered ratios decrease, there is the potential that the leverage gained with the financed debt may allow enhanced future returns. Less mature companies, especially start-ups, will tend to exhibit lower ratios because these companies typically require larger amounts of debt. This is true because income generation has not yet reached optimum levels and growth generally requires cash investments for assets such as inventories and accounts receivable.

Ways to improve the indicator: You can achieve higher ratios by paying off debt and reducing interest and principal expenses and/or increasing operations profitability.

Example

Times debt expenses covered = operating income / debt expenses

Operating income = 9,433
Debt expenses = interest expense + tax adjusted principal repayment
Interest expense = 784
Tax adjusted principal repayment = principal / (1 − tax rate)
Principal = current portion of long-term debt = 650
Tax rate = 40%

Times debt expenses covered = 9,433 / (784 + [650/(1 − 0.40)]) = 5.052 = 505%

SOLVENCY

Sector	Mid to large cap	Times Debt Expenses Covered	Small to mid cap	Times Debt Expenses Covered	Micro to small cap	Times Debt Expenses Covered
Manufacturing	General Motors	2.51	Toro	3.53	Encad	*
Retail	Wal-Mart Stores	2.05	Bed Bath & Beyond	*	TCBY Enterprises	−0.13
Food	McDonald's	2.92	Applebee's Int'l	5.93	Garden Fresh Restaurant	0.88
Technology	Microsoft	*	Cypress Semiconductor	2.54	Jmar Technologies	*
Finance	Morgan-Stanley Dean Witter	*	Franklin Resources	23.35	AmeriTrade Holding	*
Healthcare	Columbia/HCA Healthcare	2.17	Novacare	2.25	National Home Health Care	*
Service	Manpower	118.97	Air & Water Technologies	−0.87	Market Facts	7.56
Media/Publishing	McGraw Hill	9.23	Scholastic	2.34	Thomas Nelson	2.02

* Companies without any reported debt expenses.

160 Comparing Operations Cash Flow Plus Debt Expenses to Debt Expenses

Equation

Operations cash flow plus debt expenses to debt expenses = (operations cash flow + debt expenses) / debt expenses

Operations cash flow plus debt expenses to debt expenses is a measure of how readily a company can meet principal and interest payments with cash flow generated from operations. Operations cash flow and operating income can vary significantly since a number of factors affect operations cash flow. These factors include operations income, depreciation, and changes in a number of other asset and liability levels such as inventory, accounts receivable, and accounts payable.

When to use indicator: Managers, investors, and creditors can use this indicator to determine the solvency and profitability of a company.

Meaning of result: Higher ratios indicate healthy companies that generate high cash flows from operations and/or companies that employ little or no debt. As the ratio increases, there is generally less risk to creditors that debt payment schedules will not be met.

Lower ratios indicate highly leveraged firms with significant principal and interest expense and/or those firms that generate small cash flows from operations. While creditor risk typically increases as the ratio of operations cash flow plus debt expense to debt expense decreases, there is the potential that the leverage gained with the financed debt may allow enhanced future returns. Less mature companies, especially start-ups, will tend to exhibit lower ratios since these companies typically require larger amounts of debt. This is true because income generation has not yet reached optimum levels and growth generally requires cash investments for assets such as inventories and accounts receivable.

Ways to improve the indicator: You can achieve higher ratios by paying off debt, reducing interest expense levels, and/or increasing operations cash flow.

Example

Operations cash flow plus debt expenses to debt expenses = (operations cash flow + debt expenses) / debt expenses

Operations cash flow = 4,820
Debt expenses = interest expense + tax adjusted principal repayment
Interest expense = 784
Tax adjusted principal repayment = principal / (1 − tax rate)
Principal = current portion of long-term debt = 650
Tax rate = 40%
Debt expenses = 784 + (650 / [1 − 0.40]) = 1,867

Operations cash flow plus debt expenses to debt expenses = (4,820 + 1,867) / 1,867 = 3.582 = 358.2%

Sector	Mid to large cap	Operations Cash Flow Plus Debt Expenses to Debt Expenses	Small to mid cap	Operations Cash Flow Plus Debt Expenses to Debt Expenses	Micro to small cap	Operations Cash Flow Plus Debt Expenses to Debt Expenses
Manufacturing	General Motors	369%	Toro	509%	Encad	*
Retail	Wal-Mart Stores	383%	Bed Bath & Beyond	*	TCBY Enterprises	383%
Food	McDonald's	364%	Applebee's Int'l	815%	Garden Fresh Restaurant	234%
Technology	Microsoft	*	Cypress Semiconductor	1240%	Jmar Technologies	*
Finance	Morgan-Stanley Dean Witter	*	Franklin Resources	1792%	AmeriTrade Holding	*
Healthcare	Columbia/HCA Healthcare	308%	Novacare	213%	National Home Health Care	*
Service	Manpower	1782%	Air & Water Technologies	160%	Market Facts	853%
Media/Publishing	McGraw Hill	810%	Scholastic	671%	Thomas Nelson	166%

* Companies without any reported debt expenses.

161 Finding How Many Times the Long-Term Debt is Covered

Equation

Times long-term debt covered = operating income / long-term debt

Times long-term debt covered is a measure of how readily a company can pay off long-term debt with income earned from operations.

When to use indicator: Managers, investors, and creditors can use this indicator to determine the size of long-term debt relative to company earning power.

Meaning of result: Higher ratios indicate healthy companies that generate high income streams from operations and/or companies that employ little or no debt. As the times long-term debt ratio increases, there is typically less risk to creditors that debt payment schedules will not be met.

Lower ratios indicate highly leveraged firms with significant amounts of long-term debt and/or those firms that generate small income streams from operations. While creditor risk increases as times long-term debt covered ratios decrease, there is the potential that the leverage gained with the financed debt may allow enhanced future returns. Less mature companies, especially start-ups, will tend to exhibit lower ratios because these companies typically require larger amounts of debt. This is true because income generation has not yet reached optimum levels and growth generally requires cash investments for assets such as inventories and accounts receivable.

Ways to improve the indicator: You can achieve higher ratios by paying off debt and/or increasing operations profitability.

Example

Times long-term debt covered = operating income / long-term debt

Operating income = 9,433
Long-term debt = 25,180 – 12,032 = 13,148

Times long-term debt covered = 9,433 / 13,148 = 0.7174 = 71.74%

Sector	Mid to large cap	Times Long-Term Debt Covered	Small to mid cap	Times Long-Term Debt Covered	Micro to small cap	Times Long-Term Debt Covered
Manufacturing	General Motors	0.08	Toro	0.40	Encad	20.81
Retail	Wal-Mart Stores	0.49	Bed Bath & Beyond	9.45	TCBY Enterprises	–0.08
Food	McDonald's	0.42	Applebee's Int'l	2.95	Garden Fresh Restaurant	0.55
Technology	Microsoft	*	Cypress Semiconductor	0.08	Jmar Technologies	1.68
Finance	Morgan-Stanley Dean Witter	0.17	Franklin Resources	1.11	AmeriTrade Holding	*
Healthcare	Columbia/HCA Healthcare	0.14	Novacare	0.27	National Home Health Care	10.44
Service	Manpower	0.60	Air & Water Technologies	–0.07	Market Facts	0.99
Media/Publishing	McGraw Hill	0.45	Scholastic	0.18	Thomas Nelson	0.29

* Companies without any reported long-term debt.

162 Comparing Operations Cash Flow to Long-Term Debt

Equation

Operations cash flow to long-term debt = operations cash flow / long-term debt

Operations cash flow to long-term debt is a measure of how readily a company can pay off long-term debt with cash flow generated from operations. Operations cash flow and operating income can vary significantly since a number of factors affect operations cash flow. These factors include operations income, depreciation, and changes in a number of other asset and liability levels such as inventory, accounts receivable, and accounts payable.

When to use indicator: Managers, investors, and creditors can use this indicator to determine the size of long-term debt relative to company cash flow generating power.

Meaning of result: Higher ratios indicate healthy companies that generate high cash flows from operations and/or companies that employ little or no debt. As the ratio increases, there is generally less risk to creditors that debt payment schedules will not be met.

Lower ratios indicate highly leveraged firms with significant amounts of long-term debt and/or those firms that generate small cash flows from operations. While creditor risk typically increases as the ratio of operations cash flow to long-term debt decreases, there is the potential that the leverage gained with the financed debt may allow enhanced future returns. Less mature companies, especially start-ups, will tend to exhibit lower ratios since these companies typically require larger amounts of debt. This is true because income generation has not yet reached optimum levels and growth generally requires cash investments for assets such as inventories and accounts receivable.

Ways to improve the indicator: You can achieve higher ratios by paying off debt and/or increasing operations cash flow.

Example

Operations cash flow to long-term debt = operations cash flow / long-term debt

Operations cash flow = 4,820
Long-term debt = 25,180 − 12,032 = 13,148

Operations cash flow to long-term debt = 4,820 / 13,148 = 0.367 = 36.7%

Sector	Mid to large cap	Operations Cash Flow to Long-Term Debt	Small to mid cap	Operations Cash Flow to Long-Term Debt	Micro to small cap	Operations Cash Flow to Long-Term Debt
Manufacturing	General Motors	8.45%	Toro	45.92%	Encad	−233.70%
Retail	Wal-Mart Stores	67.95%	Bed Bath & Beyond	380.52%	TCBY Enterprises	168.49%
Food	McDonald's	38.13%	Applebee's Int'l	356.02%	Garden Fresh Restaurant	84.01%
Technology	Microsoft	*	Cypress Semiconductor	37.33%	Jmar Technologies	0.00%
Finance	Morgan-Stanley Dean Witter	−2.28%	Franklin Resources	80.69%	AmeriTrade Holding	*
Healthcare	Columbia/HCA Healthcare	13.31%	Novacare	13.64%	National Home Health Care	758.86%
Service	Manpower	8.50%	Air & Water Technologies	4.87%	Market Facts	98.40%
Media/Publishing	McGraw Hill	34.43%	Scholastic	44.33%	Thomas Nelson	9.61%

* Companies without any reported long-term debt.

163 Finding How Many Times Fixed Costs are Covered

Equation

Times fixed costs covered = operating income / fixed costs

Times fixed costs covered is a measure of the relative sizes of operating income and the amount of fixed costs employed to run a business. The total cost to produce a product or service includes variable and fixed costs. Fixed costs are those costs that remain relatively constant regardless of the quantity of goods or services produced while variable costs are those costs that change with volume. Examples of fixed costs are building rent, interest payments, and salaries for nonmanufacturing employees such as engineers and accountants. Variable costs include such items as raw materials, direct labor, and the fuel used to operate machinery.

When to use indicator: Managers, investors, and creditors can use this indicator to determine the size of fixed costs relative to company earning power.

Meaning of result: Higher ratios indicate healthy companies that generate high income streams from operations and/or companies that operate with smaller fixed costs. As the times fixed costs covered increases, there is typically less risk to creditors that debt payment schedules will not be met.

Lower ratios indicate highly leveraged firms with significant amounts of fixed costs given the size of operating income. Creditor risk generally increases as times fixed cost covered ratios decrease since there is greater potential that income generated from operations may not be sufficient to cover fixed costs.

Ways to improve the indicator: You can achieve higher ratios by lowering fixed costs and/or increasing operations profitability. You can lower fixed costs by shifting a portion of fixed costs to variable costs by producing more labor- and material-dependent products or services. You can also achieve this with outsourcing, using contractors for design work, manufacturing, sales and marketing, etc. Contractor use is typically more variable in nature than the use of in-house, fixed-cost expertise.

Example

Times fixed costs covered = operating income / fixed costs

Operating income = 9,433
Fixed cost = costs that are independent of the number of goods or services produced
Total cost of goods sold = 54,212
Raw material cost = 31,063
    Direct labor = 7,860
    Overhead cost = 15,164
Other direct costs = 125
R&D costs = 4,578
SG&A costs = 15,993
Depreciation & amortization = 1,204
Interest = 784

Fixed costs = overhead cost + other direct costs + R&D cost + SG&A cost + depreciation & amortization + interest = 15,164 + 125 + 4,578 + 15,993 + 1,204 + 784 = 37,848

Times fixed costs covered = 9,433 / 37,848 = 0.249 = 24.9%

Sector	Mid to large cap	Times Fixed Costs Covered	Small to mid cap	Times Fixed Costs Covered	Micro to small cap	Times Fixed Costs Covered
Manufacturing	General Motors	0.39	Toro	0.22	Encad	0.60
Retail	Wal-Mart Stores	0.26	Bed Bath & Beyond	0.37	TCBY Enterprises	−0.03
Food	McDonald's	1.11	Applebee's Int'l	1.26	Garden Fresh Restaurant	0.13
Technology	Microsoft	1.09	Cypress Semiconductor	0.10	Jmar Technologies	0.21
Finance	Morgan-Stanley Dean Witter	0.77	Franklin Resources	1.35	AmeriTrade Holding	0.66
Healthcare	Columbia/HCA Healthcare	0.17	Novacare	0.52	National Home Health Care	0.37
Service	Manpower	0.24	Air & Water Technologies	−0.19	Market Facts	0.30
Media/Publishing	McGraw Hill	0.33	Scholastic	0.10	Thomas Nelson	0.26

164 Comparing Operations Cash Flow Plus Fixed Costs to Fixed Costs

Equation

Operations cash flow plus fixed costs to fixed costs = (operations cash flow plus fixed costs) / fixed costs

Operations cash flow plus fixed costs to fixed costs is a measure of the relative size of operating cash flow and the amount of fixed costs employed to run a business. Operations cash flow and operating income can vary significantly since a number of factors affect operations cash flow. These factors include operations income, depreciation, and changes in a number of other asset and liability levels such as inventory, accounts receivable, and accounts payable. The total cost to produce a product or service consists of variable and fixed costs. Fixed costs are those costs that remain relatively constant regardless of the quantity of goods or services produced while variable costs are those costs that change with volume. Fixed costs include such items as building rent, interest payments, and salaries for nonmanufacturing employees such as engineers and accountants. Variable costs include such items as raw materials, direct labor, and the fuel used to operate machinery.

When to use indicator: Managers, investors, and creditors can use this indicator to determine the size of fixed costs relative to cash flow generated from operations.

Meaning of result: Higher ratios indicate healthy companies that generate high cash flows from operations and/or companies that employ smaller percentages of fixed costs. As the ratio increases, there is generally less risk to creditors that debt payment expenses will not be met.

Lower ratios indicate highly leveraged firms with significant amounts of fixed costs given the size of cash flow generated from operations. Creditor risk generally increases as the ratio of operations cash flow plus fixed costs to fixed costs decreases since there is greater potential that the cash generated from operations may not be sufficient to cover fixed costs.

Ways to improve the indicator: You can achieve higher ratios by lowering fixed costs and/or increasing operations cash flows. You can lower fixed costs by shifting a portion of fixed costs to variable costs by producing more labor- and material-dependent products or services. You can also achieve this with outsourcing, using contractors for design work, manufacturing, sales and marketing, etc. Contractor use is typically more variable in nature than the use of in-house, fixed-cost expertise.

Example

Operations cash flow plus fixed costs to fixed costs = (operations cash flow plus fixed costs) / fixed costs

Sector	Mid to large cap	Operations Cash Flow Plus Fixed Costs to Fixed Costs	Small to mid cap	Operations Cash Flow Plus Fixed Costs to Fixed Costs	Micro to small cap	Operations Cash Flow Plus Fixed Costs to Fixed Costs
Manufacturing	General Motors	142%	Toro	125%	Encad	93%
Retail	Wal-Mart Stores	135%	Bed Bath & Beyond	115%	TCBY Enterprises	154%
Food	McDonald's	201%	Applebee's Int'l	252%	Garden Fresh Restaurant	120%
Technology	Microsoft	208%	Cypress Semiconductor	147%	Jmar Technologies	100%
Finance	Morgan-Stanley Dean Witter	89%	Franklin Resources	198%	AmeriTrade Holding	172%
Healthcare	Columbia/HCA Healthcare	116%	Novacare	126%	National Home Health Care	127%
Service	Manpower	103%	Air & Water Technologies	113%	Market Facts	130%
Media/Publishing	McGraw Hill	126%	Scholastic	124%	Thomas Nelson	108%

Operations cash flow = 4,820
Fixed cost = costs that are independent of the number of goods or services produced
Total cost of goods sold = 54,212

Raw material cost = 31,063
Direct labor = 7,860
Overhead cost = 15,164
Other direct costs = 125

R&D costs = 4,578
SG&A costs = 15,993

Depreciation & amortization = 1,204
Interest = 784

Fixed cost = overhead cost + other direct costs + R&D costs + SG&A costs + depreciation & amortization + interest = 15,164 + 125 + 4,578 + 15,993 + 1,204 + 784 = 37,848

Operations cash flow plus fixed costs to fixed costs = (4,820 + 37,848) / 37,848 = 1.127 = 112.7%

SOLVENCY

165 Determining How Many Times Operating Expenses are Covered

Equation

Times operating expenses covered = operating income / operating expenses

Times operating expenses covered is a measure of the relative size of operating income and the operating expenses incurred in running a business. Operating expenses include all items that are incurred to provide services or manufacture products such as employee salaries, benefits, product raw materials, building rent, and utilities.

When to use indicator: Managers, investors, and creditors can use this indicator to determine the size of operating expenses relative to company earning power.

Meaning of result: Higher ratios can indicate the ready ability to pay operating expenses with income generated from operations. Lower ratios can indicate difficulty in meeting operating expenses with operating income. In such cases, it is often necessary to finance operating expenses with debt and/or issuance of stock.

Ways to improve the indicator: You can increase times operating expenses covered by increasing operating income and/or decreasing operating expenses. You can decrease operating expenses by reducing the direct costs to manufacture products or provide services and by reducing other operational expenses such as rent, travel expense, and interest payments.

Example

Times operating expenses covered = operating income / operating expenses

Operations income = 9,433

Annual pre-tax operating expenses = cost of goods sold + R&D + SG&A + interest + all other operating expenses = 54,212 + 4,578 + 15,993 + 784 = 75,567

Times operating expenses covered = 9,433 / 75,567 = 0.125 = 12.5%

Sector	Mid to large cap	Times Operating Expenses Covered	Small to mid cap	Times Operating Expenses Covered	Micro to small cap	Times Operating Expenses Covered
Manufacturing	General Motors	0.10	Toro	0.07	Encad	0.22
Retail	Wal-Mart Stores	0.05	Bed Bath & Beyond	0.13	TCBY Enterprises	−0.01
Food	McDonald's	0.30	Applebee's Int'l	0.16	Garden Fresh Restaurant	0.10
Technology	Microsoft	0.92	Cypress Semiconductor	0.03	Jmar Technologies	0.08
Finance	Morgan-Stanley Dean Witter	0.19	Franklin Resources	0.38	AmeriTrade Holding	0.29
Healthcare	Columbia/HCA Healthcare	0.09	Novacare	0.10	National Home Health Care	0.10
Service	Manpower	0.04	Air & Water Technologies	−0.04	Market Facts	0.11
Media/Publishing	McGraw Hill	0.17	Scholastic	0.05	Thomas Nelson	0.11

166 Comparing Operations Cash Flow Plus Operating Expenses to Operating Expenses

Equation

Operations cash flow plus operating expenses to operating expenses = (operations cash flow + operating expenses) / operating expenses

The ratio indicates the relationship between cash generated from operations and yearly operational expenses. Operations cash flow and operating income can vary significantly since a number of factors can affect operations cash flow. These factors include operations income, depreciation, and changes in a number of other asset and liability levels such as inventory, accounts receivable, and accounts payable. Operating expenses include all items that are incurred to provide services or manufacture products such as employee salaries, benefits, product raw materials, building rent, and utilities.

When to use indicator: Creditors and investors can use this indicator to determine how readily a company can pay operating expenses with cash generated from operations.

Meaning of result: Higher ratios can indicate the ready ability to pay operating expenses with cash generated from operations. Lower ratios can indicate difficulty in meeting operating expenses with operations cash flow. In such cases, it is often necessary to finance operating expenses with debt and/or issuance of stock.

Ways to improve the indicator: You can increase the ratio of operations cash flow plus operating expenses to operating expenses by increasing operations cash flow and/or decreasing operating expenses. You can increase operating cash flow by selling more high-profit-margin, highly demanded products or services. You can decrease operating expenses by reducing the direct costs to manufacture products or provide services and by reducing other operational expenses such as rent, travel expense, and interest payments.

Example

Operations cash flow plus operating expenses to operating expenses = (operations cash flow + operating expenses) / operating expenses

Operations cash flow = 4,820
Annual pre-tax operating expenses = cost of goods sold + R&D + SG&A + interest + all other operating expenses = 54,212 + 4,578 + 15,993 + 784 + 0 = 75,567

Operations cash flow plus operating expenses to operating expenses = (4,820 + 77,567) / 75,567 = 1.062 = 106.2%

SOLVENCY

Sector	Mid to large cap	Operations Cash Flow Plus Operating Expenses to Operating Expenses	Small to mid cap	Operations Cash Flow Plus Operating Expenses to Operating Expenses	Micro to small cap	Operations Cash Flow Plus Operating Expenses to Operating Expenses
Manufacturing	General Motors	111%	Toro	108%	Encad	98%
Retail	Wal-Mart Stores	106%	Bed Bath & Beyond	105%	TCBY Enterprises	119%
Food	McDonald's	127%	Applebee's Int'l	120%	Garden Fresh Restaurant	116%
Technology	Microsoft	191%	Cypress Semiconductor	115%	Jmar Technologies	100%
Finance	Morgan-Stanley Dean Witter	97%	Franklin Resources	127%	AmeriTrade Holding	132%
Healthcare	Columbia/HCA Healthcare	109%	Novacare	105%	National Home Health Care	108%
Service	Manpower	101%	Air & Water Technologies	103%	Market Facts	111%
Media/Publishing	McGraw Hill	113%	Scholastic	112%	Thomas Nelson	103%

167 Determining How Many Days of Operating Expense Payables are Outstanding

Equation

Days of operating expense payables = operating expenses outstanding / (annual pretax operating expenses/365)

This formula indicates how many days of average operating expenses are as yet unpaid. Operating expenses include all items that are incurred to provide services or manufacture products such as employee salaries, benefits, product raw materials, building rent, and utilities. Operating expenses outstanding include accounts payable and all other deferred operating expenses such as unpaid salaries, benefits, and rent. A manager should consider this indicator as pretax days of payables. By including taxes as an operating expense, you can determine after-tax days of payables.

When to use indicator: Creditors and investors can use this indicator to determine the size of operating expense debt that is outstanding. This ratio can help determine the financial health of a company.

Meaning of result: Higher ratios indicate larger portions of outstanding expense-related debt. High and higher trending ratios can signal the potential for financial difficulties. It may become difficult to receive trade credit when many days of payables are outstanding. High days of payables may be the result of accounting efforts to increase income statement performance. As a company defers more operating expenses, it artificially inflates net income.

Lower ratios indicate companies that quickly pay off expense-related debt. Suppliers often extend free credit for 30, 60, or more days. Very low ratios can indicate that the company is foregoing this interest-free credit benefit.

Ways to improve the indicator: You can lower days of payables by paying accounts payable balances more quickly and/or limiting deferred expense accounts such as salaries and benefits payable. You can increase days of payables by deferring payment of more operating expenses.

Example

Days of operating expense payables = operating expenses outstanding / (annual pretax operating expenses/365)

Operating expenses outstanding = accounts payable + all other deferred operating expenses = 5,633 + 2,747 (assume here that all accrued liabilities are operating expenses and that there are no notes payable that were utilized for operating expenses) = 8,380

Annual pretax operating expenses = cost of goods sold + R&D + SG&A + interest + all other operating expenses = 54,212 + 4,578 + 15,993 + 784 + 0 = 75,567

Days of operating expense payables = 8,380 / (75,567/365) = 40.5 days

Sector	Mid to large cap	Days of Operating Expense Payables	Small to mid cap	Days of Operating Expense Payables	Micro to small cap	Days of Operating Expense Payables
Manufacturing	General Motors	37.81	Toro	71.80	Encad	62.66
Retail	Wal-Mart Stores	40.99	Bed Bath & Beyond	53.28	TCBY Enterprises	33.76
Food	McDonald's	46.40	Applebee's Int'l	41.97	Garden Fresh Restaurant	44.26
Technology	Microsoft	54.09	Cypress Semiconductor	56.35	Jmar Technologies	44.03
Finance	Morgan-Stanley Dean Witter	795.42	Franklin Resources	46.79	AmeriTrade Holding	102.06
Healthcare	Columbia/HCA Healthcare	58.32	Novacare	49.99	National Home Health Care	15.41
Service	Manpower	47.96	Air & Water Technologies	125.27	Market Facts	49.92
Media/Publishing	McGraw Hill	74.53	Scholastic	58.97	Thomas Nelson	56.25

168 Finding How Many Times Asset Additions are Covered

Equation

Times asset additions covered = operating income / changes in assets

Times asset additions covered is a measure of the extent to which income generated by operations purchased asset additions. Short-term asset additions include increases in accounts such as inventory, cash, marketable securities, and accounts receivable. Long-term asset additions can include increases in accounts such as plant equipment, buildings, and other long-term investments.

When to use indicator: Managers, investors, and creditors can use this indicator to determine the size of asset additions relative to company earning power.

Meaning of result: Higher ratios indicate high income streams generated from operations and/or smaller increases in asset additions.

Lower ratios can indicate lower or negative operating income streams and/or larger asset additions.

This indicator can vary significantly with time because large dollar amount asset purchases can significantly reduce times asset additions covered. When there is a net reduction in assets, times asset additions covered is not applicable.

Ways to improve the indicator: Increasing operating income can increase this ratio, given a fixed amount of asset additions. Although asset additions can lower this ratio, this can be a positive signal, assuming the additional assets help generate larger future income streams.

Example

Times asset additions covered = operating income / changes in assets

Operating income = 9,433
Changes in assets = 56,268 − 45,464 = 10,804

Times asset additions covered = 9,433 / 10,804 = 0.873 = 87.3%

SOLVENCY

Sector	Mid to large cap	Times Asset Additions Covered	Small to mid cap	Times Asset Additions Covered	Micro to small cap	Times Asset Additions Covered
Manufacturing	General Motors	2.27	Toro	0.44	Encad	0.81
Retail	Wal-Mart Stores	0.89	Bed Bath & Beyond	0.93	TCBY Enterprises	0.25
Food	McDonald's	3.15	Applebee's Int'l	1.14	Garden Fresh Restaurant	0.56
Technology	Microsoft	0.87	Cypress Semiconductor	0.11	Jmar Technologies	0.82
Finance	Morgan-Stanley Dean Witter	0.07	Franklin Resources	0.82	AmeriTrade Holding	0.06
Healthcare	Columbia/HCA Healthcare	1.74	Novacare	0.42	National Home Health Care	4.11
Service	Manpower	0.87	Air & Water Technologies	0.19	Market Facts	0.21
Media/Publishing	McGraw Hill	5.90	Scholastic	−2.52	Thomas Nelson	−1.52

169 Comparing Operations Cash Flow to Changes in Assets

Equation

Operations cash flow to changes in assets = operating cash flow / changes in assets

The ratio of operations cash flow to changes in assets is a measure of the percentage of asset additions that cash generated from operations can pay. Operations cash flow and operating income can vary significantly since a number of factors affect operations cash flow. These factors include operations income, depreciation, and changes in a number of other asset and liability levels such as inventory, accounts receivable, and accounts payable. Asset changes include both short- and long-term asset additions/reductions. Short-term asset changes include changes in accounts such as inventory, cash, marketable securities, and accounts receivable. Long-term asset changes can include increases in accounts such as plant equipment, buildings, and other long-term investments.

When to use indicator: Managers, investors, and creditors can use this indicator to determine the size of operations cash-generating capacity relative to increases in assets.

Meaning of result: Higher ratios indicate high cash flow streams generated from operations and/or smaller increases in asset additions.

Lower ratios indicate lower operating cash flow streams and/or larger asset additions. This indicator can vary significantly with time because large dollar amount asset purchases can significantly reduce operations cash flow to asset change ratios. When there is a net reduction in assets, operations cash flow to changes in assets is not applicable.

Ways to improve the indicator: Increasing operating cash flow can increase this ratio, given a fixed amount of asset additions. Although asset additions can lower this ratio, this can be a positive signal, assuming the additional assets help generate larger future income streams.

Example

Operations cash flow to changes in assets = operating cash flow / changes in assets

Operating cash flow = 4,820
    Changes in assets = 56,268 − 45,464 = 10,804

Operations cash flow to changes in assets = 4,820 / 10,804 = 0.446 = 44.6%

Sector	Mid to large cap	Operations Cash Flow to Changes in Assets	Small to mid cap	Operations Cash Flow to Changes in Assets	Micro to small cap	Operations Cash Flow to Changes in Assets
Manufacturing	General Motors	243.91%	Toro	50.91%	Encad	−9.06%
Retail	Wal-Mart Stores	123.24%	Bed Bath & Beyond	37.31%	TCBY Enterprises	−533.48%
Food	McDonald's	285.48%	Applebee's Int'l	137.90%	Garden Fresh Restaurant	84.10%
Technology	Microsoft	86.32%	Cypress Semiconductor	50.57%	Jmar Technologies	0.00%
Finance	Morgan-Stanley Dean Witter	−0.93%	Franklin Resources	59.43%	AmeriTrade Holding	6.68%
Healthcare	Columbia/HCA Healthcare	167.38%	Novacare	21.04%	National Home Health Care	298.63%
Service	Manpower	12.25%	Air & Water Technologies	−13.23%	Market Facts	21.12%
Media/Publishing	McGraw Hill	453.67%	Scholastic	−616.23%	Thomas Nelson	−49.66%

170 Comparing Retained Earnings to Total Assets

Equation

Retained earnings to total assets = retained earnings / total assets

This ratio helps managers determine the percentage of company assets that were purchased with retained earnings instead of with other sources of cash such as the issuance of stock or debt. Retained earnings describe what remains of net income after dividends are paid.

When to use indicator: Investors can use this indicator to determine a company's financial performance. Profitable, well-run firms tend to generate healthy quantities of net income and plow back a portion of this income for the purchase of additional company assets. Reinvestment in the company can help ensure long-term revenues and earnings growth.

Meaning of result: Higher ratios indicate that retained earnings purchase larger portions of company assets. This is generally a positive sign that the company is generating positive income streams from operations and looking to the future by reinvesting a portion of profits in the company asset base. Reinvestment can take many forms such as updating obsolete equipment, acquiring a subsidiary, increasing inventories, and building new office buildings.

Lower ratios indicate larger portions of company assets are purchased with debt or from cash generated from the issuance of stock. This is often true of start-up and less mature companies whose income-generating capabilities have not yet reached full stride. This can also occur with mature companies that are experiencing difficulties in maintaining healthy profit margins.

Ways to improve the indicator: You can improve this ratio by generating higher percentages of retained earnings. You can improve retained earnings generation by providing highly demanded products or services with large profit margins. You can optimize profit margins with excellent marketing, product/service design and quality, cost control, and customer service.

Example

Retained earnings to total assets = retained earnings / total assets

Retained earnings = 18,722
Total assets = 56,268

Retained earnings to total assets = 18,722 / 56,268 = 0.333 = 33.3%

SOLVENCY

Sector	Mid to large cap	Retained Earnings to Total Assets	Small to mid cap	Retained Earnings to Total Assets	Micro to small cap	Retained Earnings to Total Assets
Manufacturing	General Motors	2.37%	Toro	30.63%	Encad	52.20%
Retail	Wal-Mart Stores	40.03%	Bed Bath & Beyond	50.76%	TCBY Enterprises	69.73%
Food	McDonald's	68.90%	Applebee's Int'l	35.67%	Garden Fresh Restaurant	−7.48%
Technology	Microsoft	34.09%	Cypress Semiconductor	34.92%	Jmar Technologies	0.00%
Finance	Morgan-Stanley Dean Witter	3.09%	Franklin Resources	56.78%	AmeriTrade Holding	5.75%
Healthcare	Columbia/HCA Healthcare	16.63%	Novacare	28.82%	National Home Health Care	23.16%
Service	Manpower	−41.44%	Air & Water Technologies	−139.72%	Market Facts	14.58%
Media/Publishing	McGraw Hill	41.42%	Scholastic	20.20%	Thomas Nelson	21.11%

CHAPTER ELEVEN

Leverage

Leverage entails using debt in the hope of increasing company revenue and profit. You can increase revenue and profit by using debt for the purchase of assets such as additional, or more efficient, machinery and for non-asset-related items such as increased advertising or additional sales force. The ratios described in this chapter detail a number of ways in which you can monitor leverage levels and types. In addition to studying these ratios, review tip #115, the debt to equity ratio.

171 Comparing Debt to the Market Value of Equity

Equation

Debt to market value of equity = total liabilities / market value of equity

This ratio describes the relationship between a company's debt and its equity. Since equity market values can be quite different from book values, the values shown on the balance sheet, this ratio can give a more accurate portrayal of debt to equity. Total liabilities include all debt such as loans payable to lenders, accounts payable to suppliers, and income taxes payable to the government.

When to use indicator: Creditors, investors, and managers can use this indicator to determine the risk level associated with a company's debt burden.

Meaning of result: Creditors generally frown on higher ratios since this indicates the company may be stretched to meet debt interest payments and because creditors like to see a substantial investment by the owners. Investors are more likely to view higher ratios in a positive light because the leverage gained with debt financing may lead to greater returns on equity investment.

Ways to improve the indicator: Paying down debt levels with operating income or owner's equity can reduce the debt-to-equity ratio. You can increase the debt-to-equity ratio, and thus increase company leverage, with the acquisition of additional debt.

Example

Debt to market value of equity = total liabilities / market value of equity

Total liabilities = 25,180
Market value of equity = (3,600 common shares × $22.50/share) + (15 preferred shares × $25.00/share) = 81,375

Debt to market value of equity = 25,180 / 81,375 = 0.3094 = 30.94%

LEVERAGE

Sector	Mid to large cap	Debt to Market Value of Equity	Small to mid cap	Debt to Market Value of Equity	Micro to small cap	Debt to Market Value of Equity
Manufacturing	General Motors	433.93%	Toro	101.64%	Encad	17.26%
Retail	Wal-Mart Stores	18.40%	Bed Bath & Beyond	4.40%	TCBY Enterprises	10.01%
Food	McDonald's	19.29%	Applebee's Int'l	12.15%	Garden Fresh Restaurant	36.52%
Technology	Microsoft	2.15%	Cypress Semiconductor	41.81%	Jmar Technologies	10.16%
Finance	Morgan-Stanley Dean Witter	538.26%	Franklin Resources	9.19%	AmeriTrade Holding	163.97%
Healthcare	Columbia/HCA Healthcare	72.61%	Novacare	72.81%	National Home Health Care	7.10%
Service	Manpower	64.11%	Air & Water Technologies	530.79%	Market Facts	17.98%
Media/Publishing	McGraw Hill	28.37%	Scholastic	73.09%	Thomas Nelson	58.58%

172 Comparing Current Debt to the Market Value of Equity

Equation

Current debt to market value of equity = current liabilities / market value of equity

This ratio describes the relationship between a company's short-term debt and its equity. Since equity market values can be quite different from the book value, the values shown on the balance sheet, this ratio can give an accurate portrayal of short-term debt to equity. Current liabilities include short-term debt such as accounts payable to suppliers, notes payable to lenders, deferred liabilities, and income taxes payable to the government.

When to use indicator: Creditors, investors, and managers can use this indicator to determine the risk level associated with a company's short-term debt burden.

Meaning of result: Higher ratios indicate larger current debt accounts. This can indicate a number of situations including the financing of both short- and long-lived assets with short-term debt, companies that are experiencing financial difficulties, and start-up firms in which high growth has caused a rapid increase in current liability accounts such as accounts payable. Creditors often frown upon very high short-term debt levels because this can indicate the company may be stretched to meet debt interest payments and because creditors like to see a substantial investment by the owners. Investors are more likely to view higher ratios in a positive light since the leverage gained with debt financing may lead to greater returns on equity investment.

Ways to improve the indicator: Paying down short-term debt with operating income or owner's equity can reduce the current-debt-to-equity ratio. Usually assets should be financed over periods close to the anticipated lifetime of the asset. When a company finances long-lived assets with short-term debt, shifting the finance terms on such assets to long-term debt can decrease the current-debt-to-equity ratio. You can increase the current-debt-to-equity ratio, and thus increase company leverage, with the acquisition of additional short-term debt.

Example

Current debt to market value of equity = current liabilities / market value of equity

Current liabilities = 12,032
Market value of equity = (3,600 common shares × $22.50/share) + (15 preferred shares × $25.00/share) = 81,375

Current debt to market value of equity = 12,032 / 81,375 = 0.1479 = 14.79%

Sector	Mid to large cap	Current Debt to Market Value of Equity	Small to mid cap	Current Debt to Market Value of Equity	Micro to small cap	Current Debt to Market Value of Equity
Manufacturing	General Motors	32.54%	Toro	57.49%	Encad	16.40%
Retail	Wal-Mart Stores	10.67%	Bed Bath & Beyond	4.06%	TCBY Enterprises	5.36%
Food	McDonald's	6.13%	Applebee's Int'l	8.72%	Garden Fresh Restaurant	17.95%
Technology	Microsoft	2.15%	Cypress Semiconductor	12.44%	Jmar Technologies	8.23%
Finance	Morgan-Stanley Dean Witter	490.11%	Franklin Resources	5.26%	AmeriTrade Holding	163.97%
Healthcare	Columbia/HCA Healthcare	14.47%	Novacare	22.64%	National Home Health Care	5.90%
Service	Manpower	45.06%	Air & Water Technologies	197.89%	Market Facts	12.37%
Media/Publishing	McGraw Hill	14.95%	Scholastic	29.70%	Thomas Nelson	20.34%

173 Comparing Long-Term Debt to the Market Value of Equity

Equation

Long-term debt to market value of equity = long-term debt / market value of equity

This ratio describes the relationship between a company's long-term debt and its equity. Since equity market values can be quite different from the book value, the values shown on the balance sheet, this ratio can give an accurate portrayal of long-term debt to equity. Long-term liabilities are those debts that are payable in full in longer than one year.

When to use indicator: Creditors, investors, and managers can use this indicator to determine the risk level associated with a company's long-term debt burden.

Meaning of result: Higher ratios indicate larger long-term debt accounts. This can indicate a number of situations including the financing of both short- and long-lived assets with long-term debt, companies that are experiencing financial difficulties, and start-up firms in which high growth rates have necessitated a rapid increase in long-term debt for the acquisition of assets such as property, plants, and machinery. Creditors often frown upon very high long-term debt levels because this can indicate the company may be stretched to meet debt interest payments and because creditors like to see a substantial investment by the owners. Investors are more likely to view higher ratios in a positive light since the leverage gained with debt financing may lead to greater returns on equity investment.

Ways to improve the indicator: Paying down long-term debt levels with operating income or owner's equity can reduce the long-term-debt-to-equity ratio. Usually assets should be financed over times close to the anticipated lifetime of the asset. When a company finances short-lived assets with long-term debt, shifting the finance terms on such assets to short-term debt will decrease the long-term-debt-to-equity ratio. You can increase the long-term-debt-to-equity ratio, and thus increase company leverage, with the acquisition of additional long-term debt.

Example

Long-term debt to market value of equity = long-term debt / market value of equity

Long-term debt = total liabilities − current liabilities = 25,180 − 12,032 = 13,148
Market value of equity = (3,600 common shares × $22.50/share) + (15 preferred shares × $25.00/share) = 81,375

Long-term debt to market value of equity = 13,148 / 81,375 = 0.1616 = 16.16%

Sector	Mid to large cap	Long-Term Debt to Market Value of Equity	Small to mid cap	Long-Term Debt to Market Value of Equity	Micro to small cap	Long-Term Debt to Market Value of Equity
Manufacturing	General Motors	401.39%	Toro	44.15%	Encad	0.86%
Retail	Wal-Mart Stores	7.73%	Bed Bath & Beyond	0.34%	TCBY Enterprises	4.65%
Food	McDonald's	13.16%	Applebee's Int'l	3.43%	Garden Fresh Restaurant	18.57%
Technology	Microsoft	0.00%	Cypress Semiconductor	29.37%	Jmar Technologies	1.93%
Finance	Morgan-Stanley Dean Witter	48.15%	Franklin Resources	3.93%	AmeriTrade Holding	0.00%
Healthcare	Columbia/HCA Healthcare	58.14%	Novacare	50.17%	National Home Health Care	1.20%
Service	Manpower	19.05%	Air & Water Technologies	332.90%	Market Facts	5.61%
Media/Publishing	McGraw Hill	13.43%	Scholastic	43.39%	Thomas Nelson	38.23%

174 Determining the Funded-Capital-to-Fixed-Asset Ratio

Equation:

Funded capital to fixed assets = (long-term liabilities + owner's equity) / fixed assets

The ratio of funded capital to fixed assets describes the percentage of fixed asset purchases that could have been made with funded capital. **Funded capital** consists of long-term liabilities and owner's equity. Long-term liabilities are those debts that are payable in full in longer than one year. Owner's equity, also known as shareholders' equity, includes all equity balance sheet items, typically the most significant of which are additional paid-in capital for stock purchases and retained earnings (generated income that a company has reinvested in itself). Fixed assets (also referred to on the balance sheet as property, plant, and equipment) include items with lifetimes of greater than three years such as land, buildings, machinery, tooling, leasehold improvements, office equipment, and vehicles.

When to use indicator: Investors and creditors can use this ratio to determine the extent to which fixed assets could have been acquired with funded capital.

Meaning of result: Higher ratios can indicate that funded capital purchased larger portions of fixed assets. Higher ratios can also result when funded capital is used to purchase asset types other than fixed assets, such as inventory or intangible assets. Lower ratios can indicate that short-term debt was used to purchase fixed assets.

Ways to improve the indicator: Acquiring additional fixed assets with capital from sources other than long-term debt or owner's equity can reduce the funded-capital-to-fixed-asset ratio. Increasing owner's equity by generating healthy profits, taking on additional long-term debt, or acquiring fewer amounts of fixed assets can increase the funded-capital-to-fixed-asset ratio.

Example

Funded capital to fixed assets = (long-term liabilities + owner's equity) / fixed assets

Long-term liabilities = total liabilities − current liabilities = 25,180 − 12,032 = 13,148
Owner's equity = 31,088
Fixed assets = 10,018

Funded capital to fixed assets = (13,148 + 31,088) / 10,018 = 4.416 = 441.6%

Sector	Mid to large cap	Funded Capital to Fixed Assets	Small to mid cap	Funded Capital to Fixed Assets	Micro to small cap	Funded Capital to Fixed Assets
Manufacturing	General Motors	312.60%	Toro	362.68%	Encad	445.16%
Retail	Wal-Mart Stores	122.79%	Bed Bath & Beyond	276.52%	TCBY Enterprises	217.07%
Food	McDonald's	101.98%	Applebee's Int'l	114.09%	Garden Fresh Restaurant	89.44%
Technology	Microsoft	1104.78%	Cypress Semiconductor	195.01%	Jmar Technologies	535.73%
Finance	Morgan-Stanley Dean Witter	2331.20%	Franklin Resources	1098.78%	AmeriTrade Holding	769.11%
Healthcare	Columbia/HCA Healthcare	179.79%	Novacare	1225.03%	National Home Health Care	6263.49%
Service	Manpower	764.32%	Air & Water Technologies	1483.29%	Market Facts	374.41%
Media/Publishing	McGraw Hill	920.31%	Scholastic	426.61%	Thomas Nelson	749.24%

175 Examining Financial Leverage

Equation

Financial leverage = change in earnings per share (%) / change in operating income (%)

Financial leverage entails using debt in an effort to increase financial returns to equity owners. As long as the financial returns achieved with the debt are greater than the cost of the debt, the financial returns realized by equity owners are increased. If the financial returns achieved with the debt do not cover the cost of the debt, financial returns to equity owners are decreased. Financial leverage thus can increase equity owner returns when things go well, but at the cost of additional risk if there is poor financial performance when events do not go as planned.

When to use indicator: Managers can use this indicator to determine the level of financial leverage employed, and more specifically, the effect of increases or decreases of operating income on the level of shareholder earnings per share. This information allows the manager to determine the magnitude of the benefits and level of risk associated with financial leveraging.

Meaning of result: Firms with higher levels of financial leverage will see dramatic increases/decreases in earnings per share for a given increase/decrease in operating income. The larger the level of debt levels relative to equity, the higher the degree of financial leverage. You can acquire debt in forms such as loans, bonds, and preferred stock. You can increase financial leverage by swapping equity financing for debt financing. For example, assume a company has determined to invest in robotic manufacturing equipment to increase manufacturing productivity. The equipment could be purchased either with debt, such as bank financing or the issuance of bonds, or with equity, such as the issuance of additional common stock or cash earned from operations. If the company finances the acquisition and increases financial leverage, the return to equity holders may increase if returns achieved with the equipment more than cover the costs associated with the financing debt. If the company instead elects to pay for the equipment with cash or an additional issuance of common stock, financial leverage is decreased and positive equity owner returns achieved with the equipment will not be magnified to the extent realized with debt financing. By increasing financial leverage, a company can generate higher equity owner returns as operating incomes rise, but at a greater risk level since poor operating income performance can result in lower returns to equity owners.

Ways to improve the indicator: You can increase financial leverage by increasing the level of debt financing relative to equity financing. While increasing financial leverage will allow greater equity owner profits when operating incomes rise, there is greater financial risk when operating incomes fall.

Example

Financial leverage = change in earnings per share (%) / change in operating income (%)

Sales level A = 85,420
Sales level B = 92,581

Variable expenses at sales level A = 38,923
Variable expenses at sales level B = 42,186

Fixed expenses at sales level A = 37,848
Fixed expenses at sales level B = 37,848

Interest expense at sales level A = 784
Interest expense at sales level B = 784

Operating income at sales level A = sales at level A − variable expenses at sales level A − fixed expenses at sales level A + interest expense at sales level A = 85,420 − 38,923 − 37,848 + 784 = 9,433
Same for operating income at sales level B = 92,581 − 42,186 − 37,848 + 784 = 13,331

Net income applicable to common stock at sales level A = 4,953

Net income applicable to common stock at sales level B = 8,067

Common shares outstanding = 3,600

Earnings per share at sales level A = net income applicable to common stock / common shares outstanding = 4,953/3,600 = 1.38

Earnings per share at sales level B = net income applicable to common stock / common shares outstanding = 8,067 / 3,600 = 2.24

Change in operating income = (change in operating income from sales level B to A) / original operating income) × 100 = [(13,331 − 9,433) / 9,433] × 100 = 41.32%

Change in earnings per share = (change in earnings per share from sales level B to A) / original earnings) × 100 = [(2.24 − 1.38) / 1.38] × 100 = 62.32%

Financial leverage = 62.32 / 41.32 = 1.51

176 Examining Operating Leverage

Equation

Operating leverage = change in operating income (%) / change in sales (%)

Operating leverage entails using fixed expense, instead of variable, investments in an effort to increase operating income. Companies measure operating leverage by determining how operating income changes with changes in the level of sales.

When to use indicator: Managers can use this indicator to determine the effect of sales increases or decreases on the level of operating income. This information allows the manager to determine the magnitude of operating leverage benefits accorded with sales increases and the risk associated with sales declines.

Meaning of result: Firms with high operating leverage will see dramatic increases/decreases in operating income for a given increase/decrease in sales. The larger the level of fixed expenses to variable expenses and sales levels, the higher the operating leverage. A manager can increase operating leverage by swapping variable expenses for fixed expenses. For example, investments in fixed assets such as robotic manufacturing equipment will tend to decrease the level of variable expenses because the robots can manufacture goods more cheaply than direct laborers. The trade-off for the increase in efficiencies achieved by acquiring additional fixed assets is that substantial investments must be made in fixed expenses such as the interest payments and maintenance of the robotic equipment. If the products produced with the robotic equipment fail to generate profitable sales levels, the company may be stuck with an expensive and useless fixed expense. By increasing operating leverage, a company will generate more operating income as sales levels rise, but it will be at greater risk as sales levels fall since larger amounts of fixed expenses must be covered.

Fixed costs remain relatively constant regardless of the quantity of goods or services produced while variable costs are those costs that change with the quantity of items produced. Fixed costs include such items as building rent, factory equipment interest payments, and salaries for nondirect manufacturing employees such as supervisors, engineers, and accountants. Variable costs include such items as raw materials, direct labor, and the fuel used to operate machinery.

Ways to improve the indicator: A company can increase operating leverage by increasing the level of fixed asset expenditures relative to variable expenses and sales levels. While increasing operating leverage will allow greater operating profits when sales levels rise, there is greater financial risk when sales levels fall.

Example

Operating leverage = change in operating income (%) / change in sales (%)

Sales level A = 85,420
Sales level B = 92,581

Variable expenses at sales level A = 38,923
Variable expenses at sales level B = 42,186

Fixed expenses at sales level A = 37,848
Fixed expenses at sales level B = 37,848

Interest expense at sales level A = 784
Interest expense at sales level B = 784

Operating income at sales level A = sales at level A − variable expenses at sales level A − fixed expenses at sales level A + interest expense at sales level A = 85,420 − 38,923 − 37,848 + 784 = 9,433

Same for operating income at sales level B = 92,581 − 42,186 − 37,848 + 784 = 13,331

Change in sales (%) = [(sales level B − sales level A) / sales level A] × 100 = [(92,581 − 85,420) / 85,420] × 100 = 8.38%

Change in operating income (%) = [(operating income at sales level B − operating income at sales level A) / operating income at sales level A] × 100 = [(13,331 − 9,433) / 9,433] × 100 = 41.32%

Operating leverage = 41.32 / 8.38 = 4.93

177 Examining Total Leverage

Equation

Total leverage = change in earnings per share (%) / change in sales (%)

Total leverage

= Financial leverage × operating leverage

= (change in earnings per share [%] / change in operating income [%]) × (change in operating income [%] / change in sales [%])

Total leverage is a measure of the combined effects of financial and operating leverage. **Financial leverage** entails using debt in an effort to increase financial returns to equity owners. As long as the financial returns achieved with the debt are greater than the cost of the debt, the financial returns realized by equity owners is increased. If the financial returns achieved with the debt do not cover the cost of the debt, financial returns to equity owners are decreased. Financial leverage thus can increase equity owner returns when things go well, but at the cost of the additional risk if there is poor financial performance when events do not go as planned.

Operating leverage entails using fixed expense, instead of variable, investments in an effort to increase operating income. Managers measure operating leverage by determining how operating income changes with changes in the level of sales.

When to use indicator: Managers can use this indicator to determine the level of financial and operating leverage employed, and more specifically, the effect of changes in sales levels on the level of shareholder earnings per share. This information allows the manager to determine the magnitude of the benefits and level of risk associated with financial and operating leveraging.

Meaning of result: Firms with higher levels of total leverage will see dramatic increases/decreases in earnings per share for a given increase/decrease in sales levels. Higher levels of total leverage indicate a company is employing higher financial and/or operating leverage.

The larger the level of debt levels relative to equity, the higher the degree of financial leverage. A company can acquire debt in forms such as loans, bonds, and preferred stock. A company essentially increases financial leverage by swapping equity financing for debt financing. For example, assume a company has determined to invest in robotic manufacturing equipment to increase manufacturing productivity. The company could purchase the equipment either with debt, such as bank financing or the issuance of bonds, or with equity, such as the issuance of additional common stock or cash earned from operations. By financing the acquisition and increasing financial leverage, the return to equity holders may increase if returns achieved with the equipment more than cover the costs associated with the financing debt. If the company instead elects to pay for the equipment with cash or an additional issuance of common stock, financial leverage is decreased, and positive equity owner returns achieved with the equipment will not be magnified to the extent realized with debt financing. By increasing financial leverage, a company can generate higher equity owner returns as operating incomes rise, but at a greater risk level since poor operating income performance can result in lower returns to equity owners.

Firms with high operating leverage will see dramatic increases/decreases in operating income for a given increase/decrease in sales. The larger the level of fixed expenses to variable expenses and sales levels, the higher the operating leverage. A company increases operating leverage by swapping variable expenses for fixed expenses. For example, investments in fixed assets such as robotic manufacturing equipment will tend to decrease the level of variable expenses because the robots can manufacture goods more cheaply than direct laborers. The trade-off for the increase in efficiencies achieved by acquiring additional fixed assets is that substantial investments must be made in fixed expenses such as the interest payments and maintenance required of the robotic equipment. If the products produced with the robotic equipment fail to generate profitable sales levels, the company may be stuck with an expensive and useless fixed expense. By increasing operating leverage, a company will generate more operating income as sales levels rise, but will be at greater risk as sales levels fall since it must cover larger amounts of fixed expenses.

Fixed costs remain relatively constant regardless of the quantity of goods or services produced while variable costs are those costs that change with the quantity of items produced. Fixed costs include such items as building rent, factory equipment interest payments, and salaries for nondirect manufacturing employees such as supervisors, engineers, and accountants. Variable costs include such items as raw materials, direct labor, and the fuel used to operate machinery.

Ways to improve the indicator: A company can increase total leverage by increasing financial and/or operating leverage. Increases in total leverage will magnify earnings to shareholders when sales levels are high, but will increase risk and reduce financial performance when sales are down.

You can increase financial leverage by increasing the level of debt financing relative to equity financing. While increasing financial leverage will allow greater equity owner profits when operating incomes rise, there is greater financial risk when operating incomes fall. You can increase operating leverage by increasing the level of fixed asset expenditures relative to variable expenses and sales levels. While increasing operating leverage will allow greater operating profits when sales levels rise, there is greater financial risk when sales levels fall.

Example

Total leverage = change in earnings per share (%) / change in sales (%)

Total leverage = financial leverage × operating leverage

Total leverage
= Financial leverage × operating leverage
= (change in earnings per share [%] / change in operating income [%]) × (change in operating income [%]) / change in sales [%])

Sales level A = 85,420
Sales level B = 92,581

Variable expenses at sales level A = 38,923
Variable expenses at sales level B = 42,186

Fixed expenses at sales level A = 37,848
Fixed expenses at sales level B = 37,848

Interest expense at sales level A = 784
Interest expense at sales level B = 784

Operating income at sales level A = sales at level A − variable expenses at sales level A − fixed expenses at sales level A + interest expense at sales level A = 85,420 − 38,923 − 37,848 + 784 = 9,433
Same for operating income at sales level B = 92,581 − 42,186 − 37,848 + 784 = 13,331

Net income applicable to common stock at sales level A = 4,953
Net income applicable to common stock at sales level B = 8,067

Common shares outstanding = 3,600

Earnings per share at sales level A = 1.38
Earnings per share at sales level B = 2.24

Change in sales (%) = [(sales level B − sales level A) / sales level A] × 100 = [(92,581 − 85,420) / 85,420] × 100 = 8.38%

Change in earnings per share = [(earnings per share at sales level B − earnings per share at sales level A) / earnings per share at sales level A] × 100 = [(2.24 − 1.38) / 1.38] × 100 = 62.32%

Financial leverage = 1.51 (see details in tip #175)

Operating leverage = 4.93 (see details in tip #176)

Total leverage = 62.32 / 8.38 = 7.44 (with first formula)

Total leverage = 1.51 × 4.93 = 7.44 (with second formula)

CHAPTER TWELVE

Accounts Receivable

Accounts receivable is money due to a company for products or services previously delivered to a customer. This chapter details a number of ratios to determine the levels and quality of accounts receivable.

178 Comparing Accounts Receivable to Sales

Equation

Accounts receivable to sales = accounts receivable / net sales

The formula is a measure of the relative sizes of accounts receivable and the size of the company. Accounts receivable is money due to the company for products or services delivered to a customer.

When to use indicator: Creditors, investors, and managers can use this indicator to track trends in the size of accounts receivable.

Meaning of result: Higher ratios can indicate liberal credit policies and lenient collection activities. Low ratios can indicate that management allows little or no credit and practices timely and/or aggressive collections of accounts receivable. Management should take particular note of higher trending accounts receivable. Such trends can signal customers experiencing financial difficulties and having problems meeting debt payments. Early identification and communication with such customers may increase chances of full payment. Higher trending ratios may also be the result of changes in credit policies and/or changes in the customer base.

Ways to improve the indicator: You can reduce the ratio of accounts receivable to sales by tightening credit policies and by more proactively seeking payment of outstanding accounts. Note that tighter credit policies may have the undesirable effect of reducing sales since some customers are likely to seek other suppliers with more liberal credit.

Example

Accounts receivable to sales = accounts receivable / net sales

Accounts receivable = 24,878
Net sales = 85,420

Accounts receivable to sales = 24,878 / 85,420 = 0.2912 = 29.12%

Sector	Mid to large cap	Accounts Receivable to Sales	Small to mid cap	Accounts Receivable to Sales	Micro to small cap	Accounts Receivable to Sales
Manufacturing	General Motors	37.25%	Toro	24.65%	Encad	24.69%
Retail	Wal-Mart Stores	0.83%	Bed Bath & Beyond	0.00%	TCBY Enterprises	9.66%
Food	McDonald's	4.24%	Applebee's Int'l	3.18%	Garden Fresh Restaurant	0.00%
Technology	Microsoft	10.08%	Cypress Semiconductor	12.47%	Jmar Technologies	20.08%
Finance	Morgan-Stanley Dean Witter	185.24%	Franklin Resources	10.81%	AmeriTrade Holding	358.78%
Healthcare	Columbia/HCA Healthcare	13.40%	Novacare	24.05%	National Home Health Care	23.31%
Service	Manpower	19.80%	Air & Water Technologies	16.80%	Market Facts	20.07%
Media/Publishing	McGraw Hill	27.78%	Scholastic	11.03%	Thomas Nelson	25.01%

179 Determining the Turnover of Accounts Receivable

Equation

Accounts receivable turnover = net credit sales / accounts receivable

Accounts receivable turnover describes the relative size of net credit sales and accounts receivable, and more specifically, how many times a company achieves, or turns over, the value of accounts receivable in net credit sales. Net credit sales are often essentially the same as net sales; this relationship is increasingly accurate as the percentage of credit sales to total sales increases. Accounts receivable is money due to the company from customers for products or services delivered to those customers.

When to use indicator: Creditors, investors, and managers can use this indicator to track trends in the size of accounts receivable.

Meaning of result: Lower ratios can indicate liberal credit policies and lenient collection activities. High ratios can indicate that management allows little or no credit and practices timely and/or aggressive collections of accounts receivable. Management should take particular note of lower trending accounts receivable turnover. Such trends can signal customers experiencing financial difficulties and having problems meeting debt payments. Early identification and communication with such customers may increase chances of full payment. Lower trending ratios may also be the result of changes in credit policies and/or changes in the customer base.

Ways to improve the indicator: You can increase accounts receivable turnover by tightening credit policies and by more proactively seeking payment of outstanding accounts. Note that tighter credit policies may have the undesirable effect of reducing sales since some customers are likely to seek other suppliers with more liberal credit.

Example

Accounts receivable turnover = net credit sales / accounts receivable

Net credit sales ~ net sales = 85,420
Accounts receivable = 24,878

Accounts receivable turnover = 85,420 / 24,878 = 3.4336 = 343.4%

Sector	Mid to large cap	Accounts Receivable Turnover	Small to mid cap	Accounts Receivable Turnover	Micro to small cap	Accounts Receivable Turnover
Manufacturing	General Motors	2.68	Toro	4.06	Encad	4.05
Retail	Wal-Mart Stores	120.86	Bed Bath & Beyond	*	TCBY Enterprises	10.35
Food	McDonald's	23.60	Applebee's Int'l	31.47	Garden Fresh Restaurant	*
Technology	Microsoft	9.92	Cypress Semiconductor	8.02	Jmar Technologies	4.98
Finance	Morgan-Stanley Dean Witter	0.54	Franklin Resources	9.25	AmeriTrade Holding	0.28
Healthcare	Columbia/HCA Healthcare	7.46	Novacare	4.16	National Home Health Care	4.29
Service	Manpower	5.05	Air & Water Technologies	5.95	Market Facts	4.98
Media/Publishing	McGraw Hill	3.60	Scholastic	9.07	Thomas Nelson	4.00

* Companies with no reported accounts receivable.

180 Determining How Many Days of Credit Sales are in Accounts Receivable

Equation

Days of credit sales in accounts receivable = accounts receivable / average credit sales per day

Days of credit in accounts receivable describes the size of accounts receivable in terms of how many days' worth of credit sales are outstanding. Average credit sales per day are often essentially the same as average net sales per day; this relationship is increasingly accurate as the percentage of credit sales to total sales increases. Accounts receivable is money due to the company from customers for products or services delivered to those customers.

When to use indicator: Creditors, investors, and managers can use this indicator to track trends in the size of accounts receivable.

Meaning of result: Higher ratios can indicate liberal credit policies and lenient collection activities. Low ratios can indicate that management allows little or no credit and practices timely and/or aggressive collections of accounts receivable. Management should take particular note of higher trending days of credit sales in accounts receivable. Such trends can signal customers experiencing financial difficulties and having problems meeting debt payments. Early identification and communication with such customers may increase chances of full payment. Higher trending ratios may also be the result of changes in credit policies and/or changes in the customer base.

Ways to improve the indicator: You can reduce days of credit sales in accounts receivable by tightening credit policies and by more proactively seeking payment of outstanding accounts. Note that tighter credit policies may have the undesirable effect of reducing sales since some customers are likely to seek other suppliers with more liberal credit.

Example

Days of credit sales in accounts receivable = accounts receivable / average credit sales per day

Accounts receivable = 24,878
Net sales = 85,420
Average credit sales per day ~ average net sales per day = net sales / 365 = 85,420 / 365 = 234.0

Days of credit sales in accounts receivable = 24,878 / 234 = 106.3

Sector	Mid to large cap	Days of Credit Sales in Accounts Receivable	Small to mid cap	Days of Credit Sales in Accounts Receivable	Micro to small cap	Days of Credit Sales in Accounts Receivable
Manufacturing	General Motors	135.95	Toro	89.98	Encad	90.12
Retail	Wal-Mart Stores	3.02	Bed Bath & Beyond	*	TCBY Enterprises	35.26
Food	McDonald's	15.47	Applebee's Int'l	11.60	Garden Fresh Restaurant	*
Technology	Microsoft	36.79	Cypress Semiconductor	45.50	Jmar Technologies	73.28
Finance	Morgan-Stanley Dean Witter	676.14	Franklin Resources	39.46	AmeriTrade Holding	1,309.53
Healthcare	Columbia/HCA Healthcare	48.91	Novacare	87.78	National Home Health Care	85.09
Service	Manpower	72.28	Air & Water Technologies	61.33	Market Facts	73.27
Media/Publishing	McGraw Hill	101.41	Scholastic	40.25	Thomas Nelson	91.29

* Companies with no reported accounts receivable.

181 Examining the Ages of Accounts Receivable (Aging Schedule)

Equation

Age	Percentage of accounts receivable
Current	45%
1–30 past due	38%
31–60 past due	8%
61–90 past due	5%
over 90 past due	4%

The chart is a visual tool used to describe and communicate quickly the status of accounts receivable. You may use varying categories for ages. For example, those companies with more lenient credit policies may want to track longer term accounts receivable ages such as 91–120 days and 121–180 days. You can use the aging schedule for all accounts (as shown above) as well as for individual customers. Accounts receivable is money due to the company from customers for products or services delivered to those customers.

When to use indicator: Managers can use this tool to track accounts receivable trends and the effects of changes in accounts receivable collection and credit policies. When used to track individual customers, this tool can alert management to overdue customers.

Meaning of result: Higher percentages of accounts receivable in longer age categories can indicate liberal credit policies and lenient collection activities. Higher percentages in shorter age categories can indicate that management allows little or no credit and practices timely and/or aggressive collections of accounts receivable. Management should take particular note of higher trending percentages in longer age categories. Such trends can signal customers experiencing financial difficulties and having problems meeting debt payments. Early identification and communication with such customers may increase chances of full payment. Higher trending percentages in longer age categories may also be the result of changes in credit policies and/or changes in the customer base.

Ways to improve the indicator: You can lower percentages of longer aged accounts receivable by tightening credit policies and by more proactively seeking payment of outstanding accounts. Note that tighter credit policies may have the undesirable effect of reducing sales since some customers are likely to seek other suppliers with more liberal credit.

182 Determining What Percentage of Current-Period Sales Will Be Collected in the Current Period

Equation

Percentage of current-period sales collected in current period = collected current-period accounts receivable / net sales current period

This formula indicates the portion of current-period sales a company collects from accounts receivable in the same period. Accounts receivable is money due to the company from customers for products or services delivered to those customers.

When to use indicator: Managers can use this ratio to determine the average historical change in the size of accounts receivable as a function of sales levels. When sales levels are rising, you can use this information to ensure appropriate cash is available for increases in accounts receivable according to forecasted sales levels. This ratio can also indicate trends in accounts receivable aging.

Meaning of result: Lower ratios can indicate rising sales levels, liberal credit policies, and lenient collection activities. Higher ratios can indicate that management allows little or no credit and practices timely and/or aggressive collections of accounts receivable. It can also signal falling sales levels. Management should take particular note of lower trending current-period collection ratios. Such trends can signal customers experiencing financial difficulties and having problems meeting debt payments. Early identification and communication with such customers may increase chances of full payment. Lower trending ratios may also be the result of changes in credit policies and/or changes in the customer base.

Ways to improve the indicator: You can increase current-period collection ratios by tightening credit policies and by more proactively seeking payment of outstanding accounts. Note that tighter credit policies may have the undesirable effect of reducing sales because some customers are likely to seek other suppliers with more liberal credit.

Example

Percentage of current-period sales collected in current period = collected current-period accounts receivable / net sales current period

Collected current-period accounts receivable = 7,600
Net sales current period = 8,100

Percentage of current-period sales collected in current period = 7,600 / 8,100 = 0.9383 = 93.83%

183 Determining What Percentage of Current-Period Sales Will Not Be Collected in the Current Period

Equation

Percentage of current-period sales not collected in current period = (net sales current period − collected current-period accounts receivable) / net sales current period

This ratio indicates the portion of current-period sales that are not collected from accounts receivable in the same period. Accounts receivable is money due to the company from customers for products or services delivered to those customers.

When to use indicator: Managers can use this ratio to determine the average historical change in the size of accounts receivable as a function of sales levels. When sales levels are rising, you can use this information to ensure appropriate cash is available for increases in accounts receivable according to forecasted sales levels. This ratio can also indicate trends in accounts receivable aging.

Meaning of result: Higher ratios can indicate rising sales levels, liberal credit policies, and lenient collection activities. Lower ratios can indicate that management allows little or no credit and practices timely and/or aggressive collections of accounts receivable. It can also signal falling sales levels. Management should take particular note of higher trending current-period collection ratios. Such trends can signal customers experiencing financial difficulties and having problems meeting debt payments. Early identification and communication with such customers may increase chances of full payment. Higher trending ratios may also be the result of changes in credit policies and/or changes in the customer base.

Ways to improve the indicator: You can increase current-period collection ratios by tightening credit policies and by more proactively seeking payment of outstanding accounts. Note that tighter credit policies may have the undesirable effect of reducing sales because some customers are likely to seek other suppliers with more liberal credit.

Example

Percentage of current-period sales not collected in current period = (net sales current period − collected current-period accounts receivable) / net sales current period

Collected current-period accounts receivable = 7,600
Net sales current period = 8,100

Percentage of current-period sales not collected in current period = (8,100 − 7,600) / 8,100 = 0.0617 = 6.17%

184 Examining Bad Debt and Accounts Receivable

Equation

Bad debts to accounts receivable = bad debt / accounts receivable

The ratio of bad debts to accounts receivable is a measure of the risk level associated with credit extended to customers. Accounts receivable is money due to the company from customers for products or services delivered to those customers.

When to use indicator: Managers and creditors can use this indicator to determine the risk level, or dependability, of account receivable assets.

Meaning of result: Higher ratios indicate larger portions of accounts receivable are not collectable. High and higher trending ratios can alert management to investigate credit and collection policies.

Ways to improve the indicator: You can reduce bad debt ratios by tightening credit policies and by more proactively seeking payment of outstanding accounts. Note that tighter credit policies may have the undesirable effect of reducing sales because some customers are likely to seek other suppliers with more liberal credit.

Example

Bad debts to accounts receivable = bad debt / accounts receivable

Bad debt = 1,450
Accounts receivable = 24,878

Bad debt to accounts receivable = 1,450 / 24,878 = 0.0583 = 5.83%

185 Relating Bad Debts to Sales

Equation

Bad debts to sales = bad debts / net sales

The ratio of bad debts to net sales is a measure of the risk level associated with extending credit to customers.

When to use indicator: Managers and creditors can use this indicator to determine the risk level, or dependability, of account receivable assets.

Meaning of result: Higher ratios indicate larger portions of accounts receivable are not collectable. High and higher trending ratios can alert management to investigate credit and collection policies.

Ways to improve the indicator: You can reduce bad debt ratios by tightening credit policies and by more proactively seeking payment of outstanding accounts. Note that tighter credit policies may have the undesirable effect of reducing sales because some customers are likely to seek other suppliers with more liberal credit.

Example

Bad debts to sales = bad debts / net sales

Bad debts = 1,450
Net sales = 85,420

Bad debts to sales = 1,450 / 85,420 = 0.0170 = 1.70%

186 Determining if Credit Discounts Should be Accepted and Offered

Equation

Credit discount annualized interest rate = [discount % / (100% − discount %)] × [360 / (normal credit term − discount credit term)]

This formula can help you determine whether it is cost-effective to accept credit discounts from suppliers and extend credit discounts to customers. It is common to induce customers to pay bills promptly by offering a monetary incentive to do so. An example is 2/10, net 60 credit, which means customers can take a 2% discount if they pay their bills within 10 days; otherwise they must pay their bills within 60 days. By receiving earlier payment, companies can increase cash flow and reduce the costs associated with carrying large amounts of accounts receivable. A secondary benefit of offering trade discounts is a reduction in bad debt levels because financially suspect firms might be induced to pay quickly to gain discounts.

When to use indicator: Managers can use this formula to determine if offering credit discount policies and accepting supplier credit discount terms will probably increase company profitability.

Meaning of result: You may want to consider accepting credit discount policies from suppliers when such a move will increase profits. In general, you will want to accept trade credit offerings when the discount rate is greater than what must be paid on bank loans. By paying the trade account early, you may use bank loans to finance the particular purchase. Conversely, you should decline trade credits when the discount rate is lower than available bank loans.

You can offer trade credit when you need to improve cash flow and when it is financially profitable. At times companies will offer attractive trade credit rates to solidify cash flow performance. When you do not require improved cash flow, you should offer trade credit only when financially beneficial. Improved financial performance would include a situation in which the savings generated by shorter accounts payable periods outweigh the costs associated with granting trade credits. Note that there is financial risk associated with such analyses since the results are dependent upon credit term projections. Comparing actual financial performance with projections can help the manager determine whether the assumptions made in the credit discount analysis are valid.

Example

Should trade credit be taken

Credit discount annualized interest rate = [discount % / (100% − discount %)] × [360 / (normal credit term − discount credit term)]

Discount % = 2%
Normal credit term = 60 days
Discount credit term = 10 days

Credit discount annualized interest rate = [2/(100 − 2)] × [360/(60 − 10)] = 0.1469 = 14.69%

You should take this credit if a 14.69% return is higher than what must be paid on bank loans.

Determining if trade credit should be offered

Assume same 2/10, net 60 terms as above.

Credit discount annualized interest rate = 14.69%
Company cost of credit = 9%
Percent of customers who accept terms = 50%
Days of accounts receivable before discount terms are offered = 106.3
Days of accounts receivable after terms are offered = (0.5 × 106.3) + (0.5% × 10) = 58.2
Accounts receivable before discount terms are offered = 24,878

Accounts receivable after discount terms are offered = [(percentage of customers who don't accept terms × accounts receivable before discount terms × days of accounts receivable before discount terms)/days of accounts receivable before discount terms] + [(percentage of customers who accept terms × accounts receivable before discount terms × days of accounts receivable after discount terms)/days of accounts receivable before discount terms]

Accounts receivable after discount terms are offered = [(0.5 × 24,878 × 106.3)/106.3] + [(0.5 × 24,878 × 10)106.3] = 13,609
Net credit sales = 85,420

Cost to offer plan = discount × percent of customers taking discount × net credit sales = (0.02 × 0.5 × 85,420) = 854

Savings from offering plan = cost of company credit × change in accounts receivable balance because of offered discount terms = (0.09) × (24,878 − 13,609) = 1,014

Net cost/savings to offer plan = 1,014 − 854 = 160

In this case, the discount increases cash flow by $11,269 (24,878 − 13,609) while simultaneously increasing profit by $160. When the discount increases cash flow and profit, it is clearly advantageous to offer the discount. However, when the discount increases cash flow with a reduction in profit, the offering of the discount may still be desirable because of the benefits of increased cash flow.

187 Examining Accounts Receivable Factoring

Equation:

Accounts receivable factoring annualized interest rate = (factor % / [100% − factor %]) × (360 / [normal credit term − factor payment term])

Factoring is the process of selling accounts receivable to a third party, known as a factoring company, to receive cash quickly for those accounts receivable. Companies often factor to increase cash flow and, in essence, to use an independent company as a collections department. The factoring company makes money since it purchases the accounts receivable at a discount to the actual money owed and then collects the full amount of the money owed from the borrower. The discount rate is dependent on a number of issues such as the credit rating of the borrower, the size and age of the account receivable, and the track record the factor has had with the selling company and the borrower.

When to use indicator: Creditors and managers can use this indicator to determine the costs and profits associated with factoring.

Meaning of result: Higher interest rates indicate higher factoring costs. Higher costs often are the result of poor borrower credit ratings but can also arise because of issues such as small account sizes, noncompetitive rates offered by the factoring company, and a factoring company's unfamiliarity with the companies and industries involved.

Ways to improve the indicator: Seeking competitive bids with a number of factoring companies and then establishing a history with the selected company should help keep factoring rates competitive. Maintaining a customer base with excellent payment trends should also help to reduce interest rates since the factoring company's uncollectable account losses due to nonpayment should decrease.

Example

Accounts receivable factoring annualized interest rate = (factor % / [100% − factor %]) × (360 / [normal credit term − factor payment term])

Factor % = 4%
Normal credit term = 60 days
Factor payment term = 3 days

Accounts receivable factoring annualized interest rate = (4/[100 − 4]) × (360/[60 − 3]) = 0.2632 = 26.32%

CHAPTER THIRTEEN

Accounts Payable

Accounts payable is the money owed by the company for goods and services provided on credit by suppliers. Ratios in this chapter describe the levels of accounts payable.

188 Comparing Accounts Payable to Sales

Equation

Accounts payable to sales = accounts payable / net sales

This ratio of accounts payable to sales is a measure of the relative sizes of accounts payable and the size of the company. Accounts payable is the money owed by the company for goods and services provided on credit by suppliers.

When to use indicator: Creditors, investors, and managers can use this indicator to track trends in the size of accounts payable.

Meaning of result: Higher ratios indicate the company is taking advantage of credit extended by suppliers. Since this credit is often interest free, many companies seek to keep accounts payable at high levels to maximize profit. When ratios become too high, however, it can indicate companies that are experiencing difficulty in paying bills when due, which may result in adverse credit ratings and bankruptcy.

Low ratios indicate management has not used supplier credit to a significant degree, either by choice or because suppliers have elected to withhold credit.

Ways to improve the indicator: A company can increase the ratio of accounts payable to sales by seeking additional trade credit and extending payment timing to the maximum limit offered by suppliers. A company can reduce the ratio of accounts payable to sales by paying invoices sooner and by foregoing the offering of credit altogether and paying suppliers in cash.

Example

Accounts payable to sales = accounts payable / net sales

Accounts payable = 5,633
Net sales = 85,420

Accounts payable to sales = 5,633 / 85,420 = 0.0659 = 6.59%

Sector	Mid to large cap	Accounts Payable to Sales	Small to mid cap	Accounts Payable to Sales	Micro to small cap	Accounts Payable to Sales
Manufacturing	General Motors	8.86%	Toro	5.56%	Encad	8.30%
Retail	Wal-Mart Stores	7.74%	Bed Bath & Beyond	6.07%	TCBY Enterprises	2.11%
Food	McDonald's	5.70%	Applebee's Int'l	3.83%	Garden Fresh Restaurant	5.55%
Technology	Microsoft	5.24%	Cypress Semiconductor	11.18%	Jmar Technologies	5.48%
Finance	Morgan-Stanley Dean Witter	151.79%	Franklin Resources	0.00%	AmeriTrade Holding	1.47%
Healthcare	Columbia/HCA Healthcare	4.94%	Novacare	12.68%	National Home Health Care	3.80%
Service	Manpower	3.73%	Air & Water Technologies	17.53%	Market Facts	2.38%
Media/Publishing	McGraw Hill	8.35%	Scholastic	7.27%	Thomas Nelson	6.60%

189 Finding the Turnover of Accounts Payable

Equation

Accounts payable turnover = total purchases / accounts payable

Accounts payable turnover describes the relative size of total company purchases and accounts payable, and more specifically, how many times a company achieves, or turns over, the value of accounts payable in total purchases. Accounts payable is the money owed by the company for goods and services provided on credit by suppliers.

When to use indicator: Creditors, investors, and managers can use this indicator to track trends in the size of accounts payable.

Meaning of result: Lower ratios indicate the company is taking advantage of credit extended by suppliers. Since this credit is often interest free, many companies seek to reduce accounts payable turnover to maximize profit. When ratios become too low, however, it can indicate companies that are experiencing difficulty in paying bills when due, which may result in adverse credit ratings and bankruptcy.

Higher ratios indicate that management has not used supplier credit to a significant degree, either by choice or because suppliers have elected to withhold credit.

Ways to improve the indicator: You can reduce accounts payable turnover by seeking additional trade credit and extending payment timing to the maximum limit offered by suppliers. You can increase accounts payable turnover by paying invoices sooner and by foregoing the offering of credit altogether and paying suppliers in cash.

Example

Accounts payable turnover = total purchases / accounts payable

Total purchases = 37,200
Accounts payable = 5,633

Accounts payable turnover = 37,200 / 5,633 = 6.60

190 Calculating the Number of Days of Purchases in Accounts Payable

Equation

Days of purchases in accounts payable = accounts payable / average purchases per day

Days of purchases in accounts payable describes the size of accounts payable in terms of how many days' worth of purchases are outstanding. Accounts payable is the money owed by the company for goods and services provided on credit by suppliers.

When to use indicator: Creditors, investors, and managers can use this indicator to track trends in the size of accounts payable.

Meaning of result: Higher ratios indicate the company is taking advantage of credit extended by suppliers. Since this credit is often interest free, many companies seek to increase days of purchases in accounts payable to maximize profit. When ratios become too high, however, it can indicate companies that are experiencing difficulty in paying bills when due, which may result in adverse credit ratings and difficulty in obtaining future credit lines.

Lower ratios indicate that management has not used supplier credit to a significant degree, either by choice or because suppliers have elected to withhold credit.

Ways to improve the indicator: You can increase days of purchases in accounts payable by seeking additional trade credit and extending payment timing to the maximum limit offered by suppliers. You can reduce days of purchases in accounts payable by paying invoices sooner and by foregoing the offering of credit altogether and paying suppliers in cash.

Example

Days of purchases in accounts payable = accounts payable / average purchases per day

Accounts payable = 5,633
Average purchases per day = 37,200 / 365 = 101.9

Days of purchases in accounts payable = 5,633 / 101.9 = 55.3 days

191 Comparing Accounts Payable to Purchases

Equation

Accounts payable to purchases = accounts payable / total purchases

The ratio of accounts payable to purchases describes the size of accounts payable as the percentage of yearly purchases that are outstanding. Accounts payable is the money owed by the company for goods and services provided by suppliers.

When to use indicator: Creditors, investors, and managers can use this indicator to track trends in the size of accounts payable.

Meaning of result: Higher ratios indicate the company is taking advantage of credit extended by suppliers. Since this credit is often interest free, many companies seek to increase days of purchases in accounts payable to maximize profit. When ratios become too high, however, it can indicate companies that are experiencing difficulty in paying bills when due, which may result in adverse credit ratings and bankruptcy.

Lower ratios indicate that management has not used supplier credit to a significant degree, either by choice or because suppliers have elected to withhold credit.

Ways to improve the indicator: You can increase the ratio of accounts payable to purchases by seeking additional trade credit and extending payment timing to the maximum limit offered by suppliers. You can reduce accounts payable to purchases by paying invoices sooner and by foregoing the offering of credit altogether and paying suppliers in cash.

Example

Accounts payable to purchases = accounts payable / total purchases

Accounts payable = 5,633
Total purchases = 37,200

Accounts payable to purchases = 5,633 / 37,200 = 0.151 = 15.1%

192 Finding How Many Days of Purchases Have Been Paid

Equation

Days of purchases paid = accounts payable cash disbursements / average purchases per day

This ratio describes how the size of accounts payable has changed with recent payment and purchase trends.

When to use indicator: Managers and creditors can use this indicator to determine accounts payable payment and purchase trends.

Meaning of result: When the days of purchases paid are less than the days in the time period (i.e., 26 days in a 30-day time period, 338 days in a 365-day time period), it indicates the company is using accounts payable trade credit to a higher degree. Since trade credit is generally interest free, this action tends to increase overall company profitability. However, when payables become delinquent because they are much too low relative to purchases, credit ratings and further credit offerings may suffer.

Ways to improve the indicator: You can reduce the days-of-purchases-paid ratio by delaying payment of payables until the last minute and by increasing the amount of purchases. You can increase this ratio by the opposite action, paying invoices promptly and reducing purchases.

Example

Days of purchases paid = accounts payable cash disbursements / average purchases per day

Accounts payable cash disbursements = 34,488
Average purchases per day = 37,200 / 365 = 101.9

Days of purchases paid = 34,488 / 101.9 = 338.4

193 Comparing Accounts Payable Cash Disbursements to Accounts Payable

Equation

Accounts payable cash disbursement turnover = accounts payable cash disbursements / accounts payable

Accounts payable cash disbursement turnover describes the relative size of accounts payable payments and accounts payable, and more specifically, how many times a company achieves, or turns over, the value of accounts payable in total payments. Accounts payable is the money owed by the company for goods and services provided on credit by suppliers.

When to use indicator: Managers and creditors can use this indicator to determine accounts payable payment and purchase trends.

Meaning of result: Lower ratios can indicate the company is taking advantage of credit extended by suppliers and/or high levels of growth accompanied by increasing purchases and accounts payable balances. Since accounts payable credit is often interest free, many companies seek to reduce accounts payable cash disbursement turnover to maximize profit. When ratios become too low, however, it can indicate companies that are experiencing difficulty in paying bills when due, which may result in adverse credit ratings and difficulty in obtaining future credit lines.

When companies experience high levels of sales growth, purchase levels and accounts payable balances generally increase. Since cash disbursements lag behind actual purchases and since, in this scenario, purchases are on the rise, cash disbursements tend to be lower than current purchases and the disbursement turnover ratio falls.

Higher ratios indicate management has not used supplier credit to a significant degree, either by choice or because suppliers have elected to withhold generous credit terms. Higher ratios can also indicate downturns in sales levels, meaning current purchase levels are lower than historical trends.

Ways to improve the indicator: You can reduce accounts payable cash disbursement turnover by seeking additional trade credit and paying invoices as late as possible. You can increase the ratio by paying invoices quicker and by foregoing the offering of credit altogether and paying suppliers in cash.

Example

Accounts payable cash disbursement turnover = accounts payable cash disbursements / accounts payable

Accounts payable cash disbursements = 34,488
Accounts payable = 5,633

Accounts payable cash disbursement turnover = 34,488 / 5,633 = 6.12

194 Comparing Individual Accounts Payable Disbursements to Total Cash Disbursements

Equation

Individual accounts payable cash disbursements to total cash disbursements = individual accounts payable cash disbursements / accounts payable cash disbursements

Individual accounts payable cash disbursement ratios indicate expense trends companies incur. Accounts payable is the money owed by the company for goods and services provided on credit by suppliers.

When to use indicator: Managers can use this indicator to determine areas to investigate further. For example, the ratios can highlight accounts with excessively increasing payment percentages.

Meaning of result: High ratios indicate the particular account is a large and important supplier of goods or services. When the specific ratio is trending higher, it may indicate larger use of the source of goods or services. It can also indicate unusually high price increases.

Ways to improve the indicator: Higher percentage payment ratios may be the result of normal operations and/or changes in the type of product or service offered. However, high ratios can also be the result of price gouging. In this case, it is often beneficial to request supplier rebids, noting the excessive costs. Competitive bids from other suppliers may help to bring higher trending payments in line with industry standards.

Example

Individual accounts payable cash disbursements to total cash disbursements = individual accounts payable cash disbursements / accounts payable cash disbursements

Individual accounts payable cash disbursements = 4,555
Accounts payable cash disbursements = 34,488

Individual accounts payable cash disbursements to total cash disbursements = 4,555 / 34,488 = 0.1321 = 13.21%

CHAPTER FOURTEEN

Inventory

Inventory includes finished goods, work in process, and the raw materials used to manufacture finished goods. Ratios in this chapter help managers and investors monitor the levels of inventory and determine inventory carrying costs and methods of maintaining proper inventory levels.

195 Relating Inventory and Sales Levels

Equation

Inventory to sales = inventory / net sales

This ratio compares the size of inventory levels to the size of the company. Inventory includes finished goods, work in process, and the raw materials used to manufacture finished goods.

When to use indicator: Managers, creditors, and investors can use this indicator to check that inventory levels are appropriate given sales levels and historic inventory levels. Inventory levels will tend to vary depending upon the industry in which the company competes.

Meaning of result: Higher ratios can indicate inventory levels are getting out of control. Since there is a significant cost associated with the stocking of inventory, management should proactively seek methods to keep inventory levels to a minimum. However, problems can arise when inventory levels are too low. Customers may not receive the desired and prompt delivery of products they are accustomed to, and excessive manufacturing costs may result if short production runs of out-of-stock inventory become necessary.

Ways to improve the indicator: Lower inventory levels generally increase company profitability since a company can use the cash normally tied up in inventory for higher return investments. Lower inventory levels are easier to accommodate by improving a number of factors. These include production planning, scheduling, capacity planning, product quality, equipment quality, relations with raw materials suppliers, and inventory planning. Simply reducing inventory levels without improvement in these critical areas can lead to disastrous results.

Example

Inventory to sales = inventory / net sales

Inventory = 13,421
Net sales = 85,420

Inventory to sales = 13,421 / 85,420 = 0.1571 = 15.71%

Sector	Mid to large cap	Inventory to Sales	Small to mid cap	Inventory to Sales	Micro to small cap	Inventory to Sales
Manufacturing	General Motors	6.79%	Toro	15.23%	Encad	19.56%
Retail	Wal-Mart Stores	13.99%	Bed Bath & Beyond	25.35%	TCBY Enterprises	11.79%
Food	McDonald's	0.62%	Applebee's Int'l	0.93%	Garden Fresh Restaurant	3.20%
Technology	Microsoft	0.00%	Cypress Semiconductor	14.13%	Jmar Technologies	21.83%
Finance	Morgan-Stanley Dean Witter	324.40%	Franklin Resources	0.00%	AmeriTrade Holding	0.00%
Healthcare	Columbia/HCA Healthcare	2.40%	Novacare	1.73%	National Home Health Care	0.00%
Service	Manpower	0.00%	Air & Water Technologies	0.41%	Market Facts	0.00%
Media/Publishing	McGraw Hill	8.22%	Scholastic	18.83%	Thomas Nelson	27.91%

196 Determining the Turnover of the Entire Inventory

Equation

Inventory turnover = cost of goods sold / average inventory

Inventory turnover describes the relative size of the cost of goods sold and inventory, and more specifically, how many times a company achieves, or turns over, the value of inventory in the cost to produce goods that have been sold. Inventory includes finished goods, work in process, and the raw materials used to manufacture finished goods. Cost of goods sold includes the costs required to produce the product or service (i.e., raw materials, direct labor, and direct overhead).

When to use indicator: Managers, creditors, and investors can use this indicator to check that inventory levels are appropriate given sales levels and historic inventory levels. Inventory levels will tend to vary depending upon the industry in which the company competes.

Meaning of result: Lower ratios can indicate inventory levels are getting out of control. Since there is a significant cost associated with the stocking of inventory, management should proactively seek methods to keep inventory levels to a minimum. However, problems can arise when inventory levels are too low. Customers may not receive the desired and prompt delivery of products that they are accustomed to and excessive manufacturing costs may arise if short production runs of out-of-stock inventory become necessary.

Ways to improve the indicator: Higher inventory turnover ratios generally increase company profitability since a company can use the cash normally tied up in inventory for higher return investments. Higher inventory turnover is easier to accommodate by improving a number of factors. These include production planning, scheduling, capacity planning, product quality, equipment quality, relations with raw materials suppliers, and inventory planning. Simply increasing inventory turnover without improvement in these critical areas can lead to disastrous results.

Example

Inventory turnover = cost of goods sold / average inventory

Cost of goods sold = 54,212
Average inventory = 13,421

Inventory turnover = 54,212 / 13,421 = 4.04 = 404%

Sector	Mid to large cap	Inventory Turnover	Small to mid cap	Inventory Turnover	Micro to small cap	Inventory Turnover
Manufacturing	General Motors	10.74	Toro	4.14	Encad	2.68
Retail	Wal-Mart Stores	5.66	Bed Bath & Beyond	2.31	TCBY Enterprises	5.66
Food	McDonald's	94.32	Applebee's Int'l	80.93	Garden Fresh Restaurant	8.14
Technology	Microsoft	*	Cypress Semiconductor	4.64	Jmar Technologies	2.70
Finance	Morgan-Stanley Dean Witter	0.20	Franklin Resources	*	AmeriTrade Holding	*
Healthcare	Columbia/HCA Healthcare	18.60	Novacare	43.71	National Home Health Care	*
Service	Manpower	*	Air & Water Technologies	203.68	Market Facts	*
Media/Publishing	McGraw Hill	5.64	Scholastic	2.69	Thomas Nelson	1.96

* Companies with no reported inventory.

197 Determining How Many Days of Inventory Are On Hand

Equation

Days of inventory = average inventory / cost of goods sold used per day

Days of inventory describes the size of inventory in terms of how many days of inventory use are available. Inventory includes finished goods, work in process, and the raw materials used to manufacture finished goods. Cost of goods sold includes the costs required to produce the sold product or service (i.e., raw materials, direct labor, and direct overhead).

When to use indicator: Managers, creditors, and investors can use this indicator to check that inventory levels are appropriate given sales levels and historic inventory levels. Inventory levels will tend to vary depending upon the industry in which the company competes.

Meaning of result: Higher ratios can indicate inventory levels are getting out of control. Higher ratios can also indicate obsolete portions of inventory that are difficult to sell. Since there is a significant cost associated with the stocking of inventory, management should proactively seek methods to keep inventory levels to a minimum. However, problems can arise when inventory levels are too low. Customers may not receive the desired and prompt delivery of products that they are accustomed to and excessive manufacturing costs may result if short production runs of out-of-stock inventory become necessary.

Ways to improve the indicator: Fewer days of inventory on hand generally increase company profitability since a company can use the cash normally tied up in inventory for higher return investments. Fewer days of inventory levels are easier to accommodate by improving a number of factors. These include production planning, scheduling, capacity planning, product quality, equipment quality, relations with raw materials suppliers, and inventory planning. Simply lowering days of inventory without improvement in these critical areas can lead to disastrous results.

Example

Days of inventory = average inventory / cost of goods sold used per day

Average inventory = 13,421
Cost of goods sold used per day = annual cost of goods sold / 365 = 54,212 / 365 = 148.5

Days of inventory = 13,421 / 148.5 = 90.4

Sector	Mid to large cap	Days of Inventory	Small to mid cap	Days of Inventory	Micro to small cap	Days of Inventory
Manufacturing	General Motors	33.97	Toro	88.13	Encad	135.98
Retail	Wal-Mart Stores	64.44	Bed Bath & Beyond	157.74	TCBY Enterprises	64.54
Food	McDonald's	3.87	Applebee's Int'l	4.51	Garden Fresh Restaurant	44.83
Technology	Microsoft	0.00	Cypress Semiconductor	78.67	Jmar Technologies	135.41
Finance	Morgan-Stanley Dean Witter	1,858.62	Franklin Resources	0.00	AmeriTrade Holding	0.00
Healthcare	Columbia/HCA Healthcare	19.63	Novacare	8.35	National Home Health Care	0.00
Service	Manpower	0.00	Air & Water Technologies	1.79	Market Facts	0.00
Media/Publishing	McGraw Hill	64.67	Scholastic	135.52	Thomas Nelson	186.18

198 Calculating the Turnover of Finished Product Inventory

Equation

Finished product inventory turnover = cost of goods sold / average finished product inventory

Finished product inventory turnover describes the relative size of the cost of goods sold and finished product inventory, and more specifically, how many times a company achieves, or turns over, the value of finished product inventory in the cost to produce goods that have been sold. Inventory includes finished goods, work in process, and the raw materials used to manufacture finished goods. **Finished goods** are fully manufactured products that are in stock and ready for delivery. Cost of goods sold includes the costs required to produce the product or service (i.e., raw materials, direct labor, and direct overhead).

When to use indicator: Managers can use this indicator to check that finished product inventory levels are appropriate given sales levels and historic inventory levels. Finished product inventory levels will vary depending upon the industry in which the company competes.

Meaning of result: Lower ratios can indicate finished product inventory levels are getting out of control. Since there is a significant cost associated with the stocking of finished product inventory, management should proactively seek methods to keep such inventory levels to a minimum. However, problems can arise when finished product inventory levels are too low. Customers may not receive the desired and prompt delivery of products that they are accustomed to and excessive manufacturing costs may result if short production runs of out-of-stock finished product inventory become necessary.

Ways to improve the indicator: Higher finished product inventory turnover ratios generally increase company profitability since the company can use the cash normally tied up in inventory for higher return investments. Higher finished product inventory turnover is easier to accommodate by improving a number of factors. These include production planning, scheduling, capacity planning, product quality, equipment quality, relations with raw materials suppliers, and inventory planning. Simply increasing finished product inventory turnover without improvement in these critical areas can lead to disastrous results.

Example

Finished product inventory turnover = cost of goods sold / average finished product inventory

Cost of goods sold = 54,212
Average finished product inventory = 4,268

Finished product inventory turnover = 54,212 / 4,268 = 12.7

Finding How Many Days of Finished Product Inventory Are Available

Equation

Days of finished product inventory = finished product inventory / cost of goods sold used per day

Days of finished product inventory describes the size of that inventory in terms of how many days of finished products are available in inventory. Inventory includes finished goods, work in process, and the raw materials used to manufacture finished goods. Finished goods are fully manufactured products that are in stock and ready for delivery. Cost of goods sold includes the costs required to produce the product or service (i.e., raw materials, direct labor, and direct overhead).

When to use indicator: Managers can use this indicator to check that finished product inventory levels are appropriate given sales levels and historic inventory levels. Finished product inventory levels will vary depending upon the industry in which the company competes.

Meaning of result: Higher ratios can indicate finished product inventory levels are getting out of control or identify high and rising obsolete portions of finished product inventory that are difficult to sell. Since there is a significant cost associated with the stocking of inventory, management should proactively seek methods to keep inventory levels to a minimum. However, problems can arise when finished product inventory levels are too low. Customers may not receive the desired and prompt delivery of products that they are accustomed to and excessive manufacturing costs may result if short production runs of out-of-stock inventory become necessary.

Ways to improve the indicator: Fewer days of finished product inventory on hand generally increase company profitability since the company can use the cash normally tied up in inventory for higher return investments. Fewer days of finished product inventory levels are easier to accommodate by improving a number of factors. These include production planning, scheduling, capacity planning, product quality, equipment quality, relations with raw materials suppliers, and inventory planning. Simply lowering days of finished product inventory without improvement in these critical areas can lead to disastrous results.

Example

Days of finished product inventory = finished product inventory / cost of goods sold used per day

Finished product inventory = 4,268
Cost of goods sold used per day = cost of goods sold / 365 = 54,212 / 365 = 148.5

Days of inventory = 4,268 / 148.5 = 28.74

200 Determining the Turnover of Work in Process Inventory

Equation

Work in process inventory turnover = cost of goods manufactured / average work in process inventory

Work in process inventory turnover describes the relative size of the cost of goods manufactured and work in process inventory, and more specifically, how many times a company achieves, or turns over, the value of work in process inventory in the cost to produce goods that have been manufactured. Inventory includes finished goods, work in process, and the raw materials used to manufacture finished goods. Partially manufactured products are considered work in process. Cost of goods manufactured includes the costs required to produce the product or service (i.e., raw materials, direct labor, and direct overhead).

When to use indicator: Managers can use this indicator to check that work in process inventory levels are appropriate given sales levels and historic inventory levels. Work in process inventory levels will vary depending upon the industry in which the company competes.

The cost of goods sold and cost of goods manufactured are different in that the cost of goods sold is composed only of those products that have been sold; whereas, the cost of goods manufactured is composed of the cost of all goods fabricated, whther they have been sold or not.

Meaning of result: Lower ratios can indicate work in process inventory levels are getting out of control. Since there is a significant cost associated with the stocking of inventory, management should proactively seek methods to keep inventory levels to a minimum. However, problems can arise when work in process inventory levels are too low. Customers may not receive the desired and prompt delivery of products that they are accustomed to and excessive manufacturing costs may result if short production runs of out-of-stock inventory become necessary.

Lower ratios can also indicate actual or anticipated increasing sales levels. In this case, management often increases work in process levels in anticipation of near-term decreases in finished goods inventory.

Ways to improve the indicator: Higher inventory turnover ratios generally increase company profitability since the company can use the cash normally tied up in inventory for higher return investments. Higher work in process inventory turnover is easier to achieve by improving a number of factors. These include production planning, scheduling, capacity planning, product quality, equipment quality, relations with raw materials suppliers, and inventory planning. Simply increasing work in process inventory turnover without improvement in these critical areas can lead to disastrous results.

Example

Work in process inventory turnover = cost of goods manufactured / average work in process inventory

Cost of goods manufactured = 55,642
Average work in process inventory = 5,845

Work in process inventory turnover = 55,642 / 5,845 = 9.52

201 Calculating How Many Days of Work in Process Are Available

Equation

Days of work in process inventory = average work in process inventory / cost of goods manufactured per day

Days of work in process inventory describes the size of that inventory in terms of how many days of work in process are available. Inventory includes finished goods, work in process, and the raw materials used to manufacture finished goods. Partially manufactured products are considered work in process. Cost of goods manufactured includes the costs required to produce the product or service (i.e., raw materials, direct labor, and direct overhead).

The cost of goods sold and cost of goods manufactured are different in that the cost of goods sold is composed only of those products that have been sold; whereas, the cost of goods manufactured is composed of the cost of all goods fabricated, whther they have been sold or not.

When to use indicator: Managers can use this indicator to check that work in process inventory levels are appropriate given sales levels and historic inventory levels. Work in process inventory levels will vary depending upon the industry in which the company competes.

Meaning of result: Higher ratios can indicate work in process inventory levels are getting out of control. Higher ratios can also lead to high levels of finished product inventory. Since there is a significant cost associated with the stocking of inventory, management should proactively seek methods to keep inventory levels to a minimum. However, problems can arise when work in process levels are too low since this can lead to depleted finished product inventory levels. Customers may not receive the desired and prompt delivery of products that they are accustomed to and excessive manufacturing costs may result if short production runs of out-of-stock inventory become necessary.

Higher ratios can also indicate actual or anticipated increasing sales levels. In this case, management often increases work in process levels in anticipation of near-term decreases in finished goods inventory.

Ways to improve the indicator: Lower days of work in process inventory generally increases company profitability since the cash normally tied up in inventory can be used for higher return investments. Lower days of work in process inventory levels are easier to accommodate by improving a number of factors. These include production planning, scheduling, capacity planning, product quality, equipment quality, relations with raw materials suppliers, and inventory planning. Simply lowering days of work in process inventory without improvement in these critical areas can lead to disastrous results.

Example

Days of work in process inventory = average work in process inventory / cost of goods manufactured per day

Average work in process inventory = 5,845
Cost of goods manufactured per day = cost of goods manufactured / 365 = 55,642 / 365 = 152.4

Days of work in process inventory = 5,845 / 152.4 = 38.4

202 Determining the Turnover of Raw Materials Inventory

Equation

Raw materials inventory turnover = cost of raw materials used / average raw material inventory

Raw materials inventory turnover describes the relative size of the cost of raw materials used to produce products and the raw materials inventory. More specifically, this ratio describes how many times a company achieves, or turns over, the value of average raw material inventory in the raw material costs to produce goods that have been sold. Inventory includes finished goods, work in process, and the raw materials used to manufacture finished goods. Raw materials inventory is the portion of total inventory that consists of purchased raw materials, components, and assemblies. Cost of raw materials is the raw materials cost portion of the cost of goods sold and includes purchased raw materials, components, and assemblies.

When to use indicator: Managers can use this indicator to check that raw material inventory levels are appropriate given sales levels and historic inventory levels. Raw materials inventory levels will vary depending upon the industry in which the company competes.

Meaning of result: Lower ratios can indicate that raw materials inventory levels are getting out of control. Since there is a significant cost associated with the stocking of inventory, management should proactively seek methods to keep raw material inventory levels to a minimum. However, problems can arise when raw materials inventory levels are too low. Customers may not receive the desired and prompt delivery of products that they are accustomed to when finished products are out-of-stock and there is inadequate raw materials inventory for the manufacture and replenishment of finished goods inventories.

Ways to improve the indicator: Higher raw materials inventory turnover ratios generally increase company profitability. Higher raw materials inventory turnover is easier to accommodate by improving a number of factors. These include production planning, scheduling, capacity planning, product quality, equipment quality, relations with raw materials suppliers, and inventory planning. Simply increasing raw materials inventory turnover without improvement in these critical areas can lead to disastrous results.

Example

Raw materials inventory turnover = cost of raw materials used / average raw material inventory

Cost of raw materials used = 31,063
Average raw material inventory = 3,308

Raw materials inventory turnover = 31,063 / 3,308 = 9.39

203 Examining How Many Days of Raw Materials Inventory Are Available

Equation

Days of raw materials inventory = average raw materials inventory / cost of raw materials used per day

Days of raw material inventory describes the size of that inventory in terms of how many days of raw materials are available in inventory. Inventory includes finished goods, work in process, and the raw materials used to manufacture finished goods. Raw materials inventory is the portion of total inventory that includes purchased raw materials, components, and assemblies. Cost of raw materials is the raw materials cost portion of cost of goods sold and includes purchased raw materials, components, and assemblies.

When to use indicator: Managers can use this indicator to check that raw materials inventory levels are appropriate given sales levels and historic inventory levels. Raw materials inventory levels will vary depending upon the industry in which the company competes.

Meaning of result: Higher ratios can indicate raw materials inventory levels are getting out of control and can identify high and rising obsolete portions of raw materials inventory that are difficult to sell. Since there is a significant cost associated with the stocking of inventory, management should proactively seek methods to keep inventory levels to a minimum. However, problems can arise when raw materials inventory levels are too low. Customers may not receive the desired and prompt delivery of products that they are accustomed to when finished products are out-of-stock and there is inadequate raw materials inventory for the manufacture and replenishment of finished goods inventories.

Ways to improve the indicator: Fewer days of raw materials inventory on hand generally increase company profitability. You can reduce days of raw materials inventory levels by improving a number of factors. These include production planning, scheduling, capacity planning, product quality, equipment quality, relations with raw materials suppliers, and inventory planning. Simply lowering days of raw material inventory without improvement in these critical areas can lead to disastrous results.

Example

Days of raw materials inventory = average raw material inventory / cost of raw materials used per day

Average raw material inventory = 3,308
Cost of raw materials used per day = cost of raw materials / 365 = 31,063 / 365 = 85.1

Days of raw materials inventory = 3,308 / 85.1 = 38.9

204 Determining the Inventory Ordering Cost

Equation

Average inventory ordering cost = all costs associated with ordering new raw materials or retail inventory / number of new orders

Inventory ordering costs include costs of ordering new raw materials or, for retailers, ordering new stock. The costs may include salaries and expenses for order placement, computerized inventory control, accounts payable, telephones, shipping, handling, and inspection. The average inventory order cost gives the manager a general indication of the costs associated with individual orders of new inventory.

When to use indicator: Managers can use this indicator to determine the costs associated with ordering inventory and as an input parameter in determining the optimum size of inventory orders when using techniques such as the Economic Ordering Quantity (EOQ) method. By using inventory control methods such as the EOQ, manufacturers and retailers may be able to optimize the trade-off between inventory ordering costs and inventory carrying costs. One of the more popular theories regarding inventory control is the Just-In-Time (JIT) inventory control method, in which improvements in inventory control, vendor relations, and manufacturing methods allow for inventory minimization and the cost reductions associated with carrying less inventory.

Meaning of result: Higher ordering costs can be the result of extensive, redundant, and/or inefficient ordering, inspection, shipping, handling, and payment systems.

Ways to improve the indicator: Lowering the expenses associated with acquiring inventory can lower average inventory order costs. Improved and/or computerized systems may help streamline purchasing, accounting, and payment operations and reduce the amount of employee input and expense required to purchase, receive, and pay for inventory.

Example

Average inventory ordering cost = all costs associated with ordering new raw materials or retail inventory / number of new orders

Purchasing costs (salaries, office space, overhead, etc. used in ordering inventory) = 67,500
Accounting = 6,400
Accounts payable costs = 3,000
Telephone costs = 1,460
Computer and forms costs = 15,280
Handling = 5,800
Shipping = 16,433
Inspecting = 8,697
Other miscellaneous costs = 7,520
Number of new orders = 3,540

Average inventory ordering cost = (67,500 + 6,400 + 3,000 + 1,460 + 15,280 + 5,800 + 16,433 + 8,697 + 7,520) / 3,540 = 34.49

205 Measuring the Inventory Carrying Cost

Equation

Inventory carrying cost per unit per time period = all costs associated with storing the inventory item

Manufacturers incur inventory carrying costs when they store raw materials; retailers incur them to have available stock on-hand. Carrying costs may include warehouse rent, warehouse utilities, inventory obsolescence, interest costs associated with carrying inventory, and handling costs. The inventory carrying cost per unit gives the manager an indication of the unit costs associated with stocking inventory items.

When to use indicator: Managers can use this indicator to determine the costs associated with carrying inventory and as an input parameter in determining the optimum size of inventory orders when using techniques such as the Economic Ordering Quantity (EOQ) method. By using inventory control methods such as the EOQ, manufacturers and retailers may be able to optimize the trade-off between inventory ordering costs and inventory carrying costs. One of the more popular theories regarding inventory control is the Just-In-Time (JIT) inventory control method, in which improvements in inventory control, vendor relations, and manufacturing methods allow for cost reductions associated with carrying less inventory.

Meaning of result: Higher per-unit carrying costs can be the result of expensive and/or inefficient inventory warehousing, high handling costs, and high costs of capital.

Ways to improve the indicator: Lowering the expenses associated with storing and handling inventory can lower average inventory carrying costs. Maintaining inventory at minimum required levels and efficiently making use of warehouse space can minimize costs. You can reduce handling expenses by providing inventory personnel with the tools and training to receive, inspect, and store raw materials optimally.

Example

Inventory carrying cost per unit per time period = all costs associated with storing the inventory item

Expenses for a particular inventory item per unit per year

Time period = 1 year
Cost per unit = 54
Warehouse costs (rent, utilities, insurance, etc.) = 18.00
Inventory capital costs = (cost per unit) × (cost of capital per year) = 54 × 0.1263 = 6.82
Handling = 1.54
Obsolescence = 3.40
Other miscellaneous costs = 0.88

Inventory carrying cost per unit per year = 18.00 + 6.82 + 1.54 + 3.40 + 0.88 = 30.64

206 Determining the Optimum Inventory Order Quantity

Equation

Optimum inventory order quantity (EOQ) =
[(2 × inventory order cost × total inventory usage per period)/inventory carrying cost]^0.5

One technique for determining the optimum purchase quantity of individual inventory items is the Economic Ordering Quantity (EOQ) method. This method attempts to optimize the trade-off between inventory ordering costs and inventory carrying costs and thus minimize the expenses associated with ordering and carrying inventory. Inventory ordering costs per unit of inventory decrease with increased order size while inventory carrying costs increase with larger orders.

Manufacturers realize inventory ordering costs when they order new raw materials; retailers incur them when they order new stock. The costs may include salaries and expenses for order placement, computerized inventory control, accounts payable, telephones, shipping, handling, and inspection. Manufacturers realize inventory carrying costs when they store raw materials and retailers, when they have available stock on-hand. Carrying costs may include warehouse rent, warehouse utilities, the cost of capital to purchase and carry inventory, and handling costs.

When to use indicator: Managers can use this indicator to determine the optimum size of inventory orders. By using inventory control methods such as the EOQ, manufacturers and retailers may be able to optimize the trade-off between inventory ordering costs and inventory carrying costs. One of the more popular theories regarding inventory control is the Just-In-Time (JIT) inventory control method, in which improvements in inventory control, vendor relations, and manufacturing methods allow for cost reductions associated with carrying less inventory.

Meaning of result: The EOQ calculation indicates the optimum size of inventory orders. This information can help inventory management personnel minimize the expenses of ordering and carrying inventory. Although the EOQ is useful in helping determine inventory order size, the method has a number of shortcomings. Among these limitations and assumptions are constant and predictable inventory usage rates, carrying costs that are directly proportional to inventory size, constant ordering costs, inventory depletions to zero with no safety stock, and lack of consideration of volume discounts.

Ways to improve the indicator: You can increase the EOQ by lowering carrying costs and increasing ordering costs and inventory usage rates. You can decrease the EOQ by increasing carrying costs and decreasing ordering costs and inventory usage rates.

Example

Optimum inventory order quantity (EOQ) =
[(2 × inventory order cost × total inventory usage per period)/inventory carrying cost]^0.5

Inventory order cost = 34.49 per order
Total inventory usage per period = 2,400 units per year
Inventory carrying cost = 30.64 per year per unit

Optimum inventory order quantity (EOQ) =
[(2 × 34.49 × 2,400)/30.64]^0.5 = 74 units per order, an order every 11 days (74 × 365/2,400)

What if inventory order costs rise to $62?

Then EOQ rises to 99 units per order, an order every 15 days.

What if carrying costs rise to 45 per year per unit?

Then EOQ falls to 61 units per order, an order every 9 days.

What if usage climbs to 3,500 units per year?

Then EOQ rises to 89 units per order, an order every 14 days.

207 Determining the Total Cost of Inventory Per Item

Equation

Total cost of inventory item per period = ordering costs per item per period + carrying costs per item per period

You can estimate the costs associated with inventory by adding the expenses associated with ordering and carrying inventory. Manufacturers realize inventory ordering costs when they order new raw materials; retailers when they order new stock. The costs may include salaries and expenses for order placement, computerized inventory control, accounts payable, telephones, shipping, handling, and inspection. Manufacturers realize inventory carrying costs when they store raw materials; retailers when they have available stock on-hand. Carrying costs may include warehouse rent, warehouse utilities, the cost of capital to purchase and carry inventory, and handling costs.

When to use indicator: Managers can use this indicator to estimate the costs associated with inventorying items over a given time period.

Meaning of result: Higher inventory costs can be the result of nonoptimum inventory order sizes, high carrying costs, and high ordering costs. High carrying costs can arise with expensive and/or inefficient inventory warehousing, high handling costs, expensive inventory with high interest payments, and high costs of capital. High ordering costs can be the result of extensive, redundant, and/or inefficient ordering, inspection, shipping, handling, and payment systems.

Ways to improve the indicator: You can reduce inventory costs by using techniques to determine optimum inventory order sizes such as the Economic Order Quantity (EOQ) method. This method balances ordering and carrying costs in an effort to minimize overall inventory costs. Note that the example below uses the EOQ method to determine the optimum order quantity resulting in inventory ordering costs that are equivalent to inventory carrying costs. You can minimize total inventory costs by using the EOQ method when the ordering and carrying costs are equal.

Lowering the expenses associated with acquiring inventory can lower average inventory order costs. Improved and/or computerized systems may help streamline purchasing, accounting, and payment operations and reduce the amount of employee input and expense required to purchase, receive, and pay for inventory.

Lowering the expenses associated with storing and handling inventory can lower average inventory carrying costs. Maintaining inventory at minimum required levels and efficiently making use of warehouse space can reduce warehouse costs. You can reduce handling expenses by providing inventory personnel with the tools and training to receive, inspect, and store raw materials optimally.

Example

Total cost of inventory per item per period = ordering costs per item per period + carrying costs per item per period

Time period = 1 year
Ordering costs per item per year = (average inventory order cost × total inventory usage per period) / inventory order size

Average inventory order cost = 34.49
Total inventory usage per period = 2,400
Inventory order size = 74

Ordering costs per item per year = (34.49 × 2,400) / 74 = 1,119
Carrying cost per item per year = inventory carrying cost per unit per year × average inventory size

Inventory carrying cost per unit per year = 30.64
Average inventory size = 74 / 2 = 37

Carrying cost per item per year = 30.64 × 37 = 1,134

Total cost of inventory per item per period = 1,119 + 1,134 = 2,253

208 Determining the Timing of Inventory Reorders

Equation

Inventory reorder point = (total inventory usage per period / days per period) × inventory lead time

Inventory reorder point with safety stock = inventory reorder point + safety stock

The **inventory reorder point** defines the timing of placement of new inventory orders. By considering the amount of inventory required and the lead time required to replenish depleted inventories, a manager can determine the timing on reorders. The volume of existing inventory remaining in stock is the timing trigger for new order placement. This technique is a simple method of determining only rough reorder points since the technique as described does not allow for any safety stock or variations in demand. The method assumes new inventory arrives just when existing inventory is depleted, which could increase the potential of running out of inventory. Improvements to this method account for safety stock estimations. More sophisticated techniques use probability curves to define safety stock requirements more precisely.

When to use indicator: Managers can use this indicator to determine the timing of placing new inventory orders.

Meaning of result: Higher inventory reorder point volumes occur when inventory usage rates are high and inventory lead times are long. Reorder point volumes are also high when working days per period are low and grouped together since this increases inventory usage rates and results in the need for a large inventory supply.

Ways to improve the indicator: You can lower inventory reorder points by decreasing inventory lead times and inventory usage rates. Eliminating periodic spiked inventory use and flattening inventory demand will also allow for lower inventory reorder points.

Example

Inventory reorder point = (total inventory usage per period / days per period) × inventory lead time

Total inventory usage per period = 2,400 units per year
Inventory lead time = 7 days
Days per period = 365 days

Inventory reorder point = (2,400 / 365) × 7 = 46 units

Inventory reorder point with safety stock = inventory reorder point + safety stock

Assume safety stock = 50 units

Inventory reorder point with safety stock = 46 + 50 = 96 units

209 Estimating the Size of Inventory Safety Stock

Equation

Safety stock = demand variability over lead time × service level factor

The historical demand and variability of inventory and the level of service a company wishes to provide its customers determines this method of safety stock. By computing the mean and standard deviation of demand, you can determine the demand variability. If the demand for the particular inventory items follows a normal distribution, you can use probability curves to determine a service level factor that corresponds to the percentage of time there will be sufficient stock to meet demand. You should add the safety stock amount to the mean amount required during the lead time for inventory receipt to determine the reorder point.

When to use indicator: Managers can use this indicator to determine the timing of new inventory orders. By adding a safety stock to inventory levels, you can reduce the probability of running out of inventory.

Meaning of result: Higher safety stock requirements occur when you have higher degrees of inventory demand variability and when you increase the level of service. A company that wishes to have an amount of stock on hand that will cover demand 99% of the time will have a higher service level factor than the company that desires to cover demand only 75% of the time.

Ways to improve the indicator: You can lower safety stock requirements by smoothing demand variability and by reducing vendor inventory shipment lead times. You can also decrease safety stock needs by reducing the level of customer service provided, an often unattractive alternative.

Example

Safety stock = demand variability over lead time × service level factor

Desired service level factor = 95%
Total inventory usage per period = 2,400 units per year
Mean demand per day = 6.58 units
Standard deviation demand per day = 3.24 units
Inventory lead time = 7 days
Days per period = 365 days
Demand variability over lead time = standard deviation demand per day × (average lead time^0.5) = 3.24 × (7^0.5) = 8.57

Table of service level factors	
Service level	**Factor**
50%	0.0
75%	0.67
90%	1.28
95%	1.64
99%	2.33
99.9%	3.30

Safety stock = 8.57 × 1.64 = 14.1 units

Inventory reorder point with safety stock = ([total inventory usage per period / days per period] × inventory lead time) + safety stock

Total inventory usage per period = 2,400 units per year
Inventory lead time = 7 days
Days per period = 365 days

Inventory reorder point with safety stock = ([2,400 / 365] × 7) + 14.1 = 60.1 units

210 Examining Just-In-Time (JIT) Systems

One alternative to the Economic Ordering Quantity (EOQ) technique of determining the optimum inventory purchase quantity and carrying volume is the Just-In-Time (JIT) method of manufacturing and inventory control. Rather than attempting to optimize the trade-off between inventory ordering costs and inventory carrying costs as the EOQ system teaches, the JIT technique endeavors to reduce waste and improve quality by performing a number of actions including the minimization of inventory requirements. A company reduces inventory requirements since purchased raw materials are received just prior to being used in the manufacturing and finished goods are completed just prior to shipment to customers.

When to use indicator: Management can use JIT techniques to reduce waste and improve the quality of business processes.

Meaning of result: JIT techniques offer the potential to increase quality and reduce the costs associated with a number of manufacturing and business processes. It is critical that a manager employ JIT methods together with improvements in business operations including production planning, inventory control, scheduling, vendor relations, employee training, and manufacturing methods. Without commensurate improvements in such areas, JIT failure is more likely because there is an increased probability of running out of raw materials and finished goods.

CHAPTER FIFTEEN

Product and Service Demand Types

The elasticity ratios detailed in this chapter describe how customer demand levels for products and services change with changes in product pricing. Also included is a ratio that describes how supply levels change with price changes. This information may help you improve product and service pricing strategies.

211 Examining Elastic Demand for Goods or Services

Equation

Demand elasticity = (change in quantity demanded / base volume) / (change in price / base price)

Demand elasticity, also known as **price elasticity of demand,** describes how the level of customer demand changes with changes in price. You can think of demand elasticity as the responsiveness of demand to price changes. When the demand for a product or service is *elastic,* the size of the demand is very dependent on the pricing of the product or service. For very elastic products or services, price increases will result in large demand decreases while price cuts will result in large demand increases. For elastic products or services, total revenues (price × quantity) decrease as prices increase and increase as prices decrease.

When to use indicator: It is useful for managers to understand the elasticity of the goods or services being offered when developing pricing and product line strategies.

Meaning of result: Products are considered elastic when the demand elasticity has an absolute value greater than 1.0. Absolute values much higher than 1.0 indicate even greater elasticity. You can determine elasticity by a number of factors including the amount and the availability of substitute products or services, the percentage of income the purchaser uses to purchase the product or service, the purchaser's need for the product or service, and the length of time the purchase is made after the company changes the price.

When there are few or no substitute products available, demand tends to be less elastic, or less responsive to price changes, since customers have little choice but to pay higher prices when prices rise. When the product or service takes a smaller part of the customer's income, demand also tends to be less elastic because customers generally aren't as concerned with the price change. For example, customers would be more likely to purchase a candy bar at a price that is 40% higher than normal than they would a car or a house.

When there is great need for the product or service, demand tends to be less elastic because customers are more willing to pay higher prices. The time period after which a price change has been made will also affect elasticity. If a grocery store were to raise the price of milk significantly, demand in the short term may not drop off dramatically since many shoppers may not notice the price change or may not want to make an unscheduled additional trip to buy milk at another store on the way home. However, in the longer term, as more shoppers notice the higher price and make other plans to purchase the milk, demand will probably drop more sharply. Another longer term example of the time effect is the events that took place during the oil crisis of the 1970s. When gasoline prices first rose, many consumers paid the higher prices because they had little alternative. However, with time, carpools began and manufacturers produced more efficient cars to reduce the demand for gasoline.

Example

Highly elastic example

Demand elasticity = (change in quantity demanded / base volume) / (change in price / base price)

Price A = $75
Volume at price A = 450 units
Price B = $81
Volume at price B = 310 units

Demand elasticity = [(310 − 450) / 450] / [(81 − 75) / 75] = −3.89

212 Examining Inelastic Demand for Goods and Services

Equation

Demand elasticity = (change in quantity demanded / base volume) / (change in price / base price)

Demand elasticity, also known as price elasticity of demand, describes how the level of customer demand changes with changes in price. You can think of demand elasticity as the responsiveness of demand to price changes. When the demand for a product or service is *inelastic,* the size of the demand is independent of the pricing of the product or service. For inelastic products or services, price increases will result in small demand decreases and price cuts will result in small demand increases. For inelastic products or services, total revenues (price × quantity) increase as prices increase and decrease as prices decrease.

When to use indicator: It is useful for managers to understand the elasticity of the goods or services being offered when developing pricing and product line strategies.

Meaning of result: Products are considered inelastic when the demand elasticity has an absolute value less than 1.0. Absolute values much less than 1.0 indicate even greater inelasticity. You can determine elasticity by a number of factors including the amount and the availability of substitute products or services, the percentage of income the purchaser uses to purchase the product or service, the purchaser's need for the product or service, and the length of time the purchase is made after the price changes.

When there are few or no substitute products available, demand tends to be less elastic, or less responsive to price changes, because customers have little choice but to pay higher prices when prices rise. When the product or service takes a smaller part of the customer's income, demand also tends to be less elastic because customers generally aren't as concerned with the price change. For example, customers would be more likely to purchase a candy bar at a price that is 40% higher than normal than they would a car or a house.

When there is great need for the product or service, demand tends to be less elastic because customers are more willing to pay higher prices. The time the customer purchases the product or service after a price change will also affect elasticity. If a grocery store were to raise the price of milk significantly, demand in the short term may not drop off dramatically since many shoppers may not notice the price change or may not want to make an unscheduled additional trip to buy milk at another store on the way home. However, in the longer term, as more shoppers notice the higher price and make other plans to purchase the milk, demand will probably drop more sharply. Another longer term example of the time effect is the events that took place during the oil crisis of the 1970s. When gasoline prices first rose, many consumers paid the higher prices because they had little alternative. However, with time, carpooling began and manufacturers produced more efficient cars to reduce the demand for gasoline.

Example

Inelastic example

Demand elasticity = (change in quantity demanded / base volume) / (change in price / base price)

Price A = $75
Volume at price A = 450 units
Price B = $81
Volume at price B = 435 units

Demand elasticity = [(435 − 450)/450] / [(81 − 75)/75] = −0.42

213 Understanding Unitary Elasticity for Goods or Services

Equation

Demand elasticity = (change in quantity demanded / base volume) / (change in price / base price)

Demand elasticity, also known as price elasticity of demand, describes how the level of customer demand changes with changes in price. You can also think of demand elasticity as the responsiveness of demand to price changes. When the demand for a product or service is *unitary elastic,* percentage changes in price result in equal percentage changes in demand. For unitary elastic products or services, total revenues (price × quantity) remain the same as prices increase or decrease.

When to use indicator: It is useful for managers to understand the elasticity of the goods or services being offered when developing pricing and product line strategies.

Meaning of result: Products are considered unitary elastic when the demand elasticity has an absolute value of 1.0. You can determine elasticity by a number of factors including the amount and the availability of substitute products or services, the percentage of income the purchaser uses to purchase the product or service, the purchaser's need for the product or service, and the length of time the purchase is made after the price changes.

When there are few or no substitute products available, demand tends to be less elastic, or less responsive to price changes, because customers have little choice but to pay higher prices when prices rise. When the product or service takes a smaller part of the customer's income, demand also tends to be less elastic because customers generally aren't as concerned with the price change. For example, customers would be more likely to purchase a candy bar at a price that is 40% higher than normal than they would a car or a house.

When there is great need for the product or service, demand tends to be less elastic because customers are more willing to pay higher prices. The length of time a purchase is made after a price change will also affect elasticity. If a grocery store were to raise the price of milk significantly, demand in the short term may not drop off dramatically because many shoppers may not notice the price change or may not want to make an unscheduled additional trip to buy milk at another store on the way home. However, in the longer term, as more shoppers notice the higher price and make other plans to purchase the milk, demand will possibly drop more sharply. Another longer term example of the time effect is the events that took place during the oil crisis of the 1970s. When gasoline prices first rose, many consumers paid the higher prices, because they had little alternative. However, with time, carpooling began and manufacturers produced more efficient cars to reduce the demand for gasoline.

Example

Unitary elastic example

Demand elasticity = (change in quantity demanded / base volume) / (change in price / base price)

Price A = $75
Volume at price A = 450 units
Price B = $81
Volume at price B = 414 units

Demand elasticity = [(414 − 450)/450] / [(81 − 75)/75] = −1.0

214 Examining Cross-Elasticity for Goods or Services

Equation

Cross-elasticity = (change in quantity demanded for product X / base volume of product X) / (change in price of product Y / base price of product Y)

Cross-elasticity describes how the level of customer demand for product X changes with changes in price of product Y. You can think of cross-elasticity as a measure of the substitutability of similar products.

When to use indicator: Managers need to understand the degree of cross-elasticity of the goods or services a company offers when developing pricing and product line strategies.

Meaning of result: Products or services are considered cross-elastic when the cross-elasticity has a value larger than 0.0. Larger values indicate greater degrees of cross-elasticity. You can determine cross-elasticity primarily by the substitutability, or competitiveness, of comparable products or services. For example, the cross-elasticity of butter and margarine can be high since large price changes in one will significantly affect the demand for the other.

When products have a cross-elasticity of less than 0.0, they are considered complements to each other. An example of complementary products is ski boots and skis. When the price of skis rise, the demand for ski boots will tend to decrease.

Example

Cross-elastic example

Cross-elasticity = (change in quantity demanded for product X / base volume of product X) / (change in price of product Y / base price of product Y)

Product Y price A = $75
Volume of product X at product Y price A = 450 units
Product Y price B = $81
Volume of product X at product Y price B = 525 units

Cross-elasticity = [(525 − 450)/450] / [(81 − 75)/75] = 2.08

215 Examining Price Elasticity of Supply

Equation

Elasticity of supply = (change in quantity supplied / base volume) / (change in price / base price)

Supply elasticity describes how the level of supplied goods or services changes with changes in price. The concept is similar to demand elasticity except that the elasticity of supply occurs along the supply curve versus the demand curve.

When to use indicator: Managers need to understand the elasticity of their company's goods or services when developing pricing and product line strategies.

Meaning of result: You can think of supply elasticity as the willingness of producers to provide products or services at varying price points. When the supply for a product or service is *elastic*, the willingness of producers to supply goods or services is very dependent on the pricing of the product or service. For very elastic products or services, price increases will result in large supply increases while price cuts will result in large supply decreases.

For example, mountain bike manufacturers want to produce many more bikes when sales prices rise dramatically. Conversely, falling sales prices lead to lower mountain bike supplies as some manufacturers cannot compete and cease production.

Example

Elasticity of supply = (change in quantity supplied / base volume) / (change in price / base price)

Price A = $75
Volume at price A = 450 units
Price B = $81
Volume at price B = 580 units

Elasticity of supply = [(580 − 450)/450] / [(81 − 75)/75] = 3.61

CHAPTER SIXTEEN

Capital Investment

This chapter details a number of ratios that can help you determine the degree of financial desirability of an investment. You can use the capital investment ratios for any number of investments including products, factory equipment, and entire companies.

216 Determining the Payback Period

Equation

Payback period = investment / cash flow from investment per period

The **payback period** is one of the easiest methods of determining the financial desirability of an investment. This ratio describes the amount of time required to generate a cash flow equal to the initial investment. Cash flow is the difference between cash inflows as a result of the investment and cash expenses needed to perform the work associated with the investment. When the cash flow generated per year is constant, a manager can determine the payback period directly by dividing the initial investment by the cash flow generated per year. When there are uneven cash flow estimates per year, you can determine the payback period by adding up the full year cash flows that are required to pay back the initial investment. Then you determine the percentage of the remaining year of cash flow required to pay back the initial investment fully to find the total payback period.

When to use indicator: Managers can use this ratio to help determine the viability of proposed projects. Although the payback period ratio is a very crude analysis tool, its simplicity makes it a good method for roughly gauging the potential of proposals. Drawbacks of the payback period benchmark are that it does not take into consideration the time value of money and the cash flows received after the initial investment is paid in full.

Meaning of result: Shorter payback periods are generally desirable and indicate the company will pay off the initial investment quickly if everything goes according to forecasts. In general, shorter payback times reduce risk since a company projects that investment capital will be returned quickly and because shorter term revenue projections are often more reliable than longer term forecasts.

Ways to improve the indicator: You can obtain shorter payback periods on projects that offer greater amounts of cash-generating capability and low initial investment requirements.

Example

Even cash flows

Payback period = investment / cash flow from investment per period

Project investment = 135,000
Cash flow per year = 52,000

Payback period = 135,000 / 52,000 = 2.6 years

Uneven cash flows

Payback period = investment / cash flow from investment per period

Project investment = 135,000
Year one cash flow = 52,000
Year two cash flow = 58,000
Year three cash flow = 61,000

Payback period = 1 year (52,000) + 1 year (58,000) + [135,000 − (52,000 + 58,000)] / 61,000 = 2.41 years

217 Determining the Payback Reciprocal

Equation

Payback reciprocal = cash flow from investment per period / investment

The **payback reciprocal,** the inverse of the payback period, is another easy method of determining the financial desirability of an investment. Cash flow is the difference between cash inflows as a result of the investment and cash expenses needed to perform the work associated with the investment.

When to use indicator: Managers can use this ratio to help determine the viability of proposed projects. Although the payback reciprocal ratio is a very crude analysis tool, its simplicity makes it a good method for roughly gauging the potential of proposals. A primary drawback of the payback reciprocal benchmark is that it does not consider the time value of money.

Meaning of result: Higher payback reciprocal ratios are generally desirable and indicate the company will pay off the initial investment quickly if everything goes according to forecasts. In general, shorter payback times reduce risk since the company projects that investment capital will be returned quickly and because shorter term revenue projections are often more reliable than longer term forecasts.

Ways to improve the indicator: You can obtain higher payback reciprocal ratios on projects that offer greater amounts of cash-generating capability and low initial investment requirements.

Example

Payback reciprocal = cash flow from investment per period / investment

Cash flow per year = 52,000
Project investment = 135,000

Payback reciprocal = 52,000 / 135,000 = 0.3852 = 38.52%

Finding the Discounted Payback Period

Equation

Discounted payback period = investment / discounted cash flow from investment per period

The **discounted payback period,** another method of determining the financial desirability of an investment, is similar to the payback period ratio and also takes into account the time value of money. The discounted payback period describes the amount of time required to generate a discounted cash flow equal to the initial investment. By discounting future cash flows, you realize a more accurate measure of the value of the investment. Discounted future cash flows consider that cash flow generated in the future will be worth less in today's dollars when there is a cost associated with the money used to fund an investment. When a company or individual has no cash on hand for an investment, the discount rate is considered the cost of capital. The cost of capital is a weighted average of debt and equity financing. Alternatively, when there is a ready supply of available cash, the discount rate is considered as the rate of return that alternative investments can earn.

Cash flow is the difference between cash inflows as a result of the investment and cash expenses needed to perform the work associated with the investment. When there are uneven cash flow estimates from year to year, as there are almost always for discounted payback period analyses, a manager determines the discounted payback period by adding up the full year discounted cash flows that are required to pay back the initial investment. Then the manager determines the percentage of the remaining year of discounted cash flow required to pay back the initial investment fully in order to find the total discounted payback period. The yearly discount rates for future cash flows can be found by using an accounting table that lists the present value of $1 to be received in the future a given amount of years (see Appendix B). This factor can also be determined by using tip #229: Finding the Present Value of $1.

When to use indicator: Managers can use this ratio to help determine the viability of proposed projects. This benchmark is more sophisticated than the payback period because this ratio accounts for the time value of money. However, like the payback period, the discounted payback also ignores the cash flows received after the initial investment is paid in full, a significant drawback.

Meaning of result: Shorter payback periods are generally desirable and indicate the company will pay off the initial investment quickly if everything goes according to forecasts. In general, shorter payback times reduce risk since investment capital is projected to be returned quickly and because shorter term revenue projections are often more reliable than longer term forecasts.

Ways to improve the indicator: You can obtain shorter payback periods on projects that offer greater amounts of cash-generating capability and low initial investment requirements.

Example

Discounted payback period = investment / discounted cash flow from investment per period

Project investment = 135,000
Cash flow per year = 52,000
Discount rate = 9%

Yearly discount rates found by using table in Appendix B or tip #229

Year one discount rate = 0.917
Year two discount rate = 0.842
Year three discount rate = 0.772
Year four discount rate = 0.708

Year one discounted cash flow = 0.917 × 52,000
= 47,684
Year two discounted cash flow = 0.842 × 52,000
= 43,784
Year three discounted cash flow = 0.772 × 52,000
= 40,144
Year four discounted cash flow = 0.708 × 52,000
= 36,816

First three years discounted cash flow = 47,684 + 43,784 + 40,144 = 131,612

Percentage of fourth year required to complete payback of initial investment = (135,000 − 131,612) / 36,816 = 0.092 years = 1.1 months

Discounted payback period = 3 + 0.092 = 3.092 years = 37.1 months

219 Finding the Accounting Rate of Return

Equation

Accounting rate of return = average income from investment per period / initial investment

The **accounting rate of return** is another easy method to help determine the financial desirability of an investment. This ratio describes the rate of return an investment generates from the income the investment is projected to generate. The accounting rate of return is also known as the **simple rate of return.** At times managers determine this ratio using the average initial investment rather than the total initial investment. This has the effect of doubling the accounting rate of return.

When to use indicator: Managers can use this ratio to help determine the viability of proposed projects. Although the accounting rate of return is a very crude analysis tool, its simplicity makes it a good method for roughly gauging the potential of proposals. A primary drawback of the accounting rate of return is that it does not consider the time value of money.

Meaning of result: Higher accounting rates of return are generally desirable and indicate the company will pay off the initial investment quickly if everything goes according to forecasts. In general, shorter payback times reduce risk since investment capital is projected to be returned quickly and because shorter term revenue projections are often more reliable than longer term forecasts.

Ways to improve the indicator: You can obtain higher return rates on projects that offer greater amounts of income-generation capability and lower initial investment requirements.

Example

Accounting rate of return = average income from investment per period / initial investment

Project investment = 135,000
Cash flow per year = 52,000
Life of project = 6 years
Value of investment at end of project = 15,000
Depreciation per year = (initial investment − ending value of investment) / life of project = (135,000 − 15,000) / 6 = 20,000
Net income per year = Cash flow per year − Depreciation per year = 52,000 − 20,000 = 32,000

Accounting rate of return = 32,000 / 135,000 = 0.2370 = 23.7%

220 Determining the Net Present Value (NPV)

Equation

Net present value = sum of discounted future cash flows − initial investment

The **net present value** is used to determine the financial desirability of an investment. It is the difference between the sum of the discounted future cash flows and the initial investment. In general, projects are acceptable when the net present value is greater than zero. However, the analyst must consider other factors such as risk and the amount of capital available in deciding whether to pursue a project. Since the net present value benchmark considers the time value of money, all estimated future cash flows, and the salvage value of the investment, it can be an excellent indicator of investment desirability.

Cash flow is the difference between cash inflows as a result of the investment and cash expenses needed to perform the work associated with the investment. By discounting future cash flows, a manager can determine a more accurate measure of the value of the investment. Discounted future cash flows consider that cash flow generated in the future will be worth less in today's dollars when there is a cost associated with the money used to fund an investment. When a company or individual has no cash on hand for an investment, the discount rate can be taken as the cost of capital. The cost of capital is a weighted average of debt and equity financing. Alternatively, when there is a ready supply of available cash, the discount rate can be taken as the rate of return that alternative investments can earn. The yearly discount rates for future cash flows can be found by using an accounting table that lists the present value of $1 to be received in the future a given amount of years (see Appendix B). This factor can also be determined by using tip #229: Finding the Present Value of $1.

When to use indicator: Managers can use this ratio to help determine the viability of proposed projects. This benchmark is a reasonably sophisticated method of capital evaluation because it considers the time value of money, all cash flow estimates, and the salvage value of the investment.

Meaning of result: Larger net present values are generally desirable and indicate that the company may receive high returns on the initial investment if everything proceeds according to forecast. However, the analyst must consider other factors such as risk and the amount of capital available when deciding whether to pursue a project. Capital limitations often allow the selection of only one of many investment alternatives. This circumstance is commonly known as a **mutually exclusive investment selection**. In such a case, the project with the highest net present value for a given initial investment is often the project selected for implementation. However, this is not always the case; a much lower risk project with a slightly lower net present value may be the better choice for investment.

Ways to improve the indicator: You can obtain larger net present values projects on projects that offer greater amounts of cash-generating capability and low initial investment requirements.

Example

Net present value = sum of discounted future cash flows − initial investment

Project investment = 135,000
Cash flow per year = 52,000
Life of project = 6 years
Value of investment at end of project = 15,000
Discount rate = 9%

Yearly discount rates found by using table in Appendix B or tip #229

Year one discount rate = 0.917
Year two discount rate = 0.842
Year three discount rate = 0.772
Year four discount rate = 0.708
Year five discount rate = 0.650
Year six discount rate = 0.596

Year one discounted cash flow = 0.917 × 52,000
= 47,684
Year two discounted cash flow = 0.842 × 52,000
= 43,784
Year three discounted cash flow = 0.772 × 52,000
= 40,144
Year four discounted cash flow = 0.708 × 52,000
= 36,816
Year five discounted cash flow = 0.650 × 52,000
= 33,800
Year six discounted cash flow = 0.596 × (52,000 + 15,000) = 39,932

Sum of discounted future cash flows = 242,160

Net present value = 242,160 − 135,000 = 107,160

Since cash flows are equal in future years (before the discount rate is applied), the sum of the discounted future cash flows can also be determined by using a table for the present value of an annuity for a term of six years (Appendix C) or by using tip #230.

Present value of an annuity for six years at a discount rate of 9% = 4.486
Year six discount rate for salvage value of investment = 0.596

Sum of discounted cash flows = (52,000 × 4.486) + (15,000 × 0.596) = 242,212

Net present value = 242,212 − 135,000 = 107,212

221 Finding the Risk-Adjusted Discount Rate

Equation

Risk-adjusted discount rate = risk-free discount rate + risk premium

You can adjust discount rates for the risk associated with projects by adding a risk premium to the risk-free discount rate. In a similar manner, when a company uses its cost of capital for a discount rate, higher-than-normal risk projects may warrant adding a risk premium to that rate. By adding a risk premium to the discount rate, the financial analyst may better be able to determine the merits of pursuing projects since she is factoring risk into her analysis.

When to use the indicator: Managers can use the risk-adjusted discount rate to make better decisions in evaluating and selecting capital projects by considering the risk associated with project alternatives.

Meaning of result: Higher-risk projects will have higher risk premiums and risk-adjusted discount rates. These higher rates will reduce net present values and internal rates of return since the risk associated with the projects will make them less attractive. Alternatively, lower risk projects will have lower risk premiums, lower risk-adjusted discount rates, and higher net present values and internal rates of return.

Ways to improve the indicator: You realize lower risk-adjusted discount rates when you select projects with little or no risk. However, depending upon the cash flows offered by project alternatives and the financial health of the company in question, it may be desirable to select projects with higher risk-adjusted discount rates when those higher-risk projects offer substantially greater returns.

Example

Risk-adjusted discount rate = risk-free discount rate + risk premium

Initial investment = 76,000
Cash flow per year = 52,000
Life of project = 3 years
Value of investment at end of project = 12,000
Risk-free discount rate = 6%
Risk-adjusted discount rate = Risk-free discount rate + risk premium

Risk-free discount rate = 6%
Risk premium = 8%

Risk-adjusted discount rate = 6 + 8 = 14%
Present value of $1 received annually for three years at a discount rate of 6% = 2.673
Year three discount rate for salvage value of investment at a discount rate of 6% = 0.840
Present value of $1 received annually for three years at a discount rate of 14% = 2.322
Year three discount rate for salvage value of investment at a discount rate of 14% = 0.675

Net present value at risk-free discount rate of 6%

Net present value = ([cash flow per year] × [present value of $1 received annually for 3 years at the specified discount rate]) + ([salvage value of investment] × [present value of $1 received in 3 years at the specified discount rate])

Net present value = (52,000 × 2.673) + (12,000 × 0.840) − 76,000 = 73,076

Net present value at risk-adjusted discount rate of 14%

Net present value = ([cash flow per year] × [present value of $1 received annually for 3 years at the specified discount rate]) + ([salvage value of investment] × [present value of $1 received in 3 years at the specified discount rate])

Net present value = (52,000 × 2.322) + (12,000 × 0.675) − 76,000 = 52,844

The additional risk associated with this project has the effect of reducing the net present value from 73,076 to 52,844.

222 Ascertaining the Benefit Cost Ratio

Equation

Benefit cost ratio = present value of cash inflows / present value of cash outflows

Managers use the **benefit cost ratio,** also known as the **profitability index,** to determine the financial desirability of investment projects and to select the best choice of mutually exclusive projects.

When to use indicator: Managers can use this ratio to help determine the viability of proposed projects and the best manner in which to invest limited amounts of capital.

Meaning of result: In general, acceptable projects will have benefit cost ratios greater than the value of 1.0, with the most desirable project having the highest benefit cost ratio. However, the analyst must consider other factors such as risk and the amount of capital available when deciding whether to pursue a project. Capital limitations often allow a manager to select only one of many investment alternatives. This circumstance is commonly known as a mutually exclusive investment selection. In such cases, the manager selects the project(s) with the highest benefit cost ratios until he uses all available capital for investment. In deciding between two mutually exclusive projects, he may choose a project with a lower net present value and a higher benefit cost ratio as shown in Example 2 below. Also note that a much lower risk project with a slightly lower benefit cost ratio may be the better choice for investment.

Ways to improve the indicator: You can obtain larger benefit cost ratios on projects that offer greater amounts of cash-generating capability and lower initial investment requirements.

Example

Example 1

Benefit cost ratio = present value of cash inflows / present value of cash outflows

Project investment = 135,000
Cash flow per year = 52,000
Life of project = 6 years
Value of investment at end of project = 15,000
Discount rate = 9%

Since cash flows are equal in future years, you can determine the sum of the discounted future cash flows by using the table for the present value of an annuity for a term of six years (Appendix C).

Present value of an annuity for 6 years at a discount rate of 9% = 4.486
Year six discount rate for salvage value of investment = 0.596

Sum of discounted cash flows = present value of cash inflows = (52,000 × 4.486) + (15,000 × 0.596) = 242,212

Benefit cost ratio = 242,212 / 135,000 = 1.79

Example 2

Project A:

Initial investment = 45,000
Present value of cash inflows = 178,000
Net present value = 178,000 − 45,000 = 133,000
Benefit cost ratio = 178,000 / 45,000 = 3.96

Project B:

Initial investment = 115,000
Present value of cash inflows = 266,000
Net present value = 266,000 − 115,000 = 151,000
Benefit cost ratio = 266,000 / 115,000 = 2.31

Although project B has a net present value greater than project A, the much higher benefit cost ratio returned on project A would likely make it the project of choice. This is particularly true when you have limited available capital or if the risk level associated with both projects could result in loss of the initial investment.

223 Finding the Internal Rate of Return (IRR)

Equation

IRR = discount rate when

Net present value = 0

or

Sum of discounted future cash flows − initial investment = 0

You can use the **internal rate of return** (IRR) to determine the financial desirability of an investment. The IRR is equivalent to the discount rate when the net present value is zero, where the net present value is the difference between the sum of the discounted future cash flows and the initial investment. You can think of the IRR as the interest rate received from a project that consists of an initial investment and a series of cash flows. In general, projects are acceptable when the IRR is in excess of the minimum acceptable level of return on investment, or discount rate, the company expects. However, the analyst must consider other factors such as risk and the amount of capital available in deciding whether to pursue a project. Since the IRR benchmark considers the time value of money, all estimated future cash flows, and the salvage value of the investment, it can be an excellent indicator of investment desirability.

Cash flow is the difference between cash inflows as a result of the investment and cash expenses needed to perform the work associated with the investment. By discounting future cash flows, you can realize a more accurate measure of the value of the investment. Discounted future cash flows consider that cash flow generated in the future will be worth less in today's dollars when there is a cost associated with the money used to fund an investment.

When a company or individual has no cash on hand for an investment, the minimum acceptable IRR can be taken as the cost of capital. The cost of capital is a weighted average of debt and equity financing. Alternatively, when there is a ready supply of available cash, the minimum acceptable IRR can be taken as the rate of return that can be earned on alternative investments.

When to use indicator: Managers can use this ratio to help determine the viability of proposed projects. This benchmark is a reasonably sophisticated method of capital evaluation because it considers the time value of money, all cash flow estimates, and the salvage value of the investment.

Meaning of result: Larger IRRs are generally desirable and indicate a company may receive high returns on the initial investment if everything proceeds according to forecast. However, the analyst must consider other factors such as risk and the amount of capital available when deciding whether to pursue a project. Capital limitations often allow the selection of only one of many investment alternatives. This circumstance is commonly known as a mutually exclusive investment selection. In such a case, the project with the highest IRR for a given initial investment is often the project selected for implementation. However, this is not always the case; a much lower risk project with a slightly lower IRR may be the better choice for investment.

Ways to improve the indicator: You can obtain higher IRRs on projects that offer greater amounts of cash-generating capability and low initial investment requirements.

Example

The IRR is the discount rate at which the NPV is zero. The following example illustrates the iterative technique to determine the discount rate. Contemporary computer spreadsheets preclude the necessity of such tedious calculation.

Project investment = 135,000
Cash flow per year = 52,000
Life of project = 6 years
Value of investment at end of project = 15,000

Since cash flows are equal in future years, you can determine the sum of the discounted future cash flows by using the table for the present value of an annuity for a term of six years (Appendix C).

Discount rate = 9%

Present value of an annuity for 6 years at a discount rate of 9% = 4.486
Year six discount rate for salvage value of investment = 0.596
Sum of discounted cash flows = (52,000 × 4.486) + (15,000 × 0.596) = 242,212
Net present value = 242,212 − 135,000 = 107,212

Discount rate = 20%

Present value of an annuity for 6 years at a discount rate of 20% = 3.326
Year six discount rate for salvage value of investment = 0.335
Sum of discounted cash flows = (52,000 × 3.326) + (15,000 × 0.335) = 177,977
Net present value = 177,977 − 135,000 = 42,977

Discount rate = 40%

Present value of an annuity for 6 years at a discount rate of 40% = 2.168
Year six discount rate for salvage value of investment = 0.133
Sum of discounted cash flows = (52,000 × 2.168) + (15,000 × 0.133) = 114,731
Net present value = 114,731 − 135,000 = −20,269

Discount rate = 35%

Present value of an annuity for 6 years at a discount rate of 35% = 2.385
Year six discount rate for salvage value of investment = 0.165
Sum of discounted cash flows = (52,000 × 2.385) + (15,000 × 0.165) = 126,495
Net present value = 126,495 − 135,000 = −8,505

Discount rate = 30%

Present value of an annuity for 6 years at a discount rate of 30% = 2.643
Year six discount rate for salvage value of investment = 0.207
Sum of discounted cash flows = (52,000 × 2.643) + (15,000 × 0.207) = 140,541
Net present value = 140,541 − 135,000 = 5,541

From these calculations it is seen that the internal rate of return falls between 30% and 35%. The actual value is 31.9%, which you can determine with further iterations or with a contemporary spreadsheet program.

224 Finding the Modified Internal Rate of Return (MIRR)

Equation

MIRR = Discount rate when

Net present value = 0

or

Sum of discounted future cash flows − initial investment = 0

You can use the modified internal rate of return (MIRR) to determine the financial desirability of an investment. The MIRR is similar to the internal rate of return (IRR) but considers, at distinct interest rates, the cost of finance capital and the rates of return from reinvestment of positive cash flows. In general, projects are acceptable when the MIRR is in excess of the minimum acceptable level of return on investment the company expects. However, the analyst must consider other factors such as risk and the amount of capital available in deciding whether to pursue a project. Since the MIRR benchmark considers the time value of money, all estimated future cash flows, returns on reinvested cash flows, and the salvage value of the investment, it can be an excellent indicator of investment desirability.

Discounted future cash flows consider that cash flow generated in the future will be worth less in today's dollars when there is inflation. In other words, the present value of future cash flows is less than the dollar amount of those future cash flows. By discounting future cash flows, you can realize a more accurate measure of the value of the investment. Cash flow is the difference between cash inflows as a result of the investment and cash expenses needed to perform the work associated with the investment.

When to use indicator: Managers can use this ratio to help determine the viability of proposed projects. This benchmark is a reasonably sophisticated method of capital evaluation because it considers the time value of money, all cash flow estimates, returns generated from reinvested cash flows, and the salvage value of the investment.

Meaning of result: Larger MIRRs are generally desirable and indicate that the company may receive high returns on the initial investment if everything proceeds according to forecast. However, the analyst must consider other factors such as risk factors and the amount of capital available when deciding whether to pursue a project. Capital limitations often allow the selection of only one of many investment alternatives. This is commonly known as a mutually exclusive investment selection. In such a case, the project with the highest MIRR for a given initial investment is often the project selected for implementation. However, this is not always the case; a much lower-risk project with a slightly lower MIRR may be the better choice for investment.

Ways to improve the indicator: You can obtain higher MIRRs on projects that offer greater amounts of cash-generating capability, low initial investment requirements, and high reinvestment return rates on positive cash flows.

Example

Project investment = 135,000
Cash flow per year = 52,000
Life of project = 6 years
Value of investment at end of project = 15,000
Finance rate = 9%
Reinvestment rate = 7%

MIRR = 19.2% using a contemporary spreadsheet program

225 Determining the Certainty Equivalent

Equation

Certainty equivalent cash flow = certainty equivalent coefficient × projected risky future cash flow

Managers can use **certainty equivalent** benchmarks when determining the net present value and internal rate of return of an investment. The certainty equivalent factors allow the analyst to consider the risk associated with future cash flow estimates. These factors are found by determining where the financial analyst is indifferent in choosing between a certain, no-risk future cash flow and an uncertain but risky future cash flow. Multiplying the risky future cash flow by a certainty equivalent coefficient will give the certainty equivalent cash flow. Higher-risk projects thus have lower certainty equivalent coefficients. Use a risk-free discount rate, such as received from U.S. treasury bill investments, when determining certainty equivalent net present value calculations and internal rates of return. Use the risk-free discount rate since the cash flows received from the investment are considered risk-free.

When to use indicator: Managers can use the certainty equivalent to make better decisions in evaluating and selecting capital projects since they take into consideration the risk associated with project alternatives.

Meaning of result: Higher-risk projects will yield lower certainty equivalent coefficients and lower certainty equivalent cash flow estimates. The certainty cash flow estimates are lower since it is more likely the project will fail to meet forecasted cash flow estimates. Alternatively, lower-risk projects will yield higher certainty equivalent coefficients and higher certainty equivalent cash flows.

Ways to improve the indicator: You realize higher certainty equivalent coefficients when you select projects with little or no risk. Depending upon the certainty equivalent cash flows offered by project alternatives and the financial health of the company in question, it may be desirable to select projects with high or low certainty equivalent coefficients.

Example

Determine the certainty equivalent and normal net present values and compare results.

Initial investment = 76,000

Year	Projected risky cash flow	Certainty equivalent coefficient	Certainty equivalent cash flow
1	52,000	.90	46,800
2	65,000	.75	48,750
3	72,000	.50	36,000

Life of project = 3 years
Value of investment at end of project = 12,000
Risk-free discount rate = 6%
Normal discount rate = 9%

Certainty equivalent net present value determination

Certainty equivalent net present value = sum of discounted certain equivalent future cash flows − initial investment

Discount rate = 6%

Yearly discount rates found by using table in Appendix B or tip #229

Year one discount rate = 0.943
Year two discount rate = 0.890
Year three discount rate = 0.840

Year one discounted cash flow = 0.943 × 46,800
= 44,132
Year two discounted cash flow = 0.890 × 48,750
= 43,387
Year three discounted cash flow = 0.840 × 36,000
= 30,240

Sum of discounted certain equivalent future cash flows = 117,759

Certainty equivalent net present value = 117,759 − 76,000 = 41,759

Normal net present value determination

Net present value = sum of discounted future cash flows − initial investment

Discount rate = 9%

Year one discount rate = 0.917
Year two discount rate = 0.842
Year three discount rate = 0.772

Year one discounted cash flow = 0.917 × 52,000
= 47,684
Year two discounted cash flow = 0.842 × 65,000
= 54,730
Year three discounted cash flow = 0.772 × 72,000
= 55,584

Sum of discounted future cash flows = 157,998

Net present value = 157,998 − 76,000 = 81,998

In this case, the certainty equivalent net present value of 41,759 is about half that of the normal present value of 81,998 indicating there is a substantial amount of risk associated with the projected cash flows.

226 Determining the Future Value of $1

Equation

Future value in n years = present value × ([1 + interest rate] ^ [n years])

The **future value** is the amount accumulated on a given amount of money (present value) that is invested at a given interest rate of return and is compounded annually for a given number of years (n).

When to use indicator: Managers and investors can use this indicator to determine the future value of investments and loans.

Meaning of result: You can achieve higher future values when interest rates are higher and when the time periods are longer to allow for interest compounding.

Example

Future value in n years = present value × ([1 + interest rate] ^ [n years])

Present value = $1
Interest rate = 9%
n = 3 years
Future value = 1 × (1.09^3) = 1.295

Future value of $1 in three years at an interest rate of 9% is $1.30.

227 Finding the Future Value of an Annuity of $1

Equation

Future value of an annuity of $1 for n years = 1 + annuity × (1 + interest rate)^1 + annuity × (1 + interest rate)^2 + . . . + annuity × (1 + interest rate)^(n–1)

The **future value of an annuity** is the amount accumulated on a series of annuity payments. An **annuity** is a series of equal, periodic payments given or received at the end of each time period for a specified amount of time. The difference between an **annuity** and an **annuity due** is the timing in which the equal, periodic payments are given or received; annuities are paid at the end of the period and annuities due are paid at the beginning of the period.

When to use indicator: Managers and investors can use this indicator to determine the future value of investments and loans.

Meaning of result: You can achieve higher future values when interest rates are higher and when the time periods are longer to allow for interest compounding.

Example

Future value of an annuity of $1 for n years = 1 + annuity × (1 + interest rate)^1 + annuity × (1 + interest rate)^2 + . . . + annuity × (1 + interest rate)^(n–1)

Annuity = $1
Interest rate = 9%
n = 3 years

Future value of an annuity of $1 for 3 years = 1 + 1 × (1.09)^1 + 1 × (1.09)^2 = 3.278

Future value of an annuity of $1 in three years at an interest rate of 9% is $3.28.

CAPITAL INVESTMENT

228 Calculating the Future Value of an Annuity Due of $1

Equation

Future value of an annuity due of $1 for n years
= annuity × (1 + interest rate)^1 + annuity × (1 + interest rate)^2 + . . . + annuity × (1 + interest rate)^n

The **future value of an annuity due** is the amount accumulated on a series of annuity due payments. An annuity due is a series of equal, periodic payments given or received at the beginning of each time period for a specified amount of time. The difference between an annuity and an annuity due is the timing in which the equal, periodic payments are given or received; annuities are paid at the end of the period and annuities due are paid at the beginning of the period.

When to use indicator: Managers and investors can use this indicator to determine the future value of investments and loans.

Meaning of result: You can achieve higher future values when interest rates are higher and when the investment time is longer to allow for interest compounding.

Example

Future value of an annuity due of $1 for n years
= annuity × (1 + interest rate)^1 + annuity × (1 + interest rate)^2 + . . . + annuity × (1 + interest rate)^n

Annuity = $1
Interest rate = 9%
n = 3 years

Future value of an annuity due of $1 for 3 years
= 1 × (1.09)^1 + 1 × (1.09)^2 + 1 × (1.09)^3 = 3.573

Future value of an annuity due of $1 in three years at an interest rate of 9% is $3.57.

229 Finding the Present Value of $1

Equation

Present value = future value / ([1 + interest rate] ^ [n years])

The **present value** is the value in today's dollars of a sum of money received in the future. In present value determinations, the annually compounded interest rate is also known as the **discount rate** or the **rate of return**.

When to use indicator: Managers and investors can use this indicator to determine the present value of future cash flows generated/paid from items such as investments, lottery winnings, dividends, and loans.

Meaning of result: You can achieve higher present values when interest rates are lower and when investment timeframes are shorter. When interest rates are low, as in times of low inflation, present values of sums of money received in the future are high since there is a lack of inflationary effects that can quickly erode the value of money.

Example

Using formula

Present value = future value / ([1 + interest rate] ^ [n years])

Future value in 3 years = $1
Interest rate = 9%
n = 3 years

Present value = 1 / (1.09^3) = 0.772

Present value of $1 received in three years at an interest rate of 9% is $0.77.

Using tables

Discount rate = 0.772 = $0.77 = present value of $1 received in three years

230 Determining the Present Value of an Annuity of $1

Equation

Present value of an annuity received/paid for n years = annuity / (1 + interest rate)^1 + annuity / (1 + interest rate)^2 + . . . + annuity / (1 + interest rate)^n

The **present value of an annuity** is the value in today's dollars of the sum of the annuity payments. An annuity is a series of equal, periodic payments given or received at the end of each time period for a specified amount of time. The difference between an annuity and an annuity due is the time in which the equal, periodic payments are given or received; annuities are paid at the end of the period and annuities due are paid at the beginning of the period. The interest rate in present value determinations is also known as the discount rate or the rate of return.

When to use indicator: Managers and investors can use this indicator to determine the present value of annuities. Annuities are commonly used with investments, insurance payments, lottery winnings, dividends, and loans.

Meaning of result: You can achieve higher annuity present values with lower discount rates and more annuity payments. When interest rates are low, as in times of low inflation, present values of sums of money received in the future are high since there is a lack of inflationary effects that can quickly erode the value of money.

Example

Using formula

Present value of an annuity received/paid for n years = annuity / (1 + interest rate)^1 + annuity / (1 + interest rate)^2 + . . . + annuity / (1 + interest rate)^n

Annuity = $1
Interest rate = 9%
n = 3 years

Present value of an annuity = 1 / (1.09^1) + 1 / (1.09^2) + 1 / (1.09^3) = 2.531

Present value of an annuity of $1 received for three years at an interest rate of 9% is $2.53.

Using tables

Discount rate = 2.531 = present value of an annuity of $1 received for three years

231 Calculating the Present Value of an Annuity Due of $1

Equation

Present value of an annuity due of $1 received/paid for n years = (1 + interest rate) × [annuity / (1 + interest rate)^1 + annuity / (1 + interest rate)^2 + . . . + annuity / (1 + interest rate)^n]

Or

Present value of an annuity due of $1 received/paid for n years = 1 + [annuity / (1 + interest rate)^1 + annuity / (1 + interest rate)^2 + . . . + annuity / (1 + interest rate)^(n−1)]

The **present value of an annuity due** is the value in today's dollars of the sum of the annuity due payments. An annuity due is a series of equal, periodic payments given or received at the beginning of each time period for a specified amount of time. The difference between an annuity and an annuity due is the time at which the equal, periodic payments are given or received; annuities are paid at the end of the period and annuities due are paid at the beginning of the period. The interest rate in present value determinations is also known as the discount rate or the rate of return.

When to use indicator: Managers and investors can use this indicator to determine the present value of annuities due. Annuities due are commonly used with investments, insurance payments, lottery winnings, dividends, and loans.

Meaning of result: You can achieve higher annuity due present values with lower discount rates and more annuity due payments. When interest rates are low, as in times of low inflation, present values of sums of money received in the future are high since there is a lack of inflationary effects that can quickly erode the value of money.

Example

Using formula

Present value of an annuity due of $1 received/paid for n years = (1 + interest rate) × [annuity / (1 + interest rate)^1 + annuity / (1 + interest rate)^2 + . . . + annuity / (1 + interest rate)^n]

Annuity = $1
Interest rate = 9%
n = 3 years

Present value of an annuity due of $1 = (1 + 0.09) × [1 / (1.09^1) + 1 / (1.09^2) + 1 / (1.09^3)] = 2.759

Present value of an annuity due of $1 received for three years at an interest rate of 9% is $2.76.

Using tables

Discount rate = 1.759 = present value of an annuity of $1 received for 2 years at a discount rate of 9%

Present value of an annuity due of $1 = 1 + 1.759 = 2.759

232 Examining Perpetuities

Equation

Present value of a perpetuity of $1 = annuity / interest rate

The present value of a perpetuity is the value in today's dollars of the sum of the annuity due payments. A **perpetuity** is a series of equal, periodic payments given or received at the end of each time period; it lasts forever. The perpetuity is thus a special form of annuity in which the annuity payments continue without end. The interest rate in present value determinations is also known as the discount rate or the rate of return.

When to use indicator: Managers and investors can use this indicator to determine the present value of perpetuities.

Meaning of result: Higher perpetuity present values can be achieved with lower discount rates. When interest rates are low, as in times of low inflation, present values of sums of money received in the future are high since there is a lack of inflationary effects that can quickly erode the value of money.

Example

Present value of a perpetuity of $1 = annuity / interest rate

Annuity = 1
Interest rate = 9%

Present value of a perpetuity of $1 = 1 / 0.09 = 11.11

CHAPTER SEVENTEEN

Investment/Loan Interest Rate Information

This chapter details ratios which describe interest rates and bond yields. This information will help you make investment decisions and seek additional funding.

233 Examining Simple Interest

Equation

Simple interest earned = principal × simple interest rate × time

Simple interest is an easy method of charging or receiving interest on an investment. Few people use the method nowadays even though it is easy to use because compound methods of interest determination are much more popular. The value of simple interest investments grow linearly with time since all interest earned is based upon the principal investment. No interest is earned on previously earned interest. With compound interest, investments grow exponentially because interest is earned on the principal investment plus the interest earned previously during the term of the investment.

When to use indicator: Managers, investors, and creditors use simple interest calculations to determine returns on simple interest investments and payments on simple interest loans.

Meaning of result: You can earn higher amounts of simple interest with larger principal investments, higher simple interest rates, and longer investment terms.

Example

Simple interest earned = principal × simple interest rate × time

Principal = 1,000
Simple interest rate = 8.5% per year
Time = 1 year

Simple interest earned = 1,000 × 0.085 × 1 = 85

234 Exploring Compounded Interest

Equation

Compound interest earned = principal × {[1 + (interest rate / compounding episodes per year)]$^{\text{(compounding episodes per year} \times \text{investment time frame)}}$ − 1}

Annual compound interest rate = [1 + (interest rate / compounding episodes per year)]$^{\text{compounding episodes per year}}$ − 1

Compound interest is a common method of charging and receiving interest on an investment. With **compound interest**, investments grow exponentially because interest is earned on the principal investment plus the interest earned previously during the term of the investment. The compounded interest rate is also known as the **effective yield** and the **interest rate yield**.

When to use indicator: Managers, investors, and creditors can use compound interest calculations to determine returns on compound interest investments and payments on compound interest loans.

Meaning of result: You can earn higher amounts of compound interest with larger principal investments, higher compound interest rates, and longer investment terms.

Examples

Compound interest earned = principal × {[1 + (interest rate / compounding episodes per year)]$^{\text{(compounding episodes per year} \times \text{investment time frame)}}$ − 1}

Principal = 1,000
Interest rate = 8.5% per year
Compounding episodes per year = 365 (daily)
Investment time frame = 1 year

Compound interest earned = 1,000 × {[1 + (0.085/365)]$^{(365 \times 1)}$ − 1} = 88.71

Annual compound interest rate = [1 + (interest rate / compounding episodes per year)]$^{\text{compounding episodes per year}}$ − 1 = [1 + (0.085/365)]^{365} − 1 = 0.0887 = 8.87%

Principal = 1,000
Interest rate = 8.5% per year
Compounding episodes per year = 365 (daily)
Investment time frame = 2 years

Compound interest earned = 1,000 × {[1 + (0.085/365)]$^{(365 \times 2)}$ − 1} = 185.28

Principal = 1,000
Interest rate = 8.5% per year
Compounding episodes per year = 12 (monthly)
Investment time frame = 1 year

Compound interest earned = 1,000 × {[1 + (0.085/12)]$^{(12 \times 1)}$ − 1} = 88.39

235 Examining the Current Yield on Bonds

Equation

Current yield = annual interest / market price of bond

The **current yield** is the yield on a bond based upon the current market price for that bond. Bonds are corporate or government debt obligations that return the principal investment amount upon maturity and pay interest at typically regular intervals and/or are discounted at inception. The interest rate stated on a bond is called the **coupon rate** or **nominal yield.** When general interest rates rise, market prices on existing bonds fall since the lower interest rate bonds are attractive only at lower prices. Conversely, when general interest rates fall, market prices for existing bonds rise since the higher interest rate on bonds becomes more attractive and can demand higher prices. Bonds that sell at prices higher than the original issue price, or **par value,** are said to sell at a premium. Bonds that sell at prices lower than par value are said to sell at a discount.

When to use indicator: Managers, investors, and creditors can use this indicator to determine the current, or market price, yield on bonds.

Meaning of result: Current yields increase relative to the coupon rate as the market prices for bonds fall, and they decrease relative to the coupon rate as the market prices for bonds increase.

Example

Current yield = annual interest / market price of bond

Stated rate of interest on bond = 8.5%
Annual interest = 100 × stated rate of interest = 85
Market price of bond = 1,200

Current yield = 85 / 1,200 = 0.0708 = 7.08%

236 Examining the Yield to Maturity on Bonds

Equation

If bond is purchased at a discount

Yield to maturity = (annual interest + annual capital gain) / average of purchase price and redemption price

If bond is purchased at a premium

Yield to maturity = (annual interest − annual capital loss) / average of purchase price and redemption price

The **yield to maturity** is the yield on a bond based upon both the annual interest earned by the bond and the capital gains or losses that occur when someone purchases a bond at a discount or premium. Bonds are corporate or government debt obligations that return the principal investment amount upon maturity and pay interest typically at regular intervals and/or are discounted at inception. The interest rate stated on a bond is called the coupon rate or nominal yield. When general interest rates rise, market prices on existing bonds fall since the lower interest rate bonds are attractive only at lower prices. Conversely, when general interest rates fall, market prices for existing bonds rise since the higher interest rate bonds become more attractive and can demand higher prices. Bonds that sell at prices higher than the original issue price, or par value, are said to sell at a premium. Bonds that sell at prices lower than par value are said to sell at a discount.

When to use indicator: Managers, investors, and creditors can use this indicator to determine the yield to maturity on bonds.

Meaning of result: The yield to maturity increases relative to the coupon rate as the market prices for bonds fall, and they decrease relative to the coupon rate as the market prices for bonds increase.

Example

If bond is purchased at a premium

Yield to maturity = (annual interest − annual capital loss) / average of purchase price and redemption price

Stated rate of interest on bond = 8.5%
Annual interest = 100 × stated rate of interest = 85
Purchase price of bond = 1,200
Redemption price of bond = 1,000
20-year bond
Annual capital loss = (purchase price − redemption price) / term of bond = (1,200 − 1,000)/20 = 10
Average price of bond = (purchase price of bond + redemption price of bond) / 2 = (1,200 + 1,000)/2 = 1,100

Yield to maturity = (85 − 10) / 1,100 = 0.0682 = 6.82%

If bond is purchased at a discount

Yield to maturity = (annual interest + annual capital gain) / average of purchase price and redemption price

If bond is purchased at a discount, the annual capital gain is *added to* the annual interest instead of subtracted from it as in the previous example.

237 Examining the Effective Annual Yield on T-bills

Equation

Effective annual T-bill yield = [(par value − initial investment) × 365] / (initial investment × number of days to maturity)

The U.S. Treasury sells debt obligations to the public in the form of bills, notes, and bonds. T-bills are sold at a discount to par, with the full par value being paid at maturity. This formula allows an investor to use the discount information to determine the effective annual yield of T-bills.

When to use indicator: Investors can use this indicator to determine effective annual T-bill yields when given the discount amounts, days to maturity, and the par value of the T-bill.

Meaning of result: Larger discount amounts and shorter days to maturity can increase the effective annual T-bill yield.

Example

Effective annual T-bill yield = [(par value − initial investment) × 365] / (initial investment × number of days to maturity)

Par value = 10,000
Discount = 2.3% = 230
Initial investment = par value − discount = 10,000 − 230 = 9,770
Number of days to maturity = 181

Effective annual T-bill yield = [(10,000 − 9,770) × 365] / (9,770 × 181) = 0.0475 = 4.75%

238 Exploring the Rule of 72

Equation

Estimate of the time to double your money = 72 / interest rate yield

This indicator is commonly used to estimate roughly the amount of time required to double your money given an annual interest rate yield.

When to use indicator: Managers, creditors, and investors can use this indicator when examining the desirability of investments, loans, and any other vehicles which pay or receive interest.

Meaning of result: It takes longer to double investments when interest rates are lower. The time required to double an investment decreases as the rate of interest increases.

Example

Estimate of the time to double your money = 72 / interest rate yield

Interest rate yield = 8%

Estimate of the time to double your money = 72 / 8 = 9 years

Estimate of the time to double your money = 72 / interest rate yield

Interest rate yield = 12%

Estimate of the time to double your money = 72 / 12 = 6 years

INVESTMENT/LOAN INTEREST RATE INFORMATION

239 Exploring Interest Rates and Their Significance: Federal Funds Rate

The **federal funds rate** is the interest charged for loans between banks that belong to the Federal Reserve System (Fed). The Fed requires all banks within the system, the vast majority of U.S. banks, to maintain a certain percentage of assets on reserve with the Fed. When a bank has excess reserves on deposit at the Fed, the system allows it to lend those reserves to other banks within the system at the federal funds rate. When a bank has not met the minimum deposit requirement at the Fed, it may borrow money from banks with excess reserves at this same rate. Most of these loans are for one day only.

When to use indicator: Managers, creditors, and investors can use this benchmark to help predict the state of the economy in the near future. This information may aid in determining the timing and benefits of company acquisitions/sales, capital investments/sales, marketing programs, and product development projects.

Meaning of result: The Fed is charged with maintaining high levels of employment, stable prices, and moderate long-term interest rates in the U.S. economy. At the Fed's disposal are a number of tools it can use in an attempt to achieve these goals including the ability to control short-term interest rates and the capacity to control bank reserves by buying and selling Treasury bills in the open market. The Fed can control short-term interest rates with the federal funds rate and the discount rate. The Fed will tend to increase short-term rates when it forecasts future price instability because of an anticipated overheated, and potentially inflationary, economy. The Fed will tend to decrease short-term rates when it foresees the potential of a sluggish economy with increasing unemployment levels.

240 Exploring Interest Rates and Their Significance: Discount Rate

The discount rate is the interest rate charged by the Federal Reserve System (Fed) to its member banks on funds borrowed from the Fed by those banks.

When to use indicator: Managers, creditors, and investors can use this benchmark to help predict the state of the economy in the near future. This information may aid in determining the timing and benefits of company acquisitions/sales, capital investments/sales, marketing programs, and product development projects.

Meaning of result: The Fed is charged with maintaining high levels of employment, stable prices, and moderate long-term interest rates in the U.S. economy. At the Fed's disposal are a number of tools it can use in an attempt to achieve these goals including the ability to control short-term interest rates and the capacity to control bank reserves by buying and selling Treasury bills in the open market. The Fed can control short-term interest rates with the federal funds rate and the discount rate. The Fed will tend to increase short-term rates when it forecasts future price instability because of an anticipated overheated, and anticipated inflationary, economy. The Fed will tend to decrease short-term rates when it foresees the potential of a sluggish economy with increasing unemployment levels.

241 Exploring Interest Rates and Their Significance: Treasury Bills/Notes/Bonds

The U.S. Treasury sells debt obligations to the public in the forms of bills, notes, and bonds. The primary differences between bills, notes, and bonds are the terms to maturity: bills mature in one year or less, notes mature in 2 to 10 years, and bonds mature in 10 years and longer. Most investors consider U.S. treasuries the safest type of investment possible because they are backed by the full faith and credit of the U.S. government.

When to use indicator: Managers, creditors, and investors can use this benchmark to help predict the state of the economy in the near future. This information may aid in determining the timing and benefits of company acquisitions/sales, capital investments/sales, marketing programs, and product development projects.

Meaning of result: Short-term rates often closely track the Federal Reserve's (Fed's) policy with regard to the two short-term rates it controls: the federal funds rate and the discount rate. The Fed will tend to increase short-term rates when it forecasts future price instability because of an anticipated overheated, and potentially inflationary, economy. The Fed will tend to decrease short-term rates when it foresees the potential of a sluggish economy with increasing unemployment. The Fed can also control short-term interest rates by buying and selling Treasury bills in the open market. Longer-term Treasury notes and bond rates tend not to be as closely linked to the short-term actions of the Fed. High and higher trending longer term rates can indicate anticipated inflation while lower long-term rates, particularly when the yield curve is inverted, can indicate a higher likelihood of recession. Inverted yield curves occur when short-term interest rates are higher than long-term rates.

CHAPTER EIGHTEEN

External Indicators

This chapter details a number of ratios that help indicate the state of the economy, the business climate, and the stock markets. This information can help business owners and investors gauge the timing of their investments and strategic decisions. For example, when the leading economic indicators strongly indicate a downturn in the economy, a business might delay a capital investment program such as the construction of a new factory until business conditions become more favorable.

242 Examining the Index of Leading Economic Indicators

The **index of leading economic indicators**, published monthly by the Conference Board, a leading business membership and research organization, is designed to indicate the state of the near-future economy by signaling high and low points in the business cycle. This index is composed of 10 individual indicators that tend to lead changes in the state of economy. While all of the indicators generally tend to lead the economy, it is common for one to a number of the individual indicators to give false forecasts regarding the direction of the economy. The number of unique economic predictors in the index improves its reliability. The 10 leading economic indicators are 1) average weekly hours worked by manufacturing workers, 2) average new unemployment claims, 3) manufacturers' new orders for consumer goods, 4) vendor performance, 5) manufacturers' new orders for plants and equipment, 6) new residential building permits, 7) S&P 500, 8) M2 money supply, 9) short- and long-term interest rate spreads, and 10) index of consumer expectations.

When to use indicator: Managers, creditors, and investors can use this benchmark to help predict the state of the economy in the near future. This information may aid in determining the timing and benefits of company acquisitions/sales, capital investments/sales, marketing programs, and product development projects.

Meaning of result: High and/or rising leading economic index values indicate the probability of a healthy economy in the near-term future. Low and/or falling values can indicate near-term future downturns for the business economy. The index tends to be more reliable in forecasting upturns than downturns in the business cycle.

It is best to follow indicator trends over a number of months to reduce the possibility of false economic forecasts. Trends become more reliable when they become longer in duration, larger in percentage change, and broader in economic scope. One very rough rule of thumb is that, for recession verification, the index must fall for at least three consecutive months. The Conference Board suggests a potentially more reliable recession prediction method: a 1% decline in the leading index (2% when annualized) together with declines in the majority of the 10 index components.

243 Examining the Index of Coincident Economic Indicators

The **index of coincident economic indicators**, published monthly by the Conference Board, a leading business membership and research organization, is designed to verify the state of the economy and location in the business cycle. Four individual indicators comprise this index. They tend to occur at the same time as do changes in the state of economy. While all of the indicators generally trend in this manner, it is common for one to a number of the individual indicators to give false forecasts regarding the state of the economy. The number of unique economic predictors improves the reliability of the index. The four coincident economic indicators are 1) employees on nonagricultural payrolls, 2) personal income, 3) industrial production, and 4) manufacturing and trade sales.

When to use indicator: Managers, creditors, and investors can use this benchmark to help confirm the current state of the economy. This information may aid in determining the timing and benefits of company acquisitions/sales, capital investments/sales, marketing programs, and product development projects.

Meaning of result: High and/or rising coincident economic index values can indicate a currently healthy economy. Low and/or falling values can indicate current low points in the business cycle.

It is often best to follow indicator trends over a number of months to reduce the possibility of false economic readings. Trends become more reliable when they become longer in duration, larger in percentage change, and broader in economic scope.

244 Examining the Index of Lagging Economic Indicators

The **index of lagging economic indicators**, published monthly by the Conference Board, a leading business membership and research organization, is designed to verify the state of the past economy and high or low points in the business cycle. This index is composed of six individual indicators that tend to lag behind changes in the state of the economy. While all of the indicators generally trend in this manner, it is common for one to a number of the individual indicators to give false forecasts regarding the state of the economy. The number of unique economic predictors increases its reliability. The six lagging economic indicators are 1) unemployment duration, 2) inventory-to-sales ratio for manufacturing and trade, 3) manufacturing labor cost per unit of output, 4) installment credit outstanding-to-personal income ratio, 5) prime rate, and 6) changes in the consumer price index.

When to use indicator: Managers, creditors, and investors can use this benchmark to help confirm the near-past state of the economy. This information, while not as obviously beneficial as predictors of the future state of the economy, may aid in determining the timing and benefits of company acquisitions/sales, capital investments/sales, marketing programs, and product development projects.

Meaning of result: High and/or rising lagging economic index values indicate a near-past healthy economy. Low and/or falling values can indicate near-past low points in the business cycle.

It is often best to follow indicator trends over a number of months to reduce the possibility of false economic readings. Trends become more reliable when they become longer in duration, larger in percentage change, and broader in economic scope.

245 Assessing the Gross Domestic Product (GDP)

The **gross domestic product** (GDP) is a measure of all of the goods and services earned by a country within its boundaries whereas the gross national product (GNP) includes earnings produced both domestically and internationally.

When to use indicator: Managers, creditors, and investors can use this benchmark to help determine the state of the economy.

Meaning of result: Higher percentage increases in GDP levels often indicate a growing and healthy economy. When the economy becomes overheated and the percentage increases in GDP become unsustainably high, however, there is often a tendency for higher rates of inflation and an economic downturn.

246 Examining the Gross National Product (GNP)

The **gross national product** (GNP) is a measure of all of the goods and services earned by a country, both domestically and internationally.

When to use indicator: Managers, creditors, and investors can use this benchmark to help determine the state of the economy.

Meaning of result: Higher percentage increases in GNP levels often indicate a growing and healthy economy. When the economy becomes overheated and the percentage increases in GNP become unsustainably high, however, there is often a tendency for higher rates of inflation and an economic downturn.

247 Examining the Producer Price Index (PPI)

The **producer price index** (PPI) is a group of indexes that measures the average change over time of selling prices that domestic goods manufacturers and service providers receive. Each month more than 10,000 PPIs are released for individual products and groups of products.

When to use indicator: Managers, creditors, and investors can use this benchmark to help determine the state of the economy. The PPI can also be used to deflate other economic indicators to negate the effects of inflation. This allows the easier communication of real changes in those economic series. Another use of the PPI is for price escalation in long-term contracts. For example, a supplier that uses aluminum sheeting in manufacturing a product may base the contract financial terms on the PPI pricing for aluminum.

Meaning of result: Higher percentage increases in the PPI indicate climbing prices for the individual or group of products in question. As producers can realize changes in prices before retailers and consumers, the PPI can indicate future changes in the state of the economy.

248 Assessing the Consumer Price Index (CPI)

The **consumer price index** (CPI) is a measure of the average change over time of prices paid by domestic consumers for a fixed basket of goods and services. Each month prices for about 90,000 consumer goods and services are taken from around the country as data in determining the CPI.

When to use indicator: Managers, creditors, and investors can use this benchmark to help determine the state of the economy and the rate of inflation. The CPI can also be used to deflate other economic indicators such as retail sales and hourly earnings in order to negate the effects of inflation. This allows for the easier communication of real changes in those economic series. The CPI is also used for adjusting dollar values such as adjusting Social Security payments and determining cost-of-living wage adjustments.

Meaning of result: Higher percentage increases in the CPI indicate climbing prices for the consumer's basket of goods and services, an indication of rising inflation.

249 Examining the Dow Jones Industrial Average (DJIA)

The **Dow Jones Industrial Average** (DJIA) is one of the most popular stock market indicators. Although only 30 companies comprise the DJIA, and it is widely criticized as too narrow in scope when compared with broader indexes such as the S&P 500, the DJIA often tracks the overall performance of the market quite closely.

When to use indicator: Managers, creditors, and investors can use this benchmark to help predict the state of the economy in the near future since many economists indicate the DJIA tends to lead economic activity. This information may aid in determining the timing and benefits of company acquisitions/sales, capital investments/sales, marketing programs, and product development projects. Investors often use the DJIA as a comparative tool, or benchmark, in determining the performance of other investments.

Meaning of result: High percentage increases in the DJIA result from market price increases of the 30 industrial companies that comprise the DJIA. Market price increases can be the result of anticipated increases in corporate earnings, which may result from an expanding economy. DJIA increases can also result from falling interest rates; when interest rates fall, investors tend to look for alternatives that may generate higher yields. The result is often increased demand for securities, which drives up market prices for stocks and increases the DJIA.

250 Exploring the Russel 2000 Average

The **Russel 2000** is one of the most popular indicators of small company stocks. It is considered the small stock equivalent of the Dow Jones Industrial Average (DJIA) although significantly more companies comprise the Russel 2000 than the 30 industrials which comprise the DJIA.

When to use indicator: Managers, creditors, and investors can use this benchmark to help predict the state of the economy in the near future. This information may aid in determining the timing and benefits of company acquisitions/sales, capital investments/sales, marketing programs, and product development projects. Investors often use the Russel 2000 as a comparative tool, or benchmark, in determining the performance of small company investments.

Meaning of result: High percentage increases in the Russel 2000 result from market price increases of the 2,000 companies that comprise the index. Market price increases can be the result of anticipated increases in corporate earnings, which may result from an expanding economy. Russel 2000 increases can also result from falling interest rates; when interest rates fall, investors tend to look for alternatives that may generate higher yields. The result is often increased demand for securities, which drives up market prices for stocks and increases the Russel 2000.

251 Exploring the Wilshire 5000 Average

The **Wilshire 5000** average is a popular indicator of the overall performance of the stock market, from the largest to very small companies. It is considered the overall stock equivalent of the Dow Jones Industrial Average (DJIA). Since significantly more companies comprise the Wilshire 5000 than the 30 industrials which comprise the DJIA, it should more closely track the performance of the total market.

When to use indicator: Managers, creditors, and investors can use this benchmark to help predict the state of the economy in the near future. This information may aid in determining the timing and benefits of company acquisitions/sales, capital investments/sales, marketing programs, and product development projects. Investors often use the Wilshire 5000 as a comparative tool, or benchmark, in determining the performance of company investments.

Meaning of result: High percentage increases in the Wilshire 5000 result from market price increases of the 5,000 companies that comprise the index. Market price increases can be the result of anticipated increases in corporate earnings, which may result from an expanding economy. Wilshire 5000 increases can also result from falling interest rates; when interest rates fall, investors tend to look for alternatives that may generate higher yields. The result is often increased demand for securities, which drives up market prices for stocks and increases the Wilshire 5000.

CHAPTER NINETEEN

Company Valuation

This chapter details a number of methods of valuing, or pricing, companies. This information can help the investor determine the value of potential investments. It can also help the business manager determine the value of his company and/or companies considered for acquisition. Typically, investors use no single method of valuation in determining the price of a company. Instead, they employ a number of methods to find the "right" value. Be careful in employing rule of thumb valuation ratios, such as "two times sales" or "five times operations cash flow" since valuations tend to vary greatly with considerations such as company growth potential, industry type, and the degree of "entry barriers" a company possesses. When competition can readily copy a company's core competencies, such as its manufacturing methods, innovation potential, and distribution methods, entry barriers are small and valuation ratios tend to fall.

252 Determining the Book Value of a Company

Equation

Book value of a company = balance sheet value of owner's equity

Book value per share = book value of company / number of common shares issued and outstanding

The **book value** of a company is equal to the owner's equity portion of the balance sheet. You can determine it by subtracting liabilities and preferred stock commitments from total company assets.

When to use indicator: Managers, creditors, and investors can use this indicator to help determine the value of a company. This information can be a basis for pricing the company for acquisition or sale, for creditworthiness, and for stock investment analysis. It is generally desirable to use a number of valuation techniques in arriving at a company value.

Meaning of result: Higher book values often indicate companies with strong balance sheets. Such companies have often had a history of excellent earnings and have plowed those earnings back into additional company assets and reductions in liabilities. The book value of a company can be far from the company's market value. Investors can value companies with excellent current and forecasted earnings potential much in excess of book value while they may value those that are experiencing difficulties less than book value.

Example

Book value of a company = balance sheet value of owner's equity

Balance sheet value of owner's equity = total shareholder equity − liquidation value of preferred stock − preferred stock dividends in arrears = 31,088 − 375 − 0 = 30,713

Book value of a company = 30,713

Book value per share = book value of company / number of common shares issued and outstanding

Book value of a company = 30,713
Number of common shares issued and outstanding = 3,600

Book value per share = 30,713 / 3,600 = 8.53

Sector	Mid to large cap	Book Value Per Share	Small to mid cap	Book Value Per Share	Micro to small cap	Book Value Per Share
Manufacturing	General Motors	24.19	Toro	19.79	Encad	5.63
Retail	Wal-Mart Stores	8.26	Bed Bath & Beyond	2.14	TCBY Enterprises	3.28
Food	McDonald's	12.91	Applebee's Int'l	9.23	Garden Fresh Restaurant	8.01
Technology	Microsoft	6.28	Cypress Semiconductor	7.10	Jmar Technologies	0.70
Finance	Morgan-Stanley Dean Witter	23.27	Franklin Resources	7.36	AmeriTrade Holding	2.31
Healthcare	Columbia/HCA Healthcare	11.30	Novacare	8.32	National Home Health Care	4.45
Service	Manpower	7.69	Air & Water Technologies	−3.40	Market Facts	6.06
Media/Publishing	McGraw Hill	14.48	Scholastic	20.60	Thomas Nelson	9.77

253 Finding the Liquidation Value of a Company

Equation

Liquidation value of company = cash + marketable securities + (70% of inventory, accounts receivable, and prepaid expenses) + (50% of other assets) − total liabilities

Liquidation value per share = liquidation value of company / number of common shares issued and outstanding

The **liquidation value** is the money that remains after a company sells all of its assets and pays all of its debts. Liquidation value is generally pertinent only when a company has failed or is near failing since asset liquidation is generally the poorest method of returning value to equity holders.

When to use indicator: Managers, creditors, and investors can use this indicator to help determine the value of a company, particularly when failure is imminent. This information can be used as a basis for pricing the company for acquisition or sale, for creditworthiness, and for stock investment analysis. It is generally desirable to use a number of valuation techniques in arriving at a company value.

Meaning of result: Higher liquidation values often indicate companies with large amounts of current assets such as cash and marketable securities, significant amounts of longer term assets, and smaller liability balances. However, companies that exhibit such characteristics are generally not in immediate danger of failure, thus reducing the usefulness of liquidation valuations.

Example

Liquidation value of company = cash + marketable securities + (70% of inventory, accounts receivable, and prepaid expenses) + (50% of other assets) − total liabilities

Cash = 4,139
Marketable securities = 524
70% of inventory, accounts receivable, and prepaid expenses = $0.7 \times (13,421 + 24,878)$ = 26,809
50% of other assets = $0.5 \times$ other assets = $0.5 \times (56,258 - 4,139 - 524 - 13,421 - 24,878) = 0.5 \times (13,296) = 6,648$
Total liabilities = 25,180

Liquidation value of company = 4,139 + 524 + 26,809 + 6,648 − 25,180 = 12,940

Liquidation value per share = liquidation value of company / number of common shares issued and outstanding

Liquidation value of company = 12,940
Number of common shares issued and outstanding = 3,600

Liquidation value per share = 12,940 / 3,600 = 3.59

Source: J. Wilcox's "Gambler's Ruin Formula" from the Prentice Hall book, *Handbook of Financial Analysis, Forecasting and Modeling*.

Sector	Mid to large cap	Liquidation Value Per Share	Small to mid cap	Liquidation Value Per Share	Micro to small cap	Liquidation Value Per Share
Manufacturing	General Motors	−99.22	Toro	−0.48	Encad	2.90
Retail	Wal-Mart Stores	0.88	Bed Bath & Beyond	1.06	TCBY Enterprises	1.81
Food	McDonald's	0.02	Applebee's Int'l	3.68	Garden Fresh Restaurant	1.11
Technology	Microsoft	5.14	Cypress Semiconductor	3.25	Jmar Technologies	0.42
Finance	Morgan-Stanley Dean Witter	−100.87	Franklin Resources	2.70	AmeriTrade Holding	−1.94
Healthcare	Columbia/HCA Healthcare	−3.53	Novacare	1.16	National Home Health Care	3.29
Service	Manpower	−0.59	Air & Water Technologies	−8.64	Market Facts	3.66
Media/Publishing	McGraw Hill	−1.72	Scholastic	0.08	Thomas Nelson	3.77

254 Ascertaining the Market Value of a Company

Equation

Market value of company = market price per share × number of common shares issued and outstanding

Market value per share = market value per share

The company's **market value** is equivalent to the free market valuation of a firm's equity. Buyers and sellers determine the price of a company's stock in the open market. The market value of a company is also known as the **market capitalization**.

When to use indicator: Managers, creditors, and investors can use this indicator to help determine the value of a company. This information can be used as a basis for pricing the company for acquisition or sale, for creditworthiness, and for stock investment analysis. It is generally desirable to use a number of valuation techniques in arriving at a company value.

Meaning of result: Companies with excellent current and forecasted revenues and earnings growth are generally valued highly in the marketplace, oftentimes much in excess of book value. Growth of revenues and earnings can occur when a company provides highly demanded products or services at competitive prices, yet maintains good profit margins.

Example

Market value of company = market price per share × number of common shares issued and outstanding

Market value per share = 22.50
Number of common shares issues and outstanding = 3,600

Market value of company = 22.50 × 3,600 = 81,000

Market value per share = 22.50

COMPANY VALUATION

Sector	Mid to large cap	Market Value Per Share	Small to mid cap	Market Value Per Share	Micro to small cap	Market Value Per Share
Manufacturing	General Motors	68.88	Toro	33.94	Encad	12.88
Retail	Wal-Mart Stores	60.50	Bed Bath & Beyond	26.81	TCBY Enterprises	9.25
Food	McDonald's	71.00	Applebee's Int'l	22.75	Garden Fresh Restaurant	18.13
Technology	Microsoft	107.25	Cypress Semiconductor	8.25	Jmar Technologies	2.63
Finance	Morgan-Stanley Dean Witter	90.19	Franklin Resources	53.56	AmeriTrade Holding	14.50
Healthcare	Columbia/HCA Healthcare	29.88	Novacare	11.31	National Home Health Care	5.00
Service	Manpower	27.75	Air & Water Technologies	2.88	Market Facts	21.00
Media/Publishing	McGraw Hill	81.44	Scholastic	39.63	Thomas Nelson	13.75

255 Assessing the Price-to-Earnings Value of a Company

Equation

Price to earnings value of the company = price-to-earnings ratio × forecasted earnings per share × number of common shares issued and outstanding

Companies base price-to-earnings (P/E) valuations on estimates of the open market's appropriate P/E valuation of a company. Companies base P/E valuations in part upon the industry in which a company competes and the present and predicted financial performance of the company relative to its competitors.

When to use indicator: Managers, creditors, and investors can use this indicator to help determine the value of a company. This information can be a basis for pricing the company for acquisition or sale, for creditworthiness, and for stock investment analysis. It is generally desirable to use a number of valuation techniques in arriving at a company value.

Meaning of result: Investors often value companies that operate in growth industries and that exhibit excellent current and forecasted revenues and earnings growth at high P/E ratios, and hence high price-to-earnings valuations.

Example

Current-year earnings valuation

Price-to-earnings value of the company = estimated appropriate price-to-earnings ratio × present-year earnings per share × number of common shares issued and outstanding

Estimated appropriate price-to-earnings ratio = 18
Current-year earnings per share = 4,953 / 3,600 = 1.38
Number of common shares issued and outstanding = 3,600

Price-to-earnings value of the company, current-year's earnings estimate = 18 × 1.38 × 3,600 = 89,424

Next-year earnings valuation

Price-to-earnings value of the company = estimated appropriate price-to-earnings ratio × forecasted earnings per share × number of common shares issued and outstanding

Estimated appropriate price-to-earnings ratio = 18
Forecasted earnings per share = 1.65
Number of common shares issued and outstanding = 3,600

Price-to-earnings value of the company, next year's earnings estimate = 18 × 1.65 × 3,600 = 106,920

256 Valuing a Company on Discounted Future Cash Flow

Equation

Discounted future cash flow valuation: determined by applying the discounting method to a future estimated value of the company and a stream of revenue such as cash flow, operating income, or net income

You can value companies by discounting future estimates of company value and revenue streams. The revenue streams used in these estimates can be operating income, net income, operating cash flow, or any other indicator that fairly represents the income-generating capability of a company. As a company's value is in large part due to the income it generates, this method of company valuation can yield solid results as long as the estimates of future income generation and company value are accurate.

Discounted future cash flows consider that cash flow generated in the future will tend to be worth less in today's dollars. By estimating future cash flows and company value estimates, and then applying the discounting method to those estimates, you can make a valuation of the worth of the company in today's dollars. When a company or individual has no cash on hand for an investment, you can consider the discount rate as the cost of capital. The cost of capital is a weighted average of debt and equity financing. Alternatively, when there is a ready supply of available cash, you can consider the discount rate as the rate of return an alternative investment could earn.

When to use indicator: Managers, creditors, and investors can use this indicator to help determine the value of a company. This information can be a basis for pricing the company for acquisition or sale, for creditworthiness, and for stock investment analysis. It is generally desirable to use a number of valuation techniques in arriving at a company value.

Meaning of result: With this valuation method, investors generally highly value companies with excellent current and forecasted earnings growth because the present value of the future income streams will increase as long as the growth rate exceeds the discount rate. Growth of revenues and earnings can occur when a company provides highly demanded products or services at competitive prices, yet maintains good profit margins. High earnings growth will also tend to increase the future estimate of company value, further increasing the discounted future cash flow valuation.

Example

Discounted future cash flow valuation: determined by applying the discounting method to a future estimated value of a company and a stream of revenue such as cash flow, operating income, or net income

Year one operating income estimate = 9,433
Year two operating income estimate = 10,848
Year three operating income estimate = 12,475
Year four operating income estimate = 13,723
Year four value of company = 120,000

Discount rate = 9%

Yearly discount rates found by using table in Appendix B or tip #229

Year one discount rate = 0.917
Year two discount rate = 0.842
Year three discount rate = 0.772
Year four discount rate = 0.708

Year one discounted operating income = $0.917 \times 9{,}433 = 8{,}650$

Year two discounted operating income = $0.842 \times 10{,}848 = 9{,}134$

Year three discounted operating income = $0.772 \times 12{,}475 = 9{,}631$

Year four discounted operating income = $0.708 \times (13{,}723 + 120{,}000) = 94{,}676$

Discounted future cash flow valuation = 8,650 + 9,134 + 9,631 + 94,676 = 122,091

257 Determining the Value of a Company with No-Earnings-Per-Share Dilution

Equation

No-earnings-per-share dilution value = (annual earnings of company to be acquired / earnings per share of purchasing company) × share price of purchasing company

When one company acquires another, one method of valuation is to maintain equivalent earnings per share of the new, larger company after the acquisition. This is often a very rough estimate of valuation since the valuation of the acquiring company may have little correlation with that of the company being acquired.

When to use indicator: Managers, creditors, and investors can use this indicator to help determine the value of a company. This information can be a basis for pricing the company for acquisition or sale, for creditworthiness, and for stock investment analysis. It is generally desirable to use a number of valuation techniques in arriving at a company value.

Meaning of result: Higher no-earnings-per-share-dilution valuations can indicate the company to be acquired is earning high profits and/or the acquiring company's earnings per share are low and share prices are low. Conversely, when a profitable company acquires a company with poor earnings performance, the no-earnings-per-share-dilution valuation will tend to be lower.

Example

No-earnings-per-share-dilution value = (annual earnings of company to be acquired / earnings per share of purchasing company) × share price of purchasing company

Company #1, purchaser of company #2

$$\text{Earnings} = 7,864$$
$$\text{Shares} = 5,150$$
$$\text{Earnings per share} = 7,864 / 5,150 = 1.527$$
$$\text{Share price} = 25.75$$

Company #2, company being acquired

$$\text{Earnings} = 4,953$$
$$\text{Shares} = 3,600$$
$$\text{Earnings per share} = 4,953 / 3,600 = 1.376$$

No-earnings-per-share-dilution-value = (4953 / 1.527) × 25.75 = 83523

COMPANY VALUATION

Appendix A

Argo, Inc. Financial Statements	
Balance sheet (dollars in thousands)	**31-Dec-97**
Cash	4,139
Marketable securities	524
Accounts receivable	24,878
Inventories	13,421
raw materials	3,308
work in process	5,845
finished goods	4,268
Notes receivable	125
Other current assets	1,048
Total current assets	**44,135**
Property, plant, equipment	12,065
Less accumulated depreciation	2,047
Net Property, plant, equipment	10,018
Other noncurrent assets	45
Deferred charges	88
Intangibles	520
Less accumulated amortization	85
Net intangibles	435
Deposits and other assets	1,547
Total assets	**56,268**
Notes payable	1,000
Accounts payable	5,633
Current portion of long-term debt	650
Current portion of capital leases	0
Accrued liabilities (payroll, vacation pay, property taxes)	2,747
Income taxes payable	1,420
Other current liabilities	582
Total current liabilities	**12,032**
Deferred charges/income taxes	185
Long term debt, less current charges	12,513
Other long-term liabilities	450
Total liabilities	**25,180**
Preferred stock	300

Common stock, $.01 par value:
     5,000,000 shares authorized
     3,600,000 issued and outstanding
	36

Additional paid-in capital	12,085
Retained earnings	18,722
Less treasury stock	55
Other equities	0
Total shareholder equity	**31,088**
Total liabilities and net worth	**56,268**

Appendix A (continued)

Income Statement
(dollars in thousands)

Fiscal year ending	31-Dec-97
Net sales	85,420
Cost of goods sold	54,212
Gross profit	**31,208**
R&D expenses	4,578
Selling, G&A expenses	15,993
Depreciation & amortization	1,204
Operating income	**9,433**
Non-operating income	455
Interest expense	784
Pre-tax income	**9,104**
Provision for income taxes	3,529
Net income before extraordinary items	**5,575**
Extraordinary items	−592
Net income	**4,983**
Preferred dividends	30
Net income applicable to common stock	**4,953**

Cash flow statement
(dollars in thousands)

Fiscal year ending	31-Dec-97
Cash flow by operations	
Net income (loss)	4,953
Depreciation/amortization	1,204
Net increase (decrease) assets/liabilities	−1,337
Cash provided (used) by discontinued operations	0
Other adjustments, net	0
Net cash provided (used) by operations	**4,820**
Cash flow by investing	
(Increase) decrease in property, plant, and equipment	−6,275
(Acquisition) disposal of subsidiaries, businesses	0
(Increase) decrease in securities investments	2
Other cash inflow (outflow)	−321
Net cash provided (used) by investing	**−6,594**
Cash flow by financing	
Issue (purchase) of equity	0
Issue (repayment) of debt	0
Increase (decrease) in borrowing	3,793
Dividends, other distributions	−1,002
Other cash inflow (outflow)	0
Net cash provided (used) by financing	**2,791**
Effect of exchange rate on cash	0
Net change in cash or equivalents	**1,017**
Cash or equivalents at year start	3,122
Cash or equivalents at year end	4,139

Appendix B

Present Value of $1 Received in n Years

Discount rate (%)

		1	2	3	4	5	6	7	8	9	10	12	15	20	25	30
	1	0.990	0.980	0.971	0.962	0.952	0.943	0.935	0.926	0.917	0.909	0.893	0.870	0.833	0.800	0.769
	2	0.980	0.961	0.943	0.925	0.907	0.890	0.873	0.857	0.842	0.826	0.797	0.756	0.694	0.640	0.592
	3	0.971	0.942	0.915	0.889	0.864	0.840	0.816	0.794	0.772	0.751	0.712	0.658	0.579	0.512	0.455
	4	0.961	0.924	0.888	0.855	0.823	0.792	0.763	0.735	0.708	0.683	0.636	0.572	0.482	0.410	0.350
	5	0.951	0.906	0.863	0.822	0.784	0.747	0.713	0.681	0.650	0.621	0.567	0.497	0.402	0.328	0.269
	6	0.942	0.888	0.837	0.790	0.746	0.705	0.666	0.630	0.596	0.564	0.507	0.432	0.335	0.262	0.207
	7	0.933	0.871	0.813	0.760	0.711	0.665	0.623	0.583	0.547	0.513	0.452	0.376	0.279	0.210	0.159
	8	0.923	0.853	0.789	0.731	0.677	0.627	0.582	0.540	0.502	0.467	0.404	0.327	0.233	0.168	0.123
	9	0.914	0.837	0.766	0.703	0.645	0.592	0.544	0.500	0.460	0.424	0.361	0.284	0.194	0.134	0.094
	10	0.905	0.820	0.744	0.676	0.614	0.558	0.508	0.463	0.422	0.386	0.322	0.247	0.162	0.107	0.073
Years	11	0.896	0.804	0.722	0.650	0.585	0.527	0.475	0.429	0.388	0.350	0.287	0.215	0.135	0.086	0.056
(n)	12	0.887	0.788	0.701	0.625	0.557	0.497	0.444	0.397	0.356	0.319	0.257	0.187	0.112	0.069	0.043
	13	0.879	0.773	0.681	0.601	0.530	0.469	0.415	0.368	0.326	0.290	0.229	0.163	0.093	0.055	0.033
	14	0.870	0.758	0.661	0.577	0.505	0.442	0.388	0.340	0.299	0.263	0.205	0.141	0.078	0.044	0.025
	15	0.861	0.743	0.642	0.555	0.481	0.417	0.362	0.315	0.275	0.239	0.183	0.123	0.065	0.035	0.020
	16	0.853	0.728	0.623	0.534	0.458	0.394	0.339	0.292	0.252	0.218	0.163	0.107	0.054	0.028	0.015
	17	0.844	0.714	0.605	0.513	0.436	0.371	0.317	0.270	0.231	0.198	0.146	0.093	0.045	0.023	0.012
	18	0.836	0.700	0.587	0.494	0.416	0.350	0.296	0.250	0.212	0.180	0.130	0.081	0.038	0.018	0.009
	19	0.828	0.686	0.570	0.475	0.396	0.331	0.277	0.232	0.194	0.164	0.116	0.070	0.031	0.014	0.007
	20	0.820	0.673	0.554	0.456	0.377	0.312	0.258	0.215	0.178	0.149	0.104	0.061	0.026	0.012	0.005
	25	0.780	0.610	0.478	0.375	0.295	0.233	0.184	0.146	0.116	0.092	0.059	0.030	0.010	0.004	0.001
	30	0.742	0.552	0.412	0.308	0.231	0.174	0.131	0.099	0.075	0.057	0.033	0.015	0.004	0.001	0.000
	40	0.672	0.453	0.307	0.208	0.142	0.097	0.067	0.046	0.032	0.022	0.011	0.004	0.001	0.000	0.000
	50	0.608	0.372	0.228	0.141	0.087	0.054	0.034	0.021	0.013	0.009	0.003	0.001	0.000	0.000	0.000

Appendix C

Present Value of $1 Received Annually for n Years

Discount rate (%)

		1	2	3	4	5	6	7	8	9	10	12	15	20	25	30
	1	0.990	0.980	0.971	0.962	0.952	0.943	0.935	0.926	0.917	0.909	0.893	0.870	0.833	0.800	0.769
	2	1.970	1.942	1.913	1.886	1.859	1.833	1.808	1.783	1.759	1.736	1.690	1.626	1.528	1.440	1.361
	3	2.941	2.884	2.829	2.775	2.723	2.673	2.624	2.577	2.531	2.487	2.402	2.283	2.106	1.952	1.816
	4	3.902	3.808	3.717	3.630	3.546	3.465	3.387	3.312	3.240	3.170	3.037	2.855	2.589	2.362	2.166
	5	4.853	4.713	4.580	4.452	4.329	4.212	4.100	3.993	3.890	3.791	3.605	3.352	2.991	2.689	2.436
	6	5.795	5.601	5.417	5.242	5.076	4.917	4.767	4.623	4.486	4.355	4.111	3.784	3.326	2.951	2.643
	7	6.728	6.472	6.230	6.002	5.786	5.582	5.389	5.206	5.033	4.868	4.564	4.160	3.605	3.161	2.802
	8	7.652	7.325	7.020	6.733	6.463	6.210	5.971	5.747	5.535	5.335	4.968	4.487	3.837	3.329	2.925
	9	8.566	8.162	7.786	7.435	7.108	6.802	6.515	6.247	5.995	5.759	5.328	4.772	4.031	3.463	3.019
	10	9.471	8.983	8.530	8.111	7.722	7.360	7.024	6.710	6.418	6.145	5.650	5.019	4.192	3.571	3.092
Years	11	10.368	9.787	9.253	8.760	8.306	7.887	7.499	7.139	6.805	6.495	5.938	5.234	4.327	3.656	3.147
(n)	12	11.255	10.575	9.954	9.385	8.863	8.384	7.943	7.536	7.161	6.814	6.194	5.421	4.439	3.725	3.190
	13	12.134	11.348	10.635	9.986	9.394	8.853	8.358	7.904	7.487	7.103	6.424	5.583	4.533	3.780	3.223
	14	13.004	12.106	11.296	10.563	9.899	9.295	8.745	8.244	7.786	7.367	6.628	5.724	4.611	3.824	3.249
	15	13.865	12.849	11.938	11.118	10.380	9.712	9.108	8.559	8.061	7.606	6.811	5.847	4.675	3.859	3.268
	16	14.718	13.578	12.561	11.652	10.838	10.106	9.447	8.851	8.313	7.824	6.974	5.954	4.730	3.887	3.283
	17	15.562	14.292	13.166	12.166	11.274	10.477	9.763	9.122	8.544	8.022	7.120	6.047	4.775	3.910	3.295
	18	16.398	14.992	13.754	12.659	11.690	10.828	10.059	9.372	8.756	8.201	7.250	6.128	4.812	2.928	3.304
	19	17.226	15.678	14.324	13.134	12.085	11.158	10.336	9.604	8.950	8.365	7.366	6.198	4.843	3.942	3.311
	20	18.046	16.351	14.877	13.590	12.462	11.470	10.594	9.818	9.129	8.514	7.469	6.259	4.870	3.954	3.316
	25	22.023	19.523	17.413	15.622	14.094	12.783	11.654	10.675	9.823	9.077	7.843	6.464	4.948	3.985	3.329
	30	25.808	22.396	19.600	17.292	15.372	13.765	12.409	11.258	10.274	9.427	8.055	6.566	4.979	3.995	3.332
	40	32.835	27.355	23.115	19.793	17.159	15.046	13.332	11.925	10.757	9.779	8.244	6.642	4.997	3.999	3.333
	50	39.196	31.424	25.730	21.482	18.256	15.762	13.801	12.233	10.962	9.915	8.304	6.661	4.999	4.000	3.333

Abbreviations

CPI	consumer price index
DJIA	Dow Jones Industrial Average
EBIT	earnings before interest and taxes
EOQ	Economic Ordering Quantity method of inventory control
EVA	economic value added
G&A	general and administrative
GDP	gross domestic product
GNP	gross national product
IRR	internal rate of return
JIT	Just-In-Time method of inventory control
MIRR	modified internal rate of return
NPV	net present value
P/E	price-to-earnings ratio
PEG	price-to-earnings-to-growth rate ratio
PPI	producer price index
R&D	research and development
ROA	return on assets
ROE	return on equity
ROIC	return on invested capital
S&P500	Standard & Poor's 500
SG&A	selling, general, and administrative

References and Suggested Reading

Robert C. Higgins. *Analysis for Financial Management, 4th Edition.* Chicago: Irwin, 1995.

Jae K. Shim, Ph.D. and Joel G. Siegel, Ph.D., CPA. *Handbook of Financial Analysis, Forecasting and Modeling.* Paramus, New Jersey: Prentice Hall, 1988.

Susan M. Jacksack, J.D., editor. *Start, Run and Grow a Successful Small Business, 2nd Edition.* Chicago: CCH, 1998.

Michael R. Tyran. *The Vest-Pocket Guide to Business Ratios.* Paramus, New Jersey: Prentice Hall, 1992.

Jae K. Shim, Ph.D., Joel G. Siegel, Ph.D., CPA, and Abraham J. Simon, Ph.D., CPA. *The Vest-Pocket MBA, 2nd Edition.* Paramus, New Jersey: Prentice Hall, 1997.

John A. Tracy, CPA. *Accounting for Dummies.* Foster City, CA: IDG Books, 1997.

Robert N. Anthony, James S. Reece, and Julie H. Hertenstein. *Accounting: Text and Cases, 9th Edition.* Chicago: Irwin, 1995.

The Conference Board. www.conference-board.org (web page for The Conference Board). Internet web page, 1998.

Index

A

Abbreviations, 326
Absolute value, 269
Accounting rate of return, 278
Accounts payable, 40, 243–250
Accounts payable cash disbursement turnover, 249–250
Accounts payable ratios, 244, 247
Accounts payable turnover, 245
Accounts receivable, 40, 200, 231–242
Accounts receivable factoring, 242
Accounts receivable ratio, 232
Accounts receivable turnover, 233
Acid test, 176
After-tax operating income, 28
Age of fixed assets, 137
Aging schedule, 235
Altman's Z-score, 181
Amortization, 148
Annual cost of assets, 28
Annuity, 289
Annuity due, 289
Annuity, present value of, 292, 293
Asset additions, 218
Asset additions, times covered, 217
Assets, 126–154
Assets, annual cost of, 28

B

Bad debt, 238–239
Bankruptcy, probability of, 181
Benefit cost ratio, 282
Beta, 70
Bonds, 298

Book depreciation, 122
Book value, 152, 317
Bottom line, 19
Break-even plan capacity, 93–94
Break-even ratio, 89–90
Break-even sales level, 87–88, 91
Break-even volume, 85–86

C

Capital employed items, 26
Capital investment, 274–294
Carrying cost, 262
Cash balance, 179
Cash conversion cycle, 187, 188, 189
Cash expenses, 184
Cash flow, 66–67
Cash flow ratios, 37, 66–67, 177
Cash reserves, 178
Cash turnover, 178
Certainty equivalent, 286–287
Certainty equivalent coefficient, 286
Common stock, 46
Common stock dividend growth rate, 53
Common stock dividend payout ratio, 59, 60
Common stock dividend return ratio, 58, 65
Company valuation, 316–322
Compounded interest, 297
Conference Board, 306
Consumer price index, 312
Contribution margin, 83–84
Cost of capital, 25, 277
Cost of debt capital, 164
Cost of goods sold, 7
Cost-of-goods-sold ratios, 96–98
Coupon rate, 298
Credit discounts, 240–241

Cross-elasticity, 272
Current assets ratio, 182, 194, 195, 198–203
Current debt ratios, 185, 186, 222
Current liabilities, 183
Current period sales, 236–237
Current ratio, 175
Current yield, 298

D

Days of credit in accounts receivable, 234
Days of finished product turnover, 256
Days of inventory turnover, 254
Days of operating expense payables, 216
Days of purchases in accounts payable, 246
Days of purchases paid, 248
Days of raw material inventory, 260
Days of sales in cash, 180
Days of work in process inventory, 258
Debt, 155–164
Debt, bad, 238–239
Debt expenses, 208
Debt expenses, times covered, 207
Debt ratios, 156–160, 162
Debt to market value of equity, 221
Debt turnover, 161
Demand elasticity, 269
Depreciation, book, 122
Depreciation expenses, 41, 123, 124–125
Desired operating income, 89–92
Direct cost ratios, 111
Direct costs, 7
Direct costs per production unit, 72
Direct labor, 72, 99
Direct labor employee percentage, 106–107
Direct labor ratios, 99–105, 108
Direct operations expenses, 74, 96
Direct overhead, 109
Direct overhead cost ratios, 109
Discount rate, 277, 291, 303
Discount rate, risk-adjusted, 281
Discounted cash flow, 277
Discounted future cash flow valuation, 321
Discounted future cash flows, 277
Discounted payback period, 277
Dividend disbursements, 49
Dividend growth rates, 53

Dividend payout ratio, 47
Dividend return ratio, 47, 58
Dividends per common share, 47–48
Dow Jones Industrial Average (DJIA), 313

E

Earnings growth rate, 51–52
Earnings per share, 46
Earnings yield, 56
Economic Ordering Quantity (EOQ), 261
Economic value added (EVA), 26–27, 28
Effective annual T-bill yield, 300
Effective yield, 297
Elasticity, price, of demand, 269
Elasticity ratios, 268
Elasticity, supply, 273
Elasticity, unitary, 271
Equity, 165–173
Equity financing, 26
Equity interest rate, 25
Equity ratios, 133, 159, 166–169, 222–223
Equity, shareholder, 31, 145, 166
Equity to sales, 166
Equity turnover, 169
Expenses, 21

F

Federal funds rate, 302
Federal Reserve System, 302
Financial leverage, 31, 225–226
Financing cash flow, 40, 43
Finished goods, 255
Finished product inventory turnover, 255
Fixed asset, 117, 121, 127
Fixed asset age, 137
Fixed asset maintenance ratios, 118–119
Fixed asset productivity, 151
Fixed asset ratios, 128–135, 224
Fixed asset reinvestment rate, 150
Fixed asset replacement costs, 152
Fixed asset turnover, 128, 136
Fixed cost ratios, 80–82
Fixed costs, 75, 78–79, 211–213
Funded capital, 224

Future value, 288
Future value of an annuity, 289, 290

G

General and administrative expenses, 114
Goodwill, 140
Gross domestic product (GDP), 309
Gross margin, 7
Gross margin ratio, 9–10
Gross national product (GNP), 310
Gross profit, 7–8
Gross profit ratio, 9–10
Growth rate of earnings, 51–52
Growth rate of revenues, 49–50

H

High risk assets, 153–154
Horizontal analysis, 3
Hours-worked ratios, 102–105

I

Income from operations, 11–12
Index of coincident economic indicators, 307
Index of lagging economic indicators, 308
Index of leading economic indicators, 306
Indirect costs, 11
Indirect labor, 99
Individual intangible assets, 147
Individual intangible assets ratios, 147–149
Individual overhead expenses, 115–116
Inelastic demand, 270
Insurance cost ratios, 120–121
Intangible assets, 140
Intangible assets ratios, 140–146
Interest earned, times, 205
Interest expenses, 203, 205
Interest rate yield, 297
Interest rates, 295–304
Internal rate of return (IRR), 283–284
Inventory, 40, 201, 251–267
Inventory carrying cost, 262
Inventory ordering costs, 261
Inventory ratios, 252
Inventory reorder point, 265

Inventory turnover, 253
Invested capital ratios, 171–173
Invested capital turnover, 170
Investing cash flow, 40, 42
Investment capital, 35

J

Just-In-Time (JIT) inventory control method, 261, 267

L

Leverage, 220–230
Liquid assets ratios, 183–184, 198
Liquidation value, 318
Liquidity ratios, 174–203
Long-term asset additions, 217
Long-term debt, 134, 162, 163, 209, 210, 223

M

Market capitalization, 319
Market price return, 65
Market price return ratio, 57
Market value, 319
Marketable securities, 199
Maturity, yield to, 299
Modified internal rate of return (MIRR), 285
Mutually exclusive investment selection, 279

N

Net income, 19–20
Net income-to-sales ratio, 21–22
Net present value, 279–280
Net sales ratios, 23–24
No-earnings-per-share dilution value, 322
Nominal yield, 298
Non-operational items, 15
Notes receivable, 202

O

Operating expenses outstanding, 216
Operating expenses, times covered, 214

Operating income, 157
Operating leverage, 227–228
Operational expenses, 120, 214–215
Operations cash flow, 37, 40–41, 60, 68–69, 131, 206, 210
Operations cash flow dividend payout, 60–61, 64
Operations cash flow dividend payout ratio, 64
Operations income ratio, 13–14
Optimum inventory order quantity, 263
Overhead, 72, 110
Overhead expenses, 115–116
Owner's equity, 145, 224

P

Par value, 298
Payback period, 275
Payback reciprocal, 276
Perpetuity, 294
Plant equipment costs, 117
Preferred dividend payout ratio, 63, 64
Preferred dividend return ratio, 62
Preferred dividends, 46
Present value, 291
Present value of an annuity, 292, 293
Pretax profit, 15–16, 22
Pretax profit ratio, 17–18
Price elasticity of demand, 269
Price-to-earnings ratio (P/E), 54, 56, 320
Price-to-earnings-to-growth-rate ratio (PEG), 55
Probability of bankruptcy, 181
Producer price index (PPI), 311
Production unit ratios, 108
Profitability index, 282
Projected sales volume estimate, 89

Q

Quick assets, 176
Quick ratio, 176

R

Rate of return, 291
Ratio analysis, 5
Raw materials, 110
Raw materials cost ratios, 110
Raw materials inventory, 259
Raw materials inventory turnover, 259
Replacement cost, 152
Required equity dividend, 25
Research and development (R&D) cost ratios, 112–113
Research and development (R&D) expenses, 112
Residual income, 28–30
Retained earnings, 166, 173, 219
Return on assets (ROA), 33–34, 35
Return on equity (ROE), 31–32, 35, 56, 169
Return on invested capital (ROIC), 35–36, 170
Revenues, 21
Revenues per share, 45
Risk-adjusted discount rate, 281
Rule of 72, 301
Russel 2000 average, 314

S

Safety stock, 266
Selling expenses, 114
Selling, general, and administrative costs (SG&A) ratios, 114
Shareholder equity, 31, 145, 166
Short-lived income, 38
Short-lived sales, 39
Short-term asset additions, 217
Short-term debt, 135, 163, 183
Simple interest, 296
Simple rate of return, 278
Solvency ratios, 204–219
Supply elasticity, 273

T

Tax depreciation, 123
T-bills, 300, 304
Times asset additions covered, 217
Times debt expenses covered, 207
Times fixed costs covered, 211
Times interest earned, 205
Times long-term debt covered, 209
Times operating expenses covered, 214
Total asset coverage ratio, 139
Total asset turnover, 138
Total assets, 132, 138, 143–144, 149, 196–197
Total cost per unit, 74
Total debt, 168, 186
Total fixed costs, 87–88
Total inventory costs, 264
Total invested capital, 162
Total labor, 73
Total labor cost per unit, 73
Total leverage, 229–230
Total liabilities, 158
Total return on common stock, 65
Total shareholder equity, 145
Trade credit, 248

U

Unitary elasticity, 271
U.S. Treasury bills, 300, 304

U.S. Treasury bonds, 304
U.S. Treasury notes, 304

V

Valuation of company, 316–322
Value, book, 152, 317
Variable cost ratios, 76, 77
Variable costs, 75, 211
Variable-to-total-cost ratio, 76
Variance analysis, 4
Vertical analysis, 2
Volatility, 70

W

Wilshire 5000 average, 315
Work in process inventory turnover, 257
Working capital, 187
Working capital ratios, 189–197
Working capital turnover, 188, 189

Y

Yield to maturity, 299

Z

Z-score, 181

About the Author

Rich Gildersleeve, a registered professional mechanical engineer in California, is the director of engineering at dj Orthopedics, LLC in California. In 1997, he earned his MBA from San Diego State University. He also has a master's degree in mechanical engineering, which he earned while concurrently working as an engineer for General Dynamics Corporation. He holds nine U.S. patents and has authored various technical articles.

CD-ROM Installation Instructions

Windows

1. Insert the CD-ROM in your CD-ROM drive.
2. The Autoplay menu should run.
   If you have disabled "AutoPlay" the menu may fail to start. To start the menu, double-click "My Computer" and then double-click on the CD-ROM Drive icon.
   Double-click the file "autorun.exe."

Macintosh

1. Insert the CD-ROM in your CD-ROM drive and wait until the CD-ROM icon appears.
2. Double-click the Acrobat Reader 4.0 folder. Run Acrobat Reader 4.0. Choose File/open and select wb.pdf.